The Concept of the Spiritual:
An Essay in First Philosophy

The Concept of the Spiritual

An Essay in First Philosophy

Steven G. Smith

The King's Library

TEMPLE UNIVERSITY PRESS

Philadelphia

Temple University Press, Philadelphia 19122
Copyright © 1988 by Temple University. All rights reserved
Published 1988
Printed in the United States of America

The paper used in this publication meets the minimum
requirements of American National Standard for Information
Sciences—Permanence of Paper for Printed Library Materials,
ANSI Z39.48-1984

LIBRARY OF CONGRESS
Library of Congress Cataloging-in-Publication Data
Smith, Steven G.
The concept of the spiritual: an essay in first philosophy /
Steven G. Smith.
p. cm.
Bibliography: p.
Includes index.
ISBN 0-87722-553-2 (alk. paper)
1. Spirit. I. Title.
B105.S64S63 1988 88-1117
110—dc19 CIP

To
Carlon Jeanette Smith
and
Robert Starr Smith

Contents

Preface

"To the reader." At one time, in rebellion against what seemed like a forgetful sort of prose "objectivity," I thought I could write a book wholly as a letter to its readers. I came to see weighty reasons why this cannot be, foremost among them the impossibility of addressing in that way, with that force, persons one doesn't know. Letter gestures can be put in—"What do you think of this?"—but their true import is not what they would have in a letter. Really a book is written for a great Reader-Judge in heaven out of a desire to ensure that the Universal Record contains some true and telling entries. Of course there is also a hope that one's fellow mortals will admire it and give advice on it from the sidelines.

On the web spun out of this authorial folly actual readers land and pick their way about, and communication takes place in spite of everything. I know you are there behind the screen of the "you" I write; but how do I know it, and just what difference does this make to me? What is the nature of the actuality of communication, of community of beings? This turns out to be one form of an unsurpassably original question. If we could answer it, we would be on our way to a superior understanding of everything, particularly prefaces: we would face the conditions of the possibility of saying something *to the reader*.

A book cannot exactly be a letter, but at least it can take up this question and be an occasion for readers to occupy themselves with it as well.

Why is this essay represented as "first philosophy"? Negatively: Why is it not contributed to the literature of theology or religious edification, as might be expected from its invocation of the "spiritual"?

Sometimes theology is taken to include any fundamental orientation of thought or practice, and in this unhelpfully broad signification it certainly swallows up first philosophy. However, theology in the sharper sense involves specific life-shaping claims about *who* we primarily and overridingly have to deal with, and how we should be comporting ourselves in that relationship. In my view such claims can be made only confessionally, and it is not my business here either to make them or to consider systematically how others have made them.

Instead of attending to an encounter with a certain being (or with Being wearing a certain face), I inquire here into the generic meanings of encounter with beings—meanings that are adduced and traded on by all kinds of talk, also by theology. To see relationships between meanings is the point, not to change our lives in a particular way, on a particular basis. (Need it be said that our lives, which so evidently need changing, can be changed only in particular ways? But thoughtfulness and reasonableness are necessary for this, even if not sufficient.)

A "first" philosophy, a discourse on the ultimate conditions on thought, arises in the quest for the most fully satisfactory reasoning. The drive toward first philosophy is always with us, although circumstances usually cut us off before we get to it in anything like an explicit way. Whatever it is that requires right thinking and speaking at every moment is finally satisfied with nothing less than first philosophy.

Granting this premise, the interesting question becomes: How should first philosophy be conducted? When we pay attention not only to the original urgency that impels us to think and speak rightly but also to philosophy's history, a twofold proposition emerges as our most promising point of departure: that the ultimate reasons are rooted in the basic structure of the problem of relationship between intentional beings, and that thought about this problem is after all inseparable from the concept of the spiritual.

Suppose that "the spiritual" is the theme of choice for first philosophy; still, if we mean coherently to conceive the spiritual, we have to resolve a number of difficulties. The eight chapters of the present essay deal with these difficulties in order.

(1) In formulating a definition of the spiritual, we must do justice to the complexity and controversy in the philosophical history of spirit-notions. Only in the measure that we stay in contact with the concerns of earlier philosophers of the spiritual will we also be entitled to take over the intellectual territories they have opened up.

(2) In order not to disappoint legitimate expectations concerning the meaning and relevance of a philosophy of the spiritual, our use of spirit-words must be shown to have some foundation in ordinary talk.

(3) We must be able to exhibit the spiritual as the original "what" of thinking, an underived concreteness to which there is no prior starting-point for philosophy —and face the implications of doing so.

(4) The concept of the spiritual must also determine the fundamental "how" of thinking, which (in philosophy) must function as a justification procedure. It must be possible to conceive reason itself out of, or on the basis of, the spiritual; the very exercise of reasoning must manifest and confirm the spiritual frame of reference.

(5) In view of the supremely authoritative meaning that we propose to recognize in this "first" concept, it must be possible to show a spiritual conditioning of the basic orientation and most prominent experienced meanings of our personal lives.

(6) For the same reason, we must be able to relate our judgments of validity

and worth to the spiritual frame of reference. (Conceptions of the spiritual have typically had the role of anchoring such judgments.) But this means that different forms of validity must be examined to see how spiritual conditions affect each one.

(7) If thinking about the spiritual is not to be discontinuous with thinking about the world, we must understand the conditions of spirit's materialization; and we must see whether the dualism that inevitably attends talk of the spiritual can be articulated without falsely estranging the spiritual from the natural.

(8) Finally, spirit's relation to the world, if positive, cannot be lacking a causal dimension; it must be possible to conceive spirit's contribution to the determination of what occurs in the world. And since the worldly work of spirit is the domain of the human sciences, an account of spiritual causation should show the possibility of "human science" as such, that is, should show how human action can reasonably be understood and explained as spiritual.

The task, then, is to vindicate the starting proposition by rising to these challenges.

I am grateful for the allowances made by North Carolina Wesleyan College and Millsaps College to enable me to devote to the book the time it required. It was mostly written in other people's houses; for their hospitality I thank Clementine and Paul Luyckx in Brussels and Elise Lawton in Tallahassee. Crucial support, financial and otherwise, was provided in 1984–85 by my wife, Elise Lawton Smith, and my parents, Carlon and Robert Smith.

William Poteat and David Jones helped me in the planning stages. The manuscript was much improved in response to the suggestions of Edith Wyschogrod, who read the whole first draft; of Steven Esthimer, H. J. Adriaanse, and Theodore G. Ammon, who read parts; and of the Temple University Press readers. I thank all of these good people for their collaboration, and also Jane Cullen and Doris Braendel for making straight the way of publication. The Philosophy of Religion section of the American Academy of Religion (Southeast) let me send up a trial balloon for the whole project in a talk given in March of 1983. An earlier version of section 8.2 appeared in the *American Philosophical Quarterly* 22 (October 1985), as "The Causation of Finality."

My greatest intellectual debts are to Emmanuel Levinas, for my noncomprehension of exteriority, and to J. L. Austin, Stephen Toulmin, and R. M. Hare, who shaped my perspective on language and argument. During the time of writing I renewed my acquaintance with Buber's *I and Thou*—a book that I used to consider (in my ignorance) of little or no philosophical interest—and found there many pointers to positions I was in the process of occupying. My account of "primary objectivity" in Chapter 3 owes much to Buber's neglected thoughts on the possibility of saying You to nonhuman beings. I was also much struck some years ago by a beautifully careful and well-oriented book, *The Possibility of Altruism* by Thomas Nagel (New York: Oxford University Press, 1970), which helped to set me on the track of trying what I've tried.

S. G. S.
Jackson, Mississippi
August 1987

The Concept of the Spiritual:
An Essay in First Philosophy

Prologue: The Theme of First Philosophy

One question may be called prior to another if we necessarily make an assumption about its meaning in addressing the other. For example, the meaning of a question about a particular text's content is always conditioned by the assumed meaning of prior questions concerning the nature of writing and reading, expression and understanding. This order of meaning holds whether or not we have answers to the questions at any level, although it certainly seems to clear our way in dealing with posterior questions if we think we have answers to the prior ones or unproblematically act as though we do.

An essential mark of philosophical thinking is that it shifts attention to prior questions. This philosophical gesture is provisionally completed when we bring into view a question or set of questions to which none prior can be conceived. The attempt to elucidate and, if possible, answer such a question or questions is first philosophy; its results are normative for all other thinking.

To contest the possibility of first philosophy is one way of engaging in it.

The Western tradition has brought forth three great positive approaches to first philosophy. One starts from the question of the nature of *being:* since everything that is, *is,* can we understand anything at all unless we first clarify being itself? Another puts the question of *knowing* first: can we make valid statements about being or beings without first establishing what we are capable of knowing about anything? A third approach urges the question of *saying:* can we formulate standards of knowledge without ascertaining the rules according to which it is possible to assert existence or knowledge? And then two or more of these approaches may be woven together, as for instance when Heidegger in *Being and Time* states the first question not as "What is Being?" but as "What is the meaning of Being?"— that is, What can be said and understood of Being?[1]

The rejection of first philosophy is not a true fourth way but always a retort to one or more of the three positive ways, a negation of primal being or foundational knowledge or univocal utterance.

Let us consider more closely the shift of priority to saying, which is the most conspicuous development in the philosophy of our century. Language would surely not be taken so seriously in principle unless it were taken for something more than a mere instrument of our living. As an indispensable instrument it would need to have an organon worked out for it, but it would not for that reason deserve to be the site of first philosophy. No—if language matters this much, it must be because it is itself the reality of our living as it is most fully or crucially exposed for understanding. Of course, a like presumption would accompany ontological and epistemological first philosophy, namely, that being and knowing respectively matter most, as indeed Parmenides' passion for being and Descartes' dedication to knowing model for us. On what grounds, then, would one identify saying as not just the medium but the object of the first questions? By what characteristic that is decisive with respect to the order of priority among questions does saying differ from knowing and being? The salient difference in saying is that it is essentially interpersonal, or to be more specific, essentially an activity of creating and maintaining forms of commonality among persons. Interpersonal commonality is not just what language is *for;* it is *in* language, and in it more than in anything else. Thus the question of what can be linguistically formulated with respect to knowing and being has priority primarily because it is also the question concerning the positions that can be taken by communicators with respect to the contents of their minds and the beings they encounter, including and especially each other. Concretely, as I now presume to address an audience, what other question could impose itself as prior to this one?

But to thematize first philosophy as philosophy of language masks the factor in language that bestows priority on it. There are mechanical uses of language that are not (directly) of fundamental interest; on the other hand, there are more forms of interpersonal commonality than appear in language. If we accept the priority of the question of relationship—How will we live (together)?—what then will be the most perspicuous way to define the theme of first philosophy?

It so happens that a particular term regularly occurs in nonphilosophical English discourse to designate the most singular and authoritative dimension in human existence, our more or less vague conception of which determines our sense of what matters most in and about human life. It also happens that equivalents of this term have been introduced on pivotal occasions in Western intellectual history to express theses on what is fundamental in our existence or commanding about it— including the thesis presented early in this century by Buber and other so-called dialogical philosophers that interpersonal relationship as such is the ground and norm of meaning. The term is "spirit."

"Spirit" suffers philosophical neglect today in the English-speaking world for a variety of reasons. Insofar as it carries a generally intelligible meaning it is considered redundant to "mental," on the one hand, or "social," on the other. Probably it is generally assumed that any distinctive meaning of "spirit" would have to pertain to esoteric religious principles or experiences. The distinctive philosophical meaning of "spirit" in nineteenth-century idealism is now a liability for the concept of the spiritual, given the contemporary perception of that mode of thought as insupportably theological and unscientific.

In spite of its lapse from favor in English-speaking philosophical circles, I claim here, in advance of the argument, that the term "spiritual" remains uniquely suited to bear an adequate conception of the original situation where the order of priority in questions begins. To say that we are spiritual beings is to attain the correct orientation for addressing the question that imposes itself as a condition on all others—How will we live?—remaining aware that this first consideration is indeed a *question* (How—) concerning not simply you or me but all of *us* as *intenders* (—will we—) and in every aspect of our existence (—live?). When we allow our attention to be wholly occupied by other putatively fundamental conceptions, we invariably repress one or more features of our original situation from which the first question arises. "Reason," like "language," is embedded in relationship without exhausting it; it is only part of our life. "Mind," "consciousness," and "experience" are typically conceived in such a way that they can belong to the self alone; to mean more, they require the qualification of another conception. "Society" and "culture" represent collective behavior in its factual and fixed-normative aspects but not the *open question* of how to live among, with, and toward others as *free intenders*.

If, encouraged by philosophical tradition and everyday utterance, we are to adopt spirit as the theme of first philosophy, we must discover precisely what we are saying when we say we are spiritual and we must look into all that saying that implies. I propose, therefore, first to prepare the concept of the spiritual for use by examining philosophical and ordinary talk about the spiritual with some care, and then to work out the main lines of a comprehensive philosophy of the spiritual. Let it be said at the start that in carrying out this project we can neither resurrect idealism nor simply repeat the anti-idealist proclamations of dialogical philosophy. We will have to dispute with the one for its conceptual centerpiece and draw the other into new relations and applications.

The weightier task of this essay is, of course, to explain and defend the conception just sketched of the origin of priority in meaning. To justify the adoption of a certain term for that conception might seem to be a relatively trivial matter, but the conception is not arrived at apart from the term. The term delivers it to us. Moreover, the term is our guide if we wish to follow the history of the conception, and from that history we have much to learn about the affinities and disaffinities of the conception in the field of philosophical thinking. The word "spiritual" also must serve as a bridge between philosophical and everyday discourse.

Our investigations in Part One will bring to light the problems and opportunities that constitute the agenda of first philosophy. That agenda will be addressed in Part Two.

I
Preparation of the Concept of the Spiritual

Chapter 1

Historical Introduction of the Concept of the Spiritual

A historical survey of the meanings of spirit-words in the languages and philosophies of the West can be neither straightforward nor complete. Not only do the important spirit-words (*ruach, pneuma, psyche, thumos, spiritus, Geist, esprit,* and "spirit," to name a few) have significantly different histories, but a conception borne by a spirit-word at one time may be inherited from words in different families—as, for instance, Hegel's *Geist* owes so much to Aristotle's *nous* and Heraclitus' *logos*. Thus a comprehensive history of "spirit" would have to deal with "mind" and "reason" as well. The picture is further complicated when we consider that spirit-words are not the ordinary sort of referring words, the object of which could be demonstrated, but rather belong to that interesting class of ideological words that exist precisely in order to be postured with and argued about rather than settled by stipulation. This means that the essential history of these words includes the ways in which religious, philosophical, and cultural communities have used them to define themselves and advance their interests.

For our purposes, the history of the concept of the spiritual can be brought out perspicuously by focusing on moments in the development of the philosophical tradition when a spirit-word was deliberately introduced as the vehicle of a new thought or argument. At six such moments we will examine the uses of such words and their legacies (sections 1.2–1.7). This survey will put us in a position to identify the chief issues involved in any future use of the concept of the spiritual (1.8).

But the necessary preliminary to entering into this history is to inquire into the sense of the old spirit-words that were available from the beginning for philosophical appropriation.

1.1 The Root Metaphor in Spirit-Terms and the Questions It Raises

Our ancestral spirit-terms—in Hebrew, *ruach;* in Greek, *psyche* and *pneuma;* in Latin, *anima* and *spiritus*—all borrow metaphorically the phenomenon of moving air, breath and wind, to characterize human life most decisively. *Geist* springs from a root meaning of being moved powerfully, as in fear or amazement.[1] The common idea is that of an invisible power that has important visible effects. We do often encounter events of great consequence that have invisible causes. In natural experience the air is by far the most impressive invisible force, and so offers itself as a parable of all others. Living things, which move themselves, do so because they have a special wind inside them, the breath of life; when the breath is gone, so is the life. Since the self or (in its more recent sense) "soul" is the moving principle of the human body, it seems natural that a word for wind would eventually be adopted as a word for selfhood. But the metaphor has other implications as well. For one thing, the wind blows far and wide; the same wind can affect many different things in its one way, and so can be a principle of union and of a certain style. Under the north wind, all the trees in a forest lean south, notwithstanding their individual differences; with a spirit dwelling among them, a people are equal to a great feat or a distinctive mode of social existence. In addition, breath's process of inhaling and exhaling implies an exchange by which beings are intimately linked with exterior reality. A breathing being is more fundamentally dependent on air than on food. Air is normally the element in which it moves, the condition of its existence at every moment. Further, by means of little explosions and transmissions in air, people communicate by language, which is the most mysteriously powerful in its effects of all invisible forces. A word is, like air, imperceptible in its motion, but, stranger even than air, also imperceptible in its action. We do not feel words pressing into our faces.

Breathing and blowing is thus an image for the life-force or life-principle that is pregnant with particular implications. People who think of the life-principle in this way will undoubtedly arrive at different conclusions about it than people who think of it as, say, the heat of the blood. But we must realize that conceiving the life-principle is not as simple as fitting one image to one phenomenon. For the last few thousand years at least, human beings have felt themselves confronted with alternative *kinds* of life proceeding from alternative principles. Yahweh's invitation to the Israelites, "Therefore choose life," is embedded in a lengthy explanation of the conduct that constitutes true or righteous life and that differs from what people would do if left to themselves.[2] The very offering of choice removes this "life" from the province of biology. God's *ruach,* distinct from the original "breath of life" animating human beings and the ordinary intelligence with which they are gifted, is not immanent in humanity as such; when this spirit, like the *pneuma hagion* of the New Testament, gets into people, they lead the extraordinary lives of prophets and saints. Such a "wind" is leading, authoritative. But just as there can be more than one wind and a competition between winds, because of the way wind supervenes on the landscape, so there can be rivalry between alternative kinds of life.

———————

If "spirit" or "spirits" are thought to be abroad in the world, or if a "spiritual" dimension is thought to qualify human life—invisibly effective, communicating and unifying, authoritative—then certain questions are bound to arise pertaining to the character and relations of spirit. Any serious attempt to think the spiritual through must sooner or later confront all of them.

How precisely is the spiritual to be defined, especially in relation to concepts closely akin such as "soul" and "mind"? And what ontological presumption about spirit will underlie the attempt to define it?

How does the spiritual influence or frame of reference affect our conception of the starting point of thought—the real, the given, the concrete?

What is the relation of the spiritual influence or frame of reference to rationality?

How does spirit determine the meaning of personal life?

What is the relation of the authority of spirit or spirits to our judgments of validity and worth?

What is the relation between the spiritual and the material?

How is spirit causally active in the world?

We will now see how the most noteworthy precedents in the history of conceptions of the spiritual equip us to answer these questions.

1.2 Anaximenes—*Pneuma* and *Psyche*

Ancient accounts make it appear that Thales of Miletus was so impressed with unexpected phenomena of spontaneous motion, like magnetic attraction, that he proclaimed: "All things are full of gods" (or, as Plato wanted to say, of *psyche*, soul.)[3] But he is also reported by Aristotle to have held that everything arises from water.[4] On the basis of such scanty and inconsistent testimony, we cannot make any claims about the substance of Thales' thought, although he might have entertained the notion of a spiritual principle. Probably his successor Anaximenes was the first to posit a world-substance, air, which at the same time could be the active ingredient in human life. Given Anaximenes' commitment to air, the breath-word *psyche* and wind-word *pneuma* naturally assumed importance in his thought.

Air for Anaximenes is both the prime stuff and the prime movement, which (for a Greek) is equivalent to the immortal divine being and the most powerful divine agency. He claims, according to Aetius, that "as our soul (*psyche*), being air, holds us together and controls us, so does wind (*pneuma*) and air enclose the whole world."[5] We find here not only an appropriation of the Homeric notion of a breath-soul for cosmology, but the conception of a world-soul—divine, of course —ingredient in or mirrored by the human soul, which in a few centuries will be cultivated in Stoicism. Diogenes of Apollonia is said to have held that "men and the other living creatures live by air, through breathing it. And this is for them both soul (*psyche*) and intelligence (*noesis*)"—an idea that is at least implicit in the fragment from Anaximenes.[6]

Anaximenes bequeathes to his successors the task of correlating the principle of an individual's life, *psyche* or "soul," with a transpersonal or cosmic principle of life, *pneuma* or "spirit." Yet these two themes are not held together in subsequent Greek philosophy. Although there is a continuing attempt to relate the individual's *psyche* to something greater, the divine, *pneuma* is replaced by other transcending realities. For example, Empedocles' great theme is cosmic Love, principle alike of the divine Sphere and the rightly ordered human life.[7] Heraclitus prefers to discourse upon the *logos*, word or reason, *according to which* "all things are one."[8] The Pythagoreans in Italy are so impressed by the measure and proportion discoverable in the world that they identify the reality of everything, including *psyche*, with *number*. (They do, however, relate the soul to the divine in ascribing to it immortality and perpetual motion.)[9] And in Athenian philosophy from Anaxagoras through Aristotle the dominant problem becomes the relationship between soul, mind (*nous*), and *form* as such.

Anaximenes' *pneuma* is, however, prominent in the thinking of the Greek physicians, who find it a serviceable term for a material life-force amenable to medical treatment. For Hippocrates, *pneuma* is a universal moving air that human beings imbibe through nose, mouth, and pores. The soul is nothing other than "the inner *pneuma*, continuously renewed by inspiration and exhalation, which lends the whole organism movement and life."[10] The physicians' reflection on *pneuma* passes back into the philosophical tradition in Stoicism, where the notion of a world-soul is kept alive, and not just the individual soul but reason itself can be derived from it.[11]

The implication of the ways in which *pneuma* and *psyche* do and do not claim attention after Anaximenes is that in Greek thought the metaphorical affinity of wind and air remains strictly material and vital. When interest turns to intellectual and formal principles that would transcend and unify individuals, other words, and with them other notions, gain priority.

1.3 Anaxagoras to Aristotle—*Nous;* Plato—*Thumos*

The origin of *nous*, a word meaning "mental perception" already in Homer and best translated in philosophical texts as "mind," is unknown.[12] Although *nous* is not a moving-air word, the Greek conception of mind has so dominated the modern Western conception of the spiritual that we have no alternative but to treat it as a spirit-word. As will appear, this is a deeply problematic development, but one that must be thought through.

Nous is suddenly installed as the primary agency and authority in the world by Anaxagoras. He claims that in a cosmos in which everything is mixed up with everything else, mind alone is separate from everything: pure, therefore unlimited, therefore self-ruled. It has power over matter in much the same way that people who know what they want have power over people who do not; its fast and steady rotation, which got the world going in the beginning, now expands to govern more and more of the world's motion. All living things are under its control. Anaxagoras does not declare that mind is incorporeal, only (in the fashion then prevailing) that it is the finest and most subtle of substances. It stands to reason for him that mind knows everything, since mind arranged everything.[13]

Socrates' and Plato's references to Anaxagoras are sometimes derogatory because of the shallowness and inconsistency they perceive in his teachings, yet they are fundamentally at one with him in their commitment to the principle of mind. In the *Phaedo* Socrates relates how he came across Anaxagoras' assertion that mind is cause and controller of everything, and how this pleased him:

> Somehow it seemed right that mind should be the cause of everything, and I reflected that if this is so, mind in producing order sets everything in order and arranges each individual thing in the way that is best for it. Therefore if anyone wished to discover the reason why any given thing came or ceased or continued to be, he must find out how it was best for that thing to be, or to act or be acted upon in any other way. On this view there was only one thing for a man to consider, with regard both to himself and to anything else, namely the best and highest good.[14]

In this text the Socratic shift to moral philosophy (which became the dominant thread in the fabric of Plato's thought) is accomplished by marrying the theme of a rational cosmological principle to the theme of excellence, and human excellence in particular. Mind is *authoritative,* not only because of its unity with the world's constitutive measure and proportion, but because it intends the best. By taking this perspective on mind, Socrates and Plato also open the question of the goodness of what exists in a new way; goodness is an object of dialectical investigation and moral insight, not merely an axiomatic, unexamined attribute of divine Nature.

Plato works out the position of mind in the soul, greatly refining the concept of soul in the process. Soul is still the moving force in a living thing; in book X of the *Laws*, soul is identified as the universal principle of self-motion, and thus as the cause of all motion. The quality of a soul is, moreover, the cause of the quality of a motion, so that if the motion of a heavenly body is orderly and regular, then the soul that moves it must be a wise one, subject entirely to mind's control.[15] Plato's crucial conviction about mind, the faculty of cognition, is that it is akin to the definite-therefore-definable Forms of real, that is, unchanging, being. That much is prescribed by the necessity of an a priori connection between intelligence and the intelligible. But beyond this the soul itself, as the principle of life, must be a being like the Forms, for it is, like them, invisible.[16] It is innately capable of accord with the Forms, of not only recognizing them but loving them.[17]

Platonic *nous* and *psyche* are incorporeal, which opens up a range of new insights and, at the same time, new problems. Plato's argument in the *Phaedo* that the soul must be immortal because incorporeal things, being invulnerable to decomposition, generally are, raises the suspicion that by "soul" nothing more might be meant than the *concept* of a living being. (How would a concept cause material being to move?) In the *Apology* Socrates makes the political task of attending to Athens *herself* rather than this or that of Athens' affairs, and the moral task of attending to *oneself* rather than this or that external circumstance affecting one, sound of one piece with the philosophical task explained in the *Republic* of attending to the Forms of reality. If Socrates-as-such is abstracted from this or that circumstance of Socrates' physical existence, what remains of Socrates besides what can be conceived of him, in principle by anyone? The same question can be aimed at Aristotle when he defines soul as the first grade of actuality of a living thing, the form which the living thing's matter is the matter of.[18]

Our suspicion would not be roused if it were clear that the soul only exists where there is "subjectivity," inwardness, or a making-one's-own of experience; but that is just the point that is not made in either Plato's or Aristotle's writings, a point that does not figure in their intellectual world as it does in the modern. To be sure, there is more to soul than mind: the soul is essentially capable of being affected by particular natural things, and thus can have a unique experience and history. Plato even admits in the *Philebus* that the mixed life of pleasure and intelligence, that is, the proper collusion between Limit (the Forms) and the Unlimited (the changeable stuff of Nature) is the best. But he never ceases to envision a transcending of flesh-bound existence to a condition of direct rapport with the Forms, finally with the Form of the Good underlying the Forms, wherein it becomes very difficult to conceive what could remain, in "soul," of a self. As far as one can tell, in such a condition all distinctions between souls are abolished or emptied of significance. That being so, if the soul's authentic destiny is to attain this condition, then it must be seen as a kind of mirroring of the Forms themselves, an intermediary by which they enter into the realm of becoming as conscious *logos* at the same time that they constitute the being of things by supplying due measure and proportion.[19] On the other hand, it may plausibly be claimed that the crucial theme of Plato's philosophizing is the mortal life lived under the regulative idea of immortal rapport with the Forms, rather than actual immortality; there are many hints that support this interpretation, which is more congenial to contemporary postmetaphysical views of soul.[20] But Plato himself is only indirectly "existential." His interest points outward, toward the Forms, and so accordingly does the sense he attaches to spirit-words.

That soul exists for the sake of mind is argued most clearly in the *Timaeus*, while sketches of the chain of command within the soul are offered in the *Republic* and in the *Phaedrus* myth of the chariot.[21] Mind is the divinely given, immortal part of soul, whose task is to prevail over the confounding impulsions of the soul's mortal parts—"mortal" in the sense that they are fitted specifically to bodily existence and changeable. One of these mortal parts is a type of spirit and a natural ally of mind, namely, *thumos,* the ambitious, courageous, "irascible" power of the soul. (The root sense of *thumos* is *violently* moving air.)[22] According to the chariot myth, *thumos* is the fair steed pulling the chariot upward toward truth and beauty as directed by the driver, mind. If it were not for *thumos,* the other, dark steed, base appetite, would drag the chariot-soul downward or at least deadlock the driver. Thumic ambition for undying worldly glory is noted in the *Symposium* as an early stage on the way to love of true being.[23] (The *thumos*-theory is one way to try to conceive nonselfish *motivation* in a sensuous creature such that it is free to be a subject of reason. Is the existence of a distinct *thumos* a psychological possibility? Or does it need to be? Could not *thumos* be just the partial permeation of the vital aspect of the soul with mindlikeness, translating desires and aversions into more disinterested forms within larger perspectives?[24] Or is the energy of thumic anger and zest necessarily vital? The psychology in Plato's dialogues taken together is ambiguous enough to support different interpretations, but it points mainly in this latter direction.)

The *Timaeus* story of creation resembles the account of Anaxagoras in tracing the beginning of everything to a primordial confrontation between Mind and Necessity in which Mind gains dominion through "persuasion."[25] The motion of mind itself, the principle innate in it that moves it to act creatively, is generosity.[26] It will rescue the world from disorder by implanting in it as much measure and harmony, as much mind-likeness, as it can receive.[27] We cannot finally say whether Plato's picture of the Demiurge creating the world according to the eternal pattern is meant to maintain a distinction between Mind and that which is apprehended by Mind, the Forms, or whether it is just another way of representing Mind.[28] On this point the studied mysteriousness of Plato will give way to the plain assertion by Aristotle (who has cleared the ground by denying separate being to the Forms) that mind is identical with its proper objects.

Most of Aristotle's important ideas about mind are also Plato's: that it is immaterial, that it has its own objects distinct from the objects of the senses (notwithstanding their ontological disagreement just mentioned), that it is of divine origin, that it is the naturally authoritative part of the human soul, that the life ruled by mind is the best life and dearest to the gods, that a person's mind should be considered that person's true self, that mind can be conceived as existing separately, and that a cosmic mind has in some fashion causal primacy in the universe, just as the human mind ideally rules the human being. Some of these shared ideas are given an Aristotelian twist, however, and some new ideas are added to them.

Whereas Plato always thinks of soul as the self-moving, Aristotle thinks it is an error to ascribe motion to the soul. He argues that although the soul must be considered the primordial cause of motion in several senses, nevertheless if the soul were itself supposed to be in motion, it would be impossible to understand how it could change place, alter, grow, or diminish without violating its essential nature.[29] For that essential nature is to be the very actuality of a living being. We should simply say that the living being moves and the soul is the principle of this motion. The Orphic notion entertained by Plato that souls have lives separate from bodies raises an insoluble problem, which Plato was content to leave in obscurity, as to how souls convey their motions to bodies.[30] To the contrary, the soul must be conceived in essential community with the body, just as the Forms are in nature. The soul is the formal cause of the body's life, as its definable essence; the final cause of life, through providing the goal of well-being for the sake of which the living thing acts; and the efficient cause of life, since no other power is observed that can account for vital phenomena.[31]

Mind, however, is held to be separable from the other psychic powers—among which, by the way, the Platonic *thumos* no longer appears—and from the body.[32] It "seems to be an independent substance implanted within the soul and to be incapable of being destroyed." [33] Mind is eternal because it is essentially bound to that which is wholly actual, namely, essences or Forms, and whatever is wholly actual is unchangeable since it has no potential for new determination. The mind is the very faculty of determination and its adequate objects are entirely determined things. Aristotle exploits the double meaning of determination by asserting that a cosmic Mind that *makes* all things exists in addition to the human mind that ascertains all things.[34] This divine mind is essentially activity, for activity is superior to passivity. We learn in the *Metaphysics* that its essential activity is to think itself.[35]

Mind is called the "form of forms," the actuality of actualities—which perhaps is just to say that it is the concept of concepts.[36] But could a concept as such be *active*? What precisely is the difference in predicating activity, as distinct from actuality, of mind? Activity occurs only when there is something to do, which is to say, a potential to be actualized. Activity is superior to passivity just because actuality is superior to potency. There could not be any change in a wholly actual being, such as God, and for that reason Aristotle is careful not to impute activity to God even in asserting that human mind is most like the divine mind when it is active, that is, when it possesses rather than merely receives the objects of thought.[37] Human mind must exert itself to resemble divine mind and thus is happiest when doing so, but it would be absurd to say that the divine mind exerts itself when it is perfect—unless that mind somehow acts on what is outside it as a surplus over anything that would need to be done to become what it is. Anaxagoras, we recall, held both that mind is perfect in itself and that it acts on the elements by imparting more and more of its rotation to them. Aristotle's view that God moves the world as its final cause is not, after all, dissimilar. But this means that there is a divinely powered forming of matter, and thus that both God and the "active intellect" of *On the Soul* can be understood to act on what is outside themselves without compromising their actuality in acting. The remaining difference between the "acts" of the two would be that although human mind only becomes actual in so acting, we cannot properly speak of the actualization of God, only of everything else's actualization toward and thanks to God. This is the "generosity" of the Aristotelian God, to move everything toward itself simply by existing perfectly.

But we do not yet know whether this pure actuality, either of God or of the immortal part of humanity, is to be taken as a concept. Can we conceive of an immaterial existent that is not a concept? Only by making of that immaterial existent a subject, that is, making it a thinking, and not just a thought. Aristotle does this. He claims on the one hand that the actuality of thought is life and a blessed one at that, but on the other hand that actual thought is identical with its objects, grasps itself as an object (a pure actuality or essence) like them in possessing them, and thus finally thinks itself.[38] This means that we should either allow the familiar sense of "concept" to impose an unfamiliar sense on "life," or allow the familiar sense of "life" to impose an unfamiliar sense on "concept." The latter seems to be Aristotle's intention, as it will later be Hegel's. The only confirmation of this view, but the appropriate one, is in thinking itself, which finds that concepts (forms disengaged from matter) *are* its life. "Spiritual life" is immaterializing formation of the material, as formal cause, and eternalizing consummation of the temporal, as final cause.

Because the *nous*-philosophy of Plato and Aristotle is decisive for all further philosophical thought in the West, certain of its implications must be constantly borne in mind as we proceed.

We should first observe that not only *mind* has emerged as the primordial element in the universe and the authoritative element in humanity; *philosophy* has come into its own, too, in the sense that it has gained a reflective grasp of a subject matter distinguishing it from the other sciences and has reasoned out its own unsurpassed excellence as a mode of human life. Plato and Aristotle's commitment to the study of mind is not unconnected with their sense of the special importance of being a philosopher. The theses that philosophers must rule society (the *Republic*) and that philosophers are the happiest of human beings (the *Nicomachean Ethics*) belong to the same fabric as do their theses on mind.

Mind is alive, although under the conditions of physical existence it requires a soul in which to be implanted; it is at least capable of being free of the influences of physical existence, although it can be wrongly subordinated to the lower, mortal parts of the soul, and fail in its vocation of ruling the person; it is a native citizen of an immaterial realm populated by forms or essences (or, possibly, "concepts") and is in some sense the same sort of thing that they are; because it is essentially in rapport with things which do not change, its intuitions and judgments are always right; it is not itself moved, but moves (if we may accept Aristotle's view on this, since Plato does not seem committed to disputing the point), and in this sense is creative, for it is the author of mindlikeness in everything.

The characteristic mental event is cognition of a form. Despite the differences in what they say about the provenance of knowledge of universals, both Plato and Aristotle think of cognition as a beholding, a mental equivalent of seeing, which grasps what is as what cannot be other than it is. Aristotle goes further and speaks of thought's possession of its object, by which it "makes" the object, as light in a sense "makes" color. (The subject of the parallel assertion in Plato is the Form of the Good which commonly informs thought and its objects, not thought as such.)[39] The necessity in knowledge is not a noxious, constraining one, at odds with a thing's nature, but the experience, one might say, of the strength of a thing's being and the strength of the mind knowing it. This happy necessity is the freedom of thing and mind from the distraction of sense-experience and its dilution of being; it is the elimination of possibilities that is entailed by complete actuality, as opposed to compulsion.

It will be worthwhile now to direct questions at two unresolved issues in Greek philosophy that will be crucial for us later.

First, what are the true grounds of the *authority* of soul with respect to the body, or of mind with respect to soul? Several answers that seemed of self-evident force to Plato and Aristotle but are unsatisfying to us must be placed to one side: namely, that the immortal is naturally superior to the mortal, or that the cause is superior to the effect, or that the organ of exact or certain knowledge is superior to the organs of changeable experiences like the passions. This last reason would ground the authority of mind for the purposes of science, or at least a certain kind of science, but not for living in general.

Our question, in the sense we give it, cannot be answered by any philosopher before Socrates, for not until Socrates and Plato are mind and soul defined by their orientation toward the good, or the best; and not until the Platonic dialogues do we find any extended attempt to justify the life of mind over against the rival claims of pleasure and power. Argument on this line presupposes awareness of a problem of authority that is no longer settled among enlightened Greeks by the traditional yardstick of immortality. It could be said that Plato and Aristotle have a new Parmenidean yardstick that they everywhere apply, the principle of Being or actuality, and that for them the "best" is self-evidently that which perfects or maximizes actuality, which is the fundamental good. Such an interpretation would be unavoidable were it not for the complication we brought to light earlier concerning the divine "generosity." Plato's very mention of God's "generosity" implies that there is something better than perfect being as such, which then necessarily displaces the principle of being as unconditionally authoritative. The point is also put before us by Socrates' teasing remark in the *Republic* that the Good is beyond even Being in dignity and surpassing power.[40]

The *Timaeus* and book X of the *Laws* are permeated with wonder at the existence of the universe, and this wonder sets itself up as a pious norm. Failure to appreciate the universe greatly is either sin or madness. Of course, the sheer existence of the universe is one remarkable thing about it, but not the only one. Plato appreciates its mindlikeness, the dominance on the large scale of order and proportion. Only a mindlike universe, not just any universe at all, would elicit reverence of the sort that Plato shows. Beyond this, however, there is the additional and perhaps supremely important consideration that the world arose not through a quasi-mechanical transference of rotation from a mind-principle—as Anaxagoras would have it, and Aristotle too, whose final causation works like this rotation—but from a benevolent, generous intention on the part of a God. The goodness of this God goes beyond the excellence internal to the divine existence, as God intentionally addresses other beings by deciding to bring everything into existence and by attending to even the minutest affairs of the world.[41] We speculated earlier that the soul's *thumos* might be interpreted as its vitality permeated in part by mind; reversing this order, can God be interpreted as a permeation of the principle of form by "heart," thumic generosity? Would the participation of "heart" be a condition of the goodness and authority of the spiritual dimension of existence? (Unfortunately, this suggestion has no future within Platonism, for *thumos* is mortal.)

It is an old question whether God is diminished or magnified in being credited with particular intentions, either feelings or purposes. From the Aristotelian point of view, any account of God deciding to act or attending to lesser beings is a fairy tale; on the opposed view, Aristotle's Thought Thinking Itself is not worthy of worship and obedience because it is not personally active. The point of greatest interest here, though, is that the creativity or generosity of Plato's God is *not* an attribute of mind, and therefore no part of mind's authority, *unless* mind not only is the best thing to have or be, but does the best thing to do, as Plato's God goes beyond his good being to do the good vis-à-vis other beings. In that case a mind-God would be essentially intentional. But then we might ask on Aristotle's behalf: What could be better to do than to help all things toward the best thing to have? That is precisely what Aristotle's God does, if we did not err above in speaking of that God's activity *ad extra*. And mind in humanity imitates this "generosity" by introducing mindlikeness to the world in science and politics. If by this means we can link the essence of mind to an unsurpassable conception of goodness, if mind as such is the agency of the best, then its authority for life cannot be challenged. Aristotle's conception of goodness may not be identical to Plato's, but at least the design of his philosophy permits connecting it in similar fashion with mind.

Second: For all their interest in the problematic of comprehension as such, what reason have the Greeks shown for the intersubjective uniformity of comprehension?

There are two great dimensions of the problem of the possibility of comprehension. One is the relationship that comprehension presupposes between the mind and the world, a unifying principle that would account for both the operations of mind and the structure of the world; the Athenian philosophers finally posited mind as the principle both of creation (the reason that the world is) and of order (the reason that the world is the way it is). It could not simply be a coincidence that the inner order of mind was congruent with the outer order of the cosmos. The other dimension of the problem is the relationship that comprehension presupposes between mind and mind. It cannot simply be a coincidence that the inner order of mind in me is congruent with the inner order of mind in you. This subproblem is solved before it arises if it can be shown that there is perfect congruity, rather than a partial or analogical match, between the mind of any human philosopher (B, C, or D) and what there is to be known (A); for if B = A, and C = A, and D = A, then evidently B = C = D. But if there is something less than perfect and univocal repetition of the world's order in the order of the philosopher's mind, then B's relationship to A may differ from C's and D's. In that case B and C and D have to learn how to recognize mind in each other, how to take instruction from each other, and how to decide between themselves what mind in general is, or what reason is.

One can deny that anything less than a perfect and univocal correspondence between mind and thing deserves the name of comprehension, and this is what in effect Heraclitus meant by complaining that people are pulled by their private understandings away from the common *logos,* what Socrates meant by charging humanity with ignorance ignorant of itself, and why Plato and Aristotle both remarked on the scarcity of wise persons—so great a scarcity that the notion of a wise person might seem but a regulative ideal. But Plato was at least clear what mind *would* be; it *would* see the forms as the eye sees visible things. And Aristotle claimed with less reservation that he saw mind at work. None doubted that minds B, C, and D were the same, because with certain matters, above all mathematics, there was unanimity as to the objects of mind and their characteristics just as overwhelming as would be the unanimity of a crowd of people with normal vision identifying familiar objects. For all of Plato's sensitivity to the failures of rational inquiry to attain this unanimity in matters of "right and wrong, the noble and the base, and good and bad," [42] he staked his credit to the proposition that just as greater effort of attention is required to attain knowledge of abstract mathematical objects when compared with things of sense, so an even greater effort will yield knowledge of the still more abstract forms of the right, the noble, and the good. He did not concern himself with the possibility that because of certain physiological and cultural facts of life he and his associates were *lucky* to see things of vision the same, and to conceive abstract forms, like those of a mathematical system, the same—"lucky," that is, from the point of view of the program of mind, which would be wrecked were cognitive unity not attainable or at least plausibly to be projected.

Talk of "minds" would seem wrong to Plato and Aristotle. For them there is one thing, "mind," present in various places. But in this they assume what rather has to be demonstrated, and what they acknowledge in spite of themselves to be difficult to demonstrate. They do not try to demonstrate it, not only because they are lucky enough to have a prima facie case already made by the example of mathematics, but above all because, for them, the *purpose* of the concept of mind is to be unitary. They would not be satisfied defining mind as an individual's capacity for inwardly representing and comparing forms (of whatever sort) abstracted (however) from sense-objects. Mind is in the first place the truth-organ, and only secondarily an abstracting capability. It happens to be necessary to abstract in order to reach the truth. And since mind must be one thing, the question I have asked about congruity between "minds" is ruled out from the start. It is a conceptual error to ask it.

This unification of human experience in relation to *truth* is what Athenian philosophy has mainly accomplished by concentrating on the theme of "mind." But mind's relation to impersonal truth is much clearer than its relation to personal individuality, and its passive mirroring of the structure of reality can be understood much more readily than any activity on its part in or upon the world, let alone what we earlier vaguely called its "causal primacy."

In summary, ancient Greek philosophy presents us with no fewer than four important spirit-words, each offering a distinguishable sense to the assertion that humans are spiritual beings: they are enfolded and sustained by cosmic *pneuma;* they are ruled by a universally operative faculty of rational cognition, *nous;* each is vivified by an individual *psyche;* each has an emotional attraction to the right, the noble, and the good, *thumos.* Henceforth the Greek spirit-words will serve as our rubrics for these four aspects of the concept of the spiritual.

1.4 Philo and Paul—*Pneuma;* Augustine to Descartes—*Spiritus/Esprit*

Christianity immediately brings new possibilities, and eventually enforces new norms, for all thinking in the West. Not the least part of its impact is a distinctive conception of the spiritual reflected in a new use of the word *pneuma*.

Philo of Alexandria, the most eminent philosophical exponent of Hellenistic Judaism and a major stimulus and resource for the Alexandrian Christian theologians, is a transitional figure in our spirit-history. Under the influence of Stoicism, which had already encouraged the translation of the Hebrew term for divine spirit (*ruach*) as *pneuma* in the Septuagint, Philo introduces *pneuma* as a divinely grounded, world- and person-binding element and agency; faithful to the intentions of Platonism on the one hand and to the Jewish principle of the transcendence of God on the other, however, he conceives *pneuma* as incorporeal.[43] In so doing he detaches the concept of the spiritual from literal breath and wind, which is a major innovation in the semantics of Greek philosophy.[44] He is able to identify the divine *pneuma* with *nous* and thus to unify the two routes to truth that Plato had recognized but sharply distinguished, the heteronomous "inspiration" of the prophet or poet and the rational insight of the philosopher.[45] *Pneuma* as the governing element in authentic human existence is proper to us yet derived from an absolutely Other. When Philo uses the word *pneuma* instead of *nous,* he means our rational powers as communicated to us by God.[46]

Because of its Jewish background, *pneuma* has a different mission in the New Testament than in Greek thought. Notably, it is set in antithesis to the material creation. Since it is not "natural," it can restrict its presence to particular persons or communities at particular times, under specific conditions. Both Christians and Jews could think of the divine *pneuma* as a benefit available to them by virtue of their membership in religious communities.[47] And the same *pneuma* that is especially effective among the faithful must be distinguished from unholy "spirits" claiming the same distinction, as can be seen in the writings of the Christian apostle Paul.

Paul requires a way of speaking about a new and better kind of human life that is radically different from ordinary life, beyond the barrier of sin, and which thus can only be effected by the visitation of a redeeming power outside humanity—a power already understood to be the transcendent creator of the natural order. The principle of this new life has to be the sort of thing of which there can be more than one, since it contests a rival principle or principles for dominion in humanity; it must be capable of entering and influencing the lives of human beings without impairing their personalities and so cannot be a naturally given constituent of the human personality; it must very intimately belong to, and in some sense even be, *someone,* God; and it must be not only supersensible but superintelligible. *Nous* as conceived by Plato and Aristotle does not satisfy any of these criteria. *Nous* is not the sort of thing of which there can be more than one; as Aristotle maintains, it has no contrary, because it is actual.[48] The forces that oppose *nous* do not deserve the name of principles; all principles belong to it. It is an already-given constituent of human beings, indeed, that which makes human beings human, their true selves. Yet it is entirely impersonal. Finally, since *nous* is the agency of intellection, it would be nonsense to speak of a superintelligible *nous,* an agency whose wisdom was the foolishness of men—however superficially foolish Socrates in his wisdom might sometimes appear.

The wind-word *pneuma,* however, does largely meet the criteria. The holy spirit can get into one, supervening upon and reforming the mind with which human beings are naturally endowed; but so can other spirits "inspire" one, so that a question is always present in cases where people are carried away by invisible and apparently higher powers, whether those powers are or are from the true God. The Spirit will teach us to distinguish the spirits.[49] In any event, the possibility is already acknowledged (even by Plato) that in such a visitation from above, knowledge and power may be granted that exceed the limits of the given human constitution. Paul's usage, like Philo's, breaks with the Greek heritage of the term insofar as Paul means by *pneuma* something absolutely immaterial —as the Creator is absolutely distinct from the creation—and not just the finest or most rarefied or ubiquitous of natural substances. "Spiritual reality" in Paul is programmatically separated from worldly reality in much the same way that mind is kept separate by the *nous*-philosophers, a great difference being that spirit unlike mind is not intelligible to us of itself; rather, one might almost say that it is spirit precisely because it surpasses intelligibility. For example, Paul certainly does not have specific information to give on what the "spiritual body" of the resurrection is, other than that it is imperishable.[50] The point for him is that it is better than our present existence and for that very reason impossible adequately to conceive.

From Jerome's Bible and Augustine's writings forward, the immaterial *pneuma* of Philo and Paul becomes, for the Latin world, *spiritus;* repeating *pneuma's* progress, *spiritus* moves further away from the original meanings of breath and wind which Latin Stoicism had still traded on. But Augustine does not merely transmit the New Testament conception of the spiritual; he stamps the history of the conception with two fateful new characteristics. The "spiritual" becomes for him a realm of *substance* and at the same time a realm of *subjectivity.*

As he reports in his *Confessions,* Augustine's intellectual difficulties in accepting Christianity revolved around the notion of immaterial substance. He finally infers, in a line of thinking that will later be formalized by Anselm, that God must be substance than which nothing better can be conceived, and therefore an eternal substance distinct from the material.[51] He will not identify God here as "spiritual substance," and as a matter of fact John 4:24, "God is a spirit," is never quoted in the *Confessions.*[52] But the immaterial *creation,* distinct from God yet closer to God than the material, is the "spiritual" realm, the "heaven" of the biblical creation story's "heaven and earth."[53] Spirit is thus a substance that invisible things like souls are made of.

The second dimension of the substance argument in the *Confessions* is Augustine's complaint that the bondage of his imagination to material substance prevented him from understanding his *own* true nature.[54] The *Confessions* posits a spiritual realm encompassing the soul and with it all the innumerable motions of the heart that so fascinate Augustine. But these spiritual things are not of one piece with the transcendent Creator: now there is a distinction between the eternal invisible and the created invisible. "Spiritual" primarily refers to the created invisible realm of subjectivity, a stuff of unlimited fluidity before it receives illumination from its Creator.[55] Thus "spiritual" can be an adjective applied to "soul," and "spiritual" matters can be taken to mean "matters of the soul"—an equation that is quite common to this day.

The soul (*anima*) turns out to be Augustine's primary clue to the character of the spiritual. The fact that one's own thinking is an immaterial event should alert one to the existence of a realm superior to the material.[56] From the spiritual reality of knowledge we are led to affirm the reality of Truth Itself, which is God; in the spiritual event of *love* we feel ourselves lifted up toward the Eternal Lovable.[57]

The legacy of Paul and Augustine to all future thinking about "spirit" is manifold. From Paul we inherit the ability to use the word with striking freedom from existing speculative categories, possibly as the prime means of transcending those categories, in order to talk about something else of superordinate importance; with Paul, God's impossibly good action through Christ upon humanity. Augustine likewise uses the word "spiritual" to help himself conceive the maximally and transcendently good. On the other hand, we inherit from Augustine the notion, adapted from the Greeks, of spiritual substance, and therewith the prospect of an ontology of spirit. For Augustine immediately connects the theme of the initially incredible goodness of the Christian revelation to the theme of being, claiming first that the imperishable is self-evidently the better,[58] and then that being and goodness are inseparable:

> Either corruption does no harm (which is impossible), or (which is quite certain) all things which suffer corruption are deprived of something good in them. Supposing them to be deprived of all good, they will cease to exist altogether. For, if they continue to exist and can no longer be corrupted, they will be better than before, because they will be permanently beyond the reach of corruption. What indeed could be more monstrous than to assert that things could become better by losing all their goodness?[59]

An assumption common to Augustine and the Greeks is that the better a thing is, the more being it has. If something good is conceived to be a spirit, a kind of being must be assigned to that spirit, and the greater kind of being as being ("imperishable") according as the spirit is a better kind of thing (than "matter"). "Spiritual substance" is substance par excellence; that which is superlatively good must have perfect being; hence God and Being are the same.

Most importantly, the clue to the spiritual is the soul, which is distinguished not only by the intellectual power of mind (*mens* = *nous*) in it but also by love as its principle of motion. Joining the theme of love to the moving-air-word *spiritus* can produce a blending of Platonic *eros,* that inclination of the needy human mind toward the Forms, with the impulsive and outgoing "heart," *thumos,* as can be seen later when Aquinas explains the propriety of singling out one person of the divine Trinity by the name "Holy Spirit":

> For the name spirit in things corporeal seems to signify impulse and motion; for we call the breath and the wind by the term spirit. Now it is a property of love to move and impel the will of the lover towards the object loved. . . . Therefore because the divine person proceeds by way of the love whereby God is loved, that person is most properly named *The Holy Ghost [Spirit].*[60]

When Augustine says "My weight is my love; wherever I am carried, it is my love that carries me there," one almost gets the impression that the fair steed of the *Phaedrus* is running away with the charioteer.[61] But since Augustine's Platonic understanding of the structure of the soul preserves the intrapsychic authority of mind, this issue is unresolved. The ambiguity in Augustine will flower into the medieval debate over the primacy of intellect or will.

Twelve hundred years later the *esprit* of Descartes is a "spiritual substance" much like that conceived by Augustine. For Descartes, too, the outstanding feature of this substance is that it thinks, affirms, desires, and so forth. Especially crucial for him is the nature of the thinking thing's thought of *itself,* which by virtue of its coveted indubitability becomes the controlling factor in his metaphysics.[62] Augustine had brought in the principle of self-certainty to refute Academic skepticism:[63] in his own time, Descartes responds to Montaignean skepticism.

Descartes reinforces the distinction between the spiritual and the material, largely for philosophical and religious reasons already articulated by Plato. But he is also a physicist committed, like many of his contemporaries, to mechanistic scientific explanation. This means that spirit-matter dualism, which had always rendered the causal relations between spiritual and material being difficult to conceive except according to the Aristotelian form/content distinction, is an immediate embarrassment for Cartesianism. The realm of immaterial yet substantial selves is disconnected from the realm of "nature" or objects of sense-experience. Leibniz and Berkeley try unconvincingly to remove the embarrassment by deriving the appearances of matter from spiritual substance. Hume and Kant try to resolve the problem by rejecting the notion of spiritual substance, the effect of which is to make the status of soul more mysterious than ever. In Kant the more formal, less vital notion of rational mind (*nous*), expressed in German as *Vernunft*, becomes the focus of philosophy again.

Within Kant's own time, however, the new rise in Germany of social science and idealist philosophy begins to revitalize the concept of the spiritual.

1.5 Kant, Herder, Hegel, Kierkegaard—*Geist*

For a variety of reasons, Kant almost entirely refrains from using the German spirit-word *Geist*. Negatively, he wants to reject the knowledge-claims of metaphysical supernaturalism, which he thinks lack any true cognitive foundation. Positively, he is much more interested in illuminating *objectivity*—that is, objectively valid principles in scientific and moral judgment—than subjectivity in the sense of either personal identity or personal passion. Personal subjectivity is for Kant just an obstacle to objectivity. When he does adopt the word *Geist* in the *Critique of Judgment*, he associates it with the creative power of the imagination to produce intuitions to which concepts are not adequate.[64] *Geist*-spirit is thus outside the domain of *Vernunft*.

But the place of *Vernunft* comes to be debated in Kant's time as a *Geist*-party gathers strength. In the writings of Herder, Schiller, and Goethe, *Geist* emerges as an alpha-and-omega-term referring to a higher unity of human being that comprehends creativity and the life-force as well as the rational faculty.[65] They agree with Kant that *Geist* transcends *Vernunft* but not that *Vernunft* is the absolute authority for life and discourse. Herder suggests that reason and language are governed by a collective "genius" or "spirit" of the people, a vital power reproducing the divine energy on the human scale.[66] Just as remarkable as his introduction of a suprapersonal *pneuma*-spirit in this connection is his pluralization of it into the spirits of particular ages and places. (A near ancestor of this idea is Montesquieu's sociological conception of *esprits générales* peculiar to specific cultures.)[67] The plurality of spirits poses a fundamental challenge to reason: if spirit is controlling yet plural, how can there be one true a priori philosophy? Quite apart from that problem, how can rational thought hope to comprehend the spirit, particular or not, in which it is conducted?

The idealists Fichte, Schelling, and Hegel are not distracted by the Herderian prospect of many spirits. They are united by their resolve not to exclude anything from first philosophy, neither the historical-cultural world in all its variety nor the inner life as it goes beyond Kantian categories of the understanding and duty. For each of them, the word *Geist* is at one time or other the vehicle of that unlimited philosophical ambition.[68] We will attend to the most articulate and influential of the idealist conceptions of spirit, Hegel's.

Like the Greek philosophy of *nous* and the modern philosophies of the *cogito* and *Vernunft,* Hegel's philosophy casts itself as the rightful interpreter of a supremely important reality and thus justifies and glorifies itself. But whereas these earlier mind-conceptions established a point of *critical leverage* for philosophical thinking, an Archimedean point from which to evaluate everything that exists, Hegel's *Geist* is a vehicle of unprecedented *comprehensiveness* that takes everything that exists into philosophical thinking. What remained a mere hint in Aristotle's remark that *nous* in a sense "makes all things" becomes for Hegel a program of demonstration.

The purpose of Hegelian philosophy is to know what there is to know. And everything is to be known; for even what is taken to be unknown is known as unknown, and has meaning only as known. It is impossible to think or talk of something exterior to the knowing mind. Therefore we should abandon the pretense of criticizing and limiting knowledge, in the manner of Locke and Kant. Knowledge is actual, knowledge is all there is, and knowledge is committed to overcoming every apparent limit that it encounters since it knows that these limits have been created only by itself as a stratagem for unfolding itself. To accept this principle is already to have glimpsed the standpoint of absolute knowledge, although to say this much is only to announce a task that has still to be accomplished, if spirit is actually to take possession of absolute knowledge.

Hegel speaks of "spirit" rather than "being" because to know without limit what is to be known is to know it not merely as substance but at the same time as subject. Being that is not subject, being in itself, is but a limited mode of being inasmuch as it is a dead thing artificially removed from the being-known in which known things have their reality. On the other hand, being that is purely subject, being for itself, is a limited mode of being because it is pure negativity, the other-than-the-known. Only being-in-and-for-itself is completely inclusive, unlimited being; hence the task of philosophy is to realize it. Hegelian spirit is not, therefore, discarnate subjectivity or pure rationality any more than it is pure substance. Precisely the connotations that disqualified *pneuma* for the purposes of Plato and Aristotle—its vital materiality and its uncanniness—now recommend it to Hegel, who means to overcome all dualisms.

The primary act of spirit is self-identification, in which being and knowing are synthesized. This synthesis is not accomplished all at once. In order to give itself to itself to know in its unlimited concrete richness, spirit unfolds itself in nature (its most fundamental yet still only apparent "other") and in history. Only by grasping and at the same time overcoming the manifold distinctions in the phenomena, together with the many stages of phenomenal consciousness and consciousness of self, does spirit free itself from the limitations described above and thereby become actual in the way that is proper to spirit.[69]

Hegel inherits and turns to account most of the ideas we have already discussed. He is especially Aristotle's heir, if we see the leading edge of Aristotle's thought in his remarks on the perfect actuality of *nous*—a *concept* (the later Hegel's "Idea") which is a *life*. The primary difference is that Hegel's spiritual Concept or Idea does not stand outside of history like Aristotle's; it *is* history, and could not exist except historically. In that respect it is more like Anaximenes' air and Stoic *pneuma,* subject to Hebrew-Christian temporalization. The Pauline conception of spirit as the agent of reconciliation between alienated (sinful) individuals and their ground in Absolute Spirit also informs the Hegelian project of overcoming without simply abolishing all otherness. But spirit has again become an immanent cosmological principle in a way that had been excluded by orthodox Christianity. In fact, Hegel inherits and includes so much that his conception of spirit becomes difficult to recognize, for spirit had nearly always been invoked as a function of one or another sort of dualism.[70] Consequently, even when the notion of the spiritual loses its standing in the materialistic thought of Marx, the main claim that Hegel made about the spirit—that its essential activity is to overcome its alienation from itself by working through stages of self-externalization and self-opposition—can remain, as predicated of empirical humanity.

Hegel articulates the concept of the spiritual by recognizing the three stages of subjective, objective, and absolute spirit. "Subjective spirit" takes in all the phenomena of soul and consciousness as they are experienced.[71] It corresponds to the spiritual realm as Descartes conceived it. "Objective spirit" comprises all the demands with which spirit confronts itself to produce an objective world adequate to spirit, where universal freedom is expressed in moral and political forms canceling the contradictions between his life and hers, your will and mine. Insofar as such contradictions exist, there obtains a spiritually inactual state of affairs, for the essence of spirit is to be free, that is, to determine itself, which means to be unhindered by any opposition. (Whereas Hegel concentrates on the themes of *Sittlichkeit* and the State in his philosophy of objective spirit, Dilthey later fruitfully expands his conception to include all the forms of culture.)[72] We experience the ethical order and the State not merely as givens but as spiritual self-expressions with which we may consciously identify, thereby transcending our individuality. But our individuality is not actually overcome merely by membership in this higher ordering of ourselves. Only "absolute spirit" supersedes the remaining externality that separates individuals from themselves, from each other, and from nature; here spirit attains unlimited being-in-and-for-itself, perfect actuality, no form of subjectivity or objectivity lacking from the synthesis. This condition, apprehended (though still at a distance) by religious faith, is only fully actualized in philosophy—that is, in unlimited thinking-through.[73]

Were we to apply the Aristotelian causal scheme to the Hegelian account of spirit, we would conclude that Hegel's *Geist* moves the world as formal and final cause. At least, insofar as it is appropriate to distinguish between certain phenomena and "spirit," the relationship we must posit between the phenomena to be comprehended and the principle of comprehension is one of formal and final causation. Spirit is the true meaning of things in the double sense that it constitutes their true nature and is also the end for the sake of which they were, are, and will be realized. Efficient causation, a merely external relation between the designated causes and effects, is seen through, and vanishes, when the proper standpoint is attained.[74]

Hegel consummates the Cartesian project of perfecting comprehension for its own sake. Descartes' audacity was to doubt everything; Hegel's is to know everything. Both insist on the self of "I know" that grasps itself, but Hegel has arrived at a more adequate self that can know all in knowing itself. The principle that "an out-and-out Other simply does not exist for spirit" incites the philosopher to elicit spirit's recognition of itself in everything on heaven and earth.[75] Why not throw ourselves into this project? What could be gained by holding back? Even if we cannot presently reduce this or that opposition in philosophical insight, will we not be braver and busier if we assume that we shall eventually manage to reduce it? Can a philosopher under any circumstances shrink from comprehension? And how conceive a greater aim of comprehension than that union of knowing and being for which the German language offers Hegel the word *Geist*?

Yet the spirit-words continue to be the property of Christianity. Kierkegaard, meaning to represent Christianity, takes seriously in principle the creatureliness and sinfulness of humanity as limits to comprehension and will not use the term "spirit" to *mean* the very overcoming of such limits, as Hegel does. Kierkegaard speaks not only as a theologian attempting to check the pretensions of philosophy but also as a philosopher who finds human reason in a paradoxical embrace with the very thing that Hegel had ruled out of court, a Totally-Other. This Other reason is unable to conceive (since anything it can conceive is only relatively different from it); at the same time, reason is unable to escape from it.[76]

Is there a special Kierkegaardian contribution to the history of the concept of the spiritual? His definitions of "spirit" are not very unlike Hegel's. He seems rather to have adapted the Hegelian conception to apply strictly to the existing individual, whose task of existing cannot be superseded by any speculative comprehension. The individual must synthesize soul and body, the eternal-universal and the temporal-particular, into a unity, a self—and this accomplished relation, *when* it is accomplished, is called "spirit."

Man is spirit. But what is spirit? Spirit is the self. But what is the self? The self is a relation which relates itself to its own self, or it is that in the relation that the relation relates itself to its own self; the self is not the relation but that the relation relates itself to its own self.[77]

To be *spirit* is to be *I*. God desires to have *I*'s, for God desires to be loved.[78]

The distinction between divine and human spirit returns more or less as Augustine would draw it:

> Such a relation which relates itself to its own self (that is to say, a self) must either have constituted itself or have been constituted by another.
>
> If this relation which relates itself to its own self is constituted by another, the relation doubtless is the third term, but this relation (the third term) is in turn a relation relating itself to that which constituted the whole relation.
>
> Such a derived, constituted, relation is the human self, a relation which relates itself to its own self, and in relating itself to its own self relates itself to another.[79]

The human self cannot possess itself, i.e., cannot be a self, without relating itself to its Creator who has constituted it; the heart of the eternal/temporal being cannot be quieted until it finds rest in the infinite being that created it.[80] But Hegel says the same: the dynamism of spirit is such that finite spirit cannot rest content until its finite form is grounded in its infinite form, which transcends while preserving the finite form. Kierkegaard refrains from leaping to the cognitive standpoint of the infinite but does not dispute the reality of the infinite, or that that reality is to be conceived as the self-possession of a self, or for that matter that any self has any higher aim than to be a self as a self.[81]

Kierkegaard's hesitation in contrast with Hegel's boldness remains highly significant, more significant perhaps than the assumptions they evidently share about the nature of spirit as such. For Kierkegaard's purport is that human individuals can only with great difficulty actualize themselves as spiritual beings; to comprehend humanity as it exists to be observed, it is necessary to discern its pervasive spiritlessness, its dread and despair in falling short of spirit. Kierkegaard's use of the concept is more critical and, in the Kantian sense, regulative, whereas Hegel triumphantly names "spirit" an actual and active fact.

1.6 Scheler and Hartmann—*Geist, Geistig*

The enormous increase in the explanatory power of biology and the social sciences in the nineteenth century contributed to the fall of idealism and created a new felt need to defend the "personal" and "spiritual" against scientific reduction. In this situation, philosophical anthropology increasingly became a matter of finding a home in the cosmos for an irresolute and displaced human nature. There was a return to spirit-matter dualism, as for example in Dilthey's division between the *Geisteswissenschaften* oriented to "understanding" and the *Natur-*

wissenschaften oriented to "explanation." [82] Writers like Rudolf Eucken were concerned to mark off a distinctive "spiritual" dimension of life where higher meanings are encountered.[83] Nietzsche, on the other hand, combined his attack on the credentials of this sort of separated "spirit" with a revival of the Goethean conception of spirit as nature's own highest power.[84] Such is the background from which our next two rounds of philosophical innovation arise.

Max Scheler, originally a follower of Eucken, develops his own type of phenomenology as a new means of arguing for the autonomy and supremacy of the "spiritual" in his great work of 1913, *Formalism in Ethics and Non-Formal Ethics of Values*. The "spiritual" he takes always to be bound to the "person," an unobjectifiable existential unity of intentional acts. The spiritual or personal enters experience in the recognition of *values*, which may be described and ranked a priori by the phenomenological method of intuitively researching the invariant structures of experience. His approach is Cartesian, in the sense that he absolutely trusts whatever is given to a disciplined intuition, but interestingly anti-Cartesian in some of its results, principally in the claim that "no '*ego*' at all belongs to the essence of spirit." [85] Like most of his phenomenological colleagues, Scheler is empirical in temper and not committed to perfecting knowledge as the self-grasp of a self. His basic intention is to vindicate the Augustinian thesis that persons are only as they love and know best what they love. The "spiritual" is constituted in the activity of loving, or (more broadly) valuing, which rests on a kind of insight that is different from scientific comprehension following Aristotelian, Kantian, or Hegelian rules.

Scheler also advances the concept of the "collective person" or supraindividual spirit, which is his counterpart to the Hegelian notion of objective spirit and is meant partly as a critical revision of the latter. Not just any form of human collectivity deserves the name "collective person"—this is not the sphere of the "herd," or even the "social" of empirical sociology—but only communal unities of intention in which the essential personal activity of recognizing and preferring values takes place.[86] Individual personhood is neither less valuable than collective personhood nor necessarily subordinated to it, Scheler maintains, and herein lies his main difference from Hegel. Where Hegel's dialectic advances from the individual to the universal through mediation and supersession (which conserves what is superseded and is therefore not reductive, but *is* subordinative), Schelerian personhood attains universality by virtue of the a priori membership of any person in an encompassing personal community.[87] Even Robinson Crusoe must sense his own membership in a community in the very frustration of his intentions of co-preferring, co-responding, etc. On the other hand, the member of an actual collective person (say, a patriotic German in Germany) must acknowledge that Germany is in turn a member of a wider personal community of nations, and so on, until infinite community is realized in God.

In Scheler's earlier work the "spiritual" appears as a function of personal acts rather than of a being called "spirit." This is in itself a significant turn in the history of the concept. But Scheler's approach changes in the late work, *Man's Place in Nature*. Here he accepts the challenge of providing a credible rationale for the age-old but lately undercut belief that human nature is different in kind from living nature in general. Augustine had searched for that power within him by which he could know God and found it in the "higher" mind, which he identified with memory, rather than in those "lower" parts of the soul that one shares with the brutes.[88] Scheler now posits the principle of spirit as that which divides humanity from nature. Spirit is essentially free; its freedom in the negative sense is to withdraw "ascetically" from nature, canceling the force of vital impulses and of the sheer existence of things so as to direct its attention uncoerced by them; its positive freedom is to attend to essences, and to lure the spirit-bearing organism toward its own ends by borrowing or sublimating its vital energy.[89] Although it has an ontological niche of its own, spirit is the weakest sort of being, not, as classical anthropology and theology had it, the strongest.[90] It gets its way (when it does get its way) through "cunning," but omnipotent and triumphant it is not. The testimony of the fair earth and the heavenly bodies, which overawed the Greeks, no longer counts in the modern age; neither does the testimony of history, not after World War I.

A dualism of "spirit" and "life" similar to but more extreme than Scheler's was articulated at the same time by Ludwig Klages in a book called *Spirit as the Adversary of Soul*.[91] Spirit—whether as *logos, pneuma,* or *nous,* but in any event as distinct from the vital inwardness of the soul united with the body—must negate life and soul to achieve its ends. Spirit seeks knowledge of being, which it realizes by abstracting timeless "objects" from the flow of temporal becoming; it judges, rather than experiences, and holds experience in contempt. Spirit does not peacefully coexist with soul and body in the house of human nature; it wars against them as an outsider. That it is a deathly disease of human life becomes evident in such famous precepts as "Those who really apply themselves in the right way to philosophy are directly and of their own accord preparing themselves for dying and death," and "Flesh and blood cannot inherit the kingdom of God." [92]

Klages' idea is widely discussed by German psychologists and philosophers between the world wars. Correctly to determine the natures of spirit, consciousness, and soul and the relationships between them is not, however, a task that becomes easier with time. *Geist* (like *esprit*) had by now served for decades as the standard term both for intellective mind and for the principle of culture. It had become the pennant of the highest and vaguest ideals, the word that one used to talk (not always very definitely) about what one felt (not always very distinctly) to be most important in human life. (Its chronic vagueness is cruelly and wonderfully satirized by Robert Musil in *The Man Without Qualities*.) Against the Klagesian view, Bruno Bauch protests that the German word *Geist* just *means* a unifying vital force, what Goethe called the "life of life," and that anyone who uses the word differently in effect fails to understand German.[93] But it is too late to close the issue by semantic edict; definitions too diverse and too contrasting have already taken the field. Perhaps this has happened because *Geist* is "a classic example of an idea without a corresponding intuition" (Julius Kraft).[94] It could be argued that any concept of a "high" or "highest" aspect of human nature must be indeterminate in this way, since the "height" of X for us means on the one hand that X rises above terms of comparison into a unique region, and on the other hand that X, being the controller, is exempt from any other thing's control.

But indeterminacy in a concept calls for correction when it becomes obvious. Now that it is manifestly an open question how human capacities such as cognition, valuation, response to moral and religious imperatives, and the sense of self should be allocated to the concepts of *Geist, Bewusstsein,* and *Seele,* it becomes possible to be more specific about the meaning of *Geist.* It no longer has to mean everything, even though it continues to lend itself better than any other word to the purposes of those who wish to mean everything in one word. The most important work dedicated by a German to the specification of the concept of the spiritual, in this last period before the concept almost entirely vanishes from sustained philosophical debate, is Nicolai Hartmann's book, *The Problem of Spiritual Being.*[95]

Hartmann joins Scheler's enterprise of ontologically locating the new reality that stands out from the rest of nature in human beings, and he takes over many of Scheler's themes: that the spiritual is to be grounded in or functionally related to personal act-unities rather than to consciousness or the "I"; that the spiritual is a "higher" level of being that is "weak" and dependent for its existence and effective power on lower levels (the psychic, the organic, and the inorganic), over against which it nevertheless retains autonomy; and that intuition of values, like objective cognition (from which this intuition is distinct), is a uniquely spiritual function. Hartmann also agrees with Klages that the spirit can "feed" on vital energy to a dangerous extent.[96] He disagrees with virtually the whole tradition in arguing that spirit is not eternal but shares the timefulness of events in other strata of being; that spirit is not intrinsically perfect; that it is not ontologically independent, not a substance, but rather a reality "superexisting" upon others; that we encounter it as an object in experience—not as a thingly object, to be sure, but neither as an essentially nonobjectifiable pure subjectivity; and that it does not necessarily turn to itself as its own proper object, but is open to everything in the world.[97] The phenomenon of spirit that is empirically available for description is a complex reality comprising three forms, personal, objective, and objectivated, which are quite different from each other but cannot exist apart from each other. One of the few positive things Hartmann will say about spirit in general is that it is a spontaneous seeking and finding of new forms, and a spontaneous adherence to itself.[98] Spirit also is "expansive"; it tends to spread itself.

Personal spirit is not, contrary to common opinion, the best-known form of spirit. It is in fact the most mysterious, because we do not know theoretically what a "person" is—rather, we experience persons in practical life, and in the realm of values. Moreover, introspection seems to be of little help, since self-acquaintance that deserves the name of knowledge is rare and difficult to achieve. A spiritual individual is one whose consciousness is not directly engaged with the environment, like that of animals, but is (to use Plessner's word) "eccentric," orienting itself to the world rather than the world to itself, and is thus capable of the experience of the "objective" and the concept of truth.[99] The spiritual individual or person is a free decision maker, foresighted and purposeful, sensitive and responsive to values.

Hartmann makes strong claims for the interpersonal extension of personal spirit. One's fellow human beings require attention in a way that mere things never do; to ignore them is to sin against them and to negate personal spirit. One's primordial response to other persons is an "inner righteousness" distinct from conformity to particular rules.[100]

Objective spirit is just as much a living being as personal spirit. It consists of the whole cultural apparatus, including language, law, art, science, and so forth, which must exist in order that spiritual individuals may exist as spiritual— or we should say cultural apparatuses, because many *Gemeingeisten* have come and gone, and there is for Hartmann no single *Weltgeist* such as Hegel believed in.[101] (The generic term "objective spirit" should not conceal the fact that we have to do only with *spirits,* plural, as Herder had spoken of the spirits of nations.) Personal spirit is dependent on objective spirit; for instance, no individual could invent a whole language, nor can individuals be radically original in what they manage to say in their given language. But objective spirit also requires personal spirit, for it has neither a consciousness of its own to be aware of itself nor a conscience with which to judge and purify itself apart from the consciences of individuals. For this reason Hartmann finds Scheler's notion of "collective persons" confusing, although he tries to describe the same phenomenon.[102] Objective spirit is the theme of the *Geisteswissenschaften* (history, jurisprudence, etc.) which are always interested in the identity and movements of supraindividual realities, never strictly in individuals. Since objective spirit always amounts to more than an individual consciousness could take in, no individual—no, not even Goethe—can be wholly representative of a culture. There can be no "adequate consciousness" of objective spirit.[103]

The conditions of the possibility of objective spirit include the existence of detachable and repeatable forms, such as words, which can bridge the spatial and temporal gaps between persons, and at a deeper level an abiding intersubjective commonality in experience—Heraclitus' *logos*. Hartmann does not offer a Platonic metaphysics of Forms or any other metaphysics that would account for this commonality; he merely describes the experienced fact of commonality, which he calls an "immanent a priori." [104] It constrains the thought of spiritual individuals, making them unfree with respect to the boundaries of the thought-forms that they share with others, such as the laws of logic.

Finally, objective spirit differs from personal spirit in not being purposive. There is no "reason in history" beyond the reason of individuals.[105] The evidence, soberly read, is against it.

Living spirit produces, through "objectivation," a third form of spirit that is not alive and yet, by reason of being cut loose from living spirit, attains a kind of immortality: *objectivated spirit*. Spiritual forms of this order last potentially as long as their material bearers do. The stone of the statue and the paper of the book are not literally immortal, but they can long outlast living spirits. When such "spiritual contents" (so called by Hartmann by way of insisting that they are not mere manifestations or expressions of spirit distinct from spirit itself) are felt to be important enough to preserve, they are objectivated with the aid of relatively stable materials and then become available in principle to any living spirit. In sum, the objectivity of objective spirit becomes "objectivated" spirit simply by projecting out of the situation in which it was formed into the indefinite future.[106] Somehow—Hartmann does not presume to explain it—living spirit grasps this record of past spirit as spiritual, recognizing the spiritual content borne by the material vehicle. Not that an ancient Greek poem will mean to a modern philologist precisely what it meant to its original audience. But it does have meaning, and in presenting this meaning it will stretch the horizon of those who receive it.

Hegel went beyond the Greeks in ascribing all being and power to spirit; it would seem that with Hartmann this being and power have shrunk to the point that an ontology of spirit barely survives. But what Hartmann loses in explanatory grandeur he gains back in descriptive plausibility. And whereas Hegel's *Geist* can be translated without much violence as "mind," and most of what Hegel meant can be borne by the concept of mind, the concept of spirit is not interchangeable with the concept of mind in Hartmann. The word *Geist* has a distinctive and specific job to do.[107]

1.7 Marcel, Ebner, and Buber—*Esprit, Geist;* Levinas—*Respiration, Pneuma*

We are ready to consider a sixth and final intrusion of a new conception of the spiritual into philosophical history. It is roughly contemporary with the retreat from absolute idealism to a limited conception of *Geist*, which we traced above in Scheler and Hartmann. But this movement is a fundamental rejection of idealism rather than a partial limitation of its claims. It centers on the denial of Hegel's principle that "an out-and-out Other simply does not exist for spirit," indeed uses spirit-words precisely to affirm absolute otherness or exteriority as a first condition of meaning, and thus opposes *nous*-spirit, mind, with spirit of another kind.

One of the most important roots of the movement goes back to the first generation of critics of Hegel. Having raised the issue of what is truly "concrete" for thought in brilliant fashion, it was ironically but perhaps inevitably reproached with falsifying abstractness or, as Kierkegaard said, absentmindedness. Feuerbach offered a rival principle of concreteness, asserting that concrete humanity or spirituality resides in the I-and-You sociality of mortal, sensuous beings.[108] Just as it is absent-minded to engage in theology, since God's attributes are abstracted and alienated from their home in earthly human nature, so too it is absentminded for a self to philosophize as though not with and before a You. Probably Feuerbach's sensational attack on the transcendence of God has overshadowed the other implication of his principle of concreteness, namely, that all reflection and reasoning is conditioned by its relationship with something *exterior* to it, the human You.

Feuerbach did not develop the theme of exteriority. Kierkegaard, the Christian, did make a great point of the exteriority of God to reason and the consequent "self-ironization" of reason in the *Philosophical Fragments*, but he did not connect the logic of relationship with exteriority either to the I-You relationship as such or to spirit as such.[109] Only because the human spirit is creaturely, "derived and constituted," does it necessarily relate itself to an Other. These connections are first forged by Gabriel Marcel, Ferdinand Ebner, and Martin Buber.

The *Metaphysical Journal* kept by Marcel between 1914 and 1923 is a significant document of transition. In its First Part, from 1914, his explicit study of exteriority is conducted within the ambit of the general problem of knowledge. He seeks a theory of intelligibility that will do justice to the claims of idealism by recognizing the mind-made necessity that is essential to knowledge. That which mind (*esprit*) knows, it knows as something other than itself, but then mind realizes that this very otherness is posited by mind itself—so idealism has taught us. Yet the otherness of the known remains essential to knowledge, for if the mind believes that otherness is really nothing but its own ruse, knowledge dissolves into tautology. Marcel's solution is to concede that within the realm of the intelligible the mind's own necessity cannot be escaped, for this is constitutive of "intelligibility," but the abiding requirement of an unreduced exteriority requires us to think of the mental system as "provisional and as within a constructing experience" in which mind is formed in, or rather as, the process of discovering intelligibility in interaction with the given world.[110]

So far Marcel has not slipped the net of idealism, for his decision to give exteriority priority over the legislation of thought cannot be justified in the philosophical courtroom, where thought still presides. He *wants* to think of spiritual life as a dynamic relationship between mind and something outside it, because he thinks that true intelligibility presupposes this, but he has not yet located the concrete exigency that would make the thinker realize, and not merely wish for, a "dynamic" relationship with exteriority.[111] But then one such exigency appears in the Second Part, as Marcel, at the same time that he ventures the opinion that "all spiritual life is essentially a dialogue," uses for the first time one of the words of real dialogue by referring to God as a "you." This is not to be confused with the "you" that occurs hundreds of times in Augustine's *Confessions* in the course of actually addressing God; this is "you" as a theme. He generalizes it:

> *I* seems always to be posited as being in confrontation with a *you* [*tu*], for whom in turn I myself am a *you*. And it is in function of this dialogue and in relation to it that a *he* or *it* can be defined . . . I glimpse a sort of slow transition from pure dialectics to love, in the measure in which the *you* becomes *you* more and more profoundly.[112]

The relationship with a You, which forms the context of thought, is not itself approachable by thought, which always turns "you" to "he" or "it." Marcel resorts to the idea of "invocation" to characterize the relationship. To say or call upon *You*—who must, if called upon, be a real person—is different from thinking "you" as one theme among others. Must philosophy, theme-thinking, stop at this boundary? Marcel does not stop. He can still inquire into the conditions of the possibility of this "invocation" that has gotten woven into his discourse:

> At the moment of my invocation we must admit that something more than an idea comes into play. Yet the invocation, if I may so put it, must have an ontological foundation. I cannot *really* invoke "anybody"; I can only "pretend to" do so. In other words it appears as if invocation can only be efficacious where there is community.
>
> In a deep sense that is difficult to define we must be *already together*.[113]

This is exteriority that remains unreduced by thought, and a true concrete: the presence of "you," or more precisely of the "us" in which "I" and "you" are together.[114]

Marcel stands squarely in the Platonic-Augustinian tradition insofar as he defines the "metaphysical need" generating his journal as "the appetite for Being," the desire to possess being by thought.[115] His departure from idealism consists in addressing Being as a personal mystery rather than as an objective evidence. The consequence for him is that the thought that would possess becomes something other than theoretical cognition and it does something other than possess. But it grows directly out of *nous*-spirit's search for Being and the Good.

Unlike the *Metaphysical Journal*, Ebner's "pneumatological fragments" of 1919, *The Word and the Spiritual Realities*, are devoted from beginning to end to the thesis that the "spiritual" is all and only that which essentially pertains to the

I-You relationship. Actual language is the concretely given togetherness of You and I that serves (as it had for Herder) as the starting point for thinking about the spiritual. It is the treasure-house of the "spiritual realities." Humanity was created by God in the moment when humanity gained the Word, and although original language has been corrupted, the very structures of that corruption bear witness to its original and persisting core. Thus the life of the mind, which expresses itself in the "objective" language of oblique cases, is a spiritual phenomenon, but in a privative mode. For the knowing mind, solitary and sovereign in a world of objects that have been thematized in abstraction from living dialogue, is the mode in which the I exists in sinful seclusion from the You, turned away from the original righteousness of addressing the You to preoccupation with the affairs that it can make its "own." This life of the I as mind, which Ebner calls "the dream of the spirit" and sees culminating in idealism, is a lonely, unhappy, and unreal or "deactualized" one.[116]

For Ebner, human spirit "is essentially determined by its being fundamentally intended for a relation to something spiritual *outside* it, *through* which and *in* which it exists"—that is, God.[117] Like Paul and Kierkegaard, Ebner associates the mind-transcending "outside" with God rather than with any creaturely You. The "outside" is set in thoroughgoing dualistic opposition with the "inside" of virtually everything that passes for culture, like Pauline "spirit" against Pauline "flesh." The "You-taciturn" mind, in its secluded inwardness, perhaps remembers and longs for the actuality of You-relationship, but all of its endeavors only confirm its seclusion.

Ebner's outside-inside dualism is carried further by his nontheological contemporary Eberhard Grisebach, with the difference that Grisebach makes the "outside" the habitat of *human* Others. Grisebach's "critical" philosophy is oriented toward ethical "crises" of interpersonal encounter, actual conflicts in family, school, political, and religious life. He holds that we can never possess these in reflection; we must suffer ourselves to be surprised by them in the present moment.[118]

Martin Buber's *I and Thou*, which was published shortly after Ebner's book, contains a generalized formula for the Ebnerian idea: "Spirit is not in the I but between I and You. It is not like the blood that circulates in you but like the air in which you breathe."[119] Air-like again, spirit can move between beings, and as set loose by Buber it moves between all beings. For Buber the spirit is there wherever "encounter" or "presence" (*Gegenwärtigkeit*) occurs, whether it be with a human being, a cat, or a tree. He says that "Spirit is word," but his conception of "word" is broader by far than Ebner's; it takes in all events in which "I" and "You" are actualized, whether or not anything is spoken.[120] Spoken invocation, the call of the "I" upon the "You," is the paradigm, but only the paradigm. (Buber does not get involved in the exercises of Ebner's "pneumatological grammar" or the

Sprachdenken of Rosenstock-Huessy that derive a philosophy of the spiritual from the forms of language.) [121]

Buber shares with Marcel and Ebner the idea that God alone is absolutely You, and with Ebner at least the idea that the relationship with God grounds all I-You relationships with fellow human beings, although he gives much more stress than Ebner to the interhuman. His "appetite for Being" is not the Augustinian hunger to be directly with God, nor does he turn away in disgust from human civilization. He asserts a duality of I-It and I-You relationships parallel to Ebner's duality of "inside" and "outside"; to know or experience a thing is to have it in a less-than-actual world of one's own, whereas in saying "You" one stands forth in one's whole being without turning back, without any hoarding of experience, and thus without any possibility of expressing objectively *what* You-saying is. But it is not possible to live entirely as I to You. Life consists of an alternation between being as I to You and being as I to It, and even of an intricate entanglement between the two ways of being. Buber finds the lapse of I-You to I-It relationship a "melancholy" destiny of all I-You relationship—every You becomes a he or an it, one cannot live only invoking—but he does not see this in itself as the power of sin. [122] As a result he does not have to reject culture, and philosophy in particular, as Ebner does. He finds in the encounter with the work of art, for example, not just a representation of human alienation from God, spuriously satisfying, but an actual formation and worldly availability of spirit. His account of the entry of "spiritual content" into material objects is really no more explanatory than Hartmann's account of spiritual "objectivation"; sharing Ebner's central idea as he does, however, it is remarkable that he can allow spirit into objects at all. Buber's distinction between spirit and ordinary experience is not an ascetic one. He has superseded ascesis because he understands You-saying to God to take place in the very act of You-saying to creatures. "Let us love the actual world that never wishes to be annulled, but love it in all its terror, but dare to embrace it with our spirit's arms—and our hands encounter the hands that hold it." [123]

Buber acknowledges the paradox in trying to speak of what is not a graspable theme. Nevertheless, he insists on presenting his thought as an "ontology" of the strictly relational reality of spirit, the "between." To claim an ontological status for his indications concerning spirit is for him a way of separating them from the merely psychological, to give them a normative status as the inescapable (though indemonstrable) determinant of the meaning of human existence. Whoever lives only as I to It is "not human." [124] Like earlier philosophers of spirit, he bestows being—proper being, true actuality—upon that which is most important. Conscious that his gesture may be in tension with the autonomous drive of philosophy's conceptual machinery, he says he "dares" to do this. [125]

For Buber the causality of the spiritual, freedom correlated with meaning, is grounded in relationship; natural causality becomes spiritual causality in the same

manner that an It becomes a You. (Buber's thought on this subject will be discussed more fully in Chapter 8.) Persons who turn toward You know themselves
to be free of natural necessity because they meet there the higher necessity called
fate.

> Fate and freedom are promised to each other. Fate is encountered only by
> him that actualizes freedom. That I discovered the deed that intends me,
> that, this movement of my freedom, reveals the mystery to me . . . freedom
> and fate embrace each other to form meaning; and given meaning, fate
> —with its eyes, hitherto severe, suddenly full of light—looks like grace
> itself.[126]

The alternation of I-It- and I-You-saying is spirit's oscillation between being
subject to an alien causality and being at one with the causality of fate to which
it is akin. On the cosmic scale, the oscillation is between the world's alienation
from God and its reconciliation with God.[127] Such is Buber's version of our oldest
spirit-theme, the parallel between personal and universal motion.

The principle of exteriority is implicit in Buber's criticism of the unified totality
of objective thinking and the swallowing-all-into-self of romantic inwardness.
Relationship as he understands it presupposes irreducible plurality. The You is
absolutely other than the I, this otherness figuring not as an absence of meaning,
a mere gap in intelligibility, but as the presence of the distinctive meaning of
"You." But the concept or anticoncept of exteriority as such, with its drastic
negative implications for the traditional understanding of spirit as mind, does
not get a sustained investigation from Buber. Perhaps he mistrusts it; he does
record his suspicion that the inside-outside dualism of Grisebach prevents the
latter from appreciating all aspects of the human.[128] Yet the principle of exteriority
or pluralism remains the decisive difference between the Buberian and idealist
conceptions of the spiritual. It opens up the space in which the wind can blow.

In the generation after Buber, Emmanuel Levinas develops a philosophy of
exteriority equaling Grisebach's in critical thoroughness and similar to it in many
details. Having studied under Husserl and Heidegger, he explodes the bomb of
the human You's Otherness within the frameworks of phenomenology and ontology. Thus he employs expressions such as "signification without a context" and
"otherwise than being" to mark the impossibility of comprehending the Other.[129]
Initially he keeps his distance from *esprit* as a way of avoiding entanglement with
idealism, but in his later work he is led by the very logic of exteriority to use
spirit-words in his characterization of the Other-complicated life of the self.

It is important first to note Levinas' assessment of the interpersonal situation.

He finds that Marcel and Buber illegitimately posit an original symmetry of I and You, who meet each other as equals.[130] The absolutely Other is not, however, party to any such symmetry or reciprocity: it is incomparable. Concretely, the You appears as the superior of the I—as the I's teacher, having something from beyond the I's own realm of the Same to impart, and as judge, requiring from the I an apologia. The Other is *vous,* not the familiar *tu (Du).* Levinas objects to Marcel's view that a we-relation is prior to I and You, who then derive their meaning from community. This impairs the pluralism that must be maintained at all costs. It is not necessary to overcome the I's incapacity to generate exteriority by placing the I in a we-relation—that is the sort of ontological move, restoring a comprehensible totality, that Heidegger also makes in *Being and Time* with the categories of *Mitsein* and *Miteinandersein*—but only to acknowledge that Others present themselves as Other.[131] Like his fellow Jew Buber and against the Catholics Marcel and Ebner, Levinas understands God to be an essential but as it were background partner of interpersonal relationships. God is indeed so far in the background as to take the pronoun "He" instead of "You." Yous are said to be in the "trace" left by the One who has irreversibly "passed by." [132] Against Buber, Levinas restricts You-encounter to human beings; the concrete Other is a *face,* which animals, plants, and stones as a matter of fact do not have.[133]

The mature Levinas sets out to escape ontology rather than convert it to his own purposes, despite earlier remarks that "Being is exteriority" and that moral experience is the experience of Being par excellence.[134] In this he differs from Buber and Ebner, who adapt the category of "actuality," and from Marcel, who attributes to Being the mysteriousness of the Otherness that claims us. In his 1961 book *Totality and Infinity* Levinas largely confines himself to anti-ontology, thematizing the Other as the nonevident and absent. In later writings such as *Otherwise than Being or Beyond Essence* (1974) he experiments with positive presentations of the Other in order more adequately to indicate the moral superiority of the Other's claim to Being.

The Other cannot merely be Other *than* self and mind, for then the Other would have nothing to do with them. The Other is Other as a claimant on self and mind. Thus the Other registers as a transformation of their meaning, so that, for example, "the Self is originally posited as responsibility through and through," and reason is originally a mandated way of serving the Other and an apparatus to balance the claims of plural neighbors.[135] In order to express the true position of the Other *in* the self, Levinas employs the breath-words *inspiration* for the Other's always-already-having-commanded-the-self and *expiration* for the surrender of the self to service of the Other, its breathing out and taking nothing back. The relationship with the Other that determines the meaning of selfhood is "respiration," "the very pneuma of the psyche." [136] Breathing as a being's vital self-affirmation is cut short, becomes a held breath in the Other's presence. In this sense *esprit* can be defined as "the longest breath there is." [137]

Some of Levinas' points of disagreement with Buber seem to coincide with special difficulties in his position that are worthy of notice.

By construing relationship with the Other as negation rather than actualization of the self's own powers, such that the pneumatized self completely lacks initiative and can be reduced to "ashes from which an act could not be born anew," does not Levinas put a great difficulty in the way of understanding the activity of spirit in the world?[138] Some events must occur because of their moral significance; people must do things in response to moral claims. The very concreteness of the moral relation that is crucial to Levinas must be in actual interpersonal events such as feeding the hungry, and not merely in an inward registering of the existence of the Other, which would only be another "experience," though of a queer sort. How then are we to conceive the motivation of actions that undoubtedly are performed because of their moral meaning without resurrecting the autonomy of the ego that was displaced by that same moral meaning?

Buber makes interhuman relationship the privileged locus of spirit, but he does not, like Levinas and most other I-You thinkers, restrict the spiritual to the human. He proposes saying You to the world and everything in it. While this aspect of Buber's thought has either been criticized as sentimental or simply neglected, the greater problem, in my judgment, lies on Levinas' side: do we human beings, as "spiritual," live in a world in which human existence is *all* that fundamentally matters, nonhuman beings only contributing an accidental backdrop to human affairs? Even if it is possible for human beings to live in the world on that understanding, does not the very questioning of the restriction in that understanding begin to tear it down? If so, is the "spiritual" quality of life to be identified with the restriction or with its removal? The *pneuma* blows where it will.

———

Levinas tirelessly refines his characterization of the original relationship between I and You because this characterization is, for him, first philosophy. It brings out the first meaning, the ethical meaning of the "human" or "the spiritual life," which conditions all other meanings. Levinas must be evaluated from this perspective, therefore. The two fundamental objections to be brought against Levinas' manner of performing first philosophy and which apply to all the exteriority-thinkers we have discussed are these: Is a philosophy of absolute Otherness possible? and, Can any constructive philosophical work be done on such negative or extraordinary premises as are offered by the exteriority-thinkers? We will discuss the objections in turn, introducing answers to them that will be developed in the sequel.

First, then, it seems that a philosophy admitting absolute Otherness is impossible inasmuch as philosophy is committed to rationality and intelligibility, both of which the Other defeats or eludes. Can one venture an assertion concerning the "absolutely Other" without falling into nonsense?

Levinas' answer has two major parts. On the one hand, it is necessary to remember that absolute Otherness is not a speculative theme but an actual event, the concrete togetherness of one person with another. The extremism of the language of exteriority is a function of an extremity in real life, the fact that the Other figures to me in the *first* place as a judge and as my charge, not as an object of knowledge. If the language that measures up to this extremity cannot enter philosophy, then so much the worse for philosophy. On the other hand, claims having to do with an "absolutely Other" do not have to rest on evidence or systematic consistency with other sorts of claims in order to be meaningful, *if* they are not construed as knowledge claims. But Levinas does not intend his talk of the Other to be so construed. His discourse is ethical, not theoretical, and a gesture of deferral *to* the Other, not a representation *of* the Other. As such it is not necessarily inconsistent with the representations that science, religion, and philosophy otherwise busy themselves with. (Marcel's "invocation" and Buber's "daring" must also be interpreted in this fashion.) In his later work Levinas practices what he calls an "emphatic" mode of discourse, a new *via eminentiae* or "superlative way" designed to reflect the appropriation of concepts by the ethical gesture. For example: "In a certain sense, the real world is the world which is posited [*se pose*]; its way of being is as a thesis. But to be posited in a truly superlative way . . . is that not to be exposited [*s'exposer*], posited to the point of appearing, *affirmed* to the point of becoming language?" [139] "Becoming language" is for Levinas nothing other than respiration. (Buber likewise is conscious of following a *via eminentiae* in *I and Thou*. He speaks in his afterword of "a revolutionary transformation and expansion" taking place in "every concept that, impelled by the actuality of faith, we take from the realm of immanence and apply to transcendence.") [140]

Second, it seems that even if a radically pluralist philosophy of the spiritual is possible in the sense that a kind of meaningfulness may be granted its affirmations, the fact that such a philosophy defines itself in opposition to the principles of logical coherence and evidence—the *archai* of the It-world, the realm of stable propositional meanings—entails the sterility of that manner of thinking in all the *applications* of philosophy. Repeating its master theme or its ethical gesture over and over, it can never get as far as logic or epistemology or cosmology or constructive ethics or aesthetics or theory of value; its commitment to distinguishing itself from theoretical discourse makes it at best a marginal reminder of the questionableness of all such pursuits, but it cannot help to determine answers to the questions they deal with. In that important respect, is it not philosophically irrelevant? [141]

It is true that the exteriority thinkers have remained outside the main streams of philosophical work and have not produced a literature nearly comprehensive enough to constitute an alternative to the mainstreams, although the breadth of their actual contributions is not sufficiently appreciated. Probably the chief reason for this relative infertility or narrowness is that the struggle for the right first philosophy, on which the sense of all other work done in philosophy depends, has not yet been concluded. The task that takes priority over all others still requires intense and continuing attention from those who take it up. Another reason why thinkers of this sort might never shift attention from first questions is that the exteriority principle makes its special kind of difference across the board. It does not leave everything as it is, irrelevantly; it transfigures everything equally. That is not to say, however, that the transfiguration cannot be investigated in its various branches.

The notion that exteriority-thinking is condemned to sterility because it defines itself negatively vis-à-vis theoretical thinking would be correct were it not for the positive significance of exteriority and the prospect of a *via eminentiae* on which discourse may venture. By taking this way, one should arrive at more understanding, not less, than one would otherwise have had—of everything.

1.8 Summary

At the end of our first examination of the moving-air metaphor in 1.1 we set out an array of questions that are inseparable from the attempt to conceive the spiritual. We now have a preliminary acquaintance with a number of answers.

(1) *The definition of the spiritual.* Spirit is, by consensus, an invisible suprapersonal reality that decisively affects the perceptions, intentions, and actions of persons. Whether spirit is especially or exclusively suprapersonal, or, on the contrary, the power of being an "I"; whether spirit is the whole of personal life or only a part of it; whether it is to be identified especially with the vital, or the voluntary, or the intellectual life; whether it is essentially divine; whether it is essentially human; whether it is to be conceived as one or many—all these matters are subject to disagreement. There is a conflict between the conception of the spiritual as *transcendent,* as especially in biblically influenced writers, and a *totalizing* conception that knits persons and world together. Given the remarkable variation in conceptions of the spiritual, it must be reckoned an open question whether a rationally defensible definition can be given.

One clue does emerge in the repeated differentiations of the "spiritual" from the vital or mental or soulish, and that is that there is something distinct from life, mind, and soul to talk about, or some deep-rooted reason to try to talk in this other direction. Just because of the possibility of the differentiation we should be wary of usage that renders "spiritual" redundant with other terms; we should fear losing track of that other direction.

Any definition is formed from the start by an ontological presumption concerning what there is to define; the kind of reality that is being defined determines the kind of definition that can be given for it. Is "spirit" any *thing* definable? On this point we face the contradictory assertions that spiritual being is the most fundamental being, or Being itself, and that spirit is "otherwise than Being." (Can one say: spirit *is* otherwise than Being?) In between these extremes is the notion that spiritual being is the most excellent but not the exclusive form of being. Spirit's prime entitlements to fundamental or preeminent ontological status are its activity and its incorruptibility. The basic reason for removing spirit from being altogether is that the absolute plurality requisite for the "between" in which spirit "blows" cannot be subordinated to an underlying conjunction and unity between beings, their "being"; spirit must involve the transcending of one's being. On this latter view, one is morally prohibited from theoretically subsuming moral transcendence under the concept of a structure of transcendence *in* Being or of the being of a "we." But then is a defining of spirit antithetical to it? If so, then how, lacking all definition, is a spiritual gesture in words possible?

(2) *The relation of the spiritual to the concrete*. The opposite approaches to the relation of spirit to mind are also the approaches most obviously affected by the assumption that the spiritual is the true starting point of thought. For Hegel, mind-spirit "makes all things," and so philosophical method consists of enacting this making; for Kierkegaard and the I-You thinkers, the transcendence of the theoretical realm involved in relationship with a You is the concrete first meaning, and so the right method is a matter of communicating the theoretically incommunicable by means of unusual gestures toward the reader. Both procedures are subject to challenge, the former for being insufficiently empirical and the latter for being irrational.

(3) *The relation of the spiritual to the rational*. Necessarily, all who philosophize on spirit will discover a possible positive relationship between spirit and reason, but a crucial disagreement remains between those who identify spirit with reason and those who make reason derivative or subordinate in relation to spirit. On the former view, Hegel's is by far the most successful attempt to relate moving-air characteristics to the rules of reason—Hegel's dialectical logic itself "blows"—but he could make this move only by distinguishing spirit-reason from theoretical reason as traditionally understood, the rationality of fixed terms and categories. One can ask whether the concepts of mind and knowledge stretch to fit Hegel's results; although it goes against Hegel's own interpretation to say so, they might be transcended. Alternatively, spirit may be identified with a kind of reasonableness of heart rather than intellect, as in Scheler's axiological apriorism. Those who invoke a spirit transcendent of reason can still orient and justify

rationality in the spiritual frame of reference, as Levinas has done. The most enigmatic portrayal of the relationship between spiritual and the rational is the one implicit in Buber's unelucidated remark that the I-You and I-It realms are thoroughly entangled with each other even though persistently dual.[142]

To resolve this issue one has to determine, besides the definition of the spiritual, the fundamental character of the rational: whether its principle is *form* in the sense of singular essence, or *order* in the sense of formed plurality, or *realization* in the sense of an adequate consciousness of form or order, or *justification,* that is, the pursuit of acceptable relationships between known things or (more broadly) objects of intention, between intenders and objects of intention, and between intenders.

(4) *The meaning of the spiritual qualification of personal life.* How does spirit affect the meaning of being an "I" and acting in such a way as to have a meaningful life story? Although spirit-words have often been introduced specifically to name a reality greater than individual persons, one influential party claims that the essence of spiritual existence is the power of saying "I." But the difference between these positions is not absolute, for the supraindividual spiritual reality can be taken to be, in turn, a self-possessing "I" (Hegel), *or* the individual "I" can be understood to exist only in correlation with a "You," so that there is only a fully actual "I" when that "I" addresses "You" and thus transcends itself (Buber). We must conclude that the meaning of selfhood is contingent upon the meaning of the spiritual. The self could be taken to be just consciousness of universality— the universal validity of Forms, or of Kant's categorical imperative—or it could be taken for an individuality transcending the universal, like the "knight of faith" Abraham in Kierkegaard's *Fear and Trembling.*

As for the meaningful content of spiritually qualified living, on the idealist side much is said about the individual's membership in greater forms such as family, state, culture, and finally the world Spirit, but with the consequence that individuality itself counts for nothing. Meanwhile, on the anti-idealist side comparatively little is said beyond repetition of the global thesis that all life-expectations are transfigured or shattered by relationship with the Other.[143]

The "heart," Plato's *thumos,* is the place where self-surpassing impulses arise —and as such must be considered in connection with motivation, as part of the study of the causality of the spiritual—but also the place where self-surpassing affective reception takes place. The person who can be courageous or cowardly is also the person who can glory or feel shame. Can such feelings be interpreted as quasi-theoretical value intuitions, following Scheler? If not, what is the relation between thumic feeling and that higher spirit that Plato conceived to be knowing mind but that the I-You thinkers conceive to be relationship with Others? Can such feeling be understood as part of personal "actualization"? But then what different feeling-consequences does an account of actualization like Buber's have in comparison with a mind-based account like Hegel's?

(5) *The relation of the spiritual to judgments of validity and worth.* With Socrates and Plato the exercise of mind is inseparable from the search for excellence. Then the equation of goodness with true being, joined to the principle that true being is the proper object of the intellect, secures the evaluative authority of spirit-as-mind for Augustine and consequently much Christian thinking. Like Philo before him, Augustine harmonizes the authority of *nous* with the religious pre-eminence of the biblical *ruach/pneuma*. Whether or not spirit is to be identified with intellect and correlated with being, it can be correlated with a comprehensive a priori order of value (Scheler). Then, however, the problem is how to demonstrate the reality of "values" and justify a given scheme of them. If spirit is to transcend valuation just as it transcends acts of theoretical reason—rooting its authority in the event of personal actualization (Buber) or immediately in the Other's claim (Levinas)—then the parallel problem must be solved of making valuation derivative from or subordinate to spirit. Levinas suggests that the Other is the origin of value but does not work out the derivation.[144]

(6) *The relation between the spiritual and the material.* Spirit is invariably opposed to matter, whether or not it is allocated its own manner of being. Even Hegel's overcoming of the spirit-matter difference presupposes a great self-alienation on the part of spirit, the generation of nature as an Other. Given this difference, we have to account for the inhabiting of matter by spirit, for spirit always has to be dealt with *here* or *there,* animating *this* or *that.* And on this point we meet with a rather shocking lack of accounting on the part of almost everyone who thinks of spirit as immaterial and matter as a distinct reality. No one confronts the question more earnestly than Hartmann, but even he only manages elaborately to point to the "here" and "there" of spirit without explaining it. The most coherent solution of the problem is the Aristotelian one, identifying spirit with actualization according to form, but coherence is bought at the price of a certain shallowness: the problematic of selfhood and the supraintellectual dimension of spirit are both excluded.

(7) *The causality of the spiritual.* Spirit is a cause, whether strong and universal or weak and erratic; everyone who invokes it ascribes some effect to it. The problem is to account for its power to affect the course of the world. Since Anaxagoras' theory of the "rotation" of universal mind, virtually no one has advanced the view that spirit as such is an efficient cause, unless we count the common gesture of *naming* the principle of vital motion "soul." (An exception is Descartes, who postulated an obscure gravity-like influence of mind on body.)[145] Where the causal question is addressed, the most common strategy is to associate spirit with formal and final causation. But the appeal to formal causation leads to the weakness noted above with respect to a purely formal theory of the relation of spirit to matter; and the appeal to final causation opens the problem of the relation between final and efficient causation, to which there is the dualistic Kantian answer (final causation is the rule of the intelligible world, efficient causation of

the phenomenal) and the monistic Hegelian answer, which supersedes efficient causation. Of the I-You thinkers, Buber has done the most to illuminate the causal problem, offering a dialogical adaptation of the Kantian answer.[146] It would seem that exteriority as such can only affect the world as final cause, but even supposing that a satisfactory account can be given of final causation in general, it is hard to see how it would work in this case.

Every one of our seven questions remains open. The tradition of thought about them is rife with unresolved conflicts and aporiae. The most striking result of our survey is the emergence of one overarching conflict between a spirit-as-mind conception and another conception of spirit-as-relationship formed in opposition to it. I do not imagine that *this* conflict will be settled by logical or linguistic analysis; it seems rather that the aptitude of the word "spirit" is to be the site of disagreement, the tent over the wrestling. The struggle between these two conceptions for primacy, the prize of the struggle the right to use a spirit-word that will mean "that which has primacy" whatever else it means—this must be the first-philosophical manifestation of the permanent struggle for better life, above which no one can presume to rise and from which no one can hope to be exempt.

We set out now to answer the seven questions, beginning with the definition of spirit in the English language.

Chapter 2

A Definition of the Spiritual

2.1 A Review of Definitions

Like its counterparts in other European languages, the English word "spirit" is strongly influenced by the biblical words *ruach* and *pneuma* for which it has long been the standard translation. Yet it is by no means simply equivalent to the French *esprit* or German *Geist*. Most importantly, "spirit" does not normally take the intellectual sense proper to the other two. La Rochefoucauld's maxim *L'esprit est toujours la dupe du coeur* would sound very strange if *esprit* were translated "spirit" instead of "mind." [1]

English dictionaries assign to "spirit" the following leading senses:

(1) A supernatural or intangible being.

(2) The vital principle or animating force within a living being.

(3) A volitional being as volitionally qualified; for example, "She was a defiant spirit."

(4) An abundance of energy of will, as in "He had spirit."

(5) In the plural, an individual's emotional state; for example, "She was in low spirits."

(6) An attitude or disposition: "He wrote in a malicious spirit."

(7) The mood of a group or occasion, such as the "spirit of 1776."

(8) The real (or ideal) intention underlying anything that stands to be interpreted —in other words, the principle of the right interpretation. "They obeyed the letter of the law but not its spirit."

The adjective "spiritual" is distinguished by its strong connection with the divine. "Spiritual" persons are ones with their minds and hearts set on the "highest" matters.

Obviously there is much overlapping among these senses, and they lend themselves to consolidation. A being without will could have neither energy nor characteristics of will. The will is the animating force of any being we would speak of as having spirit—it is an undue stretch of spirit even in sense number 2 to ascribe it to a worm. Attitude and mood, disposition to act and disposition to feel, intimately affect each other and run together. Looking further down the list, it would be absurd to speak of the mood of a group or occasion if emotional beings were not the constituent subjects of that mood; a supraindividual "mood" is just the mood common to persons who together are doing or undergoing something important enough to mark in this way.

Of all the ingredients of "spirit," will and mood are most different from each other, yet they are still essentially related inasmuch as mood presupposes desire and will is the strong form of desire. A being could not feel fulfilled, empty, stretched, relaxed, expansive, or depressed if it lacked any inclination toward or away from things. For even when one experiences "emotion" with regard to oneself, in apparent isolation from all else, this feeling presupposes an inclination or disinclination to exist in a certain way. Further, all desire is pregnant with the project of doing, being, or having the thing desired. To will is just to try to actualize this project. To be sure, a weak-willed person can be not less "moody" but more so if the lack of the power of adhering to a project of desire makes that desire, and other desires not sufficiently repressed, more sensitive to vicissitudes. But this sort of moodiness is not the mood envisioned by our fifth and seventh senses of spirit. The "spirit of 1776" is a mood specific to a project, that is, to the active form of a desire, if not necessarily to action. In 1776 an American patriot felt encouraged or defiant depending on how the struggle for independence was faring.

To show the common ground of these meanings we require a concept intermediate between desire, which can mean as little as the sensation of unpleasing separation from something other than the desirer, and will, which is actual exertion or the power for it. The intermediate concept is *intention,* that holding of an aim on something else on which all significant emotion and action are based. The "attitude" of sense number 6 is just a type of intention, conceived in this case rather pneumatically, that is to say, as enfolding and guiding its haver.

If intention is the core content of the second through the seventh senses, it connects these to the eighth as well. The spirit of the laws is the intention in them. (Conversely, the intention in a person's acts that we call "spirit" in the sixth sense is the principle of rightly interpreting those acts.) And the intention in the laws is invisible, for otherwise it would not be possible to flout it in one's interpretation of the visible letter; if the spirit were visible, it would just be the letter. Likewise the intention of a person, *considered as such* (because it is of interest as such, distinct if not separable from the natural bodies in which the intention is incarnate), is invisible, and "supernatural" if regarded as an invisible being or force.

The consolidated definition of spirit, then, in relation to which the various senses may be interpreted (logically if not historically) as adaptations to different contexts, is that spirit *is* intention, especially intention that is noteworthy and memorable because of its strength, the importance of its object, or something else about it. A being that is identified with its intention, or insofar as it is thought of as sheer intention, is called a spirit. Not just any invisible being can be called a "spirit"; no one would call an invisible chair a spirit, unless it crept in front of people to trip them up and thereby manifested the minimal intentionality of a poltergeist.

Now what is that which intends if not, at least in the premier instance, a "self"? Do we confirm as quickly as all that at the notion that "Spirit is the self"? But we did not say that spirit is *in the first place* that which intends. We placed spirit *in* the general field of intention. Although we have psychologically elucidated "intention" by relating it to will and desire, we have neither psychologically nor metaphysically addressed the question of where intention comes from and whither it aims. We only know that certain beings more complicated than worms, individually and in groups, are the *locus* of intention. So we may have yet to uncover the decisive ingredient of spirit.

Further, we know that "spiritual" and "intentional" are far from synonymous. "She did it intentionally" just means that she did it on purpose; most often it would be quite out of place to say that she did it "spiritually." Evidently we should be interested in the further qualification of the exceptional case that makes it "spiritual"—what *kind* of intention was operative in it, or in what *way* intention was operative in it.

Our next step must be to examine uses of the word "spirit" in contexts where it seems to be doing its distinctive job well, and revealingly.

2.2 "Spirit" and "Spiritual"

There are numerous occasions when the word "spirit" is naturally used but could easily be dispensed with. One could just as well say "He is glum" as "His spirits are low," for instance, or "the real intent of the law" instead of "the spirit of the law." But in some cases an equivalent locution without "spirit" is difficult to find. "Spirit" comes close to being essential to such expressions as:

the spirit of fair play
public spirit
school spirit
"I am with you in spirit."
"She is a very spiritual person."

We will take these expressions as representative of the special metaphorical mission of this moving-air word in English.

(1) *The spirit of fair play* is found or invoked in human dealings of all kind, including the political, legal, and economic, but the base from which its meaning

is extended is "play," sport. To act in the spirit of fair play is to be sporting, that is, to follow commonly understood rules (so as not to spoil the game constituted by the rules) and above all to give the antagonist an equal chance. Fairness as such is a rule of conduct, but the "spirit of fair play" is more than the concept or code of fairness: it is the rule envisioned as applying to everyone, the rule as something one is called upon to "enter into." In fact, one enters into the spirit in much the same way that one enters into a personal relationship. The difference is that a personal relationship exists or ceases to exist as one enters or leaves it, whereas the spirit has its own independent reality; it is present to the individual as a possible way to act and an available kind of relationship with others. ("Sporting" is at once a way to be and a way to be with others.)

What does it mean that one acts *in* the spirit of fair play? There is a sphere of commonality that one shares with the others who play fair. The commonality applies not just to acts but to intentions; one *means* to play fair. The common sphere is the intentional equivalent of the playing field, the "place" in which the players mean to play fair together. Regarding someone whose acts conformed outwardly to sportsmanlike expectation but whose commitment to acting in that fashion was not apparent or in doubt, we would more cautiously say that such a person acted "according to" the spirit of fair play—which would begin to turn that spirit into a letter. To be *in* the spirit is to live it fully and thus form oneself by entering a relationship with others for whom living in that fashion under those circumstances is likewise essential.

The same observations apply to other "procedural" spirits such as "the spirit of democracy."

(2) A *public-spirited* person feels, judges, and acts according to the interests of the community which, at least by virtue of consisting of a number of intentional beings, is an intentional reality transcending while including the individual. Transcendence of self is essential to this sense of spiritedness. One cannot be "private-spirited." One can only be *mean*-spirited, under which description one is seen to shrink spiritedness itself. Thus there is an affinity between "spirit" and "public," meaning a larger realm, as there was also with "fair play," which implied resignation of self-interest in favor of the outcome of rule-governed dealings with others.

Public-spirited persons are not now understood to be made so by divine inspiration, although there was a correlation between God's bestowal of *ruach* and political leadership in ancient Israel. One can simply choose to be public-spirited. On the other hand, one cannot be "naturally" public-spirited in the sense that one happens to be interested in public affairs in the same way that someone else is interested in model railroading. There is tension of a sort between this spirit and the flesh; otherwise, public-spiritedness would not be considered remarkable and admirable. Such people are publicly praised and cherished, which bespeaks a general understanding that they have volunteered to live this way and that it would be unfair to take it for granted as a natural fact that they will continue to live this way. By the same token, people who are not public-spirited can be challenged to become so; "public spirit" is an open question hanging before them.

The person who takes the interests of the community to heart has not been invaded by a supraindividual intentional center, some public "heart." There is no public "heart." "Public spirit" gets into people, but it is not a being that is identical across the individuals into whom it gets. The adjective "public-spirited" expands the understood reality of the individual to whom it is attached in an individual way, rather than subsuming the individual under an already-understood general reality—in contrast to most ordinary adjectives. No one knows exactly what being public-spirited will amount to in his case or her case, except that the cases will differ. Of course, one feels one can count on public-spirited people to help in charitable fund drives and the like, but which causes they will devote themselves to, how they will understand the public interest, even how they conceive the "public" are all to some extent unforeseeable.

(3) *School spirit* is one example of *esprit de corps* in which the word "spirit" is still commonly used rather than "morale." "Morale" is an equivalent for "spirits," as in high or low spirits, regarded as shared by a group by virtue of group experience; but having school spirit means more than feeling good or bad, active or sluggish, as a group. It means devotion to the *cause* of the group, for example to beating a rival school in football, in such a way that one rejoices or is cast down according to the satisfaction or frustration of intentions specific to the group. *I* cannot beat Central High in football, but my school can, and since my school can, I can want that. Not only is my repertoire of intentions enhanced in this way, my school-related intentions are amplified in being shared with schoolmates. We vividly experience this amplification while cheering together in the football stadium; wanting together is greater than wanting separately.

In this context more than any other the "spirit is the self" hypothesis is attractive, for while school spirit, like public and sportsmanlike spirit, transcends the individual self, it seems to animate individual intentions in the manner of a supraindividual self. School-spirited students are like members of the school's body and outposts of its soul. It seems that just insofar as they participate in school spirit they lose consciousness of their separateness, as though a larger self displaces their individual selves; and the thrill of this enlargement is school spirit's attraction.

The theory of a larger self founders, however, when we examine its alleged largeness. It requires me to believe that when I feel the exciting expansion of my own intention while cheering at a football game there is actually not an expansion of myself but a displacement of my own self by the larger one; so that if I think about what I mean at this moment when I say *I* want my school to win, I cannot claim that I (as bearer of my personal name) want this, only that my school (which now is my "I") does. It further requires me to believe that when I look into the eyes of my cheering neighbor I see not a different individual selfhood expanded through the cheering but instead a repetition of the same larger selfhood that has taken me over. That means that I cannot say "You" any more to my neighbor, except as a charade. It also means that if I try to arouse school spirit in anyone else I am really trying to make that person, to that extent, identical with my school-spirited self—again abolishing my individual "I" and any "You." But all of these consequences of the theory of a larger self amount to reductions, not expansions. Before the larger self comes on the scene there are numerous personal "I"s, each with its own style and outlook, and each a "You" to all the others; after the larger self is imposed there is only one "I," which has a rather restricted outlook and a monotonous way of expressing itself.

On the contrary, school spirit only enhances life because it expands the intentions of "I" and the met intentions of "You" without abolishing I or You. Cheering at a football game adds a dimension to relationships with fellow students rather than suppressing all other dimensions. If happiness in this new dimension overshadows frustrations in the others, then it may feel as though school spirit is overcoming private existence in its negative aspect, but the overcoming counts as the revelation of a new, superior possibility of life together rather than the eclipsing of the old. It excites precisely in the consciousness of its contrast with the unspirited ways that lie open alongside it. Similarly, the *togetherness* of sharers of school spirit is satisfying because it is other than the unity of the *fasces*. A fascist school spirit, one that actually submerged the individual personhoods of its members, would be as pathological and repulsive as actual fascist national spirits have been. More to the present point, it would not be a "spirit" of the same kind. It would belong to a different recognized kind of "spirit," a possessing demon.

On a Hegelian interpretation, the special meaning of "spirit" in this context would lie in school spirit's creation of a controlling but organic unity in which all individuality was preserved at the same time that it was superseded. There would be no fascist "submerging" of individuality. But a Hegelian spirit realizes itself necessarily, as a consummation of the meanings of its ingredients, whereas a school spirit's appeal is connected with its gratuitousness, the contingent and even improbable work it does in gathering free and dissimilar beings. The crucial issue here is whether the first meaning of spirit is *one*-comprehending-many (the magnitude of the *one* proportional to the dissimilarities of the many that it triumphantly overcomes) or many-*together* (the magnitude of the *together* proportional to the dissimilarities with which it coexists). Of course, this is not just a linguistic issue, and English speakers, being different sorts of people and having different outlooks, will certainly divide in the way they prefer to think about intentional commonality. But I claim that the non-Hegelian interpretation fits the generality of usage better.

We may also note in passing how a school's "spirit" is not the same as its "soul." One could speak of, say, a school's soul being laid bare as students and staff answer questions provoked by some sort of scandal. In this context "soul" means an inner essence imagined as feeling, something normally hidden from observers. Its spirit, by contrast, is its buoyancy and its proclamation, supposed to be as manifest as possible.

(4) *I am with you in spirit* would be written in a letter, for example, in the consciousness of being unable to speak or act with another person at an envisioned moment. If we are not to dismiss this statement as irony or bravado, we must take seriously the possibility of nonbodily togetherness it projects.

The statement is not flatly descriptive or predictive. It is like a promise in that it does not "come off" without the backing of the one saying it. The backing in question is not the performance of an observable deed or the readiness to perform one, however, but an unobservable intentional gesture. The invisibility of the gesture, far from cheapening it, gives it its encouraging effect in this context: both maker and recipient of the gesture are to know that intention *as such* can *in some sense* prevail over physical separation. It is more bolstering still to realize that this intention is for *togetherness as such,* the precondition of everything that would be intended together. The place in which writer and reader are together is obviously not a physical place and so can be no other than the purely intentional sphere that we have already seen to be the home of the spirit of fair play. To write or read this statement seriously is to become conscious of dwelling in that intentional "place."

The special character of the place of spiritual togetherness is worth careful attention. It is not natural but neither is it supernatural, in the sense that the writer or reader of these words expects an astral-plane encounter perceptible by higher senses. Rather, the whole point of the declaration is to create a togetherness transcending *any* kind of actual encounter. The reader is to think of the writer as attending to the reader's situation in *parallel* with the reader's experience rather than as part of it, and while the two surely feel this as a deficiency in the sense that they would prefer to be together in physical space, they feel at the same time a positive exaltation in the partial conquest of their deprivation by a mode of togetherness that is independent of all spatial contingencies. They are cheating space of its prerogative to divide, but they do this by creating a new space. The difference between "I will be thinking about you" and "I will be with you in spirit" is the difference between merely parallel living and *parallelistically common* living. The word "spirit" introduces that parallelistic commonality.

(5) *A spiritual person* is very likely to be a religiously preoccupied person, but "spiritual" is not synonymous with "religious." We can imagine a person meticulous in the observance of religious law or greatly concerned about afterlife rewards and punishments whom it would yet be odd to call "spiritual." And we can also imagine a "spiritual" person with none of the particular commitments in belief or practice that ordinarily warrant the description "religious." (Whether a normative definition of religion might equate it with being spiritual in the present

sense is another question, not to be taken up here.) Nor is a "spiritual" person necessarily "great-souled," which implies breadth and depth of sensitivity.

One is inclined to describe as "very spiritual" a person who is conspicuously abstracted from worldly affairs and especially from his or her own worldly prosperity, not from laziness or ignorance but by virtue of consistently attending to something else. Such a person is not necessarily unselfish: he or she might spend every day in meditation, oblivious to the sufferings of family and friends. The point is that the conduct of such a person, selfish or unselfish, makes the onlooker conscious of another "place" or frame of reference than the ordinary world. Again, this "place" need not be a place *like* the world except "higher"; it could be a pure creation of intention. Of course, anyone can think or imagine things in some independence of worldly experience, but the "spiritual" person gives the impression of *living* in the nonworldly frame of reference and thus encouragingly vindicates its reality for the rest of us, prisoners of an imperfect natural world, who wonder. The child who lives in an alternate "world" of innocence or make-believe is a type of the "spiritual"—less encouraging if we understand childhood as a transitory condition rather than as a permanent possibility.

The exaltation implicit in this as in most uses of spirit-words is due both to the *otherness* of the "spiritual" intention with respect to ordinary ones—a kind of exoticism—and to the *triumph* of its self-superordination to the world. These are the two basic kinds of strengthening possible for intention, internally to carry off alteration and externally to prevail over circumstances. The same qualities appear in a different form in persons considered "spirited"; one is not surprised if they change their minds and one admires the confidence implicit in their recklessness.

Although "spiritual" does not *mean* "unselfish," it does seem to strain "spiritual" to apply it to an utterly self-absorbed person, for all that he or she could be absorbed in an unworldly self. Such a person would be in pursuit of extraordinary personal power, or else blessed nothingness. But a shaman does not gain powers without having dealings with the "spirits," and a Buddhist monk does not advance toward self-extinction without developing compassion for others. In practice it may be impossible to transcend the worldly self with strictly inner resources, if "transcend" and "inner" are in real contradiction. The contradiction is not at any rate logical: an individual could bring forth a higher self from within.

On the other hand, a "spiritual" person does have an essential relationship with others insofar as he or she is always regarded as a model of human possibility, a trailblazer for all into the "space" of pure intention. "Spiritual" is an honorific term marking an exemplar. In contemplating a "spiritual" person one thinks of oneself as perhaps less "spiritual" than him or her, but never as unspiritual, for that would be to belong to a different species and to lose the ground of intense interest one has in the more spiritual individual. Being spiritual concerns everyone to a greater or lesser extent.

Our findings may be summarized as follows.

"Spirit" occurs where commonality of intention supervenes upon individual intentions without abolishing the otherness of individual persons to each other. The strength and the appeal of a "spirit" is in proportion to our sense of its exceptional achievement of gathering together what remains separate. (For example, it is more stirring to contemplate a collection of very diverse people animated by common interests than an utterly uniform collection of persons who have been molded in their very individuality by common intentions.) The distinctive sense expressed in most uses of "spirit" is oxymoronic: together-and-separate, common-and-parallel. As opposed to Hegelian spirit, a unity to which individual differences, although preserved, are made relative, the ordinary senses of "spirit" suggest a unity that is held relative to plurality.

To *be* "spirited" with such a spirit is to live in the non-natural "space" or "place" of the spirit's togetherness by sharing intentions with others. To be "spiritual" is to live in the "space" of intention as such. Whether this can be done without meeting with the intentions of others—whether meeting the intentions of others is a condition of the opening up of anything describable as a "space" in which spiritually to live—is another question, but the intentions of others at least accompany one in the appreciative judgment that one is spiritual.

Spirit-words refer to an extraordinary life that is not merely odd but *better* and more authoritative. The spirit of fair play *claims* players. Public-spirited people are *more admirable*. School spirit *enhances* school life; every student who lacks it dampens life for the others, directly or indirectly. To be with someone in spirit is a crucial and *redeeming* kind of companionship. A spiritual person is a "*higher*" kind.

2.3 Observing and Sharing Spirit

Spirit-words seem by and large to depart from the psychological realm by gathering the intentions of a plurality of persons. But if the "spiritual" has to do with shared or sharable intention, is it not then an object of social science? And inasmuch as the social sciences are already equipped with the concepts of the "social" and the "cultural," is it not unnecessary to duplicate these, and with mystic overtones, by talking of the "spiritual"?

We can demonstrate that this is not the case. Suppose that Jane asks Julia, apropos of Julia's refusal to vote in an election, "Don't you have any public spirit?" It is immediately obvious that the question could not just as well be, "Don't you belong to a democratic culture?" "Society" and "culture" are words used by detached observers to describe human behavior. Jane is not trying to describe Julia correctly; she is challenging her to join in commitment to public affairs. In asking about her spirit, she calls upon her. And it is true generally that spirit-words are used to prescribe, perform, or appreciate actions and dispositions. A purportedly objective reporter who spoke of the "spirit" of a group would thereby act as a cheerleader for it. Social scientists, on the contrary, would never use such a word except between quotation marks. Their task is to identify invariant patterns in the behavior and validity-claims of agents that correspond to what the cheerleaders call the spirit of the collectivity, and those patterns are their theoretical object, the culture or social structure of the group.[2]

Julia's capacity to refrain from concurring with the spirit of good citizenship is what raises the question of her spirit and makes it interesting. This capacity has two complementary dimensions. From Jane's side it is Julia's otherness, the fact that one never already knows what Julia is, but has always to find out; from Julia's side it is what she experiences as her free will. Julia slips out of the social-scientific frame of reference in either dimension. As an *imponderable* being she is excluded from the world-description of social science, which like any science must reduce its objects to a fixed, intelligible, objective form. Social-scientific knowledge is of limited relevance to her as a *free* being because it is not sufficient to determine her choices. She needs a kind of normative principle that mere description is not meant to provide. Jane means to place a normative principle before Julia when she challenges her on public spirit, and that is why it would be beside the point for her to ask the descriptive question whether she is a member of a certain culture. "Don't you have any public spirit?" *could* mean "Don't you have a normative principle?"—that is, one could ask it with a neutral air, acting as a sociologist of morals. But more likely the question functions as a proffering of such a principle, an invitation to join it or a challenge to decline it.

To talk of a spirit is often to prescribe an intention rather than to reflect on the ineffable felt quality of an intention that is had. That is, that in the talk of spirit that goes beyond what can be said, which is often taken for some ineffable *content*, can actually be the surpassing of any descriptive content by a prescriptive *venture*. In such cases it is quite in order that the concept of spirit lack a corresponding intuition. If I am calling upon you to intend something in a certain way, the basis of my call cannot be an intuition of your having that intention, because you have not had it yet. It may be that you have it at the moment, but insofar as I call upon you, I look forward to moments when you might not have it. However, when you do share an intention with me, participating in that "spirit," your way of intending is at the same time determinative of what the spirit is and unforeseeable: determinative of what the spirit is, because it both adds to the intentional qualities that are available to be shared and affects the manner in which unreduced interpersonal otherness is apparent as the field in which the spirit is established; unforeseeable, because your unreduced otherness just is the intending that no other subject could conceivably do for you, even by way of anticipation. Clearly, then, the spirit in which you participate is unforeseeable for the same reason that you are, *which implies that we look forward to it and promote it without knowing exactly what we are talking about.* (Even a spirit controlled by extensive explicit regulation, like moral spirit, has unforeseeable quality in its concretion.)

The corollary for social science is that it is impossible to observe a spirit, as spirit, from outside it. Jane and her fellow citizens can think of the spirit of democracy as the social reality of their polity, or their "culture," but it is *their* culture, and the regularities in it that would be interpreted by social scientists as the laws of its occurrence are, to them, the rules of its performance. They understand themselves to be motivated by it, subject to its appeal, caught in the alternative of ratifying or rejecting it, and perhaps predetermined by it in the sense that it and not other things has taken up their intentional field of vision. But to the exact extent that they perceived their enthusiasm for public affairs as a socially determined personality trait, it would not be "spirit" for them. This is partly the import of philosophical assertions of the essential freedom of spirit.

In the word of encouragement "That's the spirit!" we find a gesture of approval complementary to Jane's gesture of prescription toward Julia. Jane will say it to Julia if she sees her at the voting station. It means that what has been or is being done proceeds from an intention that ought to be the rule. It also distinguishes on the spot between "spirit" and "letter" in the text of human actions by separating from what was observed (what the social scientists saw) the intention underlying what was observed. To talk of this "spirit" is implicitly to envision an infinite number of possible actions on other occasions due to the approved intention. The lift one feels in saying these words comes from thus transcending the moment. Here the doctrine of the eternity of spirit finds a warrant.

2.4 Russell's Conception of Spirit

The use of spirit-words in English-language philosophy reflects all the meanings disclosed in Chapter 1 because of the influences of European philosophical developments upon it. For example, Locke and Berkeley follow Descartes in taking "spirit" interchangeably with "soul," "mind," and "self" to mean "thinking thing." [3] Coleridge follows German idealism in identifying "spirit" with *nous*.[4] An English philosopher contemporary with Scheler and Hartmann, Bertrand Russell, proposes a restriction of the meaning of "spirit" similar to theirs. In his case, however, the restriction is based in part on a sensitivity to the difference between the meanings of the English words "mind" and "spirit." It is therefore appropriate to appeal to him as a linguistic bellwether in this part of our investigation.

Russell's scruples concerning "spirit" are on view when he worries in his *History of Western Philosophy* whether "spirit" can stand for the *nous* of Plotinus.

It is always difficult to find an English word to represent *nous*. The standard dictionary translation is "mind," but this does not have the correct connotations, particularly when the word is used in a religious philosophy. . . . Dean Inge uses "Spirit," which is perhaps the best word available. But it leaves out the intellectual element. . . . *Nous* has an intellectual connotation which is absent from "Spirit" as usually understood.[5]

Behind this negative judgment about "spirit" is a positive understanding that Russell articulates in one of his earlier books, *Principles of Social Reconstruction*. He distinguishes three sources of human activity: instinct, mind, and spirit. Instinct is desire and the drive to succeed, which we share with all animals. Mind is disinterested curiosity and the capacity of objective knowledge; with mind we gain the ability to criticize our instinctive impulses, because we can compare them with others, but apart from sheer curiosity mind supplies no motive for restraining them. As for spirit:

> The life of the spirit centres round impersonal feeling, as the life of the mind centres round impersonal thought. . . . Reverence and worship, the sense of an obligation to mankind, the feeling of imperativeness and acting under orders which traditional religion has interpreted as divine inspiration, all belong to the life of the spirit.[6]
>
> Spirit is an antidote to the cynicism of mind: it universalizes the emotions that spring from instinct, and by universalizing them makes them impervious to mental criticism. And when thought is informed by spirit it loses its cruel, destructive quality; it no longer promotes the death of instinct, but only its purification from insistence and ruthlessness. . . . It is instinct that gives force, mind that gives the means of directing force to desired ends, and spirit that suggests impersonal uses for force.[7]

Spirit redeems the instinct of patriotism, for example, by making it inclusive, a principle of appreciation of all countries, rather than xenophobic.

More than a formal principle like the Kantian categorical imperative, the spirit brings also a profound experience of well-being.

> The life of the spirit . . . brings the solution of doubts, the end of the feeling that all is vanity. It restores harmony between mind and instinct, and leads the separated unit back into his place in the life of mankind. For those who have once entered the world of thought, it is only through spirit that happiness and peace can return.[8]

Russell's account converges with ours to a considerable extent. Spirit has interpersonal extension; it is a lifting of an individual's intention up to the plane of the collective. Spirit is made of *care* or personal commitment—reverence, devotion, and so forth, instead of detached curiosity. Spiritual beings do more than know about others, they care for others. In the correspondence between knowing about others and caring about others lies the salvific experience, for the critical mental principle has met its match; it no longer has leverage to detach the individual from the social whole.

But there are dubious points worth probing. Is it true that spirit is invariably universalized? Would we be less likely to speak of a school spirit at Riverdale if the Riverdale students thoroughly hated the students at Central? It would be a less admirable spirit in that case, as we would perhaps judge it from the standpoint of a more comprehensive spirit, but seemingly no less a spirit. It is truer to say that spirit expands intentional horizons to the widest boundaries that the nature of the intention permits. One shares *Riverdale* spirit with *any Riverdalian,* not with every being in the universe. Russell must have in mind a cosmic or at least humanistic spirit, which includes what it includes not just because it is spirit but because of the kind of spirit it is. Is it true that mind has no further questions to ask of spirit if spirit is universalized? On the contrary, it seems that the absence of an objective cognition of spirit makes the reality and validity of it gravely questionable. So the critics of aestheticism and emotivism have always contended. Finally, do we have sufficient grounds for separating spirit from mind? Cannot spirit be interpreted as the intersection of mind, the universalizing power, with instinct, the power of caring? A Kantian would say that the feelings of obligation and reverence to which Russell alludes are nothing other than the impact of mind (reason) upon instinct (inclination). Practical reason and theoretical reason are both reason.

Kantians and Hegelians would justly object that it is incomprehensible how the passive *affection* of a "feeling" could have, of itself, universal form, unless that feeling were generated by the *activity* of universalization. And this raises the crucial issue of whether the spiritual tie between one individual and others is to be conceived as an active expansion of that own individual's essence, or a passive reception by that individual of the concerns of others. On the first alternative, it would be as though there were two moments in the school spirit of Riverdalians, first the casting of the intention of each into the disinterested form of devotion to the school, then an awareness of each that his or her generalized intention is reduplicated in all other members of the spirit. This might be called the "inside-out" view.[9] On the second, "outside-in" view, the two moments would be first the awareness that other Riverdalians stand to gain or lose in relation to Riverdale's institutional welfare, and second the formulation of a general intention that accommodates the cares of others. Russell's conception of spirit, like Kant's of reason, fits the first view best. A spiritual being cares disinterestedly in principle and is not prisoner to the "accidental circumstance" that it happens to live among Riverdale and not Central students. The "feeling" in question is a "higher" feeling not liable to the Kantian criticism of inclinations. But a feeling that is not restricted by the contingent fact that this or that other definite group of persons surrounds me must be designated a priori or innate. It is an emotion in search of objects rather than an affection by something real—unless, in some occult way, the whole universe affects me before I meet its parts.

Surely the idea of an emotion in search of objects is a dangerous one. It undercuts the limited validity that emotions have as indices of the reality exterior to the one who feels them. (We are remote from Russell and truth both if we ascribe to emotion only the romantic validity of its sheer experiential content, its thrill.) Therefore Russell should either join forces with Kant and abandon the term "feeling," or he should hold that a "spiritual" being is one *capable* of entering into a community of feeling with other beings. It must be a readiness to feel, and not an actual feeling, that precedes encounter with others. But this implies that transpersonal feeling, when it is actualized, is determined as to its content by particular things that are felt about and particular others who are felt with. It seems correct to say that a subject's capacity to feel is limited by the possibilities of correlating that feeling with exterior reality as intended in perception, imagination, and conception. Even if Riverdale students do not know any students at Central High, they know of them and therefore can sympathize with them in principle. They cannot sympathize with the inhabitants of the planet Krullon, which they have never heard of.

By showing that the objects of spirits (fair play, school glory) as well as the intentional contributions of their members are determinative of them, our earlier spirit-examples authorize us to adopt the outside-in view of the spiritual. We are not therefore obliged to part company with Russell or even with Kant, however, for they do not and cannot close off to discussion how the higher feeling or reason are constituted. They talk as if moral intention were an entirely innate event in individuals, rather than a contingently conditioned activity of which individuals are innately capable, but it does not seem that either need commit himself to this view. Kantian agents are not morally reasonable until they arrive at universalized practical conclusions for a determinate practical community—be it the community of "any and all actual or potential members of a universal community of intention." Nor are they impervious to instruction and correction from each other. The marvelous attribute of moral spirit, which is designedly universal both in membership and in scope of application, is the convergence of individual intentions conforming themselves to these very demanding requirements. So much is dictated by these requirements that we might think that moral reason springs identical and full-blown in the breast of every subject. If moral reason is actually a spirit, though, this is an illusion.

Russell has pried "spirit" loose from "mind" in order to address the issues of authority and motivation. A *nous*-thinker will object that Russell's "mind" is shrunken to the analytic, calculative faculty called *dianoia* by Plato and *Verstand* by Hegel. Knowledge in the fullest sense, Plato and Hegel would say, includes knowledge of right ends and has its own impetus toward the Good. We must note that Russell disagrees with this view not in the manner of the exteriority-thinkers, by affirming a "You" transcendent of knowledge, but instead by appealing to *feeling*. Yet if we ask why feeling at the level of spirit is "impersonal," why the emotions of instinct are "universalized," *given that intellect as such does not accomplish this formation,* what can we answer except that a going-forth to Others carries feeling into the transpersonal "place" of spirit? Implicitly, then, Russell and the tradition of British moral aestheticism that he represents point toward the spirit-as-relationship conception. The particular distribution of meaning between "spirit" and "mind" in English is a prime cause of this affinity.

2.5 The Proposal

The aim of properly conceiving the commanding feature of the original situation in which the question "How will we live?" is asked; the suspicion, encouraged by noteworthy examples of philosophical innovation stretching now over millennia, that a moving-air word will be strategically well suited to bear this conception; the appreciation of the distinctive and irreducible meaning of the English words "spirit" and "spiritual" gained by a review of ordinary usage—all converge now on the task of formulating a definition of the spiritual.

We *first* approach "spirit" as a qualification of the beings asking the first question, ourselves, rather than as a problematic substance to be conceived separately from ourselves; therefore, the preferable form of the question of definition is, What does it mean to say that we must understand ourselves to be, in the *first* place, "spiritual" beings?

A spiritual being is one who intends a commonality of intention with other intenders. That shared or sharable intention is a spirit. To be spiritual as opposed to merely intentional is to have intentions with regard to the spirit itself.

Spirit is thus only a complication of intention, but one with momentous implications. The intentions of spiritual beings must be universalizable, that is, capable of generalization in abstraction from the irreducibly individual aspects of intention. For instance, Jane's invocation of "public spirit" presupposes an ability to see Julia's prospective affirmation of democratic process as the same affirmation as hers. In this very generalization, however, spiritual beings must remain, for themselves, free, and for others, other. (To be free is to be other to oneself—not knowing what one will be, having to try for it.) Their selves are not displaced or superseded by the entry into intentional community; Julia is not enlisted as a *tool* of public spirit. Therefore, we can define spirit as *the intentional togetherness of beings who are for themselves "I" and for others "You," that is, other to each other.* A being who is essentially spiritual, whose proper existence comprises membership in spirit, would thus be one for whom the otherness of others has become a condition of the meaning of existence. For the otherness of others not only makes their membership in spirit an interesting issue but seeps into spirit itself, as was shown above.

The proposed definition has two outstanding peculiarities. One is that the concept of spirit is not employed in an objectively descriptive way. As we saw, "spirit" and "spiritual" characteristically make their appearance when intentions are expressed and enacted. They then reappear when experiences of expressing and enacting intentions are reflected on, as here, but even in such reflection one does not understand what is being talked about under the heading of "public spirit" unless one has been subject to the claim of spirit like it; and further, one does not entertain "public spirit" in reflection without an attitude toward it, whether admiring, amused, contemptuous, or ambivalent. A completely detached reflective grasp of spirit would be of "culture" instead. Therefore, just as spirits are normative organizations of the intentions of spiritual beings, so the very positing of spirit in a definition of it is a normative move. The spirit principle is asserted in its distinctive way even in the claim that it exists. It vanishes if it is not received as it is offered.

Much philosophical practice to the contrary, it is impossible to rise above the distinction between normative and descriptive language-acts to a neutral position from which one can compare them. Neutrality is a descriptive tactic. Neutral philosophical accounts of normative language must always pare it down to a descriptive residue: the states of affairs wanted, and the wanting of those states of affairs, which is itself a psychological state of affairs. Then the more sensitive accounts express puzzlement over what there is in addition to the descriptive residue, since there obviously is something, though one does not know how to get at it. What there is in addition is the normative intentional act itself, which can only be performed. It is there, after all, in the expression of puzzlement that draws a boundary to the province of the describable, for this is itself a normative move. One can challenge it—why *not* rest content with the phenomenal residue?—and that too is a normative move. A "move" in this sense is not a phenomenon, though it leaves a psychological and historical trace; it is something done, or rather, to be done.

The implications of this claim will be more fully examined later (Chapter 4). Meanwhile it is important to note the type of reflexivity that is involved in defining "spirit": not the reflexivity of that which knows knowing itself, but of that which norms being brought forward as a norm, indeed the norm of the realm of norms. There is no paradox in this, but it is not a definition that can be justified by correspondence, that is, by experiential fulfillment of a propositional intention, as theoretical-descriptive definitions are.

The second peculiarity of our definition of spirit is another side of the first. It contains the concept of an Other, which is not the same as the "different." The "different" is what has been carried (ferried) apart by an act of distinguishing, and is thus subordinate to the higher synthesis implicit in this act. The "other," *ander,* or *alter,* however, is what lies *beyond,* what is *more* than that which can be designated. We shall reflect in our use of these words the distinction noted earlier between the Hegelian and counter-Hegelian interpretations of unity-in-difference—which becomes now the distinction between unity-in-difference and togetherness-with-others, and no longer precisely as *distinction* between these two, but as the *otherness* of togetherness-with-others with respect to unity-in-difference. Special care is required to sustain the otherness of otherness to difference, inasmuch as otherness only appears within a theoretical framework if it is reduced to difference. The defense of a concept of otherness other than difference will coincide with the defense of a kind of language and argument other than the theoretical-descriptive. But this makes for the odd feature that the definition indicates something that is not there; it gestures emptily toward a "beyond."

Reformulated as the problem of whether an ontology of spirit is possible, this issue divides twentieth-century philosophers of the spiritual. Buber, Marcel, and Hartmann stand on one side, Levinas on the other.[10] Buber argues for an "ontology of the between" for two reasons. The first is to assert the absolute priority of interpersonal encounter in the order of meaning, so that we will not confuse his testimonies to encounter with a psychological description—but here one could say simply that he wants to call our attention to the normative character of his claims. The second is to insist that the locus of full being for a person, "actuality" (*Wirklichkeit*), is encounter with others. Marcel's appetite for Being likewise leads him to encounter with a You who is the mystery of Being. In contrast to these two, Hartmann wishes to insist that there are spiritual *phenomena* amenable to *description*. He urges us not to conclude from the peculiarities of these phenomena that they lack being. We experience the spiritual in definite forms. It is in some ways the best known of things in our life. But Levinas protests that the specificity of the spiritual is that it is *not* known, that it comes from outside the realm of being as this realm is constituted by its partnership with thought. What does it mean to say that something *is* if not to deliver it to thought? "X is Y" is the mental capture of a subject by a predicate, accomplished in the unification of the judgment. "X is," all by itself, is still an assertion that X is there for my awareness, as a subject of possible predicates, a somehow fixed point of reference for my mind as it orients itself to the world. But the others are unforeseeable. Their meaning does not lie even in the foreseeing of their unforeseeableness, which is the negative determination by which my thought ironizes itself in relation to the others, but rather in their actual surprising of thought, their own imposition of their unforeseeableness, which produces an utterly passive "suffering" of their otherness on my part.

Although Hartmann's work deserves high honor as an extraordinarily thorough and sensitive review of spiritual issues, his ontological descriptivism is naive. Spiritual phenomena are not there to be described as he imagines they are. The ontologism of Buber and Marcel is harder to dismiss; we have seen that even Levinas at one time could say "Being is exteriority." Clearly, the concept of being is one of the interesting concepts that exists to be contested, and being cannot be attached to spirit or detached from it in a universally convincing way. Our need is to consider the situation in which we think about spirit and to judge which of the possible directions we should move in. I propose that we follow Levinas' example in his move away from ontology—which means that we will mean by "ontology" what we are able to move away from—as a way of marking the otherness of the "spiritual" with respect to other themes of discourse and its independence of some of our firmest assumptions about how it is possible to reason. If we become habitually uneasy with statements that the "spiritual" *is* this or that, we will remember that we are—no, mean to be—engaged in a special kind of reasoning.

The great temptation to ontologism in matters spiritual lies in our anxiety lest spirit prove unreal, lest spiritual togetherness, rooted in no essence, evaporate the moment we no longer are, or think we are, appropriately intending. We want to express our faith in it by giving it the ultimate guarantee, asserting that it is there no matter what anyone thinks. But this is actually our bad faith. Not only is there only "spirit" to the exact extent that we actually intend spiritually—which we might freely, irresponsibly cease to do—but even to want "spirit" to exist apart from your contingent activity and mine, or to want there to be some necessity underlying our activity, is to misunderstand and betray the spiritual. It is to trade our birthright for a mess of pottage. Yet we are not easy with our birthright; we are almost intolerably aware of the alienability and deniability of the spiritual.

The impossibility of defining spirit theoretically is the reverse side of the actual possibility of raising the issue of what spirit means and thus of defining it in a purely normative way. A common, nearly standard reaction to definitional dispute, once we recognize that it cannot be settled by making observations, is to abandon it in disgust. This at the very least aborts the joy of continuing to parley. At the most, it shirks the responsibility of determining through conscientious negotiation how our life together shall be lived, or how we shall be spiritual. Therefore, what looks like an enormous presumption in the present essay, that one can take up a much-used and historically important concept such as that of the spirit and make of it what one will, unequally responsive to different elements in its tradition, is but an acknowledgment of the invitation issued by all essentially controversial concepts, and by this one above all others. In short, we must not pretend that it is not for us to say, for ourselves, precisely at this moment, what the "spiritual" is.

To conclude our opening exposition of a normative definition of the spiritual, we will bring our definition into relation with the tradition of *nous*-thinking to see to what extent, if any, our version of the spirit-as-relationship conception is reconcilable with the spirit-as-mind conception.

2.6 Spirit-as-Relationship in Relation to Spirit-as-Mind

Spirit-as-relationship has mainly been defined in antithesis to spirit-as-mind, because exteriority defeats comprehension. But if relationship, understood as intentional togetherness of beings other to each other, is to be the first principle of our life, then we would expect this superior conception of the spiritual to establish the right context and orientation for a positive interpretation of every human reality, including mind.

A point of contact between the spirit-as-mind and spirit-as-relationship conceptions appears in their common implication that a spiritual being is self-transcending. The distinctive and higher sort of consciousness that Aristotle understands by the word *nous* is not a human possession merely but the function of some relationship with the divine, a "higher" reality than the human. This transcendence is implied whenever it is claimed that the mind is responsive to meaning or principles. Undoubtedly, Plato understood the intuitive apprehension of the Forms as a self-transcending, and the capacity for this as a human kinship with the divine:

> But we must rather fix our eyes, Glaucon, on [the soul's] love of wisdom and note how she seeks to apprehend and hold converse with the divine, immortal, and everlasting world to which she is akin, and what she would become if her affections were entirely set on following the impulse that would lift her out of the sea in which she is now sunken. . . .[11]

A spiritual being, whether understood according to Plato's fables or Levinas' formula of prophetic subjectivity, "the-Other-in-the-Same"—whether visited by a *daimon* like Socrates or by a categorical imperative like Kant—is always *one who has not been left alone*. A spiritual being is *aware* in the sense of being *awakened*, roused by a visitation. In heeding this emphasis we would regard "mind" as the avenue by which conscious beings are possessed by something "beyond" rather than as the avenue by which the world is delivered over to consciousness simply to be possessed.

To confirm this general indication it will be necessary to identify the essential characteristics of mind and evaluate each in relation to the spiritual. The *nous*-tradition testifies that mind is *reflexive, active, free, creative, intuitive, universalizing*, and—with due regard to possibilities opened up by Hegel—*historical*.

(1) *Mind is reflexive or self-conscious.* In thinking about itself, a conscious

being elaborates a "self" to think about and interprets the remainder of reality according to its connection or lack of connection with this self. The self becomes a world to itself, a realm of "inwardness" or "subjectivity" distinct in kind from the outward and objective. The "eccentric" human position in the world follows from reflexivity inasmuch as subjectivity begins in the realization that what it is different from is different from it as well, and thus that the world is not the same thing as its experience of it. Every self-aware being is capable of respect for the prima facie difference between "the" world and "my" world. The issue of "objective knowledge," of being versus seeming or truth versus opinion, only arises for self-conscious mind. Since "the" world transcends "my" world, I transcend myself in being essentially occupied with "the" world and the problem of truth—even if I solve the problem by defining myself in a new way such that "the" world and "my" world necessarily coincide.[12]

—Psychologically, we know the *reflexive* consciousness to be a product of social interaction. I know myself to be one being among others in the world because I come to know myself as a being seen by others, commanded by others, having to share things with others, and defining my sphere of power over against others. Using language, I must negotiate the names and properties of things with others and thus I learn the very meanings of things by virtue of my participation in a social field of communication. I am "eccentric" because the others have de-centered me. Through birth, weaning, and other denials I have painfully learned their separateness; through language I have learned a way of being, proper to myself or "personal," that relies on their contingent respect for me as a revealer and questioner and also on my own respect for them, acquired through training and effort. I have come to know the "objective" world through symbolizing it, approaching it with public expressions.

But my psychological condition of being one among others is at the same time a logical condition, an a priori. Alongside the problem of the formation of self in childhood is the transcendental problem of the *cogito,* the self-criticizing subject of knowledge, as well as the *respondeo,* the self-criticizing moral subject. The reflexivity and eccentricity of consciousness are a priori conditions of the meaning of its existence because its encounters with others require from it the gesture of self-separation. Out of this gesture come the distinctions between "my" world and "the" world and between inclination and duty that determine the meanings that thought and action can assume. The others are of course real beings, not to be confused with a speculative principle; they must really have come along to confront the being that becomes an "I." Having come along, though, the others have irreversibly curved the universe. One cannot think back to a state before one met the others, or make any assumptions that depend on such a state, because one is pinned by the awareness that others were always there. Such is the spiritual predetermination of the reflexivity of mind.

(2) *Mind is active.* It takes the initiative with respect to the environment rather

than reacting to it instinctively; it is the manipulator, not the manipulated. Said otherwise, the mental life-principle is self-moving in a more radical sense than that in which living things in general move themselves. This has several implications.

(a) Mind is *free* of the natural environment. It may be free to remake the world according to its own moral purpose, or merely to lift its attention from sense-experience to abstract Forms. Its freedom may show itself in engagement with the world or in ascetic renunciation. In any event, it is determined by self, perhaps also by "values," but not by the naturally given.

(b) A corollary of mind's freedom is its *creativity*. The tangible token of the mind's connection with something other than nature is its production of novelties: thoughts, actions, and goods that would never have been expected from the perceptible order of things.

(c) Being free of nature, mind serves a non-natural master, whether the master be understood as a set of ideal Forms outside of it to which it is innately attuned, or simply itself, producing Forms from itself. Mind responds to meaning or principles that do not derive immediately from nature, and it can only do this because it has its own way of perceiving, different from sense-perceiving, which can be called intellectual *intuition*.

(d) The essential act of mind is the realization of plurality-ordering unities or *universalization*. This is the structure of the cognitive act that perceives the universal (the Form, essence, or concept) by disengaging it from the manifold of individual sense-readings, of the volitional act that proposes a rule of conduct, and, fundamental to both, the category of general validity. Whether universals are discovered or created, their realization provides a solution to the problem posed by the eccentricity of consciousness. Eccentric subjects retrieve themselves, find a place in "the" world, through their grasp of the universal. Private subjects become citizens of a public world.

—From the spiritual position it can be said that the essential *activity* of mind reflects the effort of initiative and response that is demanded of me if I am to live in the "place" of encounter with others. Consciousness as spiritually qualified is a going-forth, an approaching, and thus cannot be inert or merely substantial. Mind's actuality or activity can and should be represented not as an immanent property of an individual's being but as a function of the self-transcending entry into relationship of a spiritual being. Because by virtue of being spiritual I am launched outward toward the others and inhabit a world transcending "my" world, the physical substratum of my body must be distinguished from that which is launched, and this mind that is launched cannot be interpreted as merely what it feels like to be that body (unless we want to say that the body, too, is "launched"). The fundamental division here is not that between inwardness or subjectivity and outwardness or objectivity, but that between the private, which has the locale of my body, and the public, which has only the perspective limitation of my body. Mind is active because the spirit traverses back and forth the gap between persons, it blows where it wills; and as this shows up even in the solitary reflections of a being who lives in the public, it motivates the doctrine of the essential activity of mind. It is also necessary from a moral point of view that mind as intuition of communally valid norms should act without being acted on; that is, that it should command the self, with no talking back allowed from the self's other interests. In Aristotelian language this is expressed as the total actuality-without-potency, hence immateriality, of mind. In Kantian language it is the "purity" of the a priori.

I am *free* because I am drawn out through consideration of others from my own instinctive world; freedom means freedom from the private for the public. And this de-centered consciousness has so much room to maneuver and so much receptivity to the new that it is characteristically *creative,* its acts leading continually to unforeseen yet meaningful results. Poets, for instance, are poised as public beings to discover not merely new things that they can say but new things that can be said—that is, new sayings that confront them as something said from beyond the horizon of self.

Only in the spiritual field, and shaped by it, could there be "objective" (communal) meanings or principles by which a self-consciousness would feel itself commanded. The susceptibility to this command, inexplicable apart from the spiritual field because not structurally a part of identical selfhood as such, is experienced as an openness to otherness that might be identified with intellectual *intuition.* (The root meaning of "intuition" is not to be given something but to attend or turn to something.)[13] What is intuited must, moreover, be of *universal* form, or must demand to be universalized, since under this form must be united the actual and possible perceptions and communications of the others. "Essences" are what we all ought to acknowledge, not just what a lone mind has managed to recognize and identify over a manifold of instances. "Essences" are the achievements of the politics of spiritual thinking.

(3) *Mind is historical.* For Hegel and many of his successors, mind cannot be conceived apart from its progressive actualization in worldly events, which taken together as an intelligible unity constitute history. Even before its Hegelian apotheosis, "history" stood ready to hand as a category of determinate-meaningfulness-as-a-whole, a concrete universal; inevitably, it is the one adequate frame of reference for a temporal but universalizing being.

—Spiritually regarded, the memorable pattern called *history* is constituted as the time of intenders' approaching (never grasping) each other, qualified by variations of nearness, farness, rightness, and wrongness in relationship. History is time that has been irreversibly shaped and just in that way matters. The actions of others and the consequences of my actions for them go outside my control, beyond recall; "history" is what they pass into, or what, prospectively, they promise. In any case, real history is not mere exhibition of a Form spread over time; nor is it a time-occupying realization of a Form (as in Hegel), though such realizing makes a kind of story. Mind is indeed essentially historical but primarily because it is the site of interactions transcending any Form. The spiritually qualified history of mind progresses like life itself, all of its chapters of irreducible meaning and importance, rather than as a chain of steps leading necessarily to a conclusion that controls their meaning. It is true that the owl of Minerva always flies at dusk in the sense that thinkers gain their perspective from thought that has gone before, and this enables them to know things that were hidden from their predecessors. Unfortunately, they compensate for this by erring in their own new ways, even in interpreting the thought of the past. Standing on Plato's shoulders does not guarantee understanding Plato better than he understood himself.

These preliminary soundings would, however, indicate that when we proceed from the spiritual we understand mind better than it understands itself, inasmuch as we are able to assign a positive meaning to each of its essential traits without abandoning our supramental principle. We only have to oppose the principle of unlimited comprehension. But if we are committed not to knowledge simply but to knowledge-with-account, *logos,* reason, which presupposes uncomprehended Others with whom to reason, then philosophy not only is not impaired in taking this position, it is saved.

II

First Philosophy as Philosophy of the Spiritual

Chapter 3
The Concrete

3.1 The Question of the Concrete

A philosophy's cardinal exercise of tact is its decision about the concrete, what it takes to be its prime resource and beginning point. Since the very meaning of "concreteness," not to mention the very possibility of a "prime resource and beginning point," is subject to controversy, the decision is no simple matter. I rejoice in this. However, there are evidently certain characteristics that "the concrete" must have *if* it is to be invoked as the Archimedean point of philosophy. The concrete is where thinkers, perhaps in spite of their thought, really are and what they really confront; it precedes intellectual analyses and constructions and survives them when they collapse; it is what abstractions are abstracted from. (There may nevertheless be a sense in which philosophizing itself is an essential part of what is primordially given to think about.) The concrete will not go away. Whether we begin with the concrete in our grasp or alienated from it, the concrete is what is logically nearest, dependent on no other meaning to have meaning of its own.

The philosophy that misidentifies the concrete is skewed in all its parts by this first falsehood. The good reasoning in it is like a musical score with the wrong key signature; corrective criticism will try altering the signature (as we did with the spirit-as-mind tradition) in search of the right tune. The first falsehood is of course the mistake we most want to avoid. Yet the concrete cannot be found by a method, reliable or otherwise, because any systematic interrogation of appearances or regression upon presuppositions already rests on a decision about the concrete, or else is thoughtless. That consideration by itself occasions philosophical despair. But then we are entitled to console ourselves with the thought that the concrete, even though we cannot build a bridge to it, is already under our feet. We have it somehow, whether or not we recognize it. Our problem is to form concepts and arguments that will do it justice. Here we might despair again, for only on rare occasions can these be forged afresh on the anvil of the concrete, in the heat of an epochal new awareness of it. Usually, we can hope at most to bend the thoughts provided by our tradition into what seem to be better arrangements. Fortunately for us, those thoughts have already been shaped by many such efforts and are full of a wisdom of their own; that is our second consolation.

What might be taken for the concrete?

The most common view can be called descriptivism. It assumes that besides knowers there exists something definite in its own right, and that by some avenue knowers can accurately reflect its existence and nature in their knowledge of it. Knowers are taken to be mirrors of nature. But what we know about the physiological and cultural conditioning of our perceptions as well as our processes of thought is sufficient to discredit descriptivism. Further, the descriptivist notion of the concrete is impeached if one realizes how one's own interests have determined at any given time both what appeared to one and how it appeared. The mere process of growing up and aging will teach this to anyone who pays attention. Thus the concrete, if there is one, must include our interests.

For rationalism from Descartes onward, the activity of reason itself is the concrete. Kant exposes the interest that does not just color this activity but constitutes it—the interest in thinking the entire thinkable as a unity. Reality is kept separate from thought, as the thing-in-itself, but since it is for that reason indeterminable, it becomes dispensable. Hegel, representing the extreme development of a philosophy of comprehension, appropriately conceives the concrete as the richest possible unity of knowing and being. The meaning of everything is complicit in the constitution of the meaning of everything else; thus, to attend to anything in itself rather than in its place in the dynamic, organic ensemble of the whole (the historical self-unfolding of the Idea) is not only to impoverish knowledge by excluding from view the relations between things but radically to falsify the abstracted thing. Philosophizing belongs to the concrete as its coping stone, for there the Idea possesses itself unrestrictedly, as spirit, and that very possession is its full realization. This maximally comprehensive notion of the concrete is the one best suited to the program of comprehension and is therefore to be preferred —*if* the primary exigency to which we are subject is to comprehend, and if we are in a position to try to comprehend unrestrictedly.

There are a number of reasons for thinking that we are not in such a position, each motivating a different rival form of philosophy. If, for instance, what is knowable is absolutely determined by one's actual language and literature, which make only certain meanings available to thought, then the philosophy that would comprehend must take language itself as its point of departure and become hermeneutical or language-analytic. A more interesting alternative, because it proceeds from a basically different motive, is offered by Kierkegaard. He believes that we who are sinful and in any case finite subjects are not only not in a position to attempt unrestricted comprehension, we are also subject to a higher exigency than that of comprehension, namely, to unite the universal-ideal dimension of our being with the particular-historical in a synthesis of personal *existence*. This synthesis is the Kierkegaardian "concrete." It would be a mistake to regard it as a given, because it is something to be accomplished; nor is it ever finally accomplished. But it is the veritable inescapable, detached from which all else must be wrongly understood. It is that in human life which organizes the meaning of everything else. It is that the overlooking of which makes other philosophers (such as Hegel) comical. How could one not see what is nearest? Kierkegaard's conception of the concrete belongs to the program of existence and therefore is to be preferred if we are in a position to become selves and are called upon by nothing more important.

Yet another program, akin to the Kierkegaardian but distinct from it, is associated with Marxian socialism. Possible knowledge may be limited as a function of what pressingly needs to be *done* about the human lot as a whole—for example, to alter intolerable social conditions—so that the first given for philosophy would be an actual or mandated political struggle. We are not in a position to try to comprehend reality in abstraction from the effort to change it. This effort is determined in turn both by political goals and by the actual handholds and leverages by which it happens that reality may be changed.

The programs of comprehending, existing as a self, and fighting for social justice are all unavoidable, or rather not properly declinable. Each derives from encounter with a "concreteness" that has been convincingly attested. Are these concretenesses merely diverse or can they be ordered? There seem to be two possible ways to put them in order. The first would be to show that one concreteness is most fundamental, the others being forms of it. (For example, it can be argued that the programs of comprehension and existence, with their givens, are definite and inescapable *because of* their instrumental significance in the social struggle.) The second would be to find another concreteness yet unmentioned that is fundamental with respect to all of these. (The second way becomes increasingly attractive in principle, whether or not practicable, as attempts along the first line fail.) Perhaps a third way exists: to abandon the idea of a most-fundamental-concreteness, and to arrive instead at a protocol for orienting one's thought at a given moment to the appropriate concreteness. Such a protocol would have to be grounded in a principle other than concreteness. But since any usable principle would have to reflect the structure of the actual situation comprehending the different concretenesses, it seems that it would always amount to a principle of concreteness, whatever one called it. So the third way collapses back into the second. Finally, a fourth way would be to deny grounds for the establishment of any protocol for thought whatsoever, and thus to abandon philosophy for a kind of play.

To what fundamental concreteness is the present philosophical discourse bound?

I find that I am not in a position to comprehend, or to exist as a self, or to fight for justice, apart from the determination of another program, another element in my situation that calls for the response of this rather elaborate enactment in words. I face others—the host of other beings with places of their own in the world, and among them and preeminently the others who are intenders. This first fact of my life has two dimensions, that the others are there and that I am not at liberty to ignore them. They do not offer themselves primarily as objects of comprehension, although it is because of them that I need reasons and have undertaken this search for the first, best reasons; their importance is not derivable from the importance of my project of being a self; the claims they make transcend the practical limitations of our political comportment; nevertheless, their presence conditions the meaning of comprehension, selfhood, and social justice. They cause the "givens" of my situation to be "given" in the full, *insistent* sense; they cause specificity to *matter*. This is true not only for the specificity of the contents of my experience but for my personal identity as well. I am in the first place the one whom actual others have not left alone. My existence is qualified from the ground up as existence-toward-them. I am not free not to be this, but at the same time I am only free to propose and argue, to say what is and what should be, because I am this. Philosophy as I practice it cannot swallow the others into any other program than being with them, because its own truth is that it springs (not just historically but logically) from being with them.

In one sense it is impossible to prove the correctness of one's identification of the concrete, because the concrete is that to which one appeals to prove anything. But a certain conception of the concrete will be borne out if employing it makes everything else appear right side up. And this will happen only if there is already awareness, albeit confused or disputed, of what is claimed to be the true concrete, so that the right-sidedness of the picture generated from it is felt by those to whom the argument is directed. In the present case, I must assume that the reader faces others in the spiritual predicament, is aware in some fashion of the unsurpassable importance of that predicament, and will recognize superior clarity and justice in a line of thinking that sets out to be faithful to this above all else. Reasoning will be presented to bring about the recognition, but the reasoning will have peculiarities that are of a piece with the peculiarities of the claimed concrete. In the last analysis, this concreteness will vindicate itself (or not) through the perspicuous exhibition of it. We can make clearer as we go along what is involved in agreeing or disagreeing with this inaugural claim. It will never be possible to remove the reader's freedom to reject it. On the other hand, the author may always cling to the presumption that the grounds to which he appeals already assert themselves in the reader's act of attending to his discourse.

Hegel invites his readers into a scientific scheme wherein what is can be comprehended as what cannot be otherwise. He cannot remind us too often that although opinions are cheap, demonstrations are dear. For him the special business of philosophy is the discovery and elaboration of necessitarian arguments. Readers of *The Phenomenology of Spirit* perceive, for example, the necessary relationship (grounded inwardly, in the self-development of spirit) between pietism and religious skepticism, and in perceiving this gain the power of definitively placing these forms of consciousness in the role of preparatory constituents of something surpassing them.[1] There is no certainty like the *self*-certainty of the one who can say "I passed through that phase." Hegel's project would be checked only if a meaning with a dimension of irreducible otherness impinged on the self and held it, flouting its regime of self-possession. But as long as Hegel monopolizes the tools of demonstration, such a meaning can be expressed only as cheap opinion, as sheer enunciation of principles without the conceptually coercive support that philosophy demands. What we have to do, then, is find an argument that is, as philosophy, maximally explanatory, but that establishes the principles argued for through conceptual sensitivity and rectitude instead of coercion.

Our concrete is a problematic one that promises risky relationship rather than self-certainty. The definite, "near" thing that will not go away is not a phenomenon or a concept: it is the presence of Not-to-be-knowns toward whom I must choose how to comport myself, and with some of whom I must enter into community of intention. There is a different but related way of conceiving the concrete as problematic that rests on the inextinguishable possibility of asking what self and world mean. Concreteness is here located in the freedom of the inquirer who cannot ever, qua free, take matters as settled. This thesis should not be confused with the one that we are proposing. It is related to ours because an *implication* of being with others is that anything's meaning remains a perennially open question, but it is crucially different from ours in reserving to the self the power of questioning and thus protecting the self against any questions other than its own. Descartes will never in a hundred Meditations seriously ask himself, "But *may* I doubt?"

3.2 The Exigency and Problem of Rectifying Relationships

We say that two or more things are *related* if they have something in common. A judgment of relation imposes on the particulars their common element, whether it be located in the natures of the relata, as when we perceive two dogs to be related by virtue of their caninity, or in a more inclusive scheme or system of things, as when we perceive one magnitude to vary as a function of another. The thought supplies the common element; it is impossible to *judge* that an individual dog *apart from any judgment about it* is either the same as another dog or different, or that two magnitudes have anything to do with each other. The thought unifies the disparate, bringing intuitions under a concept, or thesis and antithesis into a synthesis. A relation is in any case a theoretical object.

If I say I have a "relationship" with you, however, I mean something other than that I am related to you. Already in informal speech my "relations" are facts that anyone could know about me, namely, the overlaps of genetic identity between me and the other members of my family. We say that I am or have a relation, whereas I am *in* a relationship. What does this "in" signify? It could mean that a relationship is a relation that exists as a shared larger system rather than a partial identity of nature, my experience and conduct varying as a function of yours, and vice versa. If a relationship were a relation, it would be a relation of this type. And it seems to be the case that we often think of our relationships in this way, to some extent. Talking to another friend, I say, "Under her influence I have become more forceful, while I have given her more confidence in herself." I may even say this to her. Such an act of description constitutes our relationship a theoretical object. But normally it remains more than that; normally we remember at the same time that the term "relationship" designates an enterprise that we are engaged in, that we therefore constitute moment by moment through our practice rather than through a cognition of it (which could only be of what *has been done* in the relationship).

There is a factual dimension in relationships, but in this context we are aware of the fact as dealt with or to-be-dealt-with. Compare two reasons often formally given for terminating a marriage, "incompatibility" and "irreconcilable differences." "Incompatibility" alleges the fact that two pieces do not fit together (therefore why try?). "Irreconcilable differences" points to a fact, difference, that was wrestled with, though unsuccessfully. According to this reason, it is not the fact as such but the defeat of practice by the fact that decides the fate of the relationship.

Relation is a theoretical and ontological concept. There either is a relation between things or there is not. A relation that falls under doubt is either resolved into knowable form or pronounced nonexistent. "Relationship," however, is a practical concept; relationships are differently determinate and subject to a different kind of evaluation than relations. It is not that certain objects have something in common with each other, but that *I am,* as an intender, something in common with someone or something; and not simply that I and the other are what we are, but that we may be what we are in a variety of ways. The salient principle of relationship is that these different ways of being are unequally good; the differences matter. In order to see how they matter, we must first see what is had in common in a relationship, and, in general, how.

In the following we will exclusively consider relationships in the full sense, those to which all parties are intentional beings. Later we will ask how the concept of relationship is applicable to the togetherness of intentional beings with intentionless ones.

At first blush it seems that parties to a relationship have objects and experiences in common. "She and I have the house, and the memories." Certainly if everything of the order of houses and memories were subtracted from life, there could be no relationships. Such things provide the occasions. But beyond the having of things there is the certain way in which they are had, that is, what is actually intended with respect to them. It is the commonality of the parties' intention with respect to a thing, rather than the relatively unimportant fact that both intend something or other with respect to it, that is the "common" specific to relationship. A man and a woman make their home in their house, and own their memories as the record of their history.

We must beware, however, of biasing our interpretation of relationships in favor of one sort of attunement. Is there relationship between persons only insofar as they are identified with each other, like lovers or friends, "one soul in two bodies"? Or is there not also relationship between those who have different intentions with respect to common things, as for example between a rich, powerful, and arrogant master and a poor, powerless, and resentful slave who live in the same household? Here conflicting intentions seem to negate each other, but relationship nevertheless exists because their intentions are directed to each other (as is given in the qualifications "arrogant" and "resentful") and to the same goods (the wealth and power that the master has but the slave has not). They are in a relationship without being intentional teammates. It is right to say that this is an unhappy relationship, but not that it is not a relationship.

The master-slave example shows that the community of intention that is essential to relationship exists at a deeper level than the coincidence of intention in details that love and friendship thrive on. The master and slave do not love the same state of affairs; neither, however, do lovers simply love the same things—they love their loving of the same things. In other words, they have an intention with respect to intention. So do the master and slave. They are in relationship by virtue of the fact that the intentions of each with respect to objects like wealth and power are an issue for each. It matters to the arrogant master how the slave feels about the situation, and vice versa. The single issue correlates their intentions.

Not any specific intention, therefore, but the very question of how to intend with respect to each other is what is had in common by parties in a relationship. It is odd to say that the question is had; we should say instead that the question has the parties, for it is the claim of the question on their attention that draws them into relationship and keeps them there. How does this question impose itself? Why do masters care about the feelings of slaves? Because in their slaves they see an opportunity to win recognition of their own subjective being as essential and objective?[2] Let us suppose so. But why would they be dissatisfied in the first place with the credentials they grant themselves? Whence came the original negative movement that turned into the danger that the self would annihilate itself in its own negativity? It must have come from the check of otherness—the insistent presence of what is neither the self nor matter for the self's projects. What, in that case, distinguishes "others" from the sheer matter of experience and practice?

We have said that the other, other than the "different," is the beyond. But we have had to speak also of the "presence" of others, which implies that they are objects of experience, and of "otherness," which implies a universal instanced in experience or a transcendental category constitutive of experience. If there were presence of others in no sense, it would be impossible to speak of them at all; if there were in no sense a category of otherness, it would be impossible to speak of them philosophically. Therefore we must admit the presence and the category, but they must be carefully qualified.

The others are (in the eminent case) those beings who approach me and whom I approach as You. I exchanged a glance with a hitchhiker as I sped past him on the highway; for a moment he figured as someone who would say something *to* me or who would call on me to say something *to* him. I did not see "otherness" in him. I saw *him*. He *was* other, there and then, as the particular You that he was. He was not in the first place this-*as*-other, though he appears as such when a discourse perforce uses the general predicate "other" as a pointer to real meetings, but *this-other*. He was, precisely as that hitchhiker, uncannier and less foreseen than Death, Nothingness, or the Dark Side of the Moon. He was present as absent, as the not-to-be-known, but as the not-to-be-known on that bend of the highway at that hour. (Of course, I could set about learning his name, where he is from, and what is on his mind, but that would not reduce the not-to-be-known.) The universe at that moment consisted of no *less* (whatever more it might have been) than he and I, for he was with me; specifically because of him I was not alone. Since my existence was qualified as an existence-with-him, and since this qualification was, by virtue of its insistence and superordinate importance, different from that imposed on me by other beings in my field of attention, the question arose: how should I exist with him? His appearance was of superordinate importance because the very otherness of "others" with respect to beings figuring as mere objects of experience can only register in the separating out of "orders" in this sense. If otherness were a matter of a new predicable quality, it would only be an extra object of experience, so it must register otherwise. The issue of super- and subordination did not exist at all, not with this seriousness, before the appearance of this other. But now it exists, and in its own strangely quiet way it insists that I attend to it—that is, to him—no less than a toothache would. I have a spirit-ache.

This other whom I become aware of as other is not just an alter ego. I do not meet the other as other by noticing the resemblance between the outward appearance of this being and what I see of myself in the mirror, then taking it that consciousness like mine must exist there too—although the *theoretical* constitution of the alter ego may, in one of its moments, proceed this way. Neither, however, is this other a blank gap in the universe that is simply missed by my intentions or that annihilates my own perspective on the world. This other and the other ones of whom I am similarly aware meet me as intenders in their own right. Their intentions are not repetitions or extensions or even dialectical correlates of mine; those are all variations of the alter ego, an interpretation that

I would like for several reasons to impose on them but that is not how they come to me. What disconnects their intentions from mine is their unforeseeableness. The others come closer to me, or withdraw from me, or step aside to wait or allow something more to happen, according to themselves. They keep their own counsel. They are outside of my jurisdiction, which causes me (on account of the given issue of our togetherness) to be in theirs. The contingency of their intention with respect to mine is significant. That is how I know I am not alone. I have to wait and see whether what I do will bring them nearer or drive them away. To the extent that I keep from driving them away I manage to be together with them.

Although the appearances suggest that *I* drove away from the hitchhiker, the truth is that I drove *him* away. If I thought I was removing myself, enforcing my own discretion, that was an illusion. The meaning of the departure becomes, not *I left*, but *He is gone*. One meets with this elementary but crucial perception throughout the literature of the going wrong of relationships.

Somehow I am aware of the life of the other with respect to me, which I have schematically represented as nearness or farness of relative position and movement. But how is it possible to meet another intentionality? What is that like? Could one experience "other" intention except as a phantasmatic echo of one's own—or, in the extreme alternative, as the annihilation of one's own? In reply, I can ask you to consider what it is like to have your hand shaken. No phenomenological description of the event can prove that an other intention is present in it, or that the perception of an other intention in it permits a continuing sense of your own. There are different ways to come to a handshake, including the reductionistic and the paranoid. Yet it is not from a romantic yearning for what handshakes might be but, quite to the contrary, from the most ordinary experience of engaging in them that I say: the hand in mine carries an intention *other* than mine that *meets* mine. Do you not also rise to handshake-like occasions on the expectation of being met by another intention, and is this expectation not fulfilled over and over again? One is aware how catching his eye is other than watching him, how dancing with her is other than dancing alone, how playing poker is other than playing solitaire. One is aware from how the meetings go, according to the orientedness of one's own spirit-intention rather than by neutral beholding.

When my intention is met by another intention, there takes place "interaction" in its proper (frequently borrowed and reduced) sense. The analogy of a game recommends itself. Within the game's framework of predictability, a sequence of interactions occurs: (*a*) In your first move, you appear, *because* I am here. (I connect only your appearance-to-me, not your existence or your general significance, with my being who and where I am.) (*b*) I act in a certain way because you are there (to beat, outwit, stand off, etc.). (*c*) You do something uncontrolled by me, for reasons of your own; yet among your reasons is what I did. (*d*) Your action becomes in turn a reason for my next action. And so on. One reason that actual games are enormously interesting is that they bring interaction closer to this pure form than it otherwise is. In an everyday interaction most of the moves are never openly made but are filled in, anxiously or presumptuously, to good effect or bad, in the minds of the players.

The others come before me in perception. I also remember them, and how I dealt with them; imagine them, and how I might deal with them; and in an abstract, nominal fashion, conceive of unimagined others, as for instance the possible inhabitants of the planet Krullon. The remembering, imagining, and conceiving taken all together occupy much more of my attention than the perceiving. Do I remain in relationship with others in these mental positionings, or is their otherness annulled in the very construction of mental signifiers of otherness? Do I as a mental being exist ipso facto in *Icheinsamkeit*? Let us consider one example that makes this seem the case and another with the contrary implication.

Romeo sees Juliet for the first time, briefly, at a ball. From that moment he is aflame with love. Before he ever sees Juliet again, he heaps the perfections of womanhood on her in his imagination and forms the intention of marrying her on an absurdly slight basis. He seems a perfect illustration of Stendhal's "crystallization" theory of love, according to which a host of intentions, already in a high state of readiness in the lover, burst forth and attach themselves to the love object when it happens along, much as a substance in solution would precipitate out upon any stick one put into it.[3] With a case like this in mind we might well ask, Is not all love actually a reciprocal projection of feelings rather than a veritable "interaction"? And if all love is so, might not all relationships be so? Is this not the most plausible way to construe apparent "interaction" in view of the indubitable fact that the acquaintance of persons with each other is mediated by processes of thought and feeling that are in turn determined by neurological states, personal history, and cultural traditions?

But now think of Helen and Agatha who have worked in the same office side by side for more than twenty years, until the day Agatha unexpectedly dies, leaving her savings to Helen instead of her irresponsible younger brother. Presently the brother begins asking Helen for money for various reasons. She wants to act as Agatha would wish. In deliberating on how to deal with him, Helen represents Agatha to herself by remembering what she has done and imagining what she would do. She feels bound to Agatha as her deputy. In a case like this it seems clear that Agatha is *with* Helen even though not present for perception. Helen endeavors to respect the signs of Agatha that exist in her own consciousness, signs that are indubitably traces left by Agatha rather than artifacts of her own feeling. Of course, we cannot be sure that these traces have not been covered over or redrawn or projected by Helen, but *she* is not at liberty to dismiss any of them on that hypothesis—their meaning is that they come from Agatha—and we should show respect for the meaning of her responsibility, which has counterparts in our own lives, by not insisting dogmatically on a responsibility-annihilating explanation of all contents of Helen's mind.

The proper generalization to draw from the two examples is that while it is always possible to raise the question whether a supposed addressing of the self by an other is actually a maneuver of the self, and probable that any supposed addressing is to some extent such a maneuver, it is nevertheless always right to grant room at the same time for actual togetherness existing in the addressing, even Juliet's brief addressing of the susceptible Romeo. He did see her that once. Suppose he never saw a real person, but only dreamed or hallucinated a beauteous Juliet to whom, he claimed, he was bound to be faithful. Should he hold himself bound to this appearance of an other—is this his concreteness? Are we entitled to wield the reality/appearance distinction in such a way as to cheapen a manifestation that seems to Romeo genuinely to address him? Such a problem is not and should not be easily resolved. Many people commit their lives to an Other that is conscientiously determined to be unreal by many other people.[4] The latter party looks on the former in the manner that one who wakes looks on one who dreams. But the force of this problem does not disturb the present argument, it only confirms it; for other-claims, like diamonds, can be cut only by each other, and the wakers can awaken the dreamers only with the cold water of otherness— that is, with an interpretation of the world that is more accommodating of possible encounters with others.

My relationship with the possible inhabitants of Krullon poses a distinct problem. They have made no impression on me that I might be faithful to. Yet I already know that I should listen to them if they speak, refrain from destroying or exploiting them if I have any influence on them, and so forth. Do I fundamentally know this because I know that *I* am one who behaves thus in meeting others, or because *they* are conceivably others who claim respect? The two answers are equivalent: they are conceivably other thanks to my conception, but I conceive in that fashion because I am a spiritual, other-claimed being. The Krullonians have the conceptual force of "others" only on loan from the real others I have met, whom they prospectively resemble as intentional beings. They do not leave a trace of their own in my consciousness but creep into the trace left by real others. The same must be true of everyone I have not actually met.

An intermediate case is presented by the people who live in the apartment below mine and who are, one presumes, bothered if I throw books on the floor or run heavily from room to room. I have never met them, but I know with certainty that they are there and with near certainty that loud noises, especially in the middle of the night, are offensive to them. As I tiptoe to the kitchen at 3 A.M., they are with me. It would not be an excuse for waking them up that since I had not met them they could not be regarded as determinate others. They left a trace in my awareness through the signs that produced my knowledge: the names on the mailbox, the rattling of the pipes. I had, in a way (obviously deficient in comparison with some other ways), met them. My knowledge introduced me into a kind of relationship. Such knowledge makes a great difference in practice; there are some people, or some knowable things about people's intentions, that we want to shelter from, because of what it means we would have to do. I do not want to know about the fear of the tyrannized, the pain of the tortured, the hunger of the famine-stricken. On the other hand, I am driven to find out everything of this sort that can be known. I may divert this impulse by musing on harmlessly abstract Krullonians, but it will not go away. It is part of the spirit-ache.

Those whom I affect or am affected by unwittingly may be in relation with me, but that must not be confused with relationship. I and the others must be reasons for each other. If this condition is not met, we cannot speak of interaction or a common enterprise.

Something is given, something pricks me, when the other appears. Thus I am already roused, but at the same time I must rouse myself further to answer. The relationship exists no matter what I do, but since I must perform it rather than rely on its fixed subsistence, since I already find myself performing it, the problem of the *rectification* of the relationship is an inescapable one for me. For I can conduct myself in the relationship in different ways not equally acceptable. Of course, a gradient of rightness is imposed on any agent with a practical task, inasmuch as different means always serve the end unequally, and relationship is a practical task; but it is also a unique sort of task in that its end is approachable without being reachable. The other may draw nearer to me, but even an infinitely near (beloved) other remains, as other, infinitely distant, an irreducibly contingent intentional challenge and answer to my own intentions. Relationship with the other can always be further rectified, and should be. When you are carrying a load that is too heavy, you are forced to think constantly about getting a better grip.

The category in which relationship is evaluated is "rightness," rather than "goodness" or "value," because the point of such evaluation is to determine how practice and position stand with respect to an absolute but exterior standard that cannot itself come into question or be examined. If we could examine the others themselves, if they (*as others*) were contents of experience whose predicates could be tested and compared, we could pronounce on their "goodness" or "value" for us, which would serve as a metajustification for judging the rightness of things according to how they stand with respect to the others. Abstractly we must say that the others as other are absolutely good, just because their existence is determinative of rightness. But we do not really know what it means to say that. We can only gesture unknowingly but nevertheless affirmatively, unjealously, toward them.

We can no more know the shape of a perfectly acceptable relationship than we can know the nature of the other. Without knowing the end toward which we are drawn, however, we still usually have some more or less trustworthy sense of *direction*. (A traveler from whom the sun is hidden by clouds can still tell the difference between east and west.) Now close attention to the marching we are called upon to do reveals that the end is not a simple one, but has two sides, corresponding to what ethicists call the *supremum bonum* or unconditional good and the *summum bonum* or complete good. We can take these terms over if by a "good" we understand an actualized rightness. The unconditional good is attained by satisfying the minimum standard of moral practice, "justice." In the complete good, happiness is added to justice. This is maximal rightness. Both justice and happiness are unattainable ends; it is not as though one could get the platform of minimal rightness under one's feet and then think about realizing happiness additionally. The demand for minimal rightness does always place itself in front of the demand for happiness, however, and in that way functions as a condition on the pursuit of happiness. Whenever one must choose between justice and happiness, one should choose justice. But it is also true—and in the history of ethical thought this has proved very difficult to understand—that one *should* choose happiness when one may.

Before the other, one must conceive justice as giving due. The very existence of an other is inseparable from the coming-into-effect of something due. What is primarily due others is affirmation of their existence as others, which means both giving them attention and respecting their going their own way. Justice toward an *intentional* other means *listening* and making of the other's intention a reason of one's own. It can readily be seen how impossible of full attainment justice is as soon as there are more than two people in the world; nay, even two lovers cannot give each other their due attention, because they must sleep from time to time and will not always keep their promise to dream of each other. There are all sorts of reasonable limitations that will have to be put on the many infinite demands for attention, ordering them so as to enable the greatest possible affirmation of all. An important modification introduced by ethical theory will be the assertion of my own due insofar as I am exemplary and justice toward me is connected to justice toward others. My "right" is only what I feel obliged to respect in myself, and the only incontrovertible reason for respecting anything in myself is that the respect is owing to others who are endangered in principle if an exception is made for me.

More is involved in justice to an intentional being than listening, for the difference between true and false listening is the response that follows it, which should have been determined by what was heard. The others appear to me in their particular forms and situations. Can one affirm hungry others, whom one has heard as hungry, without giving them food? What else is one hearing from them that takes precedence over their need? To answer them in the easiest way, as though they were well-fed fellow citizens, is not to answer them at all. It is a spiritual misfire that is probably also morally wrong.

The infinite implications of the requirement to listen and make answer to the others are traced and ordered in the various sciences. Ethics has a certain priority among them because it shares some of its central concepts with the philosophy of the spiritual, which (as we now see) expresses the exigencies of relationship in terms of "justice" and "rightness." But these implications are not confined to ethics. They reach into the substance of all the human sciences, and at least as regards methodology into the natural sciences as well. The philosophy of the spiritual, although it orients ethics and all the sciences, must not follow its own implications into their territories lest its waters spread too wide and dry up. The "justice" of which we speak here is not formulated with an eye toward the drawing of moral or political precepts from it. It is an ethicist's work to formulate a conception of justice that will accord with spiritual justice and at the same time ground a comprehensive and consistent order of ethical judgments—as it is the aesthetician's work rightly and fruitfully to conceive appreciation, the logician's work so to conceive reason, and the metaphysician's work so to conceive actuality or concreteness.

To return to the standards of rightness in relationship, "justice" in its spiritual signification is a matter of maintaining the others as other, of providing the others with tenable positions so that they may *stay,* are not denied or driven out. Spiritual life is unthinkable unless a pluralism of intention is safeguarded in principle. Because of the inherent fragility of the other-recognition that is to be preserved, no amount of safeguarding is enough. But beyond the infinite care of protection there is even more that must be done, and that is that this inconceivable "good" of the others, as and not otherwise than as a good in relationships, be properly appreciated by helping them, however one can, to flourish—which means that the others flourish in and from their relationships with me.[5] For the respect in which relationship is purely actual with the bare appearance of the other is complemented by the respect in which relationship portends a potential *amplitude* of the other's intentional existence, which, in being fostered, becomes intention-in-common at the same time that it belongs to the other.

Plato's *Timaeus* story of the creation of beings can be extended to express the absolute demand to maximize their existence. Would the supremely generous agency that so maximized ontic opportunity as to create the others in the first place be satisfied with anything less than their full flourishing? God's generous benevolence, representing the principle of maximizing the existence of the other as other, is the unquestionable standard judged by which a relationship is more or less right according to the "happiness" or flourishing of the other it promotes. It is *good* that the others exist (good of God to create the others), and *better* the more fully they exist; it is *right* to serve these ends. My own happiness is connected to that of the others insofar as I promote it, for their amplified intentions become the intentions-in-common that define the spirit that moves me and in which I rejoice. My happiness is also to be promoted for the same reason that my intentions were to be respected, that is, on account of my exemplary significance.

That X promotes the existence of others as other, and that X promotes the maximization of others' existence, are the two primordial *good reasons* for X (see section 4.3 below).

We have now ventured onto ground much traveled but confusingly mapped, where the distinct but connected claims of respect and love are exerted. For another indication of their relation we may use the expressions "responsibility to" and "responsibility for." I am responsible *to* others *purely* as other. To otherness as such I owe attention, and this, on which the possibility of relationship hangs, is always the first of the two demands for rectification of relationships. That the other commands me implies that my receptiveness to the other precedes my concern for the quality of our common existence. I cannot add or subtract a whit of otherness; the other's constitution in this respect is beyond my power to influence, and it would be an intolerable presumption on my part if I set out to influence it—if, for example, feeling that my relationship with you was languishing on account of your dull predictability, I dosed your coffee with amphetamines to liven you up. On the other hand, your well-being is in both my power and my care. I promote your well-being by way of acting on my responsibility *for* you.

Evidently any responsibility for must also be a responsibility to, and vice versa. The fundamental responsibility *to* the others is *for* their being-present or being-heard; that is, it is the duty of attention. And one must be responsible *to* whomever one is responsible for, although this dimension may be complicated by an additional accountability, as a child's tutor is accountable to the parents as well as to the child, or even a clearly superior accountability, as when religious persons answer unconditionally to a divine Creator for the well-being of all creatures. We cannot now pretend to fix the controversial order of accountabilities, which can be decided only in actual encounters with the Other or others whose claims are in dispute. However, my responsibility *for* the others, even though it must also be *to* someone, is given to me whether or not I am clear on who that responsibility is finally *to*. I will necessarily want to know whose deputy I am, of course, but I do not need an answer to that question to be sure that the well-being of others is in my charge.

Relationship is an infinite double exigency of rectification. None of the others ever get sufficient attention or become as happy as they ought to be. Living under this weight understandably makes me anxious. Time and again I cheat by unilaterally positing a togetherness between the others and me that satisfies (so I say) the demand. "I did everything for him I could." "Have you ever seen her happier?" "You'd like that, wouldn't you?" One can suspect whoever says such things of trying to solve the insoluble problem of rectification and in that way get out from under it. Yet cases of cheating shade into cases of spiritual leadership —as when, in the simplest instance, you really would like what I suggest you would. The difference between cheating and leading depends on whether or not the speaker is open to the free response and influence of the other. The only proof of good faith is the persistence of genuine interaction.

3.3 Primary Objectivity

Are there "others" other than human others? Can one speak of "relationship" with nonhuman others?

Buber's *I and Thou* testifies to "relationship" (*Beziehung*) between human and nonhuman beings no less than to the interhuman. A tree and a cat command his attention exclusively, in the manner of any You; so do *geistige Wesenheiten* or cultural objects, respecting which he cites his encounter with a Doric column.[6] Buber's extremely inclusive conception of "You" is generally either ignored or rejected as a remnant of mysticism. To those who have never encountered a tree in the way Buber has, or who do not realize they have, his account of the relationship will naturally seem implausible or, at best, "lyrically" emphatic. Perhaps the greatest reason for being skeptical of relationship with the nonhuman is that the opportunities for cheating are so noticeable. What can a tree say in contradiction if a Buber rapturously perceives it proclaiming itself to him? Can true relationship be so much at the mercy of one of the partners as Buber's tree-relationship is?

But the Buberian conception of such relationships is carefully distinguished from relationships with the cultural and with other human beings by the criterion of language. Language is the threshold of interhuman relationships; short of it, beings like cats "stammer," and beings like trees are mute; cultural objects call it forth. We shall ask presently what difference language makes in the network of issues that we have brought forward, but first we must not neglect to face *the inherently infinite claim of anything and everything other,* including nonspeaking and subintentional beings. Here the norm is set by the encounters in which non-speaking beings receive their due from us, as an odd pebble gets its due from a fascinated geologist, or a ship's power plant is honored by the total concern of its engineer, or a landscape is done justice by a painter. The basic exaltation common to science, technics, and art, by which the energy of subjects is concentrated on the nature and possibilities of objects, lacks an accepted name in English but is best called "objectivity" (the usual translation for a word that comes closer and has been appropriated for the same use, the German *Sachlichkeit*).[7] By "objectivity" we mean a concern for nonspeaking others as other that tends to detach the subject from everything "subjective" that would occlude the others' manifestation. Naturally my passion for the other being is always open to the criticism that I attend to it as a way of ignoring something else or in order to express an impulse of my own, but the seriousness of the criticism derives in turn from objectivity.

We may distinguish *primary objectivity,* direct concern for others, from secondary, Kantian objectivity, by which one is detached from private experience and passion in order to be attached to a system of public intelligibility, conforming to rules of relationship with speaking others. The irony of the distinction is that primary objectivity appears here not otherwise than as a public object, while we call part of the operative concreteness of this discourse "secondary." However, public discourse does not concretely *mean* to be a coherentist conspiracy; it means to communicate, under limitations necessary for publicity, the nature and possibilities of other beings. Otherwise we would have publicity without intelligibility.

Much that has already been said about relationship applies to togetherness with anything. A tree no less than a person confronts me as a being whose existence is grounded in itself, in the sense that a tree taken to be a construction of my own consciousness would no longer carry the weightier and orienting meaning of naive perception's respectful "the tree." Certainly the tree depends on my interpretation of it to mean what it means, but my interpretation is of a distinct interpretandum that is *served* by it. (The interpretation need not be druidical, but neither can it be wholly utilitarian.) The tree therefore has an otherness to protect, whence spring simultaneously the demands for a refutation of idealism and for a critique of naive realism. Further, we encounter the tree's being as variable in such a way that the issue of its *well*-being is not only intelligible but, so long as we attend to it, pressing. Here too the tree is limited in comparison with an intentional being; it does not have the intentional relationship to its own well-being that is properly called an "interest." Again, it depends on my interest in it for the issue of its well-being to arise, but it does call forth my interest. No doubt I am susceptible to it because of the kind of being I am, also vital, with limbs to lose, and flesh that can be pink or gray. But for all the help that analogizing might provide in educating me about trees or criticizing my attitudes toward them, analogy is not what fundamentally accredits the tree as an *eidos* and interest. The tree accredits *itself* to the objective observer—not of course as a givenness fulfilling our tree-intentions, but as an incitement to the intentions that would company with the tree and a felicitation of them for the duration of the encounter.

The difference between a tree and a rock is that by virtue of the tree's vital purposiveness it offers definite and binding clues to the interpretation of the normative form of its existence that the rock does not. For the same reason, that it is a teleonomic system, the tree could be held to have greater "value" (on the premise that value corresponds to degree of organic unity), but this is only a coincidence, even if not an accidental one: we are not interested in "valuing" the tree, only in noticing what constitutes its well-being.[8] Tree and rock are both "other," but a rock keeps inaccessible counsel, and interpretations I impose on it are condemned to arbitrariness. I can only be struck by the undreamed-of form in which it confronts me; I cannot judge that one form is more perfect than another. Imagine that I come upon a huge, perfectly spherical rock balanced on the tip of a stalagmite in a cave, then accidentally bump it so that it falls and breaks into little bits. What a shame!—but what kind of shame? The rock-sphere might have been a formidable tourist attraction, but I cannot say that the rock is worse off, since for all I can tell the mineral material is just as happy existing in its broken-up form.

The ontological difference between "realms" designated "material" and "organic" or "vital" seems, therefore, to be rooted in the different possibilities of encounter, the "higher" realm being the locus of encounters in which intention is more fully and determinately engaged. The individuals we meet in the "psychic" realm show us and ask us still more.

What distinguishes a cat from trees and rocks is not in the *first* place that the cat exhibits "consciousness" by solving practical problems, being happy or unhappy in anticipation of an event, seeming to dream, and so forth, but rather that we have *dealings* with it. The cat is, in one sense, a self-interpreting intentional being. Unlike the tree, it advances its own case—we cannot yet say "argues" —and, up to a point, criticizes the interpretations we impose on it through our actions. The tree can only criticize our tree-interpretation by shriveling up, that is, passively withdrawing from the relationship as we have shaped it. The cat can actively withdraw, can say No. It can also try to catch my eye. Just as I face it, it faces me. In this reciprocal "facing" lies the precondition, and the inevitability, of having "dealings" with such a being. Normally the eye is the natural element that constitutes "face"; one cannot see that which sees, that which would only be pointed at one because it sees one, without knowing there is an intentionality over against one. (Analogues of touch exist but are more ambiguous and less universal.) A being that *looks* at me exists *toward* me, and its towardness solicits and negotiates with my own. It is You.

Clearly a cat and I can have a relationship. I have only to play with one for a while to prove to myself that intentions and corresponding manners of behavior are sharable with it. Nevertheless, in the absence of language our intentions cannot become themes; we cannot get enough distance from them to have intentions toward our intentions, and thus cannot really promise anything to each other. Our shared intention in itself can never become the reason for which something is done. We can live in a shared intention, but not in the sharing of intention. If I look into the cat's eyes at the moment just after settling down in front of the fire when we are both feeling warm and relaxed, I deceive myself if I seriously believe what I like to imagine, that the cat has and enjoys an awareness that we are both feeling good. The cat simply feels good. I have to feel good for both of us.

Language is undoubtedly a threshold, but is it the threshold of the spiritual? Does our definition of the spiritual commit us to denying that a cat's relationship with another cat is spiritual? Or is the difference between people and cats merely that people, unlike cats, can know that their relationships are spiritual? We defined a spiritual being as one existing in intentional community with others, where the otherness with respect to each other of these beings is an unreduced intrusion into the experience of each. Though the examples we used at that stage made much of subjects' knowledge of their participation in spirit and what it might mean to them, we did not explicitly require the knowledge, only the intentional participation. We left the door open for cats, and properly. The distinction between rational and nonrational beings has its importance, but it should not be overzealously applied, as it often is in attempts to define the personal. There seems to be one sense in which at least the higher animals are undoubtedly personal—they are intentional beings who interact with each other and with us—and another sense in which their personhood is, as far as we can tell, truncated in comparison with ours.

We must take note, in consequence, of the point that spirit-as-relationship is not a "higher" qualification of existence with respect to spirit-as-mind *in the sense that* rationality is a subordinate, necessary-but-not-sufficient condition of spirituality—as consciousness is a subordinate, necessary-but-not-sufficient condition of rationality, life such a condition of consciousness, and materiality such a condition of life. For spirit-as-relationship cuts across the distinction between rational and nonrational consciousness. That distinction makes an enormous difference as to the nature of the dealings that are possible or obligatory between beings, but not to the presence of dealings or to the existence of intentional community resulting from dealings. Spirit-as-mind is qualified by spirit-as-relationship because of something we share with the animals, not because of something we share only with the gods.

Primary objectivity is not relationship, but it is a spiritual principle in the sense that only spiritual beings would approach the world open to its "claims." The Others of relationship are the precedent for others in the nonintentional world. The priority of relationship asserts itself in the manifest superiority of my responsibility to intentional others over my responsibility to nonintentional others. When a cat comes into the room, everything there folds into the space between me and it and becomes matter for our dealings. The ball of yarn on the floor is not emptied of intrinsic meaning, but supervening upon its own meaning is its readiness to be our instrument of play. The cactus plant becomes something that might hurt the cat. The lamp becomes something that the cat had better not knock over. Nonintentional beings suffer this imposition of meaning without resistance or violation because the imposition occurs at a height that they do not reach, where they have nothing to contest. At this height, actions are taken that might disserve them—the cactus plant might have to be destroyed for the cat's sake— not out of disrespect for them, but out of necessarily superior respect for a more unignorably present other.

What shall we say the cat becomes when another human being walks into the room? Neither a fellow dealer with us nor mere matter for our dealing. In truth, such beings as cats are in an ambiguous position. It is not rude to talk about them in their presence, nor is it unjust to make decisions affecting their welfare without consulting them—for one *could not* consult them, one *could not* hurt their feelings by anything said. Yet it seems that one *should* approach these higher dealings with them as far as one can for the sake of those actual dealings that tell us they are about to put a foot over a threshold.[9]

Primary objectivity belongs to the concrete, for it is not a derivation or construction or alteration of some more original concreteness. Yet the fact that tree-claims as it were step in front of the claims of inorganic objects, while cat-claims and then speaker-claims take precedence in turn, means that there is a gradient of far-to-near within the concrete situation. Even when I am alone with a rock, absorbed by its shape and textures, that "I" is still one for whom rocks are occasions of discourse and means for practice in relationship with speaking others. It is not sentimental to acknowledge the original claims made by things, but it is originally impermissible to remove these claims from the horizon of higher claims in which they appear. There is a farness of the rock from me in the standing possibility that living and speaking others will step in front of it, which they in fact typically do. (My "mind" just is in part the standing of this possibility for me.)

The antinomy in which thinking about these matters is usually caught opposes the thesis of admitting the absolute importance of all existence while annihilating distinctions of importance between kinds of existence to the antithesis of insisting on the superior claim of speaking beings while making the importance of everything else merely relative to their interest. Albert Schweitzer's philosophy of "reverence for life" is a good example of the thesis. On the basis of his own affirmation of the concrete—"I am life which wills to live, in the midst of life which wills to live" [10]—Schweitzer argues thus:

> The great fault of all ethics hitherto has been that they believed themselves to have to deal only with the relations of man to man. In reality, however, the question is what is his attitude to the world and all life that comes within his reach. A man is ethical only when life, as such, is sacred to him, that of plants and animals as that of his fellow-men, and when he devotes himself helpfully to all life that is in need of help. Only the universal ethic of the feeling of responsibility in an ever-widening sphere for all that lives—only that ethic can be founded in thought. The ethic of the relation of man to man is not something apart by itself: it is only a particular relation which results from the universal one. [11]

One can criticize the metaphysical construction of a universal "will-to-life," and one can ask why the magic circle of importance extends only to the vital; still, Schweitzer's is one of the greatest of all proposals to broaden the circle decisively. So struck was he by the stepping-forward of all living things that he did not respond to the claim of the nonvital, just as the vast majority of his contemporaries failed adequately to respond to the claim of nonhuman life. However, his proposal runs afoul of our original sense of the greater nearness of human claims. The assertion that interhuman relation is only a particular case of a universal bond among living things is not directly warranted, as he suggests it is, by the concrete situation—which is not to say that the assertion may not be justified in a particular ethical or metaphysical context. At any rate, our objection to Schweitzer ought not to veer to the antithesis: only human life is absolutely important. It is possible to register the stepping-forward of a nearer other without obliterating the others that remain behind.

3.4 Four Objections to Primary Objectivity Answered

We will attain important clarifications of the principle of primary objectivity if we attend to the most serious objections to it: (1) that the principle is absurd because it demands respect for an infinity of others arrayed in an unimaginable infinity of ways; (2) that the principle absurdly forbids the destruction or rejection of anything whatsoever; (3) that the principle undermines the important distinction between real beings and mere ideas; and (4) that it unacceptably deprives selfhood of meaning.

(1) *The problem of infinite others.* There is no special difficulty in the way we envision the occasions of relationship. Naturally there will be borderline cases. A friend of mine talks to plants, finds that they flourish in "response" to being talked to, and interprets this as proof that relationship with them exists. This seems to me an unwarranted interpretation of the exchange between person and plant, but I cannot be entirely sure, and it is more reasonable when in doubt to expand rather than contract the interintentional sphere. The hardest case is the one in which certain people can *learn* to interact with (say) plants while other people, in spite of efforts in good faith, cannot, and must regard the first group as ones who act merely *as though* they are in relationship with plants. What is certain, however, is that a plant that did show itself intentionally expressive and responsive would have to be dealt with as a You. It would join a class of Yous that is marked off in principle from the nonintentional world.

The broader claim of primary objectivity is more perplexing by far because it is unlimited. The world of beings who stand to figure as "others" is not marked off from any other world, nor have we given it any a priori internal organization beyond the intentional-nonintentional distinction. In short, anything conceivable could be an "other," and it seems that this has bewildering consequences. These can be exhibited in a reductio ad absurdum objection to the conception of "others" employed here.

I see a rock. (Note incidentally the problem of how or why my attention is arrested by this individual rock rather than by any of its numerous neighbor rocks; or why I notice the precise spatial zone occupied only by what we call "the rock" rather than a nearby zone that is nine-tenths the rock and one-tenth air.) By the principles we have adopted, the rock stands over against me as an "other" claiming respect and appreciation. But "the rock" is not the only thing present in the presence of the rock. Many things are or may be immediately present in it: an aggregation of mineral bits, of molecules, of atoms, of subatomic particles; an ensemble of geometrical and physical qualities; a stimulus to vision, prospectively to other senses, and to thought; something to be thrown into a lake, kept from falling on a car, etc. Even if determined contemplation of "the rock" could abstract the whole of the rock from its parts and the independent being of the rock from its relations, why should "the rock" have any privilege over all the other beings that are equally present with it? For the mineral bits and molecules and so forth are all equally "beings." But since the spiritual *principle* of attention is simply that one must attend to the other that manifests *itself,* a spiritual being is always caught by the incoherently complex claim of the *many* "others" that manifest themselves on any occasion, which is absurd. The only point of a principle of attention is to choose what to attend to, but the principle of primary objectivity cannot choose among simultaneous claimants.

What can one say, moreover, except that it is, spiritually regarded, a physico-biologico-psychological accident that the rock or its parts or its relations figure as "the other" to me for a certain amount of time? I notice what I notice because of the way I am constituted, which has been determined by the exigencies of success in genetic reproduction. Therefore the beings that I happen to notice have no priority in principle to any other beings, except that bestowed on them by me after the fact that I noticed them. But as the reductio shows, even the priority that I want to bestow after the fact is incoherent. Because of this objection, two pillars of our argument collapse, the honorific sense that we wanted "otherness" to have and the anchoring significance that we wanted "concreteness" to have.

To answer the objection we only need to turn what it construes as a minus into a plus. "The rock" is indeed not one being but an inexhaustible complex of beings any of which may be simultaneously present for attention. The task of attention is, however, essentially inclusive rather than, as the objection assumes, exclusive. It is not necessary to the functioning of a principle of attention that it exclude every possible object but one.[12] We would much more reasonably expect it to direct us to every possible object that can, without disrespect, receive attention. The richness of "the rock," the fact that any being is the occasion of our encounter with a complex of beings, does not necessarily impose an incoherency upon attention, for actually the beings of the complex exist together coherently, and thanks to their own coherence, as *this* is present to us, attention to any ensemble of them is possible.

Primary objectivity is thus a maximal principle of attention paralleling Leibnizian monadology as a maximal principle of being. The monadology is an insane and upsetting interpretation of reality for those who wish to narrow down the range of occasions of encounter, but exhilarating for those who are rightly insatiable for encounter. Why should there *not* be worlds within worlds forever, as Leibniz proclaimed?[13] The universe, whether in itself or for attention, can just as well be infinite as finite as long as its members assort with one another. We might worry whether we can legitimately assume the independent reality of the coherencies among beings that seem to present themselves, but as long as our attention is expansionist we can have provisional confidence that apparent coherence is not the work of a reductive idealization—that, for example, the integrity of "the rock" as a whole is not a repression of the beings that we take to be making it up.

As for the other side of the objection, it cannot be denied that physically, psychologically, and biologically comprehensible dispositions of ours determine the sorts of beings that we notice. But it is not an insult to the sense of "otherness" that a rock that the evolution of my species has disposed me to see as such is baptized "other" by the principle of primary objectivity. Instead, I rejoice that I am in a position to see something and that the something is this rock.

(2) *The problem of rejection.* It may be objected that the principle of primary objectivity rules out the deliberate rejection or destruction of any being, which puts us in an absurd position with respect to beings whose rejection or destruction no one would want to forbid. For example, a gardener plants certain seeds and rejects others, cultivates certain growing things and destroys others; or an artist shows one drawing and destroys another. Plainly, imperfect plant specimens and mediocre drawings do not have prima facie entitlement to exist and flourish. It is in no sense a shame to dismiss them. But primary objectivity again proves itself an incoherent principle of selection by making it impossible to separate wheat from chaff.

In many situations we refrain from attending to and promoting certain beings for the same reason that certain persons are killed or placed in deadly danger in wartime or thrown out of an overloaded lifeboat: not because there is any defect in their primordial entitlement to attention, but because in those situations someone will necessarily be lost, and therefore secondary considerations (like innocence versus guilt or ability to perform certain needed actions) may be allowed to determine who will be lost. By the same token, the gardener can plant only so many seeds and the artist can finish only so many pictures, which entails a lot of not-planting and not-finishing. But the analogy of persons is misleading in that the necessary loss of all beings of that sort is evidently a shame; one cannot think about it without at the same time preferring that a different situation obtain in which the loss is not necessary. With an inferior seed or mediocre drawing, on the contrary, there is not only no shame involved in failing to realize it, it seems that it would actually be a shame to realize it. But how can that be, on our principles?

For the inferior seed, we could answer that if it were given its chance, it would grow into a being whose own flourishing *would* turn it into something that better plants grow nearer to. The judgment of "inferiority" would be based on the perception that the plant itself wants to be something that it will never be. Another plant, however, could come closer to perfection, and therefore the cultivation of the better seed is the true promotion of the inferior seed. It would be as though these plants' lines of prospective being all came together at the apex of the actual best plant, which would count as the flourishing of all of them.

But this answer is untenable. No judgment that one plant fulfills the promise of another can be made apart from an idealization subordinating the plants to gardening aesthetics, except perhaps in extreme cases where plants suffer life-threatening defects. All the force of the foregoing arguments renders the notion of converging lines of being utterly noxious. As we cannot accept the project of breeding a master race of human beings (with the necessary concomitant "weeding"), how can we accept so much as the breeding and weeding of gardening? For elementary respect of beings seems to demand precisely the holding apart forever of lines of being.

Although it is saner to bring our scruples from the human sphere to plants than callously to garden with humans, not all of those scruples have meaning outside of relationship. Plants, unlike intentional beings, are not beings-to-be-*dealt*-with (except in an extended, weaker sense), which entails that they are subject to our disposition, if not to our arbitrary disposition. A gardener who plucks up one plant or rejects one seed to try to grow another is usually disposing of the available possibilities so as to let the greatest amount of plant-flourishing take place. Because the plants are delivered over to the gardener's disposition, it would be a greater shame to allow the less impressive specimens and the common, all-too-hardy weeds to enjoy their own flourishing than it is to suppress these for the sake of letting the plants favored by the objective gardener have their chance. A plant cannot say what an intender tacitly says to every other intender, "Deal with me now and in future just as I am." A plant's intentions are not flouted when the gardener decides that its time is at an end; since it has no intentions, it has to fit into the gardener's scheme, which, if it is objective, will accommodate a plant's own requirements for nourishment and room to develop while it lives.

However, it *is* still a shame to suppress any plant-possibility. A gardener who felt this too acutely would go mad, but any sensitive, objective gardener feels it to some extent. The lesser shame does not belong to the feel of everyday gardening because it is decisively overshadowed by the prospective greater shame involved in refusing to select what will grow.

As for the mediocre drawing, we can compare drawings with plants and picture the artist as a gardener. The analogy works well enough by itself to rescue primary objectivity from embarrassment on this front, but we should still not be content with it, for artifacts are subject to the disposition of their makers in a more radical way than plants are subject to gardeners, and we must not overlook the distinction.

The organization and qualities of the art object are adapted to the artist's intention so that the making and perceiving of the thing are modes of flourishing for the artist and ultimately for the audience. (A thing that functions as a mere sign, in contrast, is possibly the means of the communicators' flourishing but not the very body of it.) Only because of our intentions is there an important difference between the paper smooth, image intact, and the paper ripped or reduced to ash. The drawing is a teleonomic being as an outpost of the lives of artist and audience. That is why greater shame belongs to disservice of the artist's intention than to repudiation of a particular artifact, so that artists have prima facie authority to destroy works with which they are dissatisfied. Still, an artist can wrongly underestimate the service a particular work might render an audience.

From the attempt to realize an artistic idea it is only a short step back to the idea itself. What entitlement to respect and promotion do ideas have? This question brings us to the third objection.

(3) *The problem of the ideal.* The principle of primary objectivity seems to commend to our attention anything at all that we are capable of noticing. But among the things I notice are the contents of my own mind, which not only can be "there" for me but seemingly can "strike" me just as physically present beings can. If, however, ideas (in the broad Cartesian sense), which belong to my own life and represent merely possible entities, experiences, and acts, have an original standing equal to physically real beings, then two distinctions that seem to be originally important are threatened: that between myself and the "other," and that between possibility and actuality. Let us examine the grounds and implications of these distinctions in the concrete situation to see what threat there is.

First, the zone occupied by an "other" with respect to myself depends on the nature of the encounter. When I face another living being who needs to eat, my stomach is part of my "self"; to have regard for the other's stomach is inseparable from disregarding my own. But if that sort of issue is not posed, my stomach can just as well catch my attention as a rock or plant and I can face it "objectively" provided that I stop living through it. (This is not the existence-neutralizing *epoché* that prepares the object of phenomenological insight but rather a defamiliarization that destroys both arrogance and neutrality.)

My ideas are harder to detach from the life that is myself than is my stomach. Ideation is my act, a move that I make. I do not "have" the idea of five in the sense that some *thing* swims into my field of mental vision; I produce the idea of five just in thinking it. Now the formal possibility of thinking five certainly exists apart from my mental acts, as the possibility of a home run in baseball exists apart from anyone's hitting one, and so it seems that when I attend to the formal possibility rather than to my own act I am encountering an "object," namely, "five" as such, which is completely definite. *This* possibility of counting *exists*. But it exists only as belonging to the one who counts, whose possibility it is. It is "objective" only if I defamiliarize myself with my psychic life, which I can however do only by remembering or anticipating it since in the present it always is me. My own possibilities can never be faced as actual and so are only "objective" in a deficient and misleading sense. On the other hand, when I regard possibilities of thinking in the normal way, as not just my own but anyone's, I am in effect readying myself to meet other thinkers. "Five" is properly a move in a language game. But this way of being challenged and directed outward from myself belongs to secondary objectivity, wherein an idea is the site of meeting with speaking others rather than something met in itself.

Is the fact that ideas cannot be actualities independent of my actuality sufficient reason not to recognize them as "others"? Why must a primary object or "other" be actual? Let us remember that we are not in a position to assign the status "actuality" to others; the others that claim me are the benchmark of actuality.

Their being present is the edge that cuts between the urgency of being claimed and the liberty of considering options, a division that is repeated in the metaphysical distinction between actuality and possibility. Both the ideal necessity in its structure and the practical slack in its application to life are necessary features of the order of possibility wherein the thinking part of my response to others takes place. Ideas are how I live options, ideation being the revelation of what the options are and deliberation being a play with them toward some conclusion. The ideas take on seriousness as they are marshaled in my approaches to the others. That they have aspects and implications hidden from me means that my own or our own possibilities are partly undiscovered, not that the ideas themselves are ungraspable in the manner of actual others. Grasping, assuring orientation, producing pleasure (or any experience) on demand—such is the business of ideas, and therein lies a certain kind of gratification that can tempt us away from life with others. Nominalism wants to save us from the temptation by wielding Ockham's razor: do not multiply entities by misplacing the forms of our comportment toward other beings on the other beings' side of encounter.

On this understanding of ideas the threat brought forward in the third objection is annulled, but at the cost of reminding us that the self, to whose being ideas have been assigned, does not count as others count.

(4) *The problem of the self.* The present view grants original importance only to "others," which means that the "I"—that than which the others are other—lacks original standing. My body can be an "other" if I withdraw from it, but the inner life that I am and do not actually confront, which I might well reckon more important, can never make the claim that is alleged to be the prerogative of others. However, no approach to living is tenable that so fundamentally displaces the self; paradoxically, this sort of unqualified other-concern cannot be recommended to persons, for it negates the very feature of persons, selfhood, which more than anything else requires respect.

This objection could be immediately dismissed if we were prepared to adopt the Buddhist diagnosis of selfhood as a harmful illusion. In fact the Western selfhood fetish is not obviously right-minded, and plenty of evidence from the distorted fabric of Western life could be adduced to support the Buddhist critique. Our account of primary objectivity does, however, require "self" in a certain capacity, so that the concern for selfhood is worth treating seriously.

Is it true that selfhood is to be respected in other persons? That depends on what we take "selfhood" to mean. Respect for his or her intentional energy and style is certainly essential to respect for the other person. But suppose that by a person's "selfhood" we mean his or her having a private mental world in what Ebner calls I-aloneness. It might be thought that precisely this personal privacy ensures the "otherness" of the other person and thus is the very aspect of the other most demanding of respect; but such is not the case. The hidden mental life of the other person is not the same thing as the hidden grounds of the intention of the other person. The fascination attendant upon guessing another person's thoughts should not be confused with due reverence for the other person's original claim to exist and flourish; that fascination is really a teasing of my own capacity to think my way into things, a tickling of my consciousness at its limits, rather than an encounter with the other. The truth is that if we meet another person *as withdrawn into privacy* we are aware of him or her as less than wholly actual. This inactuality might have the positive significance that it is a pause for the marshaling of potentialities or the negative significance that it is a state of distraction or alienation from the world.

The most unequivocally affirmable state of the other person, then, is not one in which the other is concerned with self. Just as my best state is the state of being claimed by others, so the best state of the other person, a claimant with respect to me, is to be a respondent to claims. While I do not have the original standing that other beings have, I belong to actuality in participating in the realization of their standing. Primary objectivity does not annihilate selfhood, in the sense of centered, thoughtful intentional life; it *saves* me from selfhood in the sense of alienated I-aloneness.

That the thoughts and feelings that belong only to me do not have the original standing of the others does not imply that they are void of meaning. It only implies that their meaning is qualified by something prior. If I have interesting and pleasant experiences, so much the better; they go to show the richness of intentional existence in general. It is important, however, to distinguish between the gratifications that keep the steeds of the *Phaedrus* chariot fed and the delights intrinsic to the motion of driving the chariot up to the other being, registering its presence. Even in ordinary speech "delight" has the lightness of freedom from self.

3.5 Concrete Generality

Our discussion of the concrete situation to this point has concentrated on the claims made by others upon the self. The self's implicit position as claim-subject has been passive. Yet one cannot be subject to something's claim unless there is a draw of some kind on one's comportment, so that one lives toward and with the claimant. Comportment-under-claim is therefore integral to the concrete situation, although it is distinguishable as the subjective correlate of the objective claim-source.

The distinction between claim and comportment-under-claim is an essential preliminary to deciding the status of generality in the concrete. We have taken general structures of reality for granted in speaking of encounter with "a rock," "a tree," and so forth. Is the fact that we refer to "this rock" and "that rock" both as "rocks" merely a convenient discursive tactic, or is the similarity between rocks itself encountered? When I encounter rocks X and Y, are their claims originally unique and incomparable or do they originally have something to do with each other—a resemblance on which the logical concept of "property" and the metaphysical concept of "essence" will be founded? It seems that the otherness of the encountered other means precisely its incomparability and unicity. If the *one* I encounter is *one of* a set, then the set is the real "one," the dominant object of attention; and if the set is defined by my prior interest, then otherness is no factor in the event, and "perception" (in the sense of "taking in") or "knowledge" occurs rather than encounter. But this would mean that I cannot encounter a *rock* as such, only an X—that encounter can in no way be informed by knowledge and experience—*unless* it is possible for me to bring to encounter, as my comportment in it and from it, my sense of resemblances. Thus the ingredience of a generality like rockness in the concrete depends on objective comportment or comportment-under-claim.

(Let us note in passing that if one could encounter a resemblance as in itself an other one—if, for instance, one could be struck by the family likeness between the faces of two brothers as such—one would necessarily attend just to that "look" and not to the beings to whom it is common, so that it would not figure as a resemblance or generality. But this is an extreme case. Normally the seeing of a resemblance must be understood as a particular way of seeing the resembling beings.) [14]

Can I respond to the claim of the incomparable other, X, by instituting the comparison implicit in seeing-X-as-a-rock? Is this not a betrayal of X? The fundamental betrayal of X would be not to respond at all, to be a null subject. To respond positively, however, is necessarily to register the impact of X on one's understanding and way of being in the world. My being with X must be reflected in what I am myself, and what I am myself in the moment that I face X is a readiness to approach other beings in certain ways, which I offer to X to qualify. My readiness to recognize a particular form or to do particular things with it is the precondition of my meeting X as a rock, so that X becomes, not in itself but *for me in the meeting*, "this particular rock." Without my own move there is no meeting, and generality belongs to my move. It is objective if I move under claim, letting X open the question of the justice of my approach.

This readiness of mine that determines the meaning of encounter is of course a product of natural, cultural, and personal history. Now in the concrete encounter we are forbidden to look away from X to the problems of the history of the rock-concept or the psychology of rock-perception; but when we do occupy ourselves with such problems, we worry whether these variable determinations of experience of X undermine all talk of a "real" X or "X in itself"—whether X no matter how indicated can only be a product of these determinations and thus unable to bear the originality we impute to it. The worry can be addressed on two fronts.

First, the *concrete* "X itself" that commands my attention is not the same as the "X in itself" that metaphysical realism would defend against absolute idealism or thoroughgoing cultural pluralism. The metaphysical "X in itself" is a solution to a conceptual problem, not immediately a way of responding to X (although it can and should be the metaphysical extension of the gesture of responding to X). Thus the difficulties one has in *saying* what X in itself would be apart from variously determined subjective representations of X do not imply that one is at liberty to dissolve X itself in the representational process in the moment in which one faces X, or that the facing of X is ambiguous at first because of doubt about X's independent being. Rather, the difficulties and doubts endemic in conceptual treatment of the theme of X are signs precisely of our own inescapable role in the original appearance of X; but our comportment, which is practically certain of X itself when it is immediately under X's claim, inevitably becomes uncertain in the domain of metaphysics or epistemology, abstracted from X, responding to different claims. Indeed, insisting on certain-knowledge-of-X is a way of being disloyal to other subjects; the doctrines of epistemic pluralism and fallibilism guard against this error.

Second, there is no reason not to credit the processes that shape my readiness to meet X with an objectivity or proto-objectivity of their own. Does not physical interaction between beings shape nature? Has not culture been shaped by encounter as well as by desire, will-to-power, linguistic and social structures, etc.? Do not having the word "rock" and seeing a "rock" signify (among other things) that a long, populous chain of predecessor subjects have found that "rock" makes many beings available to them, potentially "other" even when not actually so? Admittedly it is impossible to justify outside of encounter the trust one has to place in one's nature and culture as a revealer of the others. Comparative study shows that any natural or cultural apparatus does not simply reveal external reality but screens it out and shapes it according to its own limitations or needs. But at least one is able normatively to construe one's culture as the enterprise of maximizing the revelation and minimizing the repression of beings, and to affirm and criticize it from that standpoint. That is also how one must construe one's contribution of generality to the identity of the other in encounter.

3.6 Intention

Our reckoning with the concrete is incomplete until we determine the chief qualities of the concrete existence of *my* being as such. We have used the concept of intention all along to refer to the existence of the being who responds to and deals with other beings, but without, to this point, any elucidation of it beyond what was necessary to answer one of the objections to the principle of primary objectivity. That might have seemed dubious procedure. But it was necessary to circumscribe "intention" in advance by embedding it in a discourse on relationship and objectivity, since concrete intention is intention-in-relationship and objective intention, not an antecedently existent and comprehensible thing that wanders into encounters with others. Now that we are properly oriented, we can take up the question: What is the way of existing of a spiritual being considered as an individual? What, within the field of *pneuma*, is *psyche*?

The primordial way of existing in which we who philosophize find ourselves, our own spatio-temporalization, can of course be characterized in different ways depending on the pose we have adopted in thinking about it. The pose is all. If one gets off by oneself, sits perfectly still in a comfortable chair, and closes one's eyes, one can become within those artificial limits *res cogitans*. But now we cannot do that. We remember that there are others facing us and to be encountered; consequently we are aware of our position as (in part) selected and changeable. It is because we are primordially in motion that any position, even the placeless rest of a meditating consciousness, presents itself as an issue or problem. And it is on account of the others that we find ourselves in motion, always heading toward them or away from them, or accompanying them. There is not an immediate subjective concrete that is free of the others; a pose that seems truly solitary is, we now know (and know that we always knew), a delusion.

We also know that motion impelled entirely from within, that duress for which the nearest word is "appetite" (which mixes with interest in others as other to form the ambiguous "desire"), is not the subjective concrete. Granted, we can make it so by starving ourselves into an abnormal condition of preoccupation with internal pressures and with others as we want to assimilate them to relieve those pressures—which is to say, not as others. But this, we realize, is spiritual death, or at least a coma. It is a maddened flight from others as other. Concretely, this kind of motion is always *possible* to me; but it *is* not me.

The concrete situation thus dictates that I interpret my existence as an issue of motion, and actually always one kind of motion or another. This is superior to other favored ways of conceiving subjective or intentional existence, namely as *standing* or as *seeing*. Better than standing for two reasons: first, because if I am already in motion my reasons for acting give me places to put my feet down (which reasons can indeed give me) rather than pushes or pulls to move me from a standing center (the kind of "motivation" that reasons as such cannot give); second, because if I am essentially one who stands I can meet another only by going forth from my own place, which will uproot and alienate me. I will necessarily lose myself in having anything to do with others—which is absurd. (However, to achieve a positively significant stability, one that is not mere stasis or stagnation, it is both sufficient and necessary to parallel my motion with the motion of others, in relationship.) Better than seeing, because if I am essentially one who sees I can only meet another as "given" for inspection, which endows me with an unreal freedom from things; but on a larger view, I become nothing but a noticer, an instrument of the letting-be-shown of things, which gives me an unreal passivity, from which both common sense and spiritual responsibility revolt. There is much to be said for the primacy of motion just from an ontological point of view, to avoid the subjective equivalents of Zeno's paradoxes—this is the force of Merleau-Ponty's decisive critique of the intellectualist view of subjectivity— but the spiritual constraint coming before the constraint of intelligibility as such has already demanded motion of us, and it is only that prior constraint that here concerns us.[15] The otherness of the others opens up space between me and them; their claim on me sets me in motion in that space (the space that charges sensible space with its superior meanings).

Distinct from my motion is my *power* of motion, which I am aware of when I can reckon where I might go and then, in imagination or in fact, feel my going or its being hindered. Those are the outside and inside dimensions of motion, the first corresponding to the practical sort of seeing, which may be called surveying, and the second to "emotion." Concrete surveying, like all seeing, is generally *aiming*, turning toward something, whereas concrete "emotion" is always *riding*, moving in or on something in which the motion and the power of motion are perceptible, in which the power of motion experiences twists and turns, successes and checks, waxings and wanings. (I even ride the being-ridden of needs and drives.) In this large sense of "motion," I am nothing other than the power of it—my very being aware of it is only one exercise of it—and this means that aiming and riding are not "activities" of mine but the fundamental modes of my existence. We shall have to explore this further when we attend more systematically to the issue of the relation between the spiritual and material. But already these notions are urged on us by the two respects in which the concrete situation is problematic at root: the others being always elsewhere and therefore to be sought, through but not simply in their motions (thus as multipotential movers of their motions, or "riders" of the material of their motions), and myself being always displaced by my responsibility to and for the others, not only unable to stand but unable merely to be in motion ("standing" inertially), other kinds and different degrees of motion constantly offering themselves to me.

We thus arrive at a conception of intention—this aiming and riding—in rising to the requirements of our conception of the spiritual, bringing all phenomenological and logical considerations into this rising. Aiming and riding are what *further* we are doing when we do things, on account of which (as Anscombe says) intentional concepts are applied to our physical behavior; rising to the others is the *first* "further." [16]

Thought about subjectivity has long tended to navigate by the beacon-ideas of activity and passivity. The subject either determines the other or is determined by the other. A being is either of the determining (free) kind—that is to say, in the idealist tradition, a subject—or of the determined (unfree) kind—that is, something worldly, an object. According to this kind of thinking, otherness, the indeterminable, does not allow the subject to be free and determining with respect to it, which means that the subject is determined by it to be something other than subjective, and hence is alienated from itself. This virtually guarantees that "subjects" will be allergic to each other, and makes the concept of "intersubjectivity" nearly a contradiction. The culmination of the theory of "intersubjectivity" is reached in Sartre's *Being and Nothingness*, where it is argued that I am aware of the other subject as a subject only in becoming aware of myself as a self-alienated object of the other's gaze.[17] The other figures as other in *my* gaze only by disrupting it, wrenching all the perspective lines of my world over to a different center, robbing me of my place. Apparently I have to be either master or slave, agent or patient. But common sense is justifiably certain that sanity lies elsewhere than under the rule of these extremes. Personal existence of the most affirmable sort occurs neither in dominating nor in being dominated but in fellowship, and in this fact we should find our first conceptual clues; we should not make the fact wait for eventual, ineffectual explication with a limited conceptual scheme furnished by scientistic epistemology.

Admittedly there is no way of understanding reality without the concept of determination. Things that come to be and events that occur are determined insofar as they have any identity and distinctness from other things and events. Just as clearly, therefore, the life of an intentional being will consist of some mixture of determining and being-determined. It is reasonable to think that the significant qualities of that life will vary in some relation to the proportions of these two factors. But it is also reasonable to think that there are important differences between kinds of determining and being-determined, and that the meaning of intentional life might be just as much or more affected by these than by the difference between determining as such and being-determined as such. For instance, it makes a great difference whether I bring about an event alone or in cooperation with others—cooking the meal for a dinner party, say. But this is not the difference between determining and being determined. If someone else fixed the dessert, that is not something that just happened to me because someone else did it. It belongs to the whole meal that *we* did; although one of us is prime author of the dessert, that does not take it entirely away from the rest of us. For the dessert is part of the meal, and each of us is part of all of us—though of course not only a part. As I worked on the soup, my determining was determined by my partnership with others. It was qualified as a codetermining of a whole meal. But this codetermining was not a subtraction from my own determining, a diminution of my freedom, but rather an expansion of it. My own determining was not made to be something other than what I intended, but rather allowed to be something I intended that was not in my own power. Of all the expansions possible through the determination of one's own determining as a codetermining, of which the most glorious and affecting example is probably making music in ensemble, the really fundamental expansion is simply being reasonable and giving reasons. I give and receive reasons not just as "I" but as *one*—thinking what is to be thought, willing what is to be willed, and feeling what is to be felt by or for all.

I am not alienated from myself in being determined, when what is determined is my own determining, expansively rather than restrictively. The affirmation of the other, my first responsibility, is always an expansion, an embarkation on a greater enterprise in which the other is necessarily a partner. Nor does the intentional other's aiming at me hamper my own aiming in principle, except that it makes it more difficult for me to aim elsewhere than at this other, and thus might get in the way of this or that project. But I am not in any event permitted to ignore this other. I am not more myself if the others stay out of my way; on the contrary, my selfhood is a way of dealing with them.

Since "intention" is, for us, a question before it is a phenomenon, we are driven to look for the ingredients of answers to that basic question: the elements that constitute possible and preferable ways to intend, or, to speak Greek, the *logoi* that lay down the pattern of *nous*.

Chapter 4:

Norming

4.1 The Problem of Normative Reason

Once we admit that "spirit" is not in the ordinary sense a phenomenon and that a definition of the spiritual is therefore not ordinarily denotative, we need a theory of normative reason for self-defense. For if we exempt ourselves from the canons of descriptive rationality, our proposals will seem arbitrary and (argumentatively speaking) get in no one's way unless they can be shown to follow other rules of reason that lend them authority. To show another and superior kind of reason, of which descriptive rationality is but one derivative manifestation, is the task to which we now turn.

The challenge might give us pause, for although modern thought is not lacking in ventures on this line, there are no widely accepted results. If we ignore romantic outbursts to the effect that something like "intuition" or "experience" is higher than all reason and concentrate on arguments to an other, higher reason, the first examples to draw our notice will be the Christian writers Pascal and Kierkegaard. They conceive reasonableness as seeking God and delineate an order of reasons (of the "heart," or of subjective existence) distinct from, even opposed to, the reasons of the intellect. They remain outsiders to the philosophical tradition not so much because of their special religious commitment as because of the antithetical relation they construct between theoretical reason and the reason for which they speak. They define themselves as outsiders, and Kierkegaard in particular means to leave the relation between the two reasons vexed. (The irony in locating them "outside" philosophy, given all that philosophy has borrowed from them, is incidental to this point.)

The most successful proposal for a superior but not antithetical nontheoretical reason has been Immanuel Kant's, and his conception of "practical reason" survives rational criticism precisely because he deliberately cuts it from the same cloth as theoretical reason. Reason in either its theoretical or practical employment is the spontaneous activity of universal legislation. Theoretical reason constitutes the representation of reality according to universally valid, because necessary, rules, and practical reason directs the making of reality, so far as this lies in the power of human freedom, also according to universally valid, necessary rules.

Practical reasoning appears to be radically distinct from theoretical just as the imperative mood is distinct from the indicative; on the one hand we meet with commands, on the other with judgments of what is the case. However, it is possible to object that the distinction is more apparent than real; and the objection can be made from both sides. One can reproach Kant for founding the practical standpoint on a reduplicable and thus crypto-theoretical "I" rather than on the encounter between "I" and "You" that is the theater of true practice.[1] Or one can argue that Kant's epistemology is crypto-practical because it makes of experience a thing legislated by the "I"; what "is" the case is only what the "I" says must be the case, which estranges us from the normal sense of "is."

I suggest that our best partnership with Kant will be attained by making major adjustments in his theory in response to the first of these objections and treating the second as no objection but the diagnosis of a valid principle, at least as regards science and "experience." A general transposition of the "practical" to the "spiritual" will be necessary to carry this off, and that is in fact one dimension of the project we have in hand. But at this point let us take as our preliminary clue the Kantian discovery that a form of reason attaches directly to practice without a theoretical detour. My practical intentions are immediately rational if I successfully universalize them, that is, find that I can will for all others in relevantly similar situations what I will for myself. I do not have to represent to myself a comparison between my own nature in willing X with the nature of some true or good being in order to ground a practical judgment.

Recent British philosophy contains much sensitive investigation of the rules followed in different uses of language and of felicitous and infelicitous relations between language and events. But the very sensitivity to differences that one finds in Wittgenstein and Austin is disabling when it is necessary to determine the mutual relevance of different language uses and the protocol of their relations (especially in cases of conflict)—in other words, when a general conception of reason is needed. R. M. Hare is a partial exception in arguing forthrightly in the Kantian tradition for a distinctive prescriptive rationality having wide application.[2]

Levinas, whose critique of theoretical reason we have discussed in our first chapter, often takes the antithetical approach of the outsider. According to him, the reason by which one serves the Other diverges drastically from rationality as it exists in propositions about a known or knowable world. Nevertheless, Levinas has made important steps toward reconciling the divergent modes of reason to each other. He does this by deriving crucial categories of experience, including subjectivity and time, from the transcendental exigency of his ethics.[3] This derivation was anticipated in the foreword to his first treatise, *De l'existence à l'existant*:

The movement in which an existent is led toward the Good is not a transcendence by which the existent is raised to a superior existence, but a departure from Being and the categories by which Being is described: an *ex-cendence*. But excendence and Happiness must have a footing in Being, and that is why being is better than not-being.[4]

Like Fichte to this extent, Levinas "deduces" being from what is beyond being. Being and its categories have a reason in what is other and better than being. Once the antithetical work of arguing pluralism has been done, one can turn back and see how the sense of everything that *is* and is known comes ulteriorly from the sense of what is not and cannot be known. This program is clear in Levinas, but his attention has primarily been given to the pluralistic preconditions of the program rather than to carrying it out.

We will try to carry out the first large steps of this program by deriving reason —not only a special form of reason, but reason as such—from the spiritual. We will follow Levinas in first associating reason with a provocation or challenge issued from elsewhere than in being—to wit, the others—instead of grounding reason in the apparent structure of being. We will follow Kant in looking for the primordial form of reason in an activity of norming. Like Hare, we will treat normative uses of language as the proper field in which to begin the study of normative reason.

By "reason" we refer to the principle governing the final possible justification of claims of any sort, and, more broadly, to all actual and possible activities in which that principle is intentionally followed. (Though "reason" is also commonly associated with explanation and motivation, I take it that "rational" or "reasonable" explanation and motivation, held distinct from the psychological events of insight and desire, always refer to at least the possibility of justification.) A "norm" is a pattern that *is to be* followed (not simply that *is* followed), that is, a rule for intention. It might be asked whether "normative reason" is a redundancy, since reasoning seems in general to be a matter of following rules. The answer is that distinctions remain between making rules and merely following them and between ways of making rules. "Normative reason," if it exists, is the application of some principle of justification to the very making of rules, so that these rules are themselves neither chance nor involuntary conditions. This implies that there is at least one principle, one firstness or primordial orientation, that is not a rule. (That, of course, is what each other is.)

4.2 Normative Language

Were we aware only of what is, our language would be entirely descriptive. It would consist of nothing but statements like "It is raining" and "I hurt." Since, however, we are also aware of what could be, in addition to what is—and what could be includes the possibility that what is not be—our language contains statements like "It might rain" and "I'm afraid I might get hurt." In expressing ourselves thus we confront what could be otherwise, but still as spectators, and so we are using a mode of descriptive language. Our only interest is in knowing what actually was, is, or will come to be. The language represents the state of affairs in question, like raining, by appropriately mixing affirmation, negation, and diffidence. "It might rain" places the affirmation of future rain against a background of the possibility of saying the opposite or of an inability to say, depending on the stress on the word "might." But the very presence of what we have to call a "mode" of judgment or constative assertion signals a reflection of speakers upon themselves inasmuch as their *management* of the representation of reality becomes manifest. The statement "It might rain" does more than project a state of affairs that could be otherwise: that statement could itself be otherwise, contingent on the speaker's own acts of affirmation and negation. The one who makes it is revealed to be a self-determining being. Someone who never says anything but "It is raining" or "It is not raining" is, for all we know, only a rain-determined being. These sayings could come out of it like flowers from a watered plant. It is doubtful, therefore, whether language of the simplest descriptive sort should count as language at all, except in the sense that plants have their language. One can imagine people talking entirely in simple descriptions, but in order to think of this as a language, one must tacitly construe their utterances as chosen from among a larger range of possibilities, adding up to an intentional depiction of reality in a certain way.

We are accustomed to correlating the normative uses of language, such as exhorting, commanding, commending, advising, approving, evaluating, and appreciating, with states of affairs that are addressed as alterable. We would also normally distinguish between having an alterable *view* of a state of affairs that may or may not be alterable in itself and regarding a state of affairs as alterable. But this difference is often blurred, for an alteration in one's view of a thing can alter one's conception of the thing and thus what the thing *is* as theoretically represented. In that sense things are alterable for us in the moment that we speak in the more complicated descriptive modes, and even in the simplest description insofar as that figures as an alternative to the other types. For instance, my statement "It might rain" presupposes that I conceive rain as a contingent event. Determinists could confute me, insisting that "might" is a qualification only of my ability to know, not of the event itself (although I might persist, saying "No, it really depends on X, X on Y," and so forth, beyond all knowable conditions, so that I could never be pinned down). The issue is much clearer, of course, if *as a libertarian* I say "She might do it." Determinists and I are unlikely to reach an early agreement about what a human being is. But insofar as we argue about what a human being is, and are conscious of our arguing as a function not just of each other's stupidity but of an outstanding issue, we must regard the conception of human nature as alterable by us; and no other access to "human nature" exists, for talking purposes, than our conception.

In this sense, to describe is always to prescribe, and all language that we would want to call language is normative. We may hold to this general judgment without losing sight of the important differences that remain, on the one hand, between consciously addressing a state of affairs as alterable and only tacitly or latently doing so due to the prescriptive implication of conception as such, and on the other hand, between intending to change a state of affairs and intending to register a state of affairs as it is or could be. We will respect these differences by following the customary use of the term "normative language."

A speaker who uses normative expressions must be in a position to change something. We tend to think first of the changeable something as external to the speaker, and of the change as an action upon it; the speaker is represented as an agent addressing the question, "What shall I do?" Now although there are often good reasons, especially in ethics, for following the agent paradigm, it is misleadingly narrow, for more is alterable by intentional beings than what they "do" in the ordinary sense. A man sunk in gloom looks out of the window on a rainy day, becomes a trifle impatient with his own bad mood, and cheers up. Is cheering up something he "does"? Only in the broadest sense conceivable, by which one "does" whatever does not simply happen to one. A more adequate form of the question addressed by intentional beings is, for themselves, "How live?" and, for the world, "How could things be?" This latter question is nontheoretical because it takes in, idly perhaps, all the things the world could be if it *were* alterable. What is alterable by a speaker is merely the world as stipulated. But there is such a thing as a stipulated world. Not only the objects in this world, but their practical and emotional import, too, are subject to alteration by the beings who intend them. The true range of what could be otherwise on account of speakers, therefore, is determined by all their fancies and feelings as well as by the doings that are open to them.

The true aim of a normative utterance, on the agent model, is decision rather than action. Language does not literally kick bodies into motion; it "acts," in its way, upon the mind of the agent, who then goes kicking. (The aim of the normative intention expressed by a normative utterance, on the other hand, may well be the action.) But decision is also too restrictive a model with which to conceive the inward pole of intentional alteration. It implies established subjects confronting and comparing alternatives that come before their gaze. The gloomy man did not ponder the possibility of cheering up and then decide to; he just cheered up. There may be pulls and pushes on subjects of either a more elemental or more complicated sort, to which response is nevertheless recognizably intentional, that is, not a reflex. The claim of Being, for Heidegger, and the claims of the Other and of happiness, for Levinas, are examples. There are dimensions of decision itself other than the alternatives that present themselves for evaluation. Is my basic attitude in making this decision utilitarian or objective? Am I making this decision as though I were alone with the explicit desiderata, or in togetherness with the others with whom I pass my life as a whole?

Analyses of the situation that gives normative language its function, or of the position of the speaker that calls for normative utterance, typically stop short of the issue just glimpsed. The horizon of the others with whom the intentional subject lives is not scrutinized.[5] Yet it seems that the most important uses of normative language exist only because speakers intend, nearly or remotely, to alter *each other's* intentions, for the obvious reason that the most important thing one faces that could be otherwise is what another intentional being intends. We must say more than this. The intentions of another intender are intrinsically open to alteration in a way that nothing else can be. If I come upon some boards, I can ignore them or cut them up for firewood or nail them together to make a bench; that is one sort of alteration, but not one that radically changes the material (for even if I burn the boards I cannot get at the atoms in them). I can do many things with the boards that change them not at all or only insignificantly. What change there is is simply a departure from my life of what was, and an arrival of something different. But if I come into another intender's field of view as something to be *dealt* with, my own intentionality contributes to the motivation of that other and thus brings it about that the other lives in a different way than formerly, changing *toward* me. Since the other meets me precisely as an other intention, the very thing I attend to in this other changes by virtue of my presence. These changes are *born* in the other, and I am a sort of parent of them.

People can talk normatively just to themselves, of course. A shipwrecked boy who grows up alone on an island can (if we pass over the difficulty as to how he learned language) say, "I'd better pick those coconuts before dark." His own intentions are open to alteration, and for a person in his position, let us say not even knowing that other people or higher animals exist, nothing could be more interesting than the regulation of his own intentions. But he is surely very unlike us. For us it seems that the primary exigency that calls forth normative language is the pressing question for each of us of the others' intentions, and of the relationship between one's own and the others' intentions in which one is always already involved. I cannot so much as live among neighbors without influencing their intentions. Even if I live in an utterly passive and accepting manner, my very passivity calls out to the others in a certain way and alters their approach to me. I inevitably affect myself in this same way insofar as I am an other to myself; if, for instance, I remember how I was once passive, this motivates me now differently than other memories would.

Claims upon intention enter language in many different ways. The neatest specimens of normative utterance are those in which the norm appears explicitly in the language, but people often say things with obviously normative import yet without explicit specification of the norms involved. There are expressions verging on complete inarticulateness, like "Shucks," which nevertheless quite determinately regulate the intentions of speaker and hearers. Then there are expressions in which the norms that explicitly appear are only partial and subordinate representatives of more far-reaching norms that remain implicit. Most specific commands reach farther than they say. When I tell certain people to get out of my yard, the norm I propose to be followed goes beyond their removing themselves from my yard at this moment; it is in fact a principle of separation between our activities and affairs, in force indefinitely.

One would perhaps like to require that every true norm be a rule that can be followed on any relevantly similar occasion by any similarly placed person— that rules be essentially general. Wittgenstein says, "It is not possible that there should have been only one occasion on which someone obeyed a rule." [6] But this remark applies to the practice of rule-following, not to a particular rule. It is not possible that someone should only once do such a thing as obey a rule, but within the context of a rule-following form of life, the rules may come and go with separate occasions and separate persons. To be sure, this presupposes a rule about rules, namely, the institution of rule-obeying. But we must not prematurely hew to the requirements of logic and ethics by disallowing rules that are not universal. Norming in general is a precondition of rationality, and rational rules are a subset of the class of all rules.

Now let us think what sort of act this is, to speak to other beings with the purpose of placing before them a rule that they are to follow, in intention if not in action. Suppose you say things like the following:

> Come on, vote for Jones!
> Vote for Jones, please.
> You'll like Jones.
> If I were you, I'd vote for Jones.
> Jones is a fine candidate.
> Jones is the best candidate.
> Jones is a wonderful candidate!

Although these utterances make claims of varying stringency upon the hearer, and relate Jones himself differently to assumed standards and circumstances, they all tell the hearer what to intend. Even the "softest" of the prescriptions—"Jones is fine" and "Jones is wonderful!"—put the hearer in the potentially inconvenient position of having to disagree, which would make renegotiation of togetherness necessary. It is, with respect to the otherness of others or their sovereignty, a mammoth presumption on your part to so much as open the possibility that your intention deserves precedence over theirs. How could your intention become anyone else's? In view of the solidarity between persons and their intentions, must we not say that here the rule "to each his or her own" must be respected? Of course, that too is a rule—it turns out that we are so mixed up with each other that we cannot extricate ourself from norming *tout court*—and one offers it for general acceptance. It commends itself because it is evidently fair. But that is how any rule would commend itself. The "softness" of the claim of "Jones is wonderful!" is its yielding before the other, its refusal to press upon the other's sovereignty; it solicits rather than demands. Even the imperious "Vote for Jones!" has implicit in it conditions under which it could be evaded, that is, as long as it is a genuine normative utterance and not a would-be efficient cause. So the presumption in norming is not necessarily a domineering one. But it is unavoidably a presumption, for the "softest" norming still gets in someone's way.

Looked at from your own side, it is quite a venture to norm, and one that might well make you quail. It requires courage or gall to get in someone else's way. Usually you are already in someone's way and the question is only how best to comport yourself there. But there too you are faced with the alternatives of making stronger or weaker claims, and with greater or lesser stringency of appeal to the others—for example, whether to praise something exemplarily, advise it, or command it.

There is also a defensive aspect of norming. Your intentions are subject to alteration by others just as theirs are by you. Could you live sanely if you were unsheltered from the awful contingency of unregulated spiritual existence? Imagine a woman finding herself in a foreign city. The residents swarm around her, making bizarre motions with their heads and arms. She smiles, but this appears to make no impression at all. She holds up her hands to show her harmlessness, but this (for all she can tell) enrages some of them and draws ridicule from others. Something like this happens to many a traveler upon first contact with an alien culture; but imagine now that she must live the rest of her life in this condition, without relief. She never learns the language or customs of her "hosts," so that all means of norming are denied her; yet she continues to live among these people, who tolerate her presence for dark reasons of their own, and continue to interact with her in unintelligible ways—say, sometimes chasing her away from any food she finds, or sometimes waiting expectantly for her to do she knows not what. It is inadequate to say that she would be unhappy. Unless she took extraordinary measures of self-insulation, her personhood would go to pieces.

That could never happen, it will rightly be objected, because no human society could be so unyielding to understanding. In time, the woman would undoubtedly get the hang of some of her hosts' spiritual forms. It must be possible in principle for her to learn them because it must be possible for *them*. They could not live with each other as completely imponderable any more than she could sanely live with them under the terms of our example.

The radical alterability of the other as other, which is not reduced but is *dealt with* in following norms, is the supreme exigency for norms. The point is worth dwelling on because we are accustomed to thinking of this the other way around: we think that the fascinating and problematic alterability is one's own, the self's, while this heroic enterprise of selfhood is surrounded by a lot of more or less predictable and mediocre others who weigh the self down with their sameness and unfreedom. This perception is not without its truth, but it is not a perception of the others as other. It is a perception of the impersonal mores as such, of the "they" that both oppresses the self and occludes the others as themselves. On the contrary, when the others are perceived as others, the self feels itself in comparison to be relatively predictable and unfree. For although the self can get to know itself better, it cannot radically change itself; it is stuck with being itself.

The alterability of the self, such as it is, is thus only the second most important of the conditions that call for norming. (The third and last condition is the alterability of the world in which self and other live.) To call one condition "supreme" and another "secondary" means in this case that the supreme condition absolutely demands norms whereas the secondary one does not, except in correlation with or imitation of the supreme condition. I flatly cannot live with others as others without intentional rules in common. It is at least theoretically possible for me to live, by myself, without intentional regulation; yet, since my human way of being "spiritual" consists of facing myself as an "other" of a sort, I will always in practice norm myself. The world's alterability is the least essential. We could ignore the world, provided we did not mind dying off rather quickly. Worldly alterability becomes an ineluctable exigency for norms only when it is subsumed under the self or the other, as the alterability of my or the others' bodies, or of the instruments by which we communicate.

Normative utterance lends itself to misunderstanding because of its complexity relative to our more appealingly straightforward models of descriptive language. One issue in the interpretation of normative language is the extent to which it can be construed descriptivistically. When I say "X is good," am I making a verifiable proposition about X's possession of a "value," on the same order as "X is red"? Or am I only urging X on you? Beyond this issue, however, lies a more important one. Whether or not there is an experienceable "value" that could be contained in cognitive propositions concerning X, it is clear in most forms of normative language that I am somehow urging X on you anyway. Even the mild "X is good" usually has obvious prescriptive force on account of the occasions that evoke it, and the passive "I approve of X" is, minimally, the taking of a position from which to prescribe. The crucial question, then, concerns not content but the nature of the *performance* that takes place in normative utterances. Whether or not "values" may be assigned to their content, what kind of "spin" is put on the content when it is offered in this way?

We may distinguish between the illocutionary spin that is *in* the sense of a sentence like "Eat this plum, it's the best," which is its envisioning of the hearer choosing the indicated plum, and the perlocutionary spin that is *on* the sentence, which is the speaker's climbing up into the plum-judge's seat. But these are really two aspects of one act, the speaker's reaching in a certain way toward the intentions of the hearer. To abstract the two from each other is dangerous, for it can encourage the supposition that normative speakers are only "evincing" their attitudes with respect to the content, on the one hand, or manipulating their hearers, on the other. Undoubtedly pro and con attitudes are evinced in normative statements; undoubtedly behavior is influenced, too. But what else happens? In this, as in any other sort of language, someone is *addressed*. That in itself goes beyond the pure manipulation of pushing and shoving, and also beyond "evincing"; one reaches toward another by means of an intentional proposal. I reach toward your perception to lead it if I say so much as "There's a plum." But if, in an utterance that would be classified as normative, I commend the plum to you, the aspect of addressing or reaching becomes more prominent, since I am not just incidentally affecting what you will come to know but presuming to influence your intentions toward what you know. I am stepping deeper into your existence, having more to do with you, being towarder.

The appropriate term to apply to a move whose significance is inseparable from its being toward another is "gesture." The gesture comprises both the reaching and the twist or spin in the reach, the perlocutionary force with the illocutionary.

The gesture is a unique move toward a being in that it preserves the distance of the being toward which it moves—that is, the otherness of the other. A gesture without an audience is not a gesture at all. The movement of the gesture is a towardness that is subordinated to awayness without being simply defeated by it, and this naturally repeats the structure of relationship, where togetherness is realized subordinate to otherness. A gesture is, in fact, the only way to be with an other who remains other, for the other as other does not enter one's field of awareness as a phenomenon. One cannot have the other where one is, one must go forth from where one is to meet the other. But to be outside of "where one is" in this sense, that is, the knowable field about one, is to be blind, or, to put it positively, to be embarked on an adventure. But it must also be possible to "meet" the other; and since the phenomenal order cannot serve as the medium of meeting (even though phenomenal coordinates, such as "on this page," can often be given for where the nonphenomenal event of meeting occurs), the medium of meeting must be, not what exists, but the way in which what exists is dealt with: intention. I cannot be together with you except by soliciting your intentions with my own, and I cannot reach toward your intentions as such without gesturing—in the paradigm instance, speaking—normatively. The rectification of relationships takes place in norming. Norming is the spiritual concrete.

In speech and writing, as compared with mute bodily gestures, the matter of norming is tremendously expanded. I can say "Eat this plum" or "Accept the universe"; everything determinable by thought gets into language and receives the intentional spin that the speaker puts on it. From the normative point of view, the original requirement for language is precisely this, to be able to hand everything conceivable over to one's hearer, with a spin on it. Both facts and "values" are matter for normative gesturing. The difference between them is that "values" are already spinning in a more or less stable and reidentifiable pattern, and I can thus pile commentary on top of them, offering them to you in complex and confusing ways, such as by saying "Love your great country!" belligerently or derisively. (The purpose served by the concept of "value" is to make thus public and transferable an intentional qualification. Consequently it is at least latently contradictory to talk of "your values" and "my values.")

4.3 Normative Reason

A shift of our attention from normative language to normative reason is provoked by the question of how norming can be grounded or evaluated. By assigning both facts and "values" to be the mere "matter" of norming, we have made it impossible that either or both together could amount to sufficient justification of a norm. By analogy, nothing in the make-up of a car could justify, by itself, the way I drive it. The car's features are quite relevant, of course, to deciding what to do with it; if I own a sports car capable of going 160 miles per hour, one might go so far as to say that it would be a "shame" never to drive it at top speed— supposing that one approved of the existence of such a machine. But not even on the Bonneville salt flats would the car's capability of going 160 miles per hour constitute a justification for driving it that fast. The way in which I use the car moves at a level other than that on which the car exists, and takes other bearings than merely noting characteristics of things that exist. To persuade you that we should drive my sports car at top speed, I would have to argue not only that the car is capable of a certain speed but that that is what it is *for*. That is, I would have to adduce the way in which someone else intended or ought to intend the car in order to justify the way I intend it. Not even a "value" can, of itself, close the question of right intention. Driving the car fast serves the "value" of pleasure but not the "value" of safety; no "value" (at least of this sort) automatically justifies itself against another. An interintentional claim is needed to justify choice of "value," like "We were *meant* to have fun in this life."

It could be objected that natural goods do not have to be referred to any interintentional scheme in order to be "good," and thus have (possibly sufficient) justifying force for the one who uses them or creates them; for the intrinsic goodness of an apple is an excellent reason to eat it, and similarly the intrinsic goodness of a good deed is an excellent and sufficient reason to do it. But this is a highly misleading comparison. The apple is typically eaten in a context where the question of justification does not arise. If, to give credence to the idea that an issue of "justification" exists in such a case, we search for a principle by which the best apples are selected, what we will find is only a rationally formulated maxim of appetite, "Eat what tastes best, if no other considerations intervene." The appetite itself, treated as a mere given, determines the action and is therefore a "reason" in a theoretically explanatory sense rather than in a directly normative sense. ("I like to eat tasty things" is a truth of intention like "Heavy bodies fall" is a truth of material objects. "That's why I ate this apple" therefore cites an intraintentional *cause* rather than any taking of bearings by intention.) Whether it is *right* to accept it thus as a given is a separate question and one that does not come up very often with respect to apples. But if this question does come up, then the natural goodness of the apple, the given correlation of its characteristics with my appetite, is no longer a sufficient reason to eat it. The good deed, on the other hand, is typically done as a response to the question of what is right. Its "goodness" is actually compounded out of its judged justifiability. To the extent that natural benevolence as an "appetite" for deeds that we call good is the sole reason for which they are done, then the "reason" involved is, as with the apple, a self-descriptive citation of intraintentional causation. This may be a fine reason indeed if we judge that type of intention to be just.

It may be objected on behalf of "values" that a "value" just is a sufficient and justifying reason for being or doing something. However, there is no conceivable case where the bringing of a "value" into view renders meaningless the question "But is it right to promote this value in this case?" That question enfolds the "value" between intentions, at least the intentions of asker and audience; the justification framework thereby transcends it. "Values," like facts, are the sort of thing that must fall between intentions, for all that we set them up to govern intention. They are always thus equivocal.

If facts and "values" are not themselves justifiers—or, more precisely, if they borrow the justifying force they occasionally have from outside themselves—then what does, of itself, justify? This brings us directly to the subject of reason.

———

We call "gesture" any move toward an other as other. A gesture is necesarily symbolic inasmuch as it always adopts visible materials to be the manifesters of the invisible, namely, intention; therefore, gesture as such is already language in the broad sense. However, the standardized system of themes that we possess in word-language makes possible for the first time a gesturing toward things not present, including gestures themselves. We can have intentions toward intentions, and in that way both be conscious of consciousness itself and aware (not precisely "consciously") of spirituality. *Reason* is certainly latent in language and self-consciousness, for the standardization of themes implies the universality of the concept, and having intentions toward intentions implies the having of "principles"—how else could the intentions that are had toward intentions be distinguished in kind from the intentions they are had toward? Nevertheless, it does not seem that reason is yet actual in language and self-consciousness as such. In fact, we use the word to refer to a particular qualification of these. Reason is the totality of forms whose primary function is the approbation and justification of language and self-consciousness, and, toward this end, the rendering public of these things. Since this is not the only view one might take, we must justify it with reference to what is generally thought about reason.

The traditional aims of reason are formal, that is, having to do with how claims may be made, and material, that is, having to do with the content of claims. ("Claim" means any gesture that intends to affect in any way the intention of the ones to whom it is directed; in other words, any gesture, but regarded in light of the issue of the audience's response.)

(1) We will first consider requirements *internal* to a claim. (*a*) A general requirement that may be regarded either as formal or material, depending on whether the expression or the content is had in view, is determinacy, that is, the intelligibility of the claim's relata and relations. (*b*) Formally, a rational claim must be free from internal contradiction; the senses that it assembles and connects must assort with each other. (*c*) Materially, reason's two chief epistemological functions answer to the requirement for determinacy. They are, first, to fix and delineate the nature of the beings of which we are aware, and second, to do the same for the relations between them. In the latter category falls what is called "grounding," which is a matter of finding the relations between derived and underived things that determine the very actuality of the derived or grounded things against the possibilities of their nonexistence: to conceive what is as what cannot fail to be. Although it is clear that reason has the task of grounding, it is debatable whether reason is committed to the attempt to ground everything in such a way that a system with a maximum of necessary implications is obtained, the contingency in it shrunk (in the best case) to the point of a single *arché*, to grasp which is to grasp all. Anyone who believes this probably accepts the rationalist-idealist thesis that reason itself is the knower and doer of whatever is known and done; but alternatively, one can think that something or someone else is the knower and doer, or are the knowers and doers, who use reason as an instrument and commit it to whatever he, she, it, or they are committed to. This issue is not decided by the mere concept of reason, which only entails that wherever reason is applied there will be the greatest possible determinacy.

(2) There are formal and material conditions *external* to a claim that are also contained in the concept of reason. We shall call these conditions of "reasonableness" in distinction from the "rationality" that is internal to claims. (*a*) The

simplest illustration of this distinction concerns the general requirement of determinacy: while it is rational to *be* clear as to what one is claiming, it is reasonable
to *make it* clear to others. (A teacher rightly insists that the rationality of students' ideas can prove itself only in the reasonableness of their argumentation.)
(*b*) Corresponding to the formal requirement of rationality that a claim be free
of internal contradiction, there is the formal requirement of reasonableness that a
claim be kept as much as possible out of contradiction with other claims that are
in good standing, that is, ones that have not for one reason or another forfeited
their right to be taken seriously and borne in mind. (*c*) The material requirement
of rationality that beings and their relations be determined as knowable has its
counterpart in the requirement of reasonableness that something real, and available to be known, is outside the claim and supports it. These last two parallels,
(*b*) and (*c*), need discussion.

On (2)(b). Two obvious examples of claims outside a given claim that are in
good standing and of undisputed relevance to the given claim are other claims
made by the claimant, and claims made by those whom the claimant is addressing.
If I say now that eggs are bad for you, having said half an hour ago that eggs
are good for you, I must act to remove the contradiction to remain reasonable; I
must say something like "I was recommending eggs earlier as a source of protein,
but now I remember you have to watch your cholesterol intake." Neither could
a contradiction reasonably be left unattended between *your* earlier statement that
eggs are good and my present statement that they are bad. A burden is on me to
add, "I'm sure you had in mind the protein in eggs, but you must admit that the
cholesterol in them is dangerous for many people." If the contradiction between
us is not dealt with, then our conversation, although it might be significant or
entertaining in other ways, cannot be called a fully reasonable one. Of course,
we dare not require that every such contradiction be resolved, for then all too few
"reasonable" conversations would be left; it is enough to mobilize the intention
of overcoming them.

A choice confronts us here echoing one that faced us before when we set about
conceiving the relationship between fellow members of a spirit such as "school
spirit." It is possible to construe all my claims that are related to each other as one
great claim; and, stretching a little further, it is possible to say that all of *our* claims
are judged, for purposes of determining "reasonableness," as though they were,
for each of us, one great claim—that is, yours joined by me to mine as though
they were mine, and mine joined by you to yours as though they were yours, or all
of ours joined together as though they belonged to a super-self. On that construal,
the preceding distinction between rationality and reasonableness would wither
away, as we would ultimately have no need of it. But we decided, in our analysis
of spirit, that unity must be subordinated to otherness so as not to annul it. That
principle applies to the present question. Your claims and mine are in relationship,
but they are not unifiable, as they would have to be to collapse reasonableness into

rationality. Although our claims are common property from the moment they are spoken, since we are speaking together, they are not completely detachable from you and me, the ones who intended them and will presumably try to rescue them from all contradictions. Insofar as I am reasonable, I am still holding the string of every balloon I have sent up. *I,* not "reason in me," am accountable. If this condition of reasonableness is not enforced on actual beings such as ourselves, then the requirement to seek agreement of claims is empty; no one has to do it except "reason," which may be hard to find at the awkward moments.

Remember also that we had to relate the standard of reasonableness to the seeking, rather than the achieving, of agreement. Unless we want to go against our strong sense that an agreement-seeking conversation is properly reasonable, not just nearly or deficiently so, we will have to account somehow for the presence of reason where the consistency requirement of internal rationality is not met. You and I are certainly reasonable if we argue in good faith our respective theses that the world is getting better and that the world is getting worse, but the combined claim "The world is getting better and the world is getting worse" is irrational.

Not only would it be inconvenient to require "reasonable" conversation to resolve all differences, it would be one way of subordinating otherness to unity and thus absolutely inappropriate. The *external* relations of claims are at the same time relationships with the *exterior.* The others with whom I speak may always contradict me. This standing prerogative is how otherness is in force in conversation. But this is not a limit on reasonableness, for there is such a thing as reasonable contradiction, which tries, whether or not successfully, to remove the grounds of contradiction from its own point of view. One cannot guard against the rebuttal of one's interlocutor. The plea "Be reasonable!" can never mean only "Agree with me!"

It seems also that the demand on me to seek to remove contradiction from between my own claims presupposes the presence of the others. It is primarily for them that contradictory claims add up to an unsatisfactory discourse. If I praised eggs half an hour ago, what is that to me? My instinct is to be free of whatever I said in the past and always to start fresh. (If at the beginning of a round of golf my first drive goes awry, I can always do it over—if I am playing by myself.) But the others hold me to what I have said and done. I act as a representative of them to myself when I negate my own freedom of starting over and view my own claims as adding up to a whole discourse.

On (2)(c). The material requirement of reasonableness is that of objectivity. A claim must not hang in the air; it must be about something that is there, that can be in the appropriate way checked, and that corresponds to the claim in the appropriate way. At this point the suitability of the term "reasonableness" seems most tenuous. In our earlier application we capitalized on its affinity for interpersonal dealings. We found that some external relations of a claim are in fact embedded in relationships with other persons. But objectivity can readily be conceived to actuate solitary knowers, indeed precisely insofar as they mean to know rather than dream, and seems to have no essential grounding in the interpersonal.

Yet there is an argument for holding objectivity to be a form of reasonableness. In the first place, the others place a significant demand on me to be objective. Admittedly, this is only because they are already objective themselves, for otherwise they might be content to take over well-formed claims from me without undue concern for their truth-value. Why, though, are we *all* objective? Is it because each of us is born to respect the principle of "objective" truth—as opposed to believing what is technically or emotionally convenient—or is it because in order to meet and live with each other in the world it is necessary for us to apply the concept of "objectivity" so that each of us is bound to speak of what is there-for-anyone? The second alternative is much more probable, as a genetic proposition, and also defensible as a logical proposition, since the meaning of "really" and "truly" in sentences like "X is really there" or "X is truly like that" does analyze, in part, into "what is there in principle for anyone (in the right position) to know." The interpersonal dimension does obtain, then, and is at least one important condition of objectivity. Another important condition, however, is the direct relationship in which the claimant stands to that about which the claim is made, which we earlier designated "primary objectivity." I say "That plum is without blemish" not only to discharge my responsibility to you, in case upon hearing this you should excitedly look for it, but also out of respect for the plum itself. To witness truly to the plum is the right way of getting along with it, which is a matter of concern to me insofar as I am originally prepared to treat it as something to be gotten along with, something to be done justice. This is just what a *knower,* as opposed to a schemer or dreamer, is prepared to do. Wherever the knowing attitude comes from—whether from a process of socialization that establishes the category of others, or in some other way—this is what it stands on. We are thus assured that it is not misleading to use the word "reasonableness" in this connection as in the others.

Everything said so far may be conceded yet the fundamental issue remain, as one of originality or priority. Reason demands the subjective *grasp* of knowledge, lucid apprehension of determinate being, and also a respectful and pertinent relationship between the reasonable one and the others. If these different exigencies are merely different, then reason is two things, not one, and it is wrongheaded to offer a unitary definition of it. But reason must at least be postulated as one, for to accept incommensurable principles of justification would be to suffer a serious, permanent disorientation that must be unwelcome. If reason is one, then it is necessary to derive one of its two aspects from the other—supposing no third, more fundamental form of reason is discoverable. Our guiding pluralist principle suggests that we derive rationality from reasonableness. (It also prohibits a "third form" more original than the issue of right relationship.) This derivation should be accepted if it leaves us with a more adequate appreciation of all the matters we have touched on. It must turn things right side up and not be reductive. On this derivation, it should be remembered, depends the originality and priority of normative reason, which is a function of the rectification of relationships.

"Rectification" as we have conceived it is a movement of righting rather than a fixed position of being right. A compass needle as it swings toward the north is rectifying, even if it has infinitely far to go to reach north and so never does. "Justification," on the other hand, refers to a position that is, if not absolutely right— for we do not yet know whether a position of absolute rightness is even logically attainable—at least right *enough,* that is, sufficiently rectified with reference to a given purpose or demand. (This conceptual distinction can be made initially even though it raises the problem how "right enough" could ever be judged without some grasp of the unqualifiedly right.) We have already proposed defining reason as a principle of justification. Now the question is, does reason, which undoubtedly is an apparatus both of sufficiently rectifying propositions and of grasping reality as knowable, in fact grasp reality for the sake of justifying propositions, or justify propositions for the sake of grasping reality?

Actual reasoning practice points in both ways. For instance, scientist Ivan P. makes absolutely sure of the experimental result before his eyes *so that* his colleagues will produce the same results and be in accord with him. Yet at the same time he respects the intersubjective requirement of experimental repeatability *because* this leads to fuller and surer knowledge of reality. Suppose that Ivan's dominant attitude is the latter. Then his relationships with others become means to the end of an experience of insight and certainty, which he has alone. Since his private knowledge-experience is what mainly matters, it must also be its own justificans; that is, his scientific practice must be primarily responsible to this (prospective) experience, because that is what it endeavors to produce. External justifiers, such as his colleagues, are really only his own deputies acting for him. But now we are caught in an absurdity, for a self-justification is necessarily a pseudo-justification. Nothing justifies itself. The concept of justification, like that of rightness from which it derives, presupposes some relationship between the justificandum and a justificans exterior to it. We can preserve, at most, only a provisional meaning for justification by saying that Ivan's prospective full and sure knowledge justifies the steps he takes and experiences he has that lead toward it. But in the attaining of perfect knowledge, the concept of justification would no longer be applicable. If that knowledge would nevertheless be "rational" or "reasonable," as one would indeed wish to affirm, then justification forms no essential part of the concept of reason. This is a disquieting, apparently wrong outcome.

But suppose that this scientist's dominant attitude is one of concern for sufficiently right relationship with a justificans that remains exterior to him—which, for simplicity's sake, we may identify with his colleagues. In that case his subjective grasp of the phenomena is a means to the end of a transsubjective "reliability" in knowledge; knowledge must be sure, so that it is sharable, so that one person's knowledge may tally with another's. It might seem that in this case relationship is elevated at the price of reducing subjective grasp. If Ivan mainly cares about finding grounds of agreement with his colleagues, surely he will not peer as intently, test as resolutely, question as ruthlessly as he would for himself? After all, agreeing with one's colleagues is usually a matter of passively accepting some orthodoxy or other that happens to be established in one's field. And to call a position "rational" or "reasonable" that consisted of intersubjective justification without any essential requirement of subjective grasp would again be absurd. But knowledge is not in fact reduced in this way. It must be preserved on account of the very exigency for justification. The relationships that are to be rectified are *worldly,* not free-swinging in a void. One cannot agree with one's colleagues unless some ground of agreement has been found and held. One should not passively accept a scientific orthodoxy, because such ground always proves in the end unstable. One should brave the most ferocious opposition from one's colleagues precisely for the sake of establishing everyone in an eventually more tenable position with respect to the phenomena. Subjective insight and certainty is a subordinate but not eliminable condition of justification.[7] Thus the knowledge principle can be derived from the justification principle, which cannot in turn be derived from it. The concept of reason-as-justification is more accommodating of the essential demands of reason than reason-as-knowledge. Knowledge is the "matter" of justification as the latter can never be of the former. It follows that justification determines the final meaning of knowledge; that is, the final significance of the fact that I grasp a knowable matter is not simply that I grasp it but that others can grasp it too (or, with regard to the knowable itself, to say that it can coexist with the grasping). Knowledge must be a meeting point for us all.

Fresh from this reasoning, however, we must turn to face the possibility that we do not even know what justification means since it is a function of relationship with unknowable exteriority. Not only could a compass needle never point right at north if it did not "know" right where north is, it seems that it could never so much as begin to swing toward north. This is a nice paradox: Achilles can never even set out to overtake the tortoise unless he knows in which direction the tortoise lies ahead of him. The solution of the paradox is sufficient to give meaning to rectification and justification, but it is still only partly a solution, and this should always be remembered. Strictly speaking, one never can know more than partly what rectification and justification mean.

I do not know what you really are or what you really mean. Yet we meet, and live together. This is possible in part because the very bounds that define us as unexpected strangers to each other—you with that face, that manner, which I would never have dreamed—also limit, in some dimensions, the problem we pose for each other. We are located in space and time. Our actions occur more or less one at a time and fall into a more or less determinate sequence. The unsettleable question of what you really mean is introduced by certain apparent intentions you have manifested, and these intentions form themselves into coherent patterns. In addition to that, my intentions can go along with yours in a pattern that joins them together, a spirit. The natural limits or forms we have sketched are preconditions of spirit, which otherwise could find no purchase.

Now, a certain spirit—say, the spirit whose business it is to map the rooms, corridors, and entryways of togetherness as such, namely, the spirit of reason —always presents rules for intention to follow. The rules, as for instance the principle of noncontradiction, are graspable; they must be, because they are our rendezvous points. To the extent that you are with me in this spirit, I may meet *you* by following the rule. Of course, it is an open question, even to you, to what extent you intend in the spirit. But under normal circumstances it is more perverse and irresponsible to doubt than to accept that we are together. The rule is like the dance form, waltz or tango, that we rely on to have the dancing mode of togetherness. Though I can never in the nature of the case be sure where I stand with you absolutely, we can dance a decent waltz. By joining in a dance with me you have allowed me to be with you to this extent.

The exteriority of others would only make rectification of relationships impossible if there were no rules to follow, but without rules there would be no relationships, and so the possibility of rectification is given with relationship. A "rule" in this broad sense need not be explicit. It may only be the primal rule of respect for the other's apparent nature. All that is required is some definite pattern for intention to adhere to, as when, for instance, a lover traces faithfully the outlines of the beloved's face, repeats faithfully the beloved's words. To follow the rule is not to have the other. The lover, no matter how faithful, cannot ensure requital. But insofar as the rules of the prospective relationship allow, and so far as lies in the power of a party to that relationship, the lover can rectify the relationship and even, depending on the kind of relationship, attain a justified position. This is notoriously difficult—the most famous lovers have made slips —but not impossible in principle. Knowing the rules of love employed in love stories, we know what "perfect love" is, at least in a story, and we know that a perfect lover is right enough in that relationship.

Most relationship types comprise purposely limited thresholds of justification because of the practical impossibility of gaining a right enough position without such limits. No one could write a scholarly book if scholarship demanded an infinite search for relevant material; most scholarly claims are justified if they are based on a "reasonably" careful search in a circumscribed set of places. Such justification is obviously relative, not absolute, but then there can be no such thing as absolute justification. The fundamental problem of justification, posed by relationship with an other, is insoluble. No rules could absolutely bind those who follow them.

But now we might wonder whether any essentially relative rule can function as a true justificans in any sense. For that which justifies cannot be questionable in turn without losing its justifying force. (Here we meet with the original and true form of the problem of infinite regress, which does not really apply to causes as such, since a spontaneous cause causes just as well as a caused cause; but an unjustified justification does not justify at all.) Those who seek justification must live inside their justificans and be unable to turn elsewhere for a vantage point of evaluation. But it turns out that this requirement is met even by the only relatively binding rules of the dance. The dancers do live inside their dance. They get to be dancers, to have something to do with each other in that determinate way, by following the rules of the dance. They can criticize one dance only from the standpoint of another, superior one. The alternative is always open of exiting or ragging the dance in such a way as to impair togetherness as such, but that is not a matter of becoming unjustified so much as of losing one's hold on the whole possibility of justification. Thus relative possibilities of justification, which exist in the shadow of the absolute impossibility of sufficiently rectifying one's relationship with an other, nevertheless offer possibilities of final justification within the definite forms of togetherness where intentional beings meet. Those definite spirits are open to the essentially indefinite or anarchic question of otherness as such, which it would be a mistake to even try to answer, and which reminds us that the category of justification is inapplicable past a certain point. Past that point we approach the infinite demands of relationship empty-handed, no matter how much we are holding.

4.4 The Basic Structures of Reason

To think through the basic structures of reason, we have to shield ourselves from the dizzying thought that relationship transcends its mediation and consider which moves generally place the ones who make them in right enough positions with respect to others. All such moves must be specifying, determining acts that lead an audience toward agreement with a claim. Now, if we are to reflect our spiritual orientation in the inventory we set forth of the thought-determining aspects of reasonable claims, we cannot limit our attention to the hard reason of necessity, to which our own discourse does not conform. We must rather observe a fundamental distinction between hard reason and the sweet reason of permission or invitation, viewing both in their norming significance.

(a) Hard Reason: Noncontradiction

The truth reflected by hard reason is that not all things are compossible. This is implicit in the very fact of plurality. If white is different from black, then white cannot be black; if it could be black, it would not really be anything other than black. To *judge* that white is black is to fall short of recognizing the difference which, generically, is a condition of the existence of a world to make judgments about. Judgments depend on that difference and for that material reason must obey the principle of noncontradiction, which reaches far beyond the elementary antithesis of opposites like black and white to the most subtle repugnancies between the implications of things. To mingle incompatible ideas in a judgment is, at bottom, to disrespect the things of which one judges, in their difference which makes them what they are. A good and indeed incontrovertible reason from this point of view is one that forbids thought to violate things by conceiving them as being possibly other than what they essentially are. Obviously this is no simple matter, since things can change without ceasing to be what they are. Would we chide a fond mother for fancying that her two-year-old son might one day be accomplished and wealthy and famous? Normally there is no contradiction in that, any more than moral judgments concerning how human affairs ought to be arranged contradict the fact of their present, quite different arrangement.

There is a demand for the principle of noncontradiction from the formal-rational and formal-reasonable points of view as well. A judgment that white is black is destructive of the concepts that judgment presupposes just as it is disrespectful of the things that one makes judgments about. There must be difference between concepts paralleling the otherness of real things to each other. Difference must enter into the act of using language in yet another way: if I say to you "black is white," I am in effect unspeaking speech, failing positively to enter the circle of communication. But since communication is a condition of the existence of spirits, contradicting oneself is the fundamentally impermissible act among all prima facie communicating moves. To speak is to make a difference of some sort, to alter actually or potentially the orientation of those to whom one speaks (as to dance is to take a step). Now, noncontradictory speech presupposes the availability of noncontradictory concepts—I could not make myself clear about X if I were not clear for myself about X—but, at the same time, having noncontradictory concepts presupposes mastery of noncontradictory speech—I cannot be clear about X unless I can adequately express a judgment about X. Following the order of precedence already established, we should assert that the supreme or superordinate principle of noncontradiction is the spiritual one, having to do with *our* intentional compossibility rather than the mutual acceptance of things and their properties. The other principles follow from the spiritual one, as it would not follow from the others. That is, if we forbid speech to unsay itself by taking back what is offered, as "White is black" negates white after affirming it, then it will follow that the inner speech of thought will be kept off the paths of contradiction, and from that the world will never get grasped in a difference-annulling way. But if we rooted the principle of noncontradiction in the things themselves or private judgments about them, we could not guarantee speech in good faith. Reason would permit one to say whatever one wanted, carelessly or hypocritically, as long as one knew what one meant, or thought, or saw.

In summary, the principle of noncontradiction, which is the essential expression of reason as hard or forbidding, has three tiers: (*a*) the rule that "everything is what it is, and not another thing," as applied to all possible propositional *matters;* (*b*) the same rule applied to judgment itself, which to be what it is requires recognition of stable differences within itself (whether that is an absolute or only relative stability); and (*c*) the same rule applied to communication, which must be "positive." Everything we call fallacy stems from failure to respect these rules. The three tiers have been given in ascending order of priority. Insofar as there is relationship between them in addition to their autonomy, everything must remain just what it is *so that* judgments may be just what they are *so that* communication may take place. This ordering is implied by the absolute priority of relationship.

(b) Hard Reason: Necessitating Ground

Noncontradiction is the minimally necessary condition of reasonableness. Those who think that the essence of the universe can be grasped in such a way that all possible judgments would be analytically derivable from a true concept of the whole may also think that noncontradiction is at the same time the maximally necessary condition. Even on this scenario, however, one truth remains undetermined, namely, why the world is the way it is. To handle this question, if for no other reason, the additional principle of sufficient ground must be brought in. But the principle of sufficient ground is subject to two interpretations, one that places it on the side of necessary reason and one which does not; therefore, we should call it the principle of *necessitating* ground when it is viewed under the aspect of necessity. A sufficient ground need not be necessitating.[8] For clarity's sake we must note that the question of necessitating ground is not precisely "Why is X the way it is?" but "Why does X have to be the way it is?"

The requirement for necessary determination of an outcome by reason—ideally the conclusion of a judgment, though often directly an action—is relative to what needs to be determined. Consider the instance of asking one's way. If while traveling to Waterloo you stop at a fork to ask me which road to take, a vague gesture from me toward both of the possible roads fails to determine your decision. Since I have presumed to speak to the question instead of confessing ignorance, my answer is unreasonable. But a gesture, no matter how far it is from pointing directly to one of the roads, is perfectly determining of your choice if it leaves no doubt in your mind which one of the roads I am indicating. A wave in the general direction of the south will get you on the south road. This is a necessitating ground for taking the south road insofar as you have placed yourself under my guidance.

You wanted me to determine your choice, and I did. (It would be a different case if we discussed the relative merits of the two roads so that you could make your own decision. Then the option would be exercised within your own thinking as to whether you wanted your decision to be the necessitated outcome of a certain calculation of the factors I presented, or a spontaneous response to them.)

We sometimes need and more often delight in painting ourselves into corners with the use of necessitating grounds. It means we will not have to decide freely. Often it is the only means of bringing about agreement between parties who would otherwise exercise their options of judgment differently; and often it is very important to reach agreement.

It seems that fully to understand why a factual event *had* to take place, one must have an insight into the nature of the event and its causes that makes it possible to assert that this nature is *contradicted* if the event does not follow from its causes. The stone released at a short distance from the earth *must* fall because we *understand* both stone and earth as mass, and mass as attractive. If one is then driven back to ask why *all* these things are as they are, one is stuck without a necessarily determined answer; lacking evidence of the cause of everything, one does not contradict the nature of everything if one conceives it not to exist. The ontological argument tries to help by establishing a necessarily existing cause of all, but even this move cannot establish the necessity of things being *as* they are— the more interesting point, after all—without the help of Leibniz's nearly naked leap of faith to the notion of the "best of all possible worlds," which is made solely to protect the principle of sufficient reason![9]

The principle of necessitating ground, as opposed to a sweeter principle of sufficiency that remains to be described, is only an auxiliary to the principle of noncontradiction in the sense that it amounts to the demand that we be brought to a point of adequate, clear, and distinct knowledge where we can judge of noncontradiction. Necessity comes only from this judgment. What we call "causal necessity" presupposes a scheme of events so defined that it is contradictory to posit an effect without its cause; the causal investigations of empirical science simply fit as many phenomena as possible into such a scheme, lending them, by grace of mathematics, so much determinacy that they become necessary or impossible according to the manifest consistency of their scientific forms with the form of their causal law context. The search for a cause, inspired by the principle of necessary ground, is really a search for a scheme in which the principle of noncontradiction will hold.

The realm of the to-be-rectified—the too-vague, too-abstract, too-partial, and so forth—stretches far beyond the area where we encounter actual fallacies or can smoke them out, and thus far beyond the rule of necessity. In every case we need to attain *enough* determination of thought or action for an occasion. Once the occasion defines what is "enough," it becomes unreasonable to offer or settle for less. If, however, we cut ourselves loose from the ideal of necessity, we are adrift with the question, How much and what kind of determination of thought, on such-and-such an occasion and then on such-and-such another, *may* serve? To put ourselves in a position to answer, we must now shift our view to sweet reason.

(c) Sweet Reason: Sufficient Ground and Adequate Presentation

Contradiction, overt or implicit, is the sin of commission against reason. There are also sins of omission, of insufficiency, which only become evident once we recognize that spirit is the primary exigency for reason, reason's reason. The work of reason as of any spirit is to realize relationship. The others must not only not be rebuffed by contradiction, they must be drawn in somehow, given a place to stand as themselves and, where the alternative is present, as the most flourishing editions of themselves. The principle is one of invitation and consequent hospitality. It applies (subordinately) to the beings about which we make claims as well as (superordinately) to each other; it calls on us to perceive and conceive clearly, for example, for the sheer maximization of the *standing* of the beings we face, and not only to be clear *enough* about them so as to avoid disrespecting them or sabotaging judgment and discourse. But of prior importance are the rule that the matter of a claim should be as supportive as possible of the ones who are expected to agree with it (presenting them with the most ample opportunities of seeing for themselves what is claimed to be true), and the rule that the form of a claim, that is, how it is made, should be as inviting as possible by virtue of its affirmation of its audience.

We come to the principle of "sufficient" reason, properly speaking, when we examine the material aspect of sweet reasonableness. Our first inclination may be to say that the "sufficiency" of grounds for a judgment or action must be either a logical sufficiency, necessitating by virtue of obedience to the principle of noncontradiction, or a psychological sufficiency, necessitating according to what factually causes a subject to decide. It seems that what is "enough" for *you* to decide, if by "you" we mean no more than you, a single subject, is "subjective," and the only way to account for it is psychologically. But there are two mistakes in jumping to this conclusion. One is the dismissal of a "You" to a postlogical, empirical position, when the true position of the You as You is prelogical and spiritual. I cannot understand *you* as a matter of fact and possible object of manipulative persuasion because I am judged by you as a You. You cannot belong entirely to the matter of my claims, or even to the matter of my judgments concerning my own claims, because you define their form. Therefore what is "enough" for you is an absolute demand of reason as I face you even though it may be much less than the principle of noncontradiction would require. The second mistake is the assumption that no other ground exists besides the logical-necessitarian and the "subjective" or empirical. Spirits form this other ground. (Actually, it is misleading to represent three grounds here, since logic and facts both have spiritual extension when they serve as reasons.)

Let us now think with the aid of an example how a reason that does not even tend toward necessity can still work as a reason.

A girl walks past a crowd of her schoolmates playing dodgeball. "Janet," they cry, "come play with us!" Her inclination is not to. "Why should I?" she says. "It's fun," one of the girls replies, flinging the ball. Another girl inside the circle jumps and laughs, and says, "Come on, it's fun!"

One *could* work up the argument of the dodgeball players into syllogisms.

Theoretical: People always want to have fun.

Janet is a person.

Therefore Janet always wants to have fun.

Practical: Janet always wants to have fun.

Playing dodgeball is the presently available way of having fun.

Therefore Janet should now play dodgeball.

All the premises require further syllogized rationalization, if we want to be strict, but let us leave it at these. Rationalization of that sort is at any rate beside the point, because Janet's friends are not trying to make her play, they are inviting her to, giving an inviting reason. The actual syllogism, if there is one, could be represented thus:

Want to have fun? (Presumably she does.)

This dodgeball game is fun.

Therefore come play dodgeball.

To make this syllogism conform to the necessitarian model, we have to change it in several ways that violate the sense of the invitation. We have to make the major premise the hypothetical assertion (not a question) that Janet wants fun; the conclusion, play dodgeball, would then follow *if* she wants to have fun. But they are neither telling her to have fun nor explicitly placing a choice before her (although a choice *is* before her and she remains at liberty to choose). They are calling upon her, beckoning her to have fun. Next, we find that the minor premise is not restrictive enough to produce the conclusion. Dodgeball must be presented as the best or only way of having fun at the moment, and there is no attempt to do that. Finally, the "conclusion" was not offered as such. Though they reasoned with Janet, they did not claim that dodgeball is played for a reason. The "therefore" is misleading. Rather than retrojecting an argument that would lead to the conclusion, "Come play dodgeball," they have articulated the very playing of dodgeball, dilated the game so as to admit Janet if she will come, by affirming that it is fun. "Fun" stands as a universal to the particular of the game of dodgeball, so there is a relation like that of major premise to minor. But what has actually happened is that the particular has been expanded into the universal, rather than subsumed under a separately posited universal principle, in order to become sufficient for Janet. It is reasonable to say "It's fun!" because this re-represents the game as sufficiently inviting *in itself* to want to play. (We could as well call dodgeball the middle term between Janet and fun as call fun the middle term between Janet and dodgeball.)

The girls "reasoned" because they went to some trouble to give Janet better ground on which to accept their claim. But reasoning means giving reason. Does Janet now *have* reason to play? One way to schematize her decision is to make her evaluate the empirical probabilities that the girls are as happy as they seem to be and that she will become happier than she could otherwise be by doing the same things that they do. Then she would turn and ask herself whether she wants to be happy at that moment. If she did, she would proceed to play. But actually Janet has the intention of her schoolmates as her most important reason, and without having to establish the intention by a psychological judgment, since it *meets* her. She has not been left alone to make the judgment all by herself; they have projected their own having-fun toward her as a sharable aim. Now why, one might ask, should she believe that what is fun for them is *really* fun, fun for her too, simply because they have presumed to include her in their fun? If she is disinclined to play, why should they be right that playing dodgeball is the thing to do even for her? In other words, what authority does intention as such have in an argument?

There are at least three different ways in which a met intention can count of itself as a sufficient ground for joining or responding appropriately to it. For one, any intention is, just in being met, a self-presentation of an other and a spirit-proposing move. The others and the spirits in which one can be together with them are what is unquestionably good, and the primordial good reasons are to respect and maximize the existence of others. Not invariably, but quite often, the evident way to do that is to join with others in a spirit of their proposing. Second, when a question can be raised as to which of different possible intentions will best respect or maximize the existence of oneself or the others, there must be an initial presumption in favor of a group (like Janet's schoolmates) insofar as they exhibit a spiritual fait accompli. There may be a better spirit than the monolithic dodgeball spirit—perhaps Janet could share with them her vision of a world in which some play dodgeball while others sit under trees reading poetry by themselves—but to refrain only out of sullen solitariness cannot be a superior reason for Janet, even though *we* might be able to think of a reason why she needs to be alone. And we may add to the presumption in favor of a group as such a presumption in favor of a more inclusive group, since the spiritual fait accompli demonstrates in that case an all-the-more impressive ability to accommodate individual intentions.

Third, an intention-affirming intention must have presumptive authority against an intention-negating one. (This is an example of the reason of "surplus" that will be treated in the next section.) The buoyancy of the dodgeball players is a good reason to join them. Janet's sullenness, an intentional constriction that shrinks her existence, demands of itself—abstracting, of course, from many other factors that might shape the right way to approach her—that we change her mood if we can.

With these considerations we have entered the sphere of normative reason proper, which is the direct, explicit norming of intentional relationships according to formulable standards of sufficient rightness. There was nothing factual in the argument directed to Janet to play dodgeball, unless the players' demonstrated intention with its felicity (jumping and laughing) is treated as the "fact" in the case. In a direct norming argument the only factual premises can be intentional "facts" such as these. Yet that sort of fact was good ground for Janet to stand on; it looked as though it would support her all right if she chose to take her next step there.

The fun of dodgeball is the "matter" of the schoolgirls' claim, but the example well shows how difficult it can be to keep "matter" and "form" apart, since the infectious enthusiasm of the way in which the claim is made is part of the demonstrandum. A different example will illustrate how the form of a claim, in evident distinction from its matter, can be reasonably adequate to it. Suppose I want to tell you that Monica does not like you even though you think she is your friend. The claim is, "Monica does not like you." But there are more and less reasonable ways of presenting it. One the one hand, I may choose from a range of sparer or fuller intimations of the matter of the claim, everything from merely raising an eyebrow when you say you and Monica certainly are getting along well to a precise statement that she finds your sense of humor revolting. Note that it is not necessarily the fullest statement possible that will put you in the best position to know the truth of the claim for yourself. Then I may choose from a range of "airs" in telling you that will differently affect your appropriation of the message. I may tell you in such a solemn and doleful way that you will think you are worthless, or in such an offhand way that you will feel that Monica never mattered very much to you, anyway. Since it is false both that you are worthless and that Monica does not matter very much to you, these are, formally, relatively unreasonable ways of telling you she does not like you—"formally," because the truth and falsity in question belongs to your relationship to the truth about whether Monica likes you, rather than to the content of the immediate claim. The reasonable way is the one that puts you in the soundest position, whether that be a matter of marshaling the strength to say good-bye to Monica or of seeing what you can do to get back in her good graces.

It is loading too much onto reason to say that one is always unreasonable to the precise extent that one could have made a claim in a more other-affirming manner.

Reason is not the same as tact. Two persons equally intelligent and benevolent will not do equally well in communicating. Reason comes into it only when a possible choice looms between alternatives; without the facing of alternatives the issue of justification does not arise. If I *know* that I could tell you how Monica feels about you in unequally affirming ways, it is unreasonable of me to choose the less affirming. It is unreasonable, and not merely nasty, because it keeps you at a greater distance from truth and partnership with me.

A closing look at the reasonable general principle of fairness—like to like, like from like, all intenders prima facie alike—will illustrate sweet sufficiency and its ambiguities from another angle.

The *spirit* of fairness is a mode of togetherness for intenders. If I propose to deal with you fairly, I am approaching you in a way that affords both of us a tenable and desirable position; such is the formal reasonableness of the deal. But there is also the "fair deal" itself that is materially reasonable, which you or I can reflect on apart from our actual positioning with respect to each other in the dealing of the deal. Constituting this fair deal materially fair is the *principle* of fairness which, unlike the spirit, can be grasped by each of us in reflection. Now, the principle of fairness in itself is a hard constraint on reflection about the possibility of dealing with others, since no other universally acceptable principle of dealing can be conceived. The problem of interintentional regulation is resolved only when interintentional equilibrium is attained: that is fairness. However, the principle of fairness is not hard enough by itself to impose on any reflective subject the *problem* of interintentional regulation. Numerous philosophical assaults on egoism, two of which we will shortly consider (in section 4.5), have failed to conquer it. It does not seem to be necessary to occupy the standpoint in which the principle of fairness is necessary.

The spirit of fairness, on the other hand, is originally an opening to good common ground. It is the opportunity to realize a situation in which the principle can be applied. The fair deal I offer you is sweetly reasonable before there is anything of constraint about it. Constraint will later guard against distortions of the deal.[10]

(d) Sweet Reason: Surplus (Convergence and Fecundity)

Sweet reason furnishes a place to stand, and when it can, a better place to stand, a place to flourish.

Under the aspect of surplus, spiritual demands appear in the first place as opportunities, bonuses to seize rather than shortfalls to avoid. One gives reasons for seizing them in a second moment of turning around and contemplating the alternative of not having done so, which then would be a shortfall, so that only the chosen course was right enough. In that sense reason is always "hard" and constraining. But it should be recognized that the constraining aspect can be the correlate of an initially permissive aspect. One's zeal for a more can precede one's fear of a less, and one can give grounds for believing or doing something on this basis. Janet's friends genuinely offer her the fun of dodgeball; it would be perverse to interpret their reasoning as prospective reprobation of the alternative of not taking them up on their offer. Insofar as they reasoned with her they necessarily gave her a position that could be justified, but the reasoning in that case was an approving that was not yet a justifying.

Hume's dictum that reason is the slave of the passions is a skewed but not wholly wrong way of saying that reason is a tool of intention and that it exists in an interintentional context.[11] Praise Hume for at least pointing to this truth. By holding it in view we can understand not only the basic structures of hard reason, which reflect the conditions of the possibility of intending at all; and not only the one structure of sweet reason, the principle of sufficient ground, which most resembles hard reason; but also the specifically sweetest forms of reason, which might together be called the reasons of *surplus* insofar as they make a proposition right enough by linking it to intentional rewards in excess of what was required of intention or what it looked for. This felicitation of intention counts as reason when it occurs as an explicitated object of affirmation or action, insofar as it leads to the fundamental goods and thus is nonarbitrary. By contrast, in the implicit effect of, say, a work of art, there is a surplus of intentional amplitude without any "reasoning"—although, for *this* reason, it is a good thing to experience it, and therefore in the absence of countervailing considerations one should experience it.

The qualification "insofar as it leads to the fundamental goods" must be enforced to prevent confusion between sweetly reasonable surplus and other types of intentional excess or gratification. We do not want to say that it is reasonable for a paranoiac to move to a certain foreign country where his suspicions will be reinforced constantly by people looking at him strangely. Nor do we want to admit that someone who can numerologically transform her best friend's name into the figure "666" therefore has reason to believe that her friend is the Devil, simply because this coincidence was unlooked for. Nevertheless, amplification and felicitation of intention are good as such. The paranoiac's problem is that his paranoia constricts his intention too narrowly. The numerologist's problem is that the coincidence she has discovered is paltry in comparison with the massive coherencies of nature, history, and her personal life that contradict her claim.

Further distinctions must be drawn. An investigator who notices that things having trait A in common also tend to have trait B believes reasonably that trait B is characteristic of them, not because it is sweeter to believe so, but because a phenomenon has emerged with that shape. Observed coincidence that has the force of induction comes under hard reason, not sweet, since it is made a ground of belief or action so as not to violate the knowable. On the other hand, any scientist who believes that all phenomena available for study will turn out to conform to coherent patterns does not have that belief coerced by an induction. As a heuristic principle, rather than a thesis about nature, the belief that further coherencies among phenomena always remain to be found is sweetly reasonable. A reductionistic determinism that believes that some coherencies can eventually be dismissed for the sake of expanding others is as unreasonable in this respect as is the lazy acceptance of chance. Note that the justification of a heuristic principle is more than "pragmatic," if "pragmatic" refers only prospectively to the results that might be gained by making an assumption; a heuristic assumption has an immediate and primary justification in making us more curious and energetic.

In the range of "reason" we have to do only with moves that are right enough, and not with those that are more than sufficiently right, except when the choice of the more-than-sufficiently-right becomes the only right-enough choice. On your birthday the right thing for me to do is to give you a present, if I am your close friend or kin. It is reasonable of me to give you something of moderate cost likely to please you and, other things being equal, unreasonable not to. But suppose it is possible to give you something expensive that I know will especially please you. It would probably be quite nice to do that, you might say, but not specifically *reasonable*. Yet if I had a *choice* between pleasing you more and pleasing you less, uncomplicated by any other desiderata, the reasonable choice must be to please you more. That choice would not be arbitrary. In this claim for "more" we meet the infinity of the original demand of the other to flourish and the consequent instability of any fixed standard of sufficient rightness, which is always liable to be displaced by something righter.

Philosophical doctrines that depend on this sort of justification include the generous-God theology of Plato and Neoplatonism, paralleled by the "how much more" reasoning of the apostle Paul; Leibniz' principle of sufficient ground, together with the "best of all possible worlds" that it leads to; and Levinas' version of the Cartesian idea of the Infinite, "the thought that thinks more than it can think," which is worth remark in this connection.[12] It is not reasonable according to the theoretical requirement of adequation between thought and thing. But as both Descartes and Levinas argue, the inadequacy of thought to the Infinite does not count as a privation of the sort that reason is bound to disapprove of; it is rather a surplus of a sort that reason should glory in. Descartes claims that he conceives of God more clearly and distinctly than anything else, which is an inaccurate way of putting the point that it is to an even greater degree impossible to doubt God's reality than to doubt his own.[13] He is dazzled by brightness rather than defeated by darkness. But Levinas means to criticize the Augustinian appetite for Being that Descartes also represents. The Other is for him not something overwhelming the faculty of knowledge, but something that eludes it. Still, the import of the Other for the life of the self is positive. Living with and toward the Other is an absolute adventure.[14]

Now, the notion of adventure is an enticement, even for reason within a narrower horizon than the one we have envisioned. It is a kind of absolute promise of "more"—having more happen to one, finding more, getting more. There is an innate avidity in intention, from which spring not only the unattractive forms of ordinary greed but also romantic *Sehnsucht* and divine discontent with the world as it is. Sweet reason speaks to this avidity and lures it on but in the end tricks it by placing spiritual conditions on it, so that it becomes zeal for the others and for what is shared with them. Levinas' promise of an idea of the Infinite—a promise that Hegel also makes, with very different results—suggests to thought that it can possess just what it always wanted, an unquestionable relationship with exteriority. And this relationship is delivered, but as the unknowable: justice instead of a truth. Levinas' promise of adventure takes the essential move of intention, to aim at others and stretch toward them, and then perfects it into the aimingest aim and stretchingest stretch, a move that keeps going outward without ever heading back for home.[15] This is what one was bound for from the moment one's attention was caught by the others.

The two basic forms of justification by intentional surplus correspond to the two demands of the spiritual concrete, that for the peaceful conservation of plurality and that for its heightening via the amplification of intentions in relationship. They are, respectively, the *convergence* of different factors which all support a proposition, and the *fecundity* of a proposition in generating other supportable ones. Both are illustrated by the dodgeball option.

We find, first, convergence between the testimonies of two of the players. Janet was given good reason to play by the first girl who said it was fun. Then she was given better reason when the second girl also said it was fun. She had better reason in this sense not from the increased probability of fun brought about by a fuller induction of dodgeball players, but rather from the demonstrated capacity of the proposition to accommodate diverse intentions. The proposition becomes a fuller meeting between intentions which as such is reasonable to turn toward. We touched on this earlier in connection with the presumptive authority of a group's evident spirit; now we are regarding Janet only indirectly as a prospective member of that group but directly as a knower, one whose intentions (correlated with all actual and possible others) are, in general, better assorted when they meet, with the requisite harmony, a maximum of other intentions. This is a reflection within the subject of the positive condition of peace, which the subject should be oriented toward and attuned with.

In the second place, Janet should find the invitation approvable because of the fecundity of the action of joining the game, from which all manner of unforeseen thrills and meetings will follow. If she had a principle of joining every game she came upon, that principle would be sweetly reasonable by virtue of its fecundity in addition to its prudential reasonableness in delivering desired, specified goods. Hard practical reason would make the game a means to an end. Sweet reason makes it an end with further ends growing out of it. We can imagine a case where the two reasons pull in different directions, and one outweighs the other. Say a man is standing on a faint path deep in a forest, and his reason is, "You never know who you might meet here." Almost any way we specify who is actually available to be met, we will conclude that his spot is an unreasonable choice; for that matter, according to almost any way we specify how people should spend their time this will be found an unreasonable pastime. And yet something is right about what he does. What is right about it is that he has actually put himself in a position where a new, unforeseen meeting might occur. You never know. To stand on a busier path would probably be more sweetly reasonable as well as more "practical," but to stand ill-advisedly in the middle of the forest is not totally devoid of reasonableness. The truth actually goes further than that. While the man standing in the forest is only marginally reasonable, looked at in one way, he makes a positive impression on us at the same time because of his very foolishness, minding us of "divine simplicity." What we see in him is a purity of sweet reason uncomplicated by anything of the intelligent or prudential. Let us hold him before us to consider wherein lies the fascinating excellence and superiority of sweet reason in comparison with hard.

When one is given a sweet reason, one is not made to believe or do something, one is allowed to. It counts as a bonus, a cause for rejoicing. One expands from this floor into new space rather than contracting to fit under hard reason's ceiling. Therefore, the prospects of the man in the forest of meeting someone, miserable as they are, expand him, in a sense infinitely, because he has (foolishly) taken himself out from under the ceiling of the rules by which we limit what is worth doing. Moreover, since his action is not coerced, he can own it as his. His responsibility does not annul his individuality, for he freely becomes the distinctive individual that he is by leaping forward to specific opportunities he finds life offering him. He is spontaneous but not arbitrary. *Per contra,* those who hold to a necessitarian conception of reason are committed to the unacceptable view that exactly insofar as individuals are reasonable they are swallowed up in the universal, tamed by logic, and made indistinguishable from each other. The reason of the man in the forest creeps out of the clutches of the universal. There is a universal in it, else it would not be reason; he can match his action to a rule that justifies it; but it is a rule he has negotiated directly with life and held subordinate to himself and life. Sweet reason vindicates the priority of the individual (*as* an individual in relationship with certain others) to the universal, reminding us of the difference between togetherness and unity.

A sweet reason is the only kind one can give to an other in which the otherness of the other is directly affirmed. When the girls urge Janet to play dodgeball by saying "It's fun," they lay the proposal before her to accept or reject. This makes them vulnerable, as one properly is before an other. They open themselves to her irrefutable contradiction at the same time that they open a possibility up to her; if she says "No, it's dumb," that could spoil the game. A network of reasoning created in this way is quite a fragile one inasmuch as the assent of all parties to it, which is absolutely contingent in any case, *appears as* contingent, whereas the network of logic requires an obedience from all parties that appears as necessary. Assent arises in joy, while obedience is exacted. The whole being pours into assent, while nothing is yielded to that which exacts except that which is exacted. And intention cannot be exacted. Freedom is its essence in the self, and imponderability is its essence in the other. So the only way in which intention, the *how* of thinking, saying, and doing, can be directly normed is by sweet reason.

4.5 The Limits of Intentional Grounding Arguments

What sweet reason dares to do has also been tried by foundationalist and transcendental arguments. The differences and similarities among these approaches should be brought out.

A foundationalist argument is one that strictly derives a norm from a rationally unassailable first principle. The classic modern example would be Descartes' amassing of a system of knowledge based on indubitable intuitions. A "transcendental" argument is one that tries to determine the otherwise inderterminable margins of what is known by establishing which determinations of the unknowable are presupposed by the ways in which we necessarily determine the knowable.[16] The prototype of modern transcendental arguments is Kant's. If (says Kant) scientific judgments are valid in the way that they must be if there is to be any such thing as objective knowledge, then experience must be structured a priori according to the form of subjectivity itself. Kant also offers a moral transcendental argument. The sort of validity that we must ascribe to our moral judgments if we are to respect their sense presupposes their rootage in the universalizing legislation of free practical reason.

These are not absolutely different types of argument. There is only a difference in the evidentiary standing granted the ultimate norm. What transcendentalists arrive at becomes, for purposes of justification, their foundation; while foundationalists may (like Alan Gewirth) inquire their way toward the foundations by asking what is presupposed by ordinary thought or practice.

As has already been made clear in our discussion of the concrete, we deny the availability of the sort of basis for certainty that foundationalism seeks. But since our proposal rests on the claim of an unsurpassable and in that sense "fundamental" *problem*, there may yet be affinities to discover between the arguments available to us and those of foundationalism. We must also be partly at odds with transcendentalism, for although we will in due course consider arguments that lead from acknowledged meanings of ordinary experience to the "primary affirmations" concerning the spiritual that best make sense of these (Chapter 5), neither they nor the larger argument of the essay to which they contribute is a proper transcendental argument. Our starting point is the transcendental argument's ending point, and what is concrete for us is for the transcendental argument only derived. But in spite of this difference of approach, we are interested in the same problem that transcendental arguments handle, namely, how to relate the indeterminable to the determinable—conscious that the meaning or truth of the determinable depends on the relation.

The prime indeterminable, we have seen, is intention itself. We confront its indeterminability when we try to answer a question like "Why be moral?" which concedes a system of reasoning standards within morality but demands a determination of intention, a reason, to reason in that way. The question "Why be moral?" seems to be genuinely open, unlike the spurious question "Why be rational?" which immediately contradicts itself in asking for a reason. It seems that rational amoralists could exist, that is, people who think and communicate as validly as anyone else but are not thereby constrained to assent to moral principles or aims. (It also seems that there can be rational skeptics, but since amoralists more directly make a problem of relationships with others, we will confine our attention to them.) One way of dealing with amoralists, which has much to recommend it because of the naturalistic errors it avoids, is to leave them alone. They may be granted an invulnerable position on the far side of the "is"–"ought" gap, where "oughts" are affirmed and denied without argumentative footing in any "is" the adequate observation of which would force agreement. To the extent that agreement can be reached by demanding consistency among prescribed "oughts," they still appear to be free to refuse to play the moral language game. But rational amoralists would necessarily be converted to morality if their very rationality could be shown to be complicit with a moral principle, so that to deny the one would be to deny the other. One way to do this is to derive a supreme moral principle from a conception of practical rationality. Another way is to show that a supreme moral principle is presuppositionally accepted in any exercise of reasoning—in other words, to argue transcendentally from actual reasoning to a moral principle as the condition of its possibility. We will let the recent work of Alan Gewirth and Karl-Otto Apel represent these alternatives.[17]

(a) Foundationalism: Gewirth

According to Gewirth in *Reason and Morality*, all beings who envision and act for ends necessarily intend that they be *free* and *able* to act, that is, that the conditions of the possibility of action be met for them, regardless of which particular ends they choose or actions they would like to undertake.[18] When this intention takes into account others who might not respect one's freedom and well-being as an agent, it becomes a demand that they do. But the demand is not arbitrary. It is not rooted in private inclination, but in an intention that any agent qua agent must have. Now a nonarbitrary demand is properly called a "right," and all agents thus ascribe to themselves the right to freedom and well-being as agents. But since they ascribe this right to themselves in virtue of their agenthood, they cannot without contradiction refrain from granting it to other agents, for any other agent possesses precisely the same generic characteristics of agency that furnished grounds for the right in the first place. On the basis of this reasoning Gewirth arrives at a substantive moral principle, a categorical obligation to regard the interests of others favorably, which he calls the Principle of Generic Consistency: "Act in accord with the generic rights of your recipients as well as yourself." [19]

Gewirth employs a "dialectically necessary" method.[20] On the one hand its point of departure is given in the audience's recognition of the canons of inductive and deductive logic and the empirical phenomenon of purposiveness, but on the other hand it necessarily commits them to a supreme moral principle once the starting point is granted. Further, the starting point contains the contingent factual *truth* of agency and its conditions, which *theoretically* justifies "ought"-propositions in a way commonly thought impossible. Inasmuch as anyone with whom we can reason is in fact a rational agent, and the facts of agency appear to be as Gewirth represents them, his argument is quite strong.

The most questionable steps in the argument are the interpretation of the agent's necessary interest in the conditions of purposive action as a "demand" and then of the demand as a "right." The "right" is the hardest to swallow, because it depends on an allegedly nonmoral practical prescription that anything that is intended "ought" to happen, that any good one necessarily pursues (such as the necessary conditions of agency as such) one "must" bring about or have brought about, and that this hard "must" just means that one has a nonmoral "right" to the good. Let us pause to examine Gewirth's odd use of "right" in a prudential sense. He argues that if one denies the statement "I have rights to freedom and well-being," one must also deny the proposition that "All other persons ought at least to refrain from interfering with my freedom and well-being." That means that one accepts the proposition "It is *permissible* for others to interfere with my freedom and well-being." But this is incompatible with the belief, already shown to be inescapable, that one's own freedom and well-being as an agent are necessary goods.[21]

It does seem correct to say that if we have gotten as far as talking about what is and is not permissible for other people to do with regard to me, it would be irrational for me to give them permission to act against my necessary interests. We could put the same point a little differently by saying that once talk of rights (in the usual moral sense) exists, then it would be absurd to overlook the necessary goods of agency as objects of rights. But have we actually gotten this far in a prudential practical reckoning? Do the concepts of permission and right have any sense in a purely prudential framework? They do not if we interpret "prudence" egoistically. But Gewirth rules this out in claiming that I can make prudential prescriptions to others; and we now realize that anyone who prescribes to another is a *spiritual* being and that, whether or not "spiritual" existence entails "moral" existence, the standard interpretation of the "prudential" point of view as purely self-regarding is inadequate. If, therefore, Gewirth is explicating a nonmoral point of view that leads through universalization to a moral one, this nonmoral perspective is already one in which people are essentially concerned with each other's intentions, and where, therefore, talk of permission and right has meaning. But this also means that the question has been begged as to what consideration is sufficient to motivate an out-and-out egoist to give standing of any sort to others. Concern for the *intentions* of others, not just for their actions regarded like natural events, is built into Gewirth's concept of rationality, and from regarding them as intenders we may be led to regard them as havers of interests, simply through reflection on the conditions of agency.

Not even so much as a "demand" can be intelligibly asserted unless relationships are already in place. Indeed, self-acknowledged "rational agents" already regard themselves as some among others who all *share* in the transpersonal concept of agency. To see you as deserving of the same consideration that I demand because you also are an agent, I must already have detached from myself the concept of agency so that it is transferable to you. My view must be "objective" or "impersonal" to that extent. Not only that: the full concept of agency is already inter-agentic, and a purely selfish agency of the sort Gewirth wants to start with (to have the strongest possible argumentative position) is an artificial abstraction from it—not really where any agent is, but a way of conceding something to agents with whom one is arguing. Of course, Gewirth can admit that a system of interpersonal cognizance must already be in place if "rationality" exists but then go on to claim that he has succeeded where others have failed in deriving a specifically moral principle from the implications of rational agency as such by binding rationality as closely to empirical agency as he has. However, even if we grant that his conception of morality follows from his conception of rationality, that may simply redirect our interest to the derivation or grounding of rationality, which has the crucial features (for Gewirth's purposes) already loaded into it. Which points to an investigation like our own.

The crucial question for us, and the fascinating aspect of all arguments of this sort, is, Has Gewirth managed to norm intention by hard reason? He has caught agents in a double trap: they have to acknowledge the generic properties and presuppositions of their intending, which are independent of their specific aims, and they have to respect generic agency wherever they find it on pain of inconsistency. They transcend themselves willy-nilly first into the concept of agency and second toward the others to whom the concept applies.

It is a fact that intention exists. It is also true that logical relations exist between intentions so that they can contradict each other—for example, by willing an end but not the necessary means to it. It seems to be true, further, that once a person is committed to "rationality" as a matter of *subjective* consistency in judgments, that subjective order can only by an unusual effort of dissociation be kept nonobjective; once I see myself as "an agent" merely for the sake of planning my own life, it is quite difficult not to see you as "an agent" too. That implies that I can hardly fail to see you as having necessary interests just as I do. But the generalization that unifies my agency and its necessary interests with yours is not the same as the generalization "one" that unifies "I" and "you," in a judgment like "One ought to respect the necessary interests of agents." The difference is masked in Gewirth's argument by the way he sticks with the concept of "an agent"; if we state it perspicuously, the mistake will appear.

(1) I ought to respect the necessary conditions of my purposive action for the sole and sufficient reason that I am an agent.

(2) You are also an agent.

(3) Therefore you also have sufficient reason to respect the necessary conditions of your purposive action.

(4) The necessary conditions of my purposive action are the same as those of yours.

(5) Therefore, each of us has sufficient reason to respect the other's necessary conditions of purposive action.

But step 4 is false as it stands. The necessary conditions of my purposive action include, to name but one thing, a regular influx of food to my address, while you need something to eat at your address. What is required for the argument is that we interpret "necessary conditions" *generically*. Gewirth thinks that my conditions, if defined as my "freedom and well-being as an agent," are identical with your conditions if they are also generically defined. He would say that the generic definition is motivated in the first place not by the search for something common between agents, but by the search for the truly necessary condition of the individual's agency; for no particular thing is more than a contingent condition of my agency. But although it is true that we must conceive the conditions of my agency as a generic principle in order for them to be necessary, it remains true at the same time that the principle is concretely specified for me *and is necessary only because it is so specified*. I need food at my address not because of anything about the food, but because I would otherwise starve and fail of all my purposes; it is the principle that makes the food necessary to the contingent extent that it is necessary; but the principle is nothing without something to make necessary. Nor could you excuse yourself for preventing me from eating by saying, "You know, it's not anything specific like food that you necessarily require to act, but only your generic freedom and well-being as an agent." And what is made necessary is always something in *my* circumstances. Though we define the conditions generally, they always amount to specific conditions that tie them to me rather than to you, or to you rather than to me. Therefore, the generalization of the necessary conditions of action does not bridge the gap between *my* freedom and well-being as an agent and *yours*. What would agency matter to me if it were not mine? The "necessary" conditions are still necessary to *me* or to *you*, but not yet to "one." [22]

The generic concept that embraces I and You is agency. But it does not appear that any syllogism can require individuals so to identify with the concept of agency that the specifying, distinguishing features of their own agency are suspended, so that they respect the interests of agency as such rather than their personal interests. Gewirth thus requires from the start more good will toward reason than minimally rational amoralists would be obliged to have. In order to address the problem of eliciting this good will by reasoning, it is necessary to complement Gewirth's hard inferences from the nature of purposive action with some sort of mediation of separate purposivenesses, or intentions. That I will is one great fact, but that the others will in imponderable relationship with my will is a second great problematic "fact" that overshadows the first without offering the possibility of justification by correspondence with observable fact that the first does. We are not yet shown the reasoning by which You and I can invite each other to go together as "one" and do what "one" ought to do; there is no unchallengeable "foundation" in which this "one-ness" is already incorporated. And yet simply to accept the ordinary discourse in which the term "one" appears would be arbitrary and would not help us to understand, criticize, and repair breakdowns in this discourse.

Let us now investigate the transcendental approach.

(b) Transcendentalism: Apel

Apel's thought is in part a response to the "critical rationalist" school's denial of the possibility of fundamentally grounding any truth or principle.[23] According to Karl Popper and Hans Albert, the essential rational attitude is one that is ready to doubt everything and remains open to revision, not one that justifies itself so as to be impervious to correction. The appeal to indubitable evidence is always a "dogma" because such evidence can always be doubted. The will to truth is distinct from the will to certainty; it is adventurous. But the decision to be rational is therefore an irrational act, an ungrounded act of "faith." Since, however, the critical rationalists put the idea of criticism in place of the idea of fundamental grounding, rationality or reasonableness is constituted by the fallibilist principle, and the decision to adhere to it is the primordial reasonable act.

Apel points out against this view that criticism itself must be grounded somehow if it is to have any sense and not be an idle or "paper" doubt. Thus although a Cartesian reliance on indubitable evidences robs the principle of criticism of its right, an unbounded criticism undercuts itself. The solution is to allocate to the grounding principle of evidence and the principle of criticism their proper places as interwoven moments of rational inquiry. But this must be done from a *transcendental* perspective, that is, by establishing the conditions of the possibility of such a thing as rational inquiry; and these inhere in the practice of a language-using community (which fact inspires Apel's program of a "transcendental pragmatics of language"). From this perspective we can understand both why individuals have to have some basis in their own experience, some evidence, for proposing or doubting anything, and why no individual's evidence may be allowed the absolute standing that intuitional foundationalists have claimed for their intuitions. One person's evidence as such is not evidence for another. It becomes public evidence only in being formulated as a proposition and has validity only insofar as standards of validity are in place as conventions of the public language-game. The community, not the individual, ultimately decides what is true and right, and so any proposition must be in principle falsifiable; it cannot be certainly true in advance of being evaluated by the others.

The virtual fallibility of all propositions, even transcendental philosophical ones, cannot be taken, however, to rule out the need for a fundamental grounding, according to Apel. For one can criticize only if there is something held not open to criticism, be it only the criticism principle. Apel therefore asks: What are the uncriticizable conditions of the possibility of intersubjectively valid philosophical criticism? Or to use a term borrowed from Wittgenstein: What are the elements of the transcendental language game? Apel finds one in the first certainty of Descartes, that one who thinks must exist, provided it is given a transcendental-pragmatic interpretation. "I do not exist" is a performative contradiction of a propositional content; the linguistic performance presupposes the existence of a community of communicators, which in turn presupposes the existence of those who communicate.

> The irrefutable certainty of the *"ego cogito, ergo sum"* rests not upon the primacy of so-called "inner experience" or "introspection" of the, in principle, solitary consciousness as is assumed in the cartesian tradition of "evidence" theory up to Brentano, but rather it rests upon the primacy of an *experience situation that is simultaneously communicative and reflexive* in which the actual self-understanding (and with it the ego-consciousness) and the understanding of the existence of another are *equally original.* . . . The confirmation of personal existence in the performatively understood *"ego cogito, ergo sum"* is only possible as an understanding with oneself about oneself, and that is to say, as part of a virtually public discussion— more precisely, as the deficient mode of such a discussion in which I am for myself the other.[24]

Subjects are always in a position to criticize an actual discussion by claiming a discrepancy between it and the normative discussion situation of the ideal communication-community. They presuppose this transcendental-pragmatic norm, in fact, whenever they criticize; they can remain irrational only by remaining silent, which is to undergo personal destruction. We can therefore transcendentally justify any principle—the denial of which makes membership in the ideal communication-community impossible.

Apel believes that transcendental reflection can establish an a priori ethical norm that is a precondition of the validity of all argumentation, and even of logic (which he conceives, following Peirce, as the "ethics of thinking"). That ethical norm arises in the reflection that all who participate in an argument are committed not only to justifying their own claims but also to entertaining the justifications of claims made by others, and, further, to being ready to be concerned with all *potential* claims that could be interpersonally communicated. "The meaning of moral argument could almost be expressed in the by no means novel principle that all human *needs*—as potential *claims*—i.e. which can be reconciled with the needs of all the others by argumentation, must be made the concern of the communication community." [25] Thus the ideal communication community presupposed in any attempt to communicate gives ethical standing to all its members. At the same time, the act of communication necessarily presupposes the existence of that *real,* socially and historically determinate communication community in which the speaker has been socialized; there is a "dialectical contradiction" between the real community with all its limitations and the ideal community in which claims are definitively understood and judged.[26] The guiding ethical regulative principle, by which actual moral efforts are to be measured, is the resolution of this contradiction in the realization of the ideal communication community, where communication would be maximally open and undistorted. Solitary agents make decisions justifiable by this principle insofar as they "realize the possible critique of the ideal communication community in [their] own reflexive self-understanding." [27]

Apel contrasts his "transcendental reflection" or "contemplation" with deductive grounding. It does not determine the will, but it does rationally ground it.[28] This non-necessitarian reason is held out as a third way between Popperian decisionism and foundationalism. What precisely is the "ground" that Apel gives? He offers what should be a superior interpretation of the position thinker-speakers find themselves in, in two ways: positively or regulatively, he provides a goal, the ideal or unlimited communication community, which is maximally rewarding to the truth-seeking and arguing intention; negatively or constrainingly, he explains what has gone wrong when truth-seeking and arguing go awry—which conditions should have been respected but were not.

Has Apel found genuinely transcendental conditions of the possibility of argument, given his admission that no necessary deduction is possible? And just what are his transcendental conditions the conditions of—are they after all the conditions only of an arguably interpreted concrete? These two questions are closely related, since the lack of necessity in the derivation of transcendental conditions may be rooted in the non-necessity of Apel's interpretation of the concrete reality of argumentation. It seems to be *possible* to place science, Apel's prime example of argumentation, on the methodologically solipsistic footing that he rejects. The scientific community could be an aggregation of Cartesian researchers who have banded together strictly to use each other as checks and sources of suggestions as to what might be looked into. I freely grant that this looks like a very deficient sort of scientific community, but for all I can tell a number of scientists and scholars do act on this understanding. How could we convert them to the view that "intersubjective validity," defined in such a way as necessarily to transcend private evidence, is an a priori condition of scientific truth? Apel claims that the meaning of all the language used by scientists has already been mediated by the language-community; this is a sociological fact that, for him, has transcendental import. But what is to prevent scientists from acknowledging the facts of their socialization while at the same time remaining determined to use what their communication community has provided them without being responsible to that community? One's minimal responsibility toward the meanings of the words one uses, which is necessary to keep language usable, is distinct from maximal responsibility in the ideal community, which is toward all other actual and possible hearers. Therefore, it seems that the transcendental import of the factual conditions of argument is what must be argued. If that were certain, then our orientation to the ideal communication community (which Apel postulates in much the same way that Kant postulates the highest good in his dialectic of practical reason) would have a firm warrant. We could speak of "rational faith" in it. As matters stand, however, the whole transcendentalization of the problem could be dismissed as a smokescreen. What is stated in terms of the "a priori conditions of the possibility of argument" might only amount to an optional interpretation of the givens of argument.

(Interestingly, the absolute otherness of others *could* be argued as a transcendental condition of intersubjective validity as Apel conceives it. On the one hand this otherness is nonevident and as such invites a transcendental interpretation; on the other hand, some such ingredient as this seems necessary to distinguish in principle the realm of the intersubjective from the subjective. Nevertheless, we are bound to treat otherness as the concrete rather than as something inferred or postulated. For Apel, what we call otherness must be a function of the transcendental language-game. But that is to say, impermissibly, that a You is constituted by a We. For a suitably transposed "you" and "we" this could be a compelling sociological or linguistic thesis, but it is false for "You" in its first-philosophical sense.)

(c) Conclusions

Both Gewirth and Apel try to norm intention by "grounding" some kind of other-regarding intention. The point of departure for both is an intentional fact—

for Gewirth the fact of practical rationality, for Apel the fact of argumentation. By pointing to a fact of intention, each finds a way to cross the logical fence between "is" and "ought"; an intention that one can take for granted with any possible interlocutor is an "ought" that "is." Criticism of their arguments tries to establish the possibility of the assumed intention's persistent absence, and succeeds. Interlocutors can escape after all. But that is not to say that interlocutors who do not wish to escape have not been given good ground for sharing the intention that is proposed. Gewirth and Apel both show us that all who are prepared to speak *to* the intentions of others—that is, to use language as more than a stimulus-system—must also be prepared to relate their own intentions to those of others in a fair way. Needed to complement these arguments is a weighing of the attractions of their conception of language and reasoning, and a counting of the cost of disagreement with it. Gewirth and Apel do not get to this because their arguments are supposed to be strong enough to forbid any disagreement worth talking back to.

It has been pointed out that the project of grounding, or giving finally good reasons, leads to a trilemma.[29] Either there must always be a new reason given to justify any reason, which leads to infinite regress; or one stops giving reasons at a selected point, which is an "arbitrary" move because exempted from the justification question; or one goes in a circle, grounding reasons that need grounding with each other. Gewirth and Apel offer groundings of the second sort, where the cessation of reason-giving at the level of a certain principle is defended as nonarbitrary (even though it is unjustifiable) because it is pragmatically necessary. But whole schools of thought arise through making virtues out of these embarassments. Popperian critical rationalism endorses an infinite process of reasoning and renounces final grounding. Postcritical philosophy influenced especially by the later Wittgenstein and Michael Polanyi proceeds on the principle that beyond a certain point justifications neither can nor need be given, inasmuch as questioning is possible only on an unquestioned, tacitly trusted, and opaque base (a social form of life; one's body). Defenders of cumulative arguments hold that independently insufficient lines of reasoning can lean into and support one another much like the arms of an arch. In each case, philosophical practice assumes when it does not actually announce that what fails to satisfy the principle of sufficient ground in one sense does satisfy it in another, or satisfies a preferable version of it. Looking for reasons rather than having them is the perfect form of reason for critical rationalism. Knowing when to stop, when it makes no further sense to ask for justification, is the perfection of postcritical reason.[30] Appreciating relationships among reasons and not singlemindedly insisting on deduction is, finally, a fullness of reason, not a privation of it, for those who argue cumulatively.

Everybody is right. We only have to put these principles of reason in some order. But this can be done only under the guidance of a preunderstanding of the situation of reasoning such as a philosophy of the spiritual offers. The spiritual preunderstanding to which we are committed suggests the following:

(1) To live together with the others means that I may never stand pat with a reason. I must always be ready to justify myself, which can never be done finally, once and for all; and I must always be open to learn. Reason, just as critical rationalism maintains, is a function of the irreducible plurality of subjects that constitutes the normative meaning of the term "intersubjective." But the reason for this is that

(2) The others are present, bindingly, as other. This is a foundation of all rational considerations which is unquestionable (though deniable), and yet which is essentially opaque, since the others as such are precisely the beings who remove themselves from my knowledge. Though I tacitly rely on social forms of life, these are still objects of knowledge for the social sciences, and so too is my body an object of knowledge for physiology. It must be admitted that the sciences do not study the empirical aspects of my existence in the same quality as they have for me, supporting my personal life. But this personal life is in any case a queer thing of vanishing significance if it is not launched in communication toward the others. The others are the permanently positive unknowable.

I am practically justified in saying all this because

(3) You, sir, and you, madam, are listening. You, sir, might confirm this of what I say; you, madam, might add that. No one of us individually may speak finally for all. We have to lean into each other. But in the leaning, the matching up of only partially valid reasons, a sufficient whole is made for us. Yet this view of our relationships presupposes the radical plurality affirmed in the first point, and thus the circle is closed.

Gewirth and Apel have to beg the question to succeed, as do we. If one cannot coerce assent to a proposition, one can only beg it. The task is to find a sweet enough way of begging.

4.6 Groundlessness and the Jolly Gesture

Philosophies of groundlessness are multiplying. One reason for this is the intra-philosophical failure of the final-grounding project, which has been much studied in the case of one of the last great foundationalists, Edmund Husserl, whose quest for certainty and mental self-possession gets entangled in social, historical, and natural conditions that defeat it.[31] The failure of this or that philosophical system to secure its objectives could always act as a spur to new efforts in the same direction, yet what we observe in many quarters is a renunciation of the direction. The intraphilosophical reason for this could be a perception that the strategies and tactics available for grounding have been exhausted—a rather weak reason by itself, because one ought not to doubt that new ideas will come along. More important is the perception that one *can* philosophize apart from grounding, and not just as a shoddy equivalent for what used to be called philosophy but for new reasons of high importance. There is the looming possibility that the *logical* development of philosophical argumentation points in this direction. And at the same time weighty reasons come from outside philosophy, from the historical realities of which philosophy is an expression and to which it addresses itself. Among our reasons are the fact that European civilization lost its ground in the two World War paroxysms of death, one hideously absurd because willed by no one, the other more hideous still because willed by some—with an endless sequel of threatened global destruction; the fact that modern forms of social organization and technology oppress us apart from any overt violence; and the fact that our nontraditional culture cannot put its weight down on any ground other than what it has made for itself, its powers however being unequal to this task. These elements produce two related though sharply contrasting motives for explicitly philosophizing without a final ground: one, the desire to be *free* from the domination of an inhumane and unbalanced thought-system, and the other, the felt need to be *responsible* to the past and present victims of that system. The thought that grows out of the first motive may be designated "ironic"; out of the second, "critical."

Ironic thinkers characteristically distance themselves from what they think by devices of retraction and ambiguation: writing words then crossing them out, punning, mimicking others, mixing up rules and results from different genres of thought. In this way the performers and their performing are cut loose to be appreciated in relative independence of the fixed discursive text of something said. The performance vindicates itself in its very doing; after a word has been crossed out, one cannot any longer imprison the writer in that word; the writer is free of it. Skeptics do the same. Though one can point to a contradiction in any statement of skepticism that they make, they can always speak again to undo the statement, by which they subordinate what is said to their sovereign act of speaking. Here subjectivity seems to be absolute negativity. But it should be noted that there is a positive element of joy in the ironic performance, which goes beyond any repulsion that drives the ironist away from the philosophical system. One does this not because it is the only thing left to do, but because it is *exciting* and one *can*. Every new reach of ironic thought is a discovery not simply of subjectivity's independence but of a new mode of relationship between subjectivity and language, and through language, between subjectivity and the world.

The peril of such thought is that, left to itself, it either betrays itself by settling on the norms of a certain plateau of performance which becomes the de facto new system or else it pays the price of total irresponsibility, which is aimlessness and insanity. It must devour everything to keep itself in motion; finally it must devour itself. But the great value of ironic thought is of a piece with that of any joke or jape. We must prove to ourselves by putting an obtrusive (if not necessarily intelligible) spin on our thoughts that it is we who do the thinking, and not thoughts that do our thinking for us.

Critical thought does not risk the disintegration to which irony is liable. It is integrated by its motivating concern, something concretely given—such as the victims of the Holocaust, or the oppressed proletariat, or the hungry neighbor whoever he or she may be—to do justice to which it undercuts everything else. Its own danger is that its critical principle may become a fixed idea that interferes with serving the object of its concern. Critical thinking must pass two hurdles: it must choose a nonillusory concretum to be loyal to (which will function for it not as a ground or justification but prospectively, and perhaps unattainably, as a justifier), and it must prevent its affirmations from becoming an imprisoning, other-reducing dogmatism. Critics may develop their own ways of performatively warping language, parallel to the ways of ironists.[32] But critical aims will remain a function of prior responsibilities. They will be determined by what *ought* to be done rather than simply by what *can* be done.

The philosophy of the spiritual is groundless because the others to whom it is offered are no ground to have or stand on. Like other forms of critical thought, it is defined by what it is for or to rather than by what it is on or from. It is also "critical" in being bound before it is free, and consequently dogged in form before it is playful. But here lies sanity, both philosophical and personal. If we are bound, we can play freely without losing our bearings, and irony can teach us and save us. But freedom that starts with itself can never really bind itself so as to become a move in a definite direction.

A groundless reflection or discourse is perforce sensitive to its gestural quality. The naive assumption that in reasoning one refers to "the things themselves," which either do or do not back one up, is lost to it. The referential, descriptive, and correspondential dimension of reasoning is not done away with, of course, but it is enfolded by the dimension in which intention meets intention. The sense in which intention itself, both yours and mine, is enfolded by the natural and social factuality of our real intentions is in turn inevitably enfolded by our intentions with respect to this factuality. "What shall we make of it?" is an open question for any fact, because options (though certainly limited) always exist—including the option of pretending they do not exist, in the manner of the determinist.

Philosophy has always been, whether it knew it or not, an experimentation with gesture. It resembles the arts more nearly than the sciences to the extent that interintentional effect has been more interesting than its "objects"; or more precisely, it has tended to be conscious that the latter's significance is determined by the former. Although we customarily interpret Thales' assertion that the origin of all things is water as a protoscientific hypothesis, there is no disguising its extravagance as a willful subordination of natural plurality to a unity of principle, a gesture that is not warranted by the phenomena in an even moderately compelling way unless the project of making such a move as this sweeping unification is assumed. The Platonic theory of the Forms is a move of respect for the unconditionally valid elements of experience, not—as Plato himself often points out—a description of observable entities. (An eschatological condition of contemplating them as entities is projected.) Skepticism cannot make sense as a theoretical assertion, yet it has always been attractive and irrefutable as a move of self-withdrawal for the sake of self-possession. Descartes' *ego cogito, ergo sum* argument is best construed, as Apel argues, as a pragmatic irrefrainable rather than as a theoretical indubitable—which implies, again, that it is a move, rather than a seeing.

But the awareness of the gestural character of philosophizing has always been repressed because it is difficult to understand how a move could be reasonable except as derived from or referred to the nature of a subsisting, observable thing. It will be objected to this account that all our talk of gesture is intelligible and adjudicable only if it succeeds in making of it a theoretical object of some sort, for readers to grasp and examine in consciousness. And it is true that words are meaningful and claims adjudicable only because of the stability *for us* (not necessarily finally *for our consciousness*) of a form *of some kind*. But the commanding form, I say, is the form of the move of acknowledgment of the others who are not seen, rather than the seeing of anything. This is a move that one can do and redo. It has "objectivity" in that sense. It is that about which we speak. But at the same time the speaking *is* it; or if the speaking does not succeed here in being it, then readers will hit on it for some other reason than that they read these words. Readers cannot be referred to it by these words if they do not meet it in these words.

This same perplexity about the unobservable gesture has betrayed the concept of the spiritual. It is remarkable that although the link between the spiritual and the normative has been recognized and insisted upon in the philosophical tradition, "spirit" has nevertheless been described and theorized about as if it were a being, and the ideal realm to which it is akin has been taken to be a higher reality. The dogma has been punctured in celebrated texts—for instance, where Plato has Socrates tease Glaucon by affirming that the Good is beyond even Being, transcending it in dignity and power, and where Hume says it is impossible to discover how prescriptive statements can be deduced from descriptive ones.[33] But the implications of these remarks have always been flinched from because they are, in fact, frightening. If the ideal is not a higher reality but a frame of reference totally different from reality (and only on that account "higher"), if the "ought" is derived from no "is," then the ideal and the "ought," and the moves that offer or accept the "ought," simply hang in the air. They have no secure existence of the sort that observable reality has, and no effective causal power of the sort that observable entities have. And spirit, which is our way of inhabiting this realm—a realm with no real estate—becomes a phantasm, a hypothesis of which the social scientist has no need, a purely optional and gratuitous bonus in our language. Even transcendental arguments cannot deduce it.

When we move, we are off any ground; we are on air, or as the metaphor of spirit would have it, in the air, as air itself. But consider the happy side of this truth: we are therefore free to try to live as we should. The questions "What shall we make of this?" and "What shall we do?" are always genuine questions unforeclosed by the real, whence we leap and where we land. In our leaps we twist toward and away from each other according to the spin we put on our propositions. Whenever we speak or think, there is intention and therefore a spin on what is spoken and thought. When we speak to others as other, there is, underlying the infinity of possible specific gestures, the underlying gestural form, "Let us . . . ." This Ur-proposal that bestows spiritual form on whatever will be done assumes the otherness of the others and the availability of both self and others to do what is proposed. It is the original "ought" that promises "can" because it superordinates itself in the scheme of meaning and will not allow itself to be belied by the constraint of reality (for it cannot be immobilized); its freedom from reality is not the first thing about it, but the second, entailed by the first thing, which is the superordination of spiritual to nonspiritual existence in the event of living with others, as one intention before others.

"Let us . . ." is the minimal gesture of every proposition dealing with others as others. It corresponds to the minimal demand of respect for otherness. If I say "It's raining" to you, I mean "Let us see, say, and think that it's raining," or else I am not actually speaking. The minimal job of philosophy is thus to elucidate by reasoning the conditions under which the positing of the "Let us . . ." goes right or wrong. What then may we look forward to as the maximal task of philosophy, corresponding to the original demand that the others flourish? What would we have if the *summum bonum* of philosophy were achieved? We would have a gesture not merely acceptable but rich, expansive, and happy, and not merely expansive of the gesturer, "joyful," but convivial, "jolly."

I propose, then, that philosophy be maximally conceived as a *fröhliche Wissenschaft* of the jolly gesture. But this is to anticipate last philosophy from the standpoint of first philosophy. The fatal pitfall for this vision is to arrive at it too soon, wrongly positing a happy togetherness when the minimal conditions for togetherness have not yet been met. You cannot laugh and hand a mug of ale to someone who has been denied recognition or starved of food. On the other hand, given recognition and food, one should go on to laugh and pour the ale. The "last philosophy" that pours the ale will reach into first philosophy as much as the latter permits, but will come more into its own in constructive reasoning on the concrete loci of social experience and endeavor, touching on the forms of anger, love, and hope, of work, play, and parleying, that are susceptible of affirmation. Evidently last philosophy undisciplined by first philosophy is an ideology that requires to be unmasked for the sake of those whose interests it denies or distorts. But we cannot abstain from thinking our way toward what *would* be jolly, and in as jolly a manner as is permitted. To do this we have to embrace determinate forms of togetherness in a way that critical thinking as such forbids.

There must be something to *be* jolly. "Let us be happy!" is vapid; "Eat, drink, and be merry!" and "therefore we'll kiss" have point. As soon as we specify that which is jolly, we risk excluding some person or consideration that must not be excluded. Yet specify we must. If we wander in a blank desert of criticism we will never begin to live together.

The jolly gesture is to be characterized generally as the gesture that invites others to flourish in some indicated way. An interesting example of this gesture may be found in Hegel's philosophy. Although there is much that is unjolly in Hegel, including the normal nineteenth-century complement of sarcastic dismissals of blockheaded opponents, it was quite jolly of him to admit the principal philosophies of the past under the umbrella of the Idea, and to grant each its truth. Of course, these truths were then rigorously circumscribed as each system of thought was niched within the dialectical development of the Idea, whose absolute form was only definitively conceived at the end by Hegel himself; and this master move was perhaps not so jolly after all. But it undoubtedly remains one of the chief recommendations of Hegelianism as a general approach to philosophy that it has room in it for the conservation and affirmative interpretation of other ways of thinking while remaining (unlike the jollier but more eclectic thought of Leibniz) a system. And it is finally possible, moreover, to interpret the Hegelian dialectic as an enormous *jeu d'esprit* whose ruling necessity is in the end just freedom from necessity. What it proves is just that it can do what it does.

The necessitarian gesture is in general the opposite of jolly. Yet most philosophies threaten dissenters with intellectual death, as Nozick observes.[34] It is true that it is impossible to reason without frequent attempts to bind assent such as "must," "cannot," "only," etc. The present essay is just as full of them as any other. There are real constraints on thought, and it is crucial to identify them correctly. Thought is called upon, even constrained, to be jolly when it can, yet one cannot say that one "must" be jolly—it is unnecessary to be jolly, and that is the beauty of it. The jolly gesture *must* (and we say *must*, courting paradox, out of respect for the nature of the matter under discussion) be unnecessary. But, being a move, it does not even have a "nature" in the proper sense; it could be as different on any occasion as the intentions of the others could be. We know only this much about it, by virtue of which we have a word for it and can talk about it: it is a moreness, a waxing, of intentions together, and intention *may* take this waxing to be its final aim. To put "may" rather than "must" in that last position puts the right spin on our doctrine of the jolly and, backward from that, onto all philosophy. We are, in the final analysis, not even trying to say *how matters stand* (with regard to intention). We are *standing* in a certain way, and somehow aware of that as free movement.

The argument for a concept of spirit must commend itself on these grounds as well as on the others we have identified. "Let us conceive the spiritual in this fashion!" ought to be the jolliest alternative.

Chapter 5

Primary Affirmations of the Spiritual and Arguments Leading to Them

5.1 Five Primary Affirmations

From the original predicament of living under claims comes an overriding directive to thinking about life, either as assessment of its personal meaning or as philosophical representation of it. Thinking must show its own subjection to claim in every way possible, which means that within each domain of thought and discourse there must be a superordination of spiritual moves—as, for example, we have just given priority to spiritual considerations in our account of reasoning. This applies to the affirmations one is prepared to make concerning one's own existence, that is, the account one gives of oneself, and likewise to the general characterizations of the world one means to have priority over all others. On these affirmations depends the whole order of truth.

An affirmation is not necessarily a theoretical act, an identification, although it will have theoretical implications. Identification is the type of affirmation that divides X from not-X by fixing the nature of X. But another type of affirmation moves X into a certain posture without identifying anything, as for example "I love you" has affirmative force without nailing down what I am, what you are, or what is going to happen. For this reason it is not impossible to make affirmations respecting other beings as other. When in the course of being universalized such affirmations assume the "X is Y" form, they must be glossed in such a way as to overcome the appearance of theoretical identification. Theory does not have exclusive rights to "is" but rather gets its license from the uses of the word in the primary affirmations.

By deciding which shall be first among all possible affirmations, the philosophy of the spiritual will enter into more open and specific confrontation with alternative conceptions and ways of arguing. One can hope that dissenters will take up the challenge to articulate what they are fundamentally most committed to saying, putting seriousness against seriousness. The first affirmations will be the philosophical counters most worth arguing for, the guiding lights for one's work in devising arguments, and at the same time the flags that one's critics ought to try to capture.

The importance of primary affirmations goes beyond their role in orienting argumentation, however; the arguments that are required to justify them are of a sort (as will appear) that display the commanding form of our life ramified into its manifest, everyday structures. By bringing forward these structures as testimonies for the primary theses, we simultaneously find reason for the theses and grasp their specific consequences for our existence. Thus the arguments that we offer for our primary affirmations will go toward answering one of the questions we marked earlier as we anticipated where our project of conceiving the spiritual would lead us: how does the spiritual predicament determine the meaningful shape assumed by an individual's life?

The primary affirmations must be derived from the primary demands, which may be listed as the different aspects of the claim of others on one's attention and intention. They are, first, to notice the other, which for a speaking other, one who presents intention as such, must mean *listening* to the other, that is, receiving intention into a relationship with one's own; second, to *answer* by comporting oneself toward the other in an affirmative way. From the twin demands of listening and answering can be derived the norms of living together, respect and appreciation, and thence the norms of reason. To turn these demands into affirmations, it is only necessary to consider what they imply with respect to the place of the other and of life lived toward the other in the whole economy of one's experience, or "the world." This leads us to say:

(1) *The other—whoever or whatever it may be—is unconditionally real.* Faced by any other, it is impermissible to doubt its independent existence. One may not say that any X is not really there. (There are such things as illusions, of which there are significantly different kinds, but in every case their import is determined on the one hand by our disappointment in them, based on the a priori preference against them, and on the other by our interest in the possibility of actualities corresponding to them. Only the claims of real others A and C force the admission that B is an illusion.) This first affirmation opposes the first affirmation of the unique reality of subjectivity or the "I" that would be made by idealism; for that matter, it opposes any first affirmation of a principle of unity, because it binds itself to an actual plurality of others. It confutes idealism and monism not with a proof, which is impossible, but by making a different original gesture, determinative of all that will henceforth count as serious thought.

(2) *The other is sovereign (most-high).* It is impermissible on the face of it to attend to something else or affirm something else in preference to a self-presenting other. Inconveniently enough, there are many others, not just one, so the observance of this principle cannot be straightforward. To avoid irretrievable disorientation we must hold back from saying that each one of a plurality of others is unconditionally exigent. The others condition each other's exigency because

each is an other. The "something else" to which my attention swerves away from one other is itself an other with an original claim. However, this second other, *merely* as an other-than-the-first-other, has no claim on me: as merely that, the first other is superordinate to it. The second other makes its own claim, to respond to which is not a failure of attention to the first (even though there is something of defection here, a failure of loyalty) but a new realization of responsibility. We knew already that this was the truly serious ongoing problem of life, and the affirmation merely reminds us, in perplexing us, that the problem cannot be dispelled.

We must also say, with an eye toward the impermissibility of violation, that the other is sacred.

(3) *The intentional other is the eminent other*. The crucial generic otherness among others springs from the special superordination of intentional others within the general superordination of beings claiming attention. With intentional others, nonintentional others are things to be dealt with. The intender's gestures surround and pervade the things that are traversed by interintentional communication, as is most obvious in the paradigmatically full communications of speech and writing yet is not lacking in the simplest dealings with nonhuman animals. I may not, however, directly superordinate *myself* to any beings just because I can speak of them. A merely utilitarian attitude is forbidden by our second affirmation. I may have to cherish myself as exemplary or as one responsible—on which grounds it would, for example, be wrong, even though undeniably noble, to refuse to eat anything out of respect for the life of other beings—but I am not originally entitled to assume that anything is at my disposal.

(4) *I am what I am in relationship with others,* and I am eminently what I am in relationship with the intentional others. The *manner* of my being is thus essentially comportment toward and with the others, and the *locus* of my being is "out" in spirits and not merely "in" either my own body or my own affairs. This affirmation chooses among different possible orientations for self-identification. Different selves correspond to the different kinds of life one can live. I am not permitted to grant myself either an original or a teleologically projected reality separate from the others, because that is a way of committing the cardinal sin of ignoring them. The affirmation is not, on the one hand, ontologically necessary, because different selfhoods (such as introverted aestheticism or extroverted imperialism) remain possible; nor, once adopted, is it ontologically entirely determinative, since it leaves latitude for different theoretical constitutions of "I," "other," and "relationship." [1]

(5) *Happiness consists of living affirmatively with the others*. The idea of happiness comprehends both the subjective aspect of satisfaction and delight and the objective aspect of health and flourishing. Everything we have said so far makes inevitable the claim that success in spiritual existence is "higher" than success in any other life, but is the higher ipso facto the sweeter, the subjectively happier?

To the extent that there is a decision to be made about the comparative sweetness of modes of life, we of course are commanded to decide for this one. And perhaps one just has to decide. The pig satisfied is as happy as Socrates dissatisfied; there is nothing sweeter about the Socratic life to lead him to enter it out of the same love as that with which he now loves his slops. But once Socrates communicates with the pig, the latter is no longer at liberty merely to love his comforts. Now he must love something more complicated and elusive.

Can one make a kind of life happier just by deciding for it? This would be an unsatisfactory position to maintain if the command motivating the decision for spiritual life were an entirely alien one and not intrinsically sweet. But it is sweet. It is inseparable from the wondrous quality of the exterior encountered as exterior, which is a realm of rewards superior (because nonreductive and thus richer) to the rewards of pure satisfaction.

These five propositions show points at which the claim of the primacy of the spiritual can enter into controversy with alternative views concerning reality, value, language, subjectivity, and happiness. Although each is grammatically constative, uniting a subject with a predicate by "is," "am," or "consists of," each is actually a direction to bind subject and predicate together, an order rather than a description; or one could say that each is a posited, normative "description," and that any ontology presupposed in the use of this "is," "am," and "consists of" is a normative ontology serving supraontological aims.

Let us see now how well this set of affirmations can be argued for.

5.2 Six Dialectical Arguments

A "dialectical" argument is one that concludes to its demonstrandum from premises already accepted by its audience. Such arguments can be only as strong as the audience's commitment to the initial premises. Perhaps one would like to appeal to premises that any rational being is bound to accept, on pain of self-contradiction, but it turns out that the *interesting* content of any such premise is not included in its analytic content. For instance, Gewirth proceeds from the premise that one necessarily wants to be able to act for what one wants; but the interesting issue with regard to an agent's ability to act is how others will or will not cooperate with the agent, and, as we have seen, the initial premise construed purely analytically fails to determine this. Indeed, it could not, because the intentions of others qua other must be contingent.

The premises I choose for argument are interesting and therefore contingent; yet even though they are contingent, they seem to me very credible. There is a kind of self-contradiction in denying them in the sense that to deny them would be to negate what one after reflection still most wants to think. That is, the "wanting" in question is strong and intelligent enough to survive all possible criticism. Moreover, that we want to think in an indicated way is borne out, sometimes in spite of ideology to the contrary, by our consistently *acting* like that is what we want to think: methodologically solipsistic scientists still placing their results before their colleagues for ratification, solipsistic agents still trying to affect the intentions of other agents, solipsistic lovers still devoting themselves to their beloveds. Readers will be persuaded if they in fact want what the premises assume they want (and tacitly direct them to want), perhaps only after noticing that they do after all act as though that were what they wanted. The arguments must be non-necessary in that respect; it is possible that readers neither have those wants nor act as though they do. On the other hand, in order to be good arguments they must contain an element of necessity as well; they must exhibit patterns of relatedness among their elements that essentially constitute them the elements of a significant whole, so that to respect the latter requires assent to the arguments' conclusions. We will thus attempt to show how premises and conclusions hang inseparably together.

Premises for arguments to the primary affirmations are to be found in the relationship-structures of actual life. Six very conspicuous structures lend themselves to this occasion. They roughly map onto the four categories of subjective existence that have been current in philosophical anthropology since Kant: first, experience in general; then the theoretical, practical, and affective modes of experience, that is, knowing, doing, and feeling, with relatively active and passive, positive and negative variations on the latter. (We are bound to regard the older way of proceeding by intentional modes as a privative interpretation of our concretely interintentional life.)

(a) Experience as Realistic

How far experience is to be interpreted as a function of the experiencer and how far as a function of that which is experienced, and what, accordingly, experiencer and experienced are, are questions that have provoked the rivalry between idealism and realism. The insufficiency (for idealism) of realism lies in its naïveté with respect to the subject's bestowal and shaping of the meaning of phenomena; in a word, its failure to recognize the phenomenality of phenomena. The charge against idealism is that it undermines the very concept of experience and defeats the project of knowledge by causing that which experience is *of* to go up in smoke, leaving the subject in an unaccountable fantasy world. To exhibit necessary patterns in the fantasy, as Kant did, helps us to anticipate what will occur *in* experience but does not help us at all to know what the experience is *of* (the posited things-in-themselves) and thus does not take us toward true knowledge. But to attain knowledge by making the known wholly internal to the knowing mind, as Hegel did, reduces all knowledge to self-knowledge—which is not what knowers really want, either. This is a strange case of extremes meeting. Hegelian knowledge has the same defect that naive realism has: the former makes things to be (what the latter simply assumes them to be) wholly given over to the mind and at its disposal. Actually, unlimited givenness is the destruction, not the perfection, of knowledge, and we must see why this is so. In the following we will let "knowledge" represent all manners of being related to the experienceable.

Knowledge of X has the two dimensions, knowledge that X is, and knowledge of what X is. To know that X is is to take notice of it, to have grounds for saying that in addition to everything else, there is X. Otherwise there is no point in even speaking of X. If X turned out to be really nothing other than some already-known Y, it would be mere confusion to continue to speak of X. X should, therefore, resist a total reduction if there is any X worth speaking of, as indeed one hopes there is. Now, X must have not only a place to stand but a distinguishable way of standing, that is, a nature. We speak of X's properties *belonging* to X in the first place because its having those properties is a condition of our noticing it at all; it has to be something to be, and so if it has a warrant of its own to receive notice, it is at the same time the principle of necessary unity of its properties, or in other words the owner of the properties that make it what it is. To say that X owns its properties is already a realist assertion. The opposed idealist assertion that the knower is the real owner of the properties of any X—which is what it amounts to to say that the principle of unity of X-properties is the synthesis of the act of knowing—this assertion makes the knower the real X, and what we began calling X an illusion, unless, in order to avoid reduction of X, such binding conditions are put on the knower's constitution of X that the X-event in knowledge has an independence comparable to that which we first awarded it realistically. The more serious an idealism is about not reducing X, the harder it is to tell it apart from realism. The intrinsically reductive principle guiding such an idealism becomes an arguable, perhaps dispensable metainterpretation of the phenomena.

To speak of an X's owning its properties sounds like substance-metaphysics. But is not substance an eliminable category of experience? For after we notice X's size, solidity, color, smell, etc., together with its spatiotemporal position and its other relations with everything else, what is there left to meaningfully assert about X? What is added by speaking of X "itself" which "has" all these properties? Precisely nothing that would be a positive content of knowledge, but that is why it is necessary to speak of X itself. We speak emptily of an X independent of what we know about X so as to acknowledge that in our experience of it we are not having to do with qualities and relations that could just as well have been projected by ourselves. We have to speak of X in part as nongiven to show that X cannot be dissolved in the givenness that as such is indistinguishable from a dream. X must "subsist" so that our knowledge is about it, of it, and not about and of ourselves. It is necessary not to know X-itself so that we can have knowledge of X.

This account will provoke the objection that if X-itself is not given to knowledge, it is impossible to associate X's properties with X-itself, so that the knowledge of X that we set out to save has in fact been subverted. It is true that it would be impossible to associate alleged X-properties with an unknown X-itself, if it were entirely up to us to do so. But in fact our only basis for speaking of X-itself is the belonging-together of the X-properties that we saw when we noticed X. X is the owner of properties that are evidently owned; in that respect, the existence of X-itself is evident. X-itself calls to us precisely by associating itself with its properties.

It would be foolish to think that every experience is veridical and beyond criticism, always a matter of hearing the call of some X presenting itself as it is for itself, binding together its properties. On the contrary, it seems safe to say that every experience is partly mirage and pervasively qualified by the subject's manner of apprehension. But regardless of the qualifications of this sort that must be introduced by an adequate philosophy of experience, the crucial point is that they are, no matter how extensive, nevertheless mere *qualifications* of a presupposed transaction of some kind between the mind and an exterior X.

We assume that the distinction between true experience and dream is more fundamental to the sense of experience than the demand for givenness in experience; and we have shown how it requires a limitation of that demand. Nothing forces us to decide for this "true experience" over "dream." There must be a certain zest for encounter with otherness, which one can be invited but cannot be made to feel, in order to be moved so to decide. It cannot be denied that the dream principle has a charm of its own. Do not all reflective people toy with the notion that they are themselves God and what looks like an outer world is only a shadow-play put on for their own diversion (we cannot even say edification)? But the appeal of this notion survives only as long as it is an exotic and intriguing alternative to the common-sense acceptance of the otherness of others. It may come at first as a relief from the pressures of responsibility. If it became the truth it would be a nightmare, draining all events of significance, robbing life of all orientation. Who am I? Where am I? What am I doing? would all become unanswerable questions, because all the reference points used in answering such questions would have been abandoned. The interest of the Upanishadic thesis "That thou art" must lie in the promised adventure of leading self out of self into the other rather than in leading everything other back to the self, the old and same and alone.

The premise of this argument is: we are committed to experience rather than to dream. In all experience one has somehow to do with beings independent of oneself, and experience is veridical—which is to say, more authentic as experience —in direct proportion to the extent that these beings themselves determine its content.

From this premise we argue as follows: if one accepts the principle that experience is of independent beings, then no condition on the reality of those beings may be allowed. Whatever X our experience may be of (and we grant that great

difficulties may intrude here, from which we can never free ourselves, in ascertaining what our experience is experience of), that X is both irreducibly other
and inderivable and therefore must be affirmed to be, as other, real. Insofar as
we are committed to experience in preference to dream, we are committed to
allowing the real to determine the content of that experience, which means that
we are bound to respect it as it is in itself so far as we can. And this unconditional
claim on our respect, applying to every phase of our comportment, motivates the
affirmation that the experienced other is "sacred" or "most-high." (In the context
of the search for truth, "real" directly means "most-high.")

Thus we have given grounds for the first two primary affirmations that will
apply across all cases of experience, to what we have to do with others and
our feelings about them as well as our knowledge of them. We have not refuted
idealism—for idealism is irrefutable—but we have shown how the perennially felt
need for a refutation of idealism hangs together with the primacy of the others.
Although it would also be possible to argue toward the last three affirmations on
this same basis, it seems that the following arguments from more specific modes
of experience are stronger and more pertinent ways of arriving at them.

(b) Knowledge as Critical

In Apel's transcendental argument to a communication community we have
already met the notion that "scientific" truth or knowledge must attain to intersubjective validity, the requirements for which exceed anything attainable in private experience. But we could not see clearly what would motivate a scientist
to accept the initial portrayal of science as intersubjective from which Apel's
transcendental conditions could be inferred. We will try to see that now.

Probably the most commonly admitted reason for determining one's knowledge
as a function of the procedures of a knowledge-community of independent subjects is that in this way the finitude of the individual knower may be surpassed.
Whenever I set out to know something, I immediately need what I do not have,
eyes in the back of my head and eyes to see the back sides of things. Other subjects cover my rear, bringing to my attention anything of relevance that I would
not have noticed, and fill in the gaps in my knowledge caused by the fact that I can
be in only one place at one time. Perspectives combine to overcome perspective.

And yet it is not correct to say that I *need* the assistance of other knowers in
order to be a knower myself. As long as it is only a question of adding others'
knowledge to my own, it seems that I seek their collaboration out of sheer greed
for knowledge. It is only because I want more knowledge that I need them; it is
not that I need them to know anything at all. The strongest case we could make for
needing others as adders-to-knowledge would be to tie the project of knowledge
inseparably to the ideal of perfect knowledge, one that sees into all shadows and

around all corners. Of course no actual aggregation of finite knowers could ever possess infinite knowledge between them, but every knower would be bound to approximate as closely as possible to the ideal, which would always require one to enlist in the maximal real knowledge-community. If the investigations of the knowledge-community are prolonged into infinity, we have at least an unending approach to the ideal.

But why would a certain amount of knowledge not be enough? In practical life we recognize sufficiencies of knowledge everywhere; we call them competencies. It does not count as an impairment of the competence of farmers if they do not know the finer points of biochemistry and meteorology. If they know what benefits and what harms their crops, they *know* that, whether or not they also know theoretical explanations of the relevant phenomena. Their commitment to knowing what they know does not entail infinite curiosity in all dimensions.

On the other hand, those who are competent or expert with respect to certain phenomena do remain curious about *them*. Farmers, like scholars, keep up with their fields and compare notes with colleagues. One reason for this is their unquenchable interest in matters that have made major claims on their attention. This will be entwined with their endeavor to respect the phenomena, which means never to cease letting things show themselves. What they know is largely inductive, and they realize that no empirical induction is ever complete. But in induction and in knowledge generally there are subtractive as well as additive contingencies. One might learn that one was wrong about what one thought one knew. One might learn it from the phenomena, which is an argument for keeping one's eyes open; or one might learn it from one's colleagues, which is an argument for keeping one's ears open. Knowledge must remain liable to both sorts of correction if it is to be knowledge as opposed to opinion. This is the genuinely necessary ideal of knowledge, not directly to extend itself infinitely but to be sure of itself (and perhaps it must finally extend itself infinitely in order to be unqualifiedly sure of itself in any respect, as "the true is the whole").

The observance of knowledge's liability to correction, or "fallibilism," has, we see, two dimensions; and we are here more concerned with the second, which makes knowledge vulnerable to questioning and correction from other subjects. A purported knowledge that wants to earn the title "knowledge" wants to expose itself to the uncanniest criticism, wants to face every "But have you thought of . . ." in trying to think of everything relevant. It has a problem of never being able to get to the end of criticism from other subjects that parallels its inability to get to the end of the phenomena, which is the classic problem of the validity of induction. For just as any actual induction of phenomena is finite, with an unlimited number of possible instances yet to take into consideration, so too any actual consultation with colleagues is finite, with all of scientific history yet to come stretching out ahead without limit.

The *problem* of intersubjective fallibility exists only because other subjects exist. One would not have to worry about others' criticisms if one were alone in the world. But if one were alone, one would wish for them; and being in fact not alone, one welcomes them as a boon. For a knowledge that subjects itself to the test of the others is further toward being knowledge—*if* knowledge is defined in opposition to opinion—because it is surer. (Naturally, our being moved so to define it is influenced by our socialization.) No cultivation of evidence in private consciousness can make itself proof against the charge that its own moves dogmatically shape the evidence; nor can it ever be sure that the evidence might not be able to appear differently.

Knowledge can never be protected from the phenomena, which can embarrass it at any time no matter what anyone says. But in a sense knowledge is more vulnerable still to the criticism of other subjects, among whom the issue of the proper interpretation of phenomena will be booted interminably. The scientific community's interpretation of the phenomena is determined both by the phenomena's possible relations with each other, which are indefinitely many, and by the different approaches and attitudes—the scientific spins and twists—that will invariably be found in construals of the phenomena. Intentional beings cannot stand before things utterly passively as their perfectly duplicating recorders. They must approach them in certain ways. But this approach is in a crucial respect free and groundless and therefore requires norming if it is not to be arbitrary, a rank opinionization of knowledge. It must be at the disposal of that norming, and therefore correctible—that is to say, if it is to be right, it must have the possibility of being wrong.

The fallibilist principle thus both contributes to the demand for norming of knowledge and is implicit in norming. There is a second ingredient in the rightness of normed knowledge, distinct from its susceptibility to correction though related to it, and that is the intention proper to true knowledge (as to any spiritual enterprise) to be *justified*. "Justified" is not the same as "sure." Knowledge that is justified—or rather, belief that is justified, which makes "knowledge"— may be justified *because* it is sure, certainty being a prime standard employed in justification; this usually means that prescribed procedures have been followed for obtaining and testing the knowledge, on the basis of which everyone can have an acceptable amount of confidence in it. But it is everyone's having the confidence in it, rather than its factual freedom from correction, that *constitutes* the knowledge justified. To be justified means to be chosen and endorsed. Knowers, no less than lovers, are not content with mere being; they want to be chosen, that is, criticized (from *krinein*, to separate and choose). Each wants "his" or "her" world to be the world of others, too, and this identification can be accomplished only with their intentional concurrence. When the others say "That's right," more occurs than the ruling out of error; there is an expansion and elevation to that plenitude of confidence in belief that we call objectivity or intersubjective validity. On one level, the phenomena confirm one's belief about them simply by conforming to it. But one's believing or having of the belief, one's interpretation of the phenomena, lies on another level at which one can only be confirmed by other havers of belief, namely, other intentional beings. The phenomena are enfolded by this plural having of belief about them in just the same way that matters of discourse are enfolded by the communication of discourse, for the speaking is only the open having.

The premise of the argument from critical knowledge may be formulated as follows: knowledge as distinguished from arbitrary opinion must be subjected to every possible correction and asks for every possible confirmation. Thus far, it seems we have an unexceptionable expression of the spirit of science.

The premise may be argued from thus: belief aspiring to the status of knowledge may never close itself to correction. But that implies that it may not hold itself free from testing by the critique than which no more radical may be conceived. The most radical critique is that which is least controlled in advance, namely, that which is other than and independent from the intentions of the believer, attended to in its otherness. Therefore, the others' own showing is absolutely to be respected—which is the sense of our first and second primary affirmations. In addition, however, there is a class of others who not only show themselves but unavoidably participate in the letting-be-shown of all phenomena, namely, the intentional and especially the speaking others. Since correction is a matter not only of allowing experience to revise prejudice but also of revising experience itself in light of alternative structures imposed on it by intention, these others must also be attended to when any other is attended to. This double demand on our attention we call the "eminence" of the intentional others, as stated in our third primary affirmation. Confirmation, like correction, is significant exactly to the extent that it is not controlled by the confirmed; therefore, by parity of reasoning, the intentional others are also eminent as confirmers of knowledge.

Science is a practice, and thus the next argument, pertaining to practice or action in general, will reinforce that just given. But the main reference of that argument will be to the fourth affirmation.

(c) Actions as Deeds

Spiritual life is distinguished from bare life not only by the consciousness of self and others that qualifies it inwardly, but by what is done in it. It follows from what has already been said that spiritual life is essentially a life of action, if by "action" we mean behavior governed by and expressing intention. Behavior gains its meaning from intention. But intention as such is, though necessary, not a sufficient condition of what we want to think of as meaningful action. The sufficient condition is present only when intention somehow interacts with another intention. Let us designate intentional behavior of any sort as "action" and any fully meaningful action as a "deed." The word "deed" still carries the connotation of an accomplishment set before others to command or solicit their attention, and also of some serious or fateful action, that is, one with interintentional repercussions. In this section we shall endeavor to show that whenever life is lived in a way that we want to consider worthy or meaningful, that life is made up of deeds. We will argue in the end that the practical primacy of deeds grounds the affirmation that my own reality is inseparably connected with the reality of others through relationship.

A survey of actions ordinarily considered meaningful reveals a plurality of fields or domains of action. No doubt the map of action could be drawn in a number of different ways; hoping more to be inclusive than to do justice to nuances, I suggest that the principal domains of meaningful action are work, play, and what for want of an apt term I will call history making. I mean by this that whenever we positively evaluate an action, we interpret it as an exemplar of one or more of these three modes, and whenever we dismiss an action as meaningless or unworthy of us, we relate it privatively to one of them ("useless," "no fun," "makes no difference").

To *work* is to do something that needs to be done. It ought to be something worth doing, or so maintains any culture with a positive attitude toward work. But anything that truly needs to be done is worth doing—so any such culture, like ours, would claim. Slavery, considered as the systematic doing of necessary things that are not worth doing, has been abolished in concept, but it rears its head among us in the necessary-but-not-rewarding actions that we stigmatize, though usually not with entire seriousness, as "slaving away," "drudgery," etc. Wherever there is a necessary component of action, the attending to that component counts as work—as for instance when someone building a model sailing ship "works" on the rigging, or a politician "works" on a speech. The hobby is not work, nor is statesmanship, but there is work in them. Conversely, there are nonwork elements in occupations that count on the whole as work.

Work is a valid mode of action. One's action or inaction may be criticized as a failure to work, "idleness," or on the other hand designated as work to defend it from the charge of idleness (as when a child psychologist asserts that the play of children is really their work).[2] On occasions when it is thought that the need to work supervenes over every other practical consideration, the most joyful play or enterprising political leadership will be seen as mere idleness. More usually, some people are called "idle" with the notion that something is wrong with their lives that could best be set to rights if they strove for the life-validity attainable through work. So work-oriented are Americans that we call success in any activity "getting the job done" and congratulate an accomplishment of any sort as "good work." With so much normative investment in the ideal of working, idleness becomes a major ill or sin.

Work's dignity stems from its defining characteristic, that it needs to be done;

yet practical necessity is a menace, at least a limitation and at most a factor of oppression. As a limitation it can be benign, something to test and form oneself against.[3] But even in that case it is what is done with the necessity rather than the necessity itself that is of value. Work figures as a conquest of threat, a rescue from danger. The seriousness and value of work is therefore tied most fundamentally to what or who it rescues. (In another way the value of work is determined by the mastered difficulty and fineness of its execution; but this may be considered a virtue of artisanship subsidiary to the value of the work activity as a whole and the virtue of the worker as one who gets this done. Moreover, the fineness of a work shades into its beauty and thus comes under a different category than work.)

The work I do for myself is serious for me, greatly and irreversibly consequential, because my well-being depends on it. Under normal conditions, however, I never work solely for myself—indeed, only rarely do people even work principally for themselves. Others normally depend on what I do, so that whether or not I work and work well is a serious issue for them. This is true for all others, but eminently for my fellow human beings; on account of its interpersonal extension, the issue is a moral one. In modern industrial society the connections of dependence are myriad and indirect, so that we more naturally speak of the worker's obligation to "society" than to specified individuals (except for family dependents supported by earnings), but this does not remove the fact that real individuals are rescued from the oppression of natural or cultural necessity only by the efforts of other real individuals. Therefore, the moral issue cannot be dissolved in a purely technical "social" issue, for all that it must be addressed through social administration. Any society must have a work code; any nonslave society must have a true work ethic. Work is construed by such an ethic as service. We praise it because we are grateful for it and because we see in it the noble quality of self-sacrifice for a common good held to be greater. Work is a prime spiritual move, a way of positively being-for-others. Of course there is a contradiction here in that the nobility of work is contingent on its being done freely while its character as work is a function of the necessity that it be done. But the contradiction is overcome if I freely work for *your* necessity. The volunteer is the perfect worker. (Unfortunately, volunteering is a privilege that a leisure class largely reserves to itself, buying with the labor of the working class the choicest fruit of a work ethic.) There are those who work from necessity but work harder or better than strictly compelled to, and that is a mode of volunteering, which is commended as "good work." Idleness is a base nonvolunteering, disrespectful of the claims of others who are subject to necessity. Working is minimally valid as the avoidance of this vice, but maximally significant as the free gesture of service of others.

To work well is admirable and rewarding for the sheer expansion and concretization of the worker's own intentional existence that is accomplished in the work, but the pursuit of such goals is not properly the business of work. To work is to do what needs to be done just because it needs to be done, hence heteronomously.

But to do something because one wants to or because it belongs to one's own flourishing is the ideally spontaneous and joyful activity that we call play. Play takes in all activities that are their own reason: on the active, sporting level, everything fun, and in reception, everything on which we confer aesthetic significance. Art earns the conferral by showing intrinsic reward in our and the world's ways of existing; that is, in a sense, making of life a game that one would give oneself to.

An activity that has nothing intrinsically rewarding in it is recognized and criticized as oppressive. Even the noblest work is drained of value if it is undertaken joylessly, with no spontaneous intentional expansion in it. It is then as though the doer of the work had died. Joyless workers lead a spectral existence. Something must be done to invite them back in to occupy their own lives. This is the validity of play, that life without it is death.

Every kind of play aims at interintentional form, that is, seeks to become a game with two or more players. One might resist this thesis, objecting that no purer and stronger form of play can be found than, say, the individual ecstasy of a lad rolling down a grassy hillside on a summer's day. There is already an answer to this objection merely in observing that the lad's feelings do not expand in a vacuum, but in contact with the delightful ground and weather that felicitate him. In the strictest sense it is impossible to have fun alone; there must be something to have fun with. But it seems overwhelmingly evident that the perfect forms of play involve, in addition, the concurrence of intentional others, because we consistently seek this and rarely rest without finding it. The lad would rather be playing with a friend; the solitary beholder of a painting looks forward to meeting someone to praise it to; the musician who plays alone either practices in order to play for others or plays as though for others. To dismiss these inclinations as our sociability or herd instinct misses the issue of what constitutes our sociability and what it means to us. Of course there is a herd instinct that drives me automatically to seek the company and conversation of others, but it does not bind me. Sometimes I revolt from it and sometimes I ride it knowingly and joyfully. I can take a position with respect to it, and this taking of a position is done in awareness of the positions of others with respect to me. If I revolt from playing with others, if for example I go off to play the piano just for myself, I soon find that the revolt was from *some* others, from unsatisfactory relationships, and not from relationships *tout court;* invariably I find myself again playing to others, if only prospectively, and that not automatically and in spite of myself but most willingly from myself.

The game is play as encounter. To play with another is far more interesting than to play by oneself, because of the contingency that is introduced. To be sure, one can find one's own contingency interesting, one can stand over against oneself watching to see what one will do, but that is a deficient game, like gambling without any chips. In playing with a veritable other one hangs *as a doer* on what the other will do, which is quite a different thing from standing over against oneself as a passive observer. One cannot really interact with oneself, one can only watch oneself acting. To the extent that interaction can actually take place in imagination (in the responsible deliberations of a Helen respecting an Agatha, for example), there one is no longer playing with oneself but with traces of others.

We interact with each other in countless ways without the help of games, but we have created games and regularly resort to them in order to interact with each other in a purified, spontaneous way. With the aid of rules defining the actions of the game, the miracle occurs that we simultaneously exist wholly and fiercely in our actions and that we do this together, and together not merely as coordinated but as impinging on each other, directly constituting reasons, step by step, for each other's actions. Our togetherness is not achieved by imposing harsh and alienating constraints. It is not poisoned by necessity, as are our work relationships. The rules of the game make up a paradigmatic order that enables rather than confines activity. They give us something fun to do. When we do not have rules, we spontaneously make them up for the joy of acting vis-à-vis each other. Game rules are in fact the most attractive spirits, and every spirituality approaches the condition of a game to the extent that it meets the conditions of freedom and joy in togetherness.

One of the phenomena of play provides a transition to the domain of meaningful action that remains after work and play have been considered. That domain is history-making, and it is anticipated by the making of a kind of artificial history out of games. We play or watch what happens in a game and then afterward remember it for itself and in relation to events in other games, as greater or lesser or interestingly similar; and then we judge present games and anticipate future games in relation to past ones, taking them all together in a temporal whole that one might call a history. But while the quasi-history of a sport is set up to enhance our appreciation of the accomplishments in it by making those accomplishments make more of a difference, at the same time games must make no ultimate real difference. They would not be just games, spontaneous activities unmarred by care, if they did. Nothing could matter more within the world of baseball than that the New York Yankees have won the most world championships; but in the real world where people are born, are good or bad, and die, it has not made a whit of difference outside the organization of baseball. True history making may be defined as action that changes the fundamental conditions of life, as history is the story of what has irreversibly happened to us—making our situation what it is, and ourselves as we are—especially as a result of what we have done. "Natural history" is a stammering or mute history: we interactors are chiefly concerned with interaction. Nothing is more important to us than the effect one intention can have on another. Nothing, therefore, makes a more significant piece of news than a report of an interaction, which is what stories and histories give us.

History as written and taught is dominated by political and military events because these, as is quaintly said, have shaped our destiny. The activity of statesmen and generals is not, insofar as it transcends pure administration, an example of doing what is necessary; it is enterprise rather than work. Nor is it spontaneous, carefree, and without real effect, like play. It can be arduous and dangerous, and it certainly means to be fateful, for the reason for running its risks and spending its energy not-just-necessarily is in order to make a decisive improvement in intentional relationships or the influential conditions thereof. The facts created by political and military exploits are actual shiftings and wrinklings of the rug on which intentional beings stand. This is spirit-engineering, an attempt to act not just on intentions but on interintentionality.

History-making is not the exclusive province of political and military leaders. It occurs whenever there is leadership—in proposing marriage (successfully), in publishing a book (influentially), possibly even in selling someone something. It confers significance on action in a doubly serious way: first, by changing that which changes everything else, namely, intention; and second, by changing matters irreversibly, so that our intentional horizon is henceforth defined by the change. An irreversibly effective action is historic and meaningful even if it was frivolously done. *Crime,* intrinsically meaningful because it changes lives, can be undertaken to remedy a felt deprivation of historicity.

History is the province of the "fateful deed," or action that makes a lasting difference in the conditions of life. But all meaningful actions are fateful in some way, because it is impossible for an action to matter without the world's somehow changing on account of its happening. If I do good work, I have rescued us from not having what I made or from suffering from what I removed, and the rescue is an important part of our story. If I play well, I become irreversibly the person who flourished in just that fashion, and who approvingly contemplates his own life in just that form—forever the person who once hit a home run to win a baseball game. Work and play thus creep into real history even though their intentions are not directly historical. They are, we may say, latently historical. The paradigmatic meaningful actions in all three domains of action are "deeds" in the sense that they command attention as interintentional faits accomplis. With the category of the deed is introduced at the same time the quality of fatefulness or "greatness," and with this manner of evaluating deeds we are driven to adopt the historical point of view.

Given the reference point of the deed, we find ourselves, as regards psychic energy and affect, in the realm of *thumos.* Courage, enthusiasm, élan are the self's throwing itself into the realization of actions that others may affirm. "Noble" deeds are done by those who have submitted themselves in principle to the interintentional requirement for such actions. How one's projects fare, measured in this frame of reference, determines the level of one's thumic spirits and therewith the *feeling* of the meaning of selfhood.

The materials for an argument are now at hand. Our premises are, first, that the self must act to validate its existence, and second, that meaningful action of any sort requires both recognition from others and impact on their intentions. The "deed," the doing that is set before others and makes a difference to them, is the fulfilled form of all three modes of action.

We argue that since action is a condition of meaningful selfhood and relationship with others is a condition of meaningful action, the fourth primary affirmation, that I am what I am in relationship with others, is unavoidable. One cannot give meaning to the self's existence outside of other-regarding action, as a different primary affirmation on selfhood would attempt to do, and once it is denied any meaning of its own, the "self" drops out of our sight. This argument admittedly begs the question of the meaning of "meaningfulness" in action by stacking the deck in favor of the other-regarding interpretation. But as our discussion has shown, we do persistently, if not consistently, act in all three domains as though meaningfulness meant precisely this, and it would seem that there is no higher jurisdiction for the question of practical meaningfulness than what we mean in spite of anything to go on doing.

(d) Love as Blessed Devotion

In Western culture, shaped by a religion whose God is love, a certain form of love has come to have a preeminent importance and authority in the ideal conception of affective life. I say "a certain form" because I doubt that any culture lacks a strongly approved model of benevolent feeling, and so it seems foolish to claim normative love as the possession of the West. But there are significant differences between cultures both in the nuances of the feeling itself and in the limits prescribed for it regarding its objects and occasions. Love in the West is peculiarly unlimited in its prescribed range and validity, and at the same time peculiarly concrete, apt to attach itself definitively to individuals in the world. Both the Greek and Hebrew sources of Christian culture have determined love as worldly, although strands of both traditions aim to pull love on through the world to a higher reality. In this direction would lie rapprochement with Eastern ideals of love, such as the Hindu way of *bhakti*. But Western feeling has mainly not moved in this direction, and perhaps the single strongest proof that it has not is our centuries-long fascination with romantic love.

A formulation of what love means to us that takes in what Iseult felt for Tristan as well as what Christ felt for sinners must be rather abstract, so large are the concrete differences; yet the common traits need pointing out. In this love the beloved individuals are posited as worthy of attention in their own right, the attention demanded is unlimited solicitude, and the beloved's flourishing, in the context of a flourishing relationship, is hoped for as the supremely valuable reward. Love verges on pathology in all three respects. In positing the beloved as worthy, love is ultimately uncritical or undiscriminating (but precisely as demanded by our first two primary affirmations), and consequently threatens the lover's intellectual self-possession. In submitting to an infinite demand for solicitude, the lover is in the grip of something like obsession, a practical self-dispossession. And in hoping for the other's well-being and return of love, the lover's own happiness is staked to uncontrollable and not especially probable contingencies.[4] Love is an absurdly dangerous emotional risk.

The risks of love must be run for its special kind of payoff. Fulfilled love delivers what can only be attained in leaving oneself, which is therefore impossible, strictly speaking, to obtain. To have actually received what one cannot get, the happiness and affirmation of the other, is supreme blessedness. What more can be hoped for than to receive what is beyond all calculation? The famous "magic" of love consists of being given over to the other without having made or having to make a decision to do so (for one cannot decide to leave oneself). So precious are these boons and so widely known is their lore that they are always being counterfeited to feed the hunger for happiness. Even though one can never assume in advance that one will be in the strange position of leaving oneself, let alone that the other will be similarly launched toward oneself, one is constantly tempted to love by deciding to love and to feel oneself loved by deciding to be blessed—in order to avoid making the decisions that one really must make.

Love, whether religious or romantic, has a unique authority over the conduct of the lover, and not only for the obvious reason that it promises supreme blessedness. In this it might run afoul of morality, which does not, after all, permit one uninhibitedly to pursue one's own or any other individual's happiness. Morality could be reconciled to the project of love only if love could promise universal and permanent happiness, which no single experience of love can do. Further, the irresponsibility of lovers, insofar as they are beside themselves, constitutes no authority; it only undercuts authority. Nevertheless, lovers' special way of being beside themselves does give love a kind of positive authority in that it neutralizes that which authority is normally asserted against, namely, self-seeking. It is on the same side of a standing battle as the authority of morality. Of course, there are other battles in which love and morality are not allies, as we just noted in contrasting love's individualizing perspective with morality's universalizing one. But the fundamental motion-toward-the-other accomplished by love secures the very principle of other-interestedness that morality requires case by case for right action. The lover shows that the confidence morality might place in love is not entirely mistaken by proceeding to wish everything well, not only the beloved —as long as nothing threatens the beloved. This is the very glow of love, or its unstoppable overflowing. In love, the condition of plurality itself is positive. It is now evident that it would be bad if there were not an other; thus, all others are baptized in the good otherness of the beloved.

On the other hand, love does not disprove the imperatival, constraining interpretation of relationship with the other proposed by morality and by our own account of the concrete. At first blush, love seems to show that when interpersonal affairs stand as they should, there is no constraint or demand, only fulfillment and joy. It must be remembered, however, that the joys of love presuppose the condition of plurality that is protected by the command to respect. To prescribe love without the discipline of respect is not only unrealistic, on the grounds already given, it is cheap, that is, it takes something that has not been earned, or makes to do something without being fit to do it.

Egoistic interpretations of the experience and import of love are possible, but perverse. It might be said that the lover seeks only a completion of him- or herself in the beloved. Why then is another intentional being required for this completion? Only because the completion in question is just that which can be provided only by the other as other. Or similarly, it might be held that the lover uses the beloved for confirmation of him- or herself; but why then seek confirmation by placing oneself at the mercy of a permanently unforeseeable response? Alternatively, the self might get relief from the burden of living with itself by escaping into the ecstasy of obsession with another. But we recognize a difference between the pathological condition of obsession and love; true lovers do not fall victim to the dispossessions we alluded to above, but remain with themselves and in charge of themselves at the same time that their love-part, the "heart," is "given."

The best reason for thinking that otherness is not essential to love but rather overcome in it is the frequency with which love is described as an interweaving or fusion of the lovers. But it is just the continuing real otherness that makes the condition resembling fusion so remarkable. In love's great rush of motion toward the other, one is no longer aware of the limits that are effective in maintaining one's normal reserve or repelling one from the world so that one can be something distinctive for oneself, a self. It is not that limits vanish; it is that they are no longer felt as constraining. In love the other and one's own selfhood become sweet limits to possible action and experience; it is a joy to orient everything one does and feels toward the particular nature and needs of the beloved, by means of one's own particular powers and sensitivities. The actual loss of these self-defining limits is a foolishness of obsession that is not holy.

Even so brief a review of our experience of love is sufficient to establish these two premises: that love is a transcendence of oneself, a being-given-over of oneself that is yet distinct from loss of self, and that in "true love," love meeting these conditions, one finds supreme happiness. Taken together, these premises yield the conclusion that *supreme* happiness is attained in *a certain kind* of relationship with an other, but this is not yet to say that happiness as such is constituted by relationship as such. We have to treat what is called love, by itself, as a clue rather than an argument, and go on to show that the conditions of love are met somehow by all happiness, and that any happiness devoid of love is deficient— so that transcendence or fellowship and happiness as such are linked, as our fifth affirmation would have it.

The objective and subjective sides of the issue of happiness have to be examined separately. First, it seems to an observer that persons who devote themselves to exterior beings are in general stronger, more attractive specimens than those who are absorbed in themselves. The devotion of a lover, the primary objectivity of a scientist, engineer, or worker, and even the zeal of a builder of model ships all seem noble on their face. There are, to be sure, cases in which devotion seems to be disfiguring, as when devotees so neglect their own interests that they lead the subpersonal lives of satellites. But in such cases the mistake seems to lie not in an excess of devotion as such, but in an inauthenticity in it. The daughter who "wastes" her own life caring for her invalid mother is somehow absent from the service she has performed, has perhaps become swallowed up in her mother's egoism; whereas we know someone else who has made similar sacrifices but in the manner of an affirmatively grasped life's work, and who on that account stays bright in memory and moral reflection.

As for subjective well-being, it seems that the reward character of happiness requires that chances be taken with others. One cannot be rewarded or gratified or fulfilled unless one has stretched out one's initially empty hand. One must also avoid damaging what comes into one's hand; one has to *affirm* whatever one *has,* so long as one is to have it. (This requirement faces every tyrant as a contradiction.) There is also the negative happiness of *relief* that can be gained from getting rid of or smashing things that oppress one, but evidently a happy life is not made just by putting a minus sign in front of a minus sign, whatever momentary refreshment this may offer. The positive happiness of stretching oneself in one's new freedom from a constraint is fleeting because it has no basis outside the event of liberation.

The difficulty arises that the chances one takes with others often do not pay off. It looks, therefore, as though happiness cannot consist in any and all affirmative actions with respect to others, but only in felicitated affirmation. Who, for instance, is unhappier than unrequited and bereaved lovers? Although it is a venerable part of the ideology of love to treat the unhappy lover as better off than one who has never loved at all, unhappy lovers find this cold comfort, and we observers of love might need further convincing—especially if we have in view the inwardly cooler and outwardly less promising affirmations asked of us by morality.

We must begin by appreciating how necessary is the principle "better to have loved and lost (or failed to gain) than never to have loved" to the ideology of love, on the present interpretation of love. If love really is a venture, then we could hardly nerve ourselves to take it if we did not believe in this principle. Only by committing ourselves to the venture as such, without guaranteed results, do we put ourselves in a position to receive the unobtainable and incalculable. The venture must therefore be a good, nay, a better thing in itself. But to say this is not yet to demonstrate the value of the venture in itself; it is only to comment on the *logic* of risky love. The value remains in doubt. Indeed, to prudence the whole project of risky love seems insane. We see this most clearly in the perspective of the Buddha's lofty, compassionate prudence. We are told that a woman grieving for a lost grandchild came to the Buddha seeking consolation. He asked her if she wished she had as many grandchildren to love as there were people living in the large town of Savatthi. "Oh yes," she exclaimed. "Then," said the Buddha, "you would cry every day, for in Savatthi someone dies every day." [5] The point of the story is not that one should not love, but that one should love detachedly, in peaceful independence of the contingencies that attend love. To Western sensibility this seems heretical. We feel that a love in which one does not put oneself at risk is inauthentic. This holds for religion as well as romance: Christianity and Judaism accept suffering and attempt to bestow meaning on it, calling on one to lay oneself open to it. The Suffering Servant and martyrs are blessed figures. To the unsympathetic bystander this will appear to be nothing more than ideological cheerleading for risky love that perhaps even undercuts its essential riskiness by guaranteeing a felicitation from God to all who love. Yet this felicitation does not annul suffering.

It may be that without prevenient or promised divine love, risky love is folly. But if that is so, then from our nontheological standpoint we can say only that folly is the price of happiness, or of what deserves to be reckoned true happiness. The ultimate retort of risky love to objections is that what is gained by holding back from it is not actually happiness but some lesser good such as tranquility or contentment—a mean compensation for what one might be and have. Less than one might be, because lovers, in their ardor, stretch themselves out into their intentionally strongest forms; less than one might have, because the possibility always does exist that one will receive the unobtainable. [6]

The basic interaction in which one stretches oneself toward a thing qua unobtainable and then receives it is not confined to experiences we call "love," though it appears there in heightened form. The lessons of love apply broadly to all reward experience. For example, on the happiest sort of hike, one climbs a hill not knowing what to expect and gains an undreamed-of view.

As would be expected, the force of the love argument for the fifth affirmation depends on a disputable conception of "happiness." Readers may gauge their allegiance to the conceptions of love and happiness presented here by their reactions to the story of the Buddha's advice to the grandmother.

Because of the intensity of the experience of love and the considerable development of doctrines that have grown out of our reflection on it, love offers itself as the most favorable point of departure for a specifically effective argument to our spiritual affirmations, particularly to the one regarding happiness. There are other effective approaches that are in one sense more suitable to our purpose, in that the affections in question are evidently disinterested ones, less likely to be confused either with selfish craving or self-despair than love is. Beings who are, as we say, "moved" by perception or imagination of the violation of others, or by merely hearing of the free return of one being to another, are beings who live outside themselves in a peculiarly "spiritual" way. In comparison, the passionately interested lover seems like a man trying to jump out of his own boots—who sometimes succeeds. But those who are horrified or whose hearts are warmed already float in the space of interintentionality; they are affected even though they are not present bodily at the point where the affect is delivered.

(e) Violation as Horrible

I begin with the premise that horror is an essential part of the affective life, as it ought to be. To be unhorrifiable would be an essential defect; the thought of an unhorrifiable person is itself horrifying. I maintain this in face of the not uncommon belief that human beings can hope to attain an emotional position beyond upset, on the principle that *tout comprendre, c'est tout accepter*. We have already argued that *tout comprendre* is out of reach. Now we shall argue further that certain events are absolutely unacceptable, that the inability to accept them destabilizes the self, and that this would only happen to a being committed to living in togetherness with others as other. Having earlier separated spiritual togetherness from mere sociability or herd instinct, we will now array horror on the spiritual side and proceed on the hypothesis that subjects experience horror proper by means of, and not in spite of, cognition and norming responsibility.

Unlike other modes of intense fear such as terror and dread, horror mingles repulsion and protest. It differs from simple disgust in its threateningness, and it is unique among ways of feeling threatened in its (impotent) gesture of rejecting the threat, saying "No, this *should not* be." Horrified eyes refuse to believe what they are seeing; even while they take in the horrible, they say "No, this *is* not." Horror discloses the synthesis of "is" and "ought" in one's conception of the "nature" of things. If one did not think that the destroyed or threatened thing ought to be as it is, one would not be bothered by what happens to it, it would not count as a "violation"—therein lies the "ought." But if one did not further believe that the *nature* of things makes unthinkable the violation in question, one would not feel the vertigo, the cognitive disorientation, that comes in confronting the horrible, which produces expressions like "sick" and "warped." Horror-tale characters like the Undead directly attack our sense of how things are-and-ought-to-be.

Horrifying presentations achieve their effects easily because it makes no difference to my horror whether a zombie stalks me or someone else. The unnaturalness is what horrifies, not the threat to my person. Horror is the bystander's fear par excellence, the newspaper reader's fear.

There is an element of betrayal in that which horrifies. One discovers that one had counted on things being a certain way, one had formed one's very self on the assumption; now, how is it possible to live in this other world in which one cannot count on this certain thing, and by implication on anything? But that this question arises at all presupposes a mode of existence that was contingent to start with upon the concurrence of others. It may have been foolish to build a self on this violable foundation, like a house on sand, and then to treat the sand as though it were rock. The more sensible alternative would be not to count on anything. We find in this dilemma of suffering attachment versus seemingly mean-spirited detachment a repetition of the problem brought to light in our consideration of love. Now, to present the dilemma truly, we must purify it of elements that do not belong to it.

I am horrified by the "unnatural." But how did *that sort* of "nature," one in which will and feeling are invested, get constituted? It must have been formed by a normative gesture that either was first motivated by desire or carried desire in its train. The desire must be in the norm for the possibility of emotional offense to exist. At the same time, the desire must really have become an objective, that is, interintentional norm; it cannot be a mere principle of personal wishing. No matter how strongly and consistently I want my car to work properly, still, when it fails to start, I am never more than vexed—never actually horrified. Breaking down like this is, after all, in the *nature* of cars. But if something genuinely uncanny occurs—for instance, if the brake pedal suddenly has no effect as I approach a busy intersection—then there occurs that combination of recoil of feeling and cognitive dislocation that distinguishes horror, and only because it is the case that "one" counts on "one's" car's brakes and not just I on mine. Admittedly, if I knew more about car mechanics I would regard brake failure in the same class as a dead battery, and if I could be brought cognitively to accept it I would thereby lose my horror of it, though not my fear. Therefore, horror is relative to what horrified individuals know or think they know, and the improvability of knowledge means that at least certain horrors are eliminable.

The purely scientific attitude never insists on a certain conception of a thing but stands ready to revise concepts according to what the things themselves do, and so is invulnerable in principle to horror—it is, in fact, the modern cultural equivalent of Stoicism. Science suffers only from the marginal horror of the radically unintelligible, which it successfully excludes by holding incontrovertibly that God does not play with dice (or, alternatively, plays with dice according to laws of chance). If there is an ineliminable horror, it does not lie in the "nature" addressed by science.

It would be absurd for a scientist to will that the phenomena be different than they are, just as absurd as Canute's commanding the waves to stop. A nonabsurd prescription can be issued only to a being capable of taking direction, which is to say an intender in relationship with other intenders. Now, horror proper presupposes that a nonabsurd prescription is in force, namely, the norm, backed by the horrified individual's intention, that is threateningly contradicted in experience. Therefore the "nature" that is violated in horror must be the nature of an intentional being, which, as a "nature," is held to be something not merely changeable—hence properly a "nature"—but at the same time is not merely empirical, not merely to be observed. The intentional others are free to join us in spirit but equally free to pull the rug out from under our feet; but we are not free not to stand on that rug, and therein lies our permanent liability to horror. We are caught in the contradictory position of simultaneously treating each other as nonempirical (qua free) beings and committing ourselves to a life resting on interintentional concurrence, on agreed ways to be, for which "(human) nature" is the comprehensive formula. For example, a mother who hates her own children is, for the scientist, merely unusual, whereas to the ordinary sensibility she is "unnatural." Mother love is such a fundamental building block of our spiritual edifice that everything teeters when it is removed. Yet the norm of mother love would not have taken on such emotional force if it were not maintained by significant prescribing, which presupposes that mothers really are free to take (or reject) the prescription.

To the extent that events not in human control are lastingly horrible, they are viewed theologically. The horrible earthquake that killed thousands was something that a god did or let happen. It cannot be perceived as horrible if we think that it *just* happened.

In sum, horror is the experience of the subversion of spirit, which insofar as it is ineliminable makes acknowledgment of a primordial commitment to spiritual existence incumbent on us. One knows both that one exists in relationship with others and that one is, in a generalized way, *"one"* (not only "I"), a being spread through the whole network of relationships rather than a specific point in that network. An earthquake in Turkey, killer of hundreds, shakes me when I read about it in the newspaper; in a certain manner I *am* in Turkey as the ectoplasmic "one." This spiritual "one" is not to be confused with the *Man* of the inauthentic *Man-selbst* of which Heidegger speaks in *Being and Time*, nor with the "immersion in the spirit of the community" observable in children and "primitive" peoples that is remarked by Scheler or the primordial relationality discussed by Buber in *I and Thou*.[7] These modes of life are on the near side of the formation of a separate self, whereas the "one" is beyond that. It is not the case that I live as though I really were in Turkey, suffering the violation of the earthquake. Turkey remains far from me, but nevertheless the earthquake *matters*. It shakes the *spirit* in me, which then, perhaps, upsets my stomach.

From the premises that we are normally and normatively horrifiable and that horror presupposes the prescription of a "nature" shared by intentional beings, we argue most directly to the fourth affirmation: I am what I am in relationship with others. For otherwise I would not experience a shaking of my own foundations in the subversive action of the horrifying. But in the analysis of horror we find also a new confirmation of the eminence of intentional others, since only they can be the objects of nonabsurd prescription and thus the agents of horrification. The fifth affirmation on happiness is partially confirmed by the discovery that the subject's well-being is staked to the concurrence of others.

(f) The Return of the Other as Heartwarming

Horror is "moving," in a repulsive way. One finds one's own will unraveling in the experience, or one's vision led out over an abyss. But there is another well-known way in which one can be "moved," a positive, attractive, integrating, and grounding counterpart to horror for which the precisely accurate if banal term is "heartwarming." Like horror, it is an emotional target often aimed at by works of art because it is so easy to hit; so easy to hit, because our susceptibility to it is linked with our universalized existence as "one." However, horror is of primary interest only in comparatively trivial genres of narrative art, such as horror novels and horror films—even though it makes a crucial contribution to most of the greatest tragedies; whereas heartwarming seems to be the main point of virtually all stories that we think of as ending "happily."

A story often told in one version or another to children may serve as the prototype of them all. A little girl finds a baby robin fallen from its nest. As it grows up it becomes her dear pet. But the day comes when the robin is unhappy to be confined indoors, and the little girl realizes (or one of her wise parents counsels her) that it is time for the bird, which was born wild, to be wild again. She opens the window; it flies away; she cries. But the robin comes back, and before leaving again promises to return the following year. Sure enough, next spring it appears at her windowsill and stays with her until it is time to fly on, and the visit is repeated every year after that, first by the original robin and then by its descendants.[8]

The robin story has in common with all heartwarming stories that the otherness of the other is emphasized by a natural unlikeness, while the freedom of the other is proved by separation in order that the eventually confirmed relationship will be felt to be based on true concurrence—not habit, circumstance, or utilitarian calculation. The other returns as other, gratuitously, yet benignly, enabling and forming spirit. In the robin story these conditions are met in spectacular fashion. The robin is, according to our preunderstanding of it, barely an intentional being at all; the question hovers over the story whether relationship with it is even possible, let alone probable—it is a miraculous opportunity for the spiritual when the baby robin falls from its world into the girl's—and when the robin returns, "keeping faith," it is almost as glorious as if the stones were to start singing. The wild robin in respect of its form of life is as alien to the little girl as another intentional being could be, except for fish (whence the charm of mermaid tales) or creatures from another planet. The Montague male and Capulet female are like peas in a pod in comparison. Then the robin goes away, not just to another place but into an entirely different scheme of things (the robin itinerary of migration, the robin significance of the seasons, robin mating and family life, etc.). The eventual fidelity of the robin bridges over these differences and transcends even the first robin's life, so strong is this spiritual tie that seemed initially so frail in relation to the forces of nature.

The role of works of art in the general enterprise of rectifying relationships is to organize their elements in such a way that we feel they come out right. In stories this is a matter of producing the sense of an ending, which of course may be right without being "happy"—for tragedies come out right, given the evils with which they deal—but which is, by the testimony of popular narrative art, rightest of all when it is happy; and the happiness or flourishing of the principals is, in the most moving stories, always set in relationship. The successful knight does not just kill the monster, he then marries the princess. The cowboy does not just defeat the bronco, he tames it. The little engine does not just manage to pull the train over the mountain, it succeeds in this by way of being of service to the boys and girls waiting for the train. Christ is not just resurrected, he comes back to his disciples.

Inclusiveness, maximal extension of relationship, is a prime virtue of happy artistic presentations. In the happiest stories the villains are converted rather than destroyed. *Everyone* in the town pitches in to help a protagonist in distress. Nature herself may help at the crucial moment with a timely wind or rainfall. (Consider the parallel of the "happy" pictures made so memorable by Jan van Eyck and the Master of Flemalle, in which the smallest and most ordinary things are exalted by inclusion in a beautiful whole; or the "happy" architecture of Gothic churches, encompassing both grotesque and sublime decorations.)

Readers must decide for themselves which stories seem to them to come out rightest, to see whether the suggestions offered here are correct. In making this judgment it will be necessary to put aside any criteria other than happiness, such as realism or novelty or intricacy of design, that would militate for or against different sorts of stories. It would be absurd to demand that all stories set out to warm our hearts as much as possible; I do not mean to be setting up either an aesthetic or a moral canon. We should be mistrustful of stories that are too happy, for they are probably cheap both aesthetically and morally. However, we should not be uncritical of the *other* desires and sensitivities that stories aim to gratify. If I long for power, I will love to read about omnipotent characters (the fastest gun in the West); if I am bored with my surroundings, I will seek out stories of faraway places; if I am bored altogether, I will seek diversion in stories of fascinating complexity. Literature is pervaded with elements catering to these inclinations, too, since they are strong and perennial. But such elements are not, for all the pleasures they afford, as *moving* as the one that we have discussed here. "Moving" is the specifically aesthetic version of the event-for-and-in-intention of superordination. In its positive form, "heartwarming," it is one's sensing that "Yes, that matters most" and "Yes, that is best."

The premises of this argument are that the most moving stories are those that end in the triumph of relationship, and that the "moving" in question is testimony (which cannot be gainsaid) to one's fundamental orientation toward the important and the good. It follows that one who is thus moved is committed prior to all other commitments to relationship as we have defined it—which supports our second, fourth, and fifth affirmations.

5.3 A Transitional Remark on Spiritual Facts

For the allied purposes of letting the others be other and letting intention be free, we have denied being to spirit. We have held to an extreme form of the is-ought disjunction in construing spiritual existence itself, the medium and subject of all oughts, as a normative venture without describable foundation. Spiritual existence is standing on air, existing in a certain way purely by meaning to exist in a certain way. Accordingly, the first part of this discourse has been a proposal, rather than a description; an offering of a possibility rather than a banking on a reality. Still, it will not have escaped the reader's notice that in the dialectical arguments of this chapter certain given spiritual realities were appealed to. If there were not something *there* to appeal to, some commitment to critical knowledge, propensity to horror, and so forth, argument on these matters would be impossible. But how can something which *is not* be *there*? Are we not indirectly granting being to spirit by assuming that certain other-regarding intentions have been and will be realized in recognizable form?

Everything depends on how that assumption is made. If we do not let ourselves speak of the being of spirit, then our assuming must always be hopeful and proclamatory, a free positing of the meaning of what is assumed. If we say "This story is heartwarming," we mean "Let this story be heartwarming." If we claim that an other is there to be met as other, we go to the rendezvous point riskily and foolishly, like lovers.

In spite of its logically queer status and its tenuousness, spiritual life does have shape, as does anything that can be spoken of. We have spiritual habits and spiritual identities, as all the assuming that we do follows rules and forms into patterns. The solution of is-ought problems—those that are properly soluble—is possible thanks to the "existence" of this spiritual factuality. The grounding of any norming I offer to you must be the fact that you intend as you are invited to, or that we intend together in the way I declare possible. Those are not facts like others; I can only talk about them provisionally and look forward to them. But they are fact-like in their independence from me and the moment and in their occurrent contingency.

The last three chapters of this work investigate three major problems concerning spiritual factuality, proceeding from the basic orientation of the philosophy of the spiritual that has been achieved in the foregoing. These problems came to our notice already in the historical review of Chapter 1. We should address them just in order to reach a more adequate total understanding of the spiritual, but in doing so we will reap the extra benefit of gaining a superior perspective on a range of ethical, aesthetic, and metaphysical points of traditional interest. The three problems of spiritual factuality are:

1   How is "validity" possible, that is, how can one know in advance that a move of a certain form will be an interintentional success?

2   Under what conditions does the spiritual life take material form?

3   How does the spiritual life contribute to the determination of what happens in the world?

Chapter 6

The Essence and Forms of Validity

6.1 The Pneumatological Approach to Validity

At every moment, I am turned toward some X that is *there*. But—where am *I*? Am I someplace definite at every moment?

An unreflective being walks ahead without looking to see where it is putting its feet. The problem of its own position does not arise for it. A puppy on ice is a comical sight: slipping and slipping, it cannot think about how to walk but persists with the instinctive mechanics of forward motion. Human beings, on the other hand, not only will pay attention to the issue of how to walk on slick ice but will be so perplexed from the start that they are barely able to move. I attend to my own position, present and prospective, and find, instead of an "X that is there," multiple indefinite possibilities—an annoying and challenging state of affairs for an intender. I might go crazy if I found myself always in it; by everyday standards I rarely am. Yet, in a sense not really foreign to everyday understanding, I *am* always in it, because in addition to the sporadic difficulties I encounter in positioning myself with respect to a more or less stable environment, I am also necessarily aware, more than sporadically, of the question of my position with respect to others as other: all the individual beings inhabiting that "environment" that was a function of my purposes, and, eminently, the intentional others in collusion with whom I am embarked on spiritual existence. I am not simply where I see myself but also, since I am committed to seeing with the others, where the others see me. Since I can in principle never know exactly how the others see me, it is as though I had to walk on ice all my life.

Where shall one stand, to what spot shall one put one's foot forward, in face of these difficulties? There must be places to stand that one can have some confidence in, where one can expect not to slip and fall, and where, looking further, there is an open horizon, a freedom from infelicitous consequences—for example, the infelicity of being sought by other persons elsewhere than where one is. It must be possible to see these places in advance and to have a map of them so that one can plan journeys. A life that is *all* slipping and stumbling and lostness is unthinkable. A tenable position, a place where one can count on being able to position oneself, which holds one and where one can hold forth and avail, is a locus of *validity*.

The word "validity" derives from a word for strength, the Latin *valere*. The valid is originally the effective, what works, what can be done. But the question of what can be done draws in and increasingly relies on the enterprise of mapping positions in the practical and theoretical arts and sciences, since our sense of what can be done is determined both by our accumulating experience in relation to the environment and by how this experience figures in the interintentional network. The sense of a doing is incorporated and preserved in our positional definition of validity, because positions are meaningless except as places where things are or may be done. One occupies a position in no other way than by acting in some fashion—be that action only a waiting to receive the action of another being.

The metaphor of the "position" or "place to stand" applies here not just to theaters of action but to actions themselves. Before any perplexity about where to try to do a thing is the question of what to do; lacking the ability to perform an action (a formed movement), an intentional being is most fundamentally lost and adrift. Actions—or, to qualify them spiritually, "gestures"—are the loci of intention. When I move into the next moment of my life, I must deliver of that moment a move of a certain shape. That move is the place where my temporally projecting foot comes down. If I miss it, I lose the thread of my existence. I dither. We feel this vividly when we try some complicated movement with our bodies as complete novices—for instance, on the first attempt at riding a bicycle. The seriousness of the demand for the certification of certain positions and gestures as "valid" is measured by the helplessness and futility that we experience at such times and that we must keep at bay for the sake of coherent life.

We take up the theme of validity in order to examine this problem of coherence, especially as posed by spiritual existence, in which what one *can* do is inextricably entangled with what one *may* do. We dealt earlier with the problem of rectifying relationships, but without much regard for how it is possible to structure a spiritual life; in other words, we saw the spirit of an intentional move without seeing how it could be pulled off. We prescribed certain rules of reason, for example, without worrying how a person could engage in reasoning or recognize a reason. This is, nevertheless, a matter that requires our attention here. Furthermore, since the intentional event of the gesture is qualified by intention's encounter with others, it is necessary that our understanding of gestures (symbols, propositions, styles, and spirits or cultures) receive a first orientation from the philosophy of the spiritual.

The problem of validity is philosophically approachable in four ways.

Realism, whether natural or transcendental-ontological, would have it that the range of valid intentional moves is determined by the landscape of what is. Those moves that fit this landscape, either conforming or corresponding, are the ones that may be made repeatedly and without attendant infelicity. The weakness of realism, of course, is that we cannot check reality independently of the moves we make, so we gain nothing by positing it as a solution of this problem. If, moreover, the most important features of the landscape are unknowable others-as-other, then "conforming" and "corresponding" become inapplicable in their normal senses and the main explanatory virtue of realism is removed.

The strength of *psychologism* is to start from the truth that validity is an issue only for minds; its thesis is that we discover the tenable intentional positions by observing what intention factually succeeds in doing. For example, one establishes the validity of the law of noncontradiction by demonstrating the incapacity of the mind to conceive A and not-A simultaneously.[1] Now, it is certain that the law of noncontradiction would not be valid for mind M if it were not the case that M can clearly conceive propositions formed in accordance with it and cannot clearly conceive propositions conflicting with it. The psychological condition is necessary; it is not, however, sufficient. Psychologism is crippled by its inability to produce an interintentionally normative form of thought or expression. What I can think or say is not coextensive with what I or anyone ought to think or say, and yet public systems of intention (logic, ethics, etc.) require objective or universal or a priori validity for their forms. This sort of validity belongs to the very sense of those forms.

Idealism accepts mind as the reference point for validity but escapes the embarrassment of psychologism by positing mind objective, universal, and a priori. The valid is what is in fact intended by objective mind rather than yours or mine. We attain valid intention to the precise extent that we conform to this mind in us, which is not something formed by contingent experience but exists eternally (or with historical necessity) and therefore can be counted on in all cases and cannot even be conceived to fail us. Idealism has a difficulty in getting to this objective mind, one which seems at first less severe than the difficulty of realism, since mind is available to us in a way that exterior reality is not, but in the end proves no less so. For objective mind derives its authority over the actual minds of individuals precisely from its exteriority to them, but insofar as it is exterior it is unavailable for independent examination. After careful procedures of thinking have been followed, resulting in the deduction of transcendental categories or the enactment of the dialectic of the absolute Idea, an act of faith is still required to posit that these thought-forms are not merely what Kant and Hegel were able to produce but what all thinkers, always and everywhere, must arrive at insofar as they succeed in thinking. Idealism turns out to be just psychologism plus faith, and although there are grounds for that faith, idealism locates them wrongly. It has no vindication different from that to which psychologism looks; both stand or fall according to what the actual intender manages to intend. Although idealism rests on a *transcendental* fact of intention, it is yet only *a fact* that as such *means* a somewhat with respect to which I and the others are free, so that idealism can account no better than psychologism for the binding, normative character of "objectively valid" forms. Idealism is forced to claim that "oughtness" is experienced in the discrepancy between individual mind and objective mind, which leads it to the unacceptable conclusion that a wholly objective mind would no longer be either subject to obligation or free—that is, on a loose tether of responsibility —in the interintentional sense. Hegel's self-moving Concept, for example, can neither be moved by anything nor move in relation to anything. (My objection assumes that the interintentional sense of the crucial concepts such as obligation and freedom is superordinated to the merely intentional sense, inadequate but not incoherent with itself, on which idealism relies.)

The approach to be defended here could be called *pneumatologism* if the word were not too ugly to use. It adds, to the recognition that validity is relative to intention, the principle that normatively objective validities must somehow invite in the exteriority that the other approaches either fail to reach or try to incorporate without proper entitlement. In order to identify intentional moves that are not only makeable but makeable in principle by all and acceptable to all—the moves that are made by "one," our counterpart to *Bewusstsein überhaupt*—we need to commence negotiations with the others, or, since that can hardly be done all at once, find where these negotiations have already been begun, and what manner of results they have shown themselves capable of producing.[2] The others have to be somehow present, as my effective partners and justifying judges, in anything I mean if it is to count as valid in the fullest sense.

In the next four sections we will build up the order of validity forms, from the simplest to the most comprehensive, both to establish a perspicuous overview *clear,*valid* of validity and also to give ourselves insight, as each appropriate vantage point appears, into related philosophical problems. Then in sections 6.6–6.8 we will turn from what *can* be meant to what *should* be meant, seeking an alternative to "values" theory as a frame of reference for judgments of worth.

6.2 Propositions. Symbols and the Critique of Art

Every gesture may be called a "proposition" since it puts something forward, something, moreover, that is itself a position, namely, a way of perceiving, think-ing, willing, acting, or feeling. Whether I speak a sentence, write a book, paint a painting, wave my hand, or scratch my chin, I simultaneously occupy a position relative to others (which may be warm or cool, right or wrong, etc.) and publicly establish a position as possible and perhaps desirable to occupy. I may at times risk improvising novel propositions to see how they will turn out, but that is out-side our present concern: we seek the conditions under which a proposition may be anticipated as a success, or what makes it valid.

It is a freezing morning in December. My next-door neighbor emerges from his house at the same moment I come out of mine, and I see that while we are making our respective ways to the sidewalk, words of some kind must pass between us. I finally think of a serviceable remark: "Cold enough for you?" I would never venture on such irony with a semi-stranger like my neighbor, except that this particular irony is hallowed by so much general use that no one should take it differently than the way I mean it, as a harmless, friendly comment on the weather. I am confident that this gesture will assert an acceptable sort of comradeship with my neighbor because I have often accepted it and seen it accepted. The gesture's validity is obviously not absolute in the sense that it is certain to achieve what I mean to achieve by it. My neighbor may be abnormally cranky this morning and resent my presumption. Or I may speak in a slightly wrong tone that makes him suspect an active irony on top of the standardized irony of the phrase. But, in principle, one *may* say "Cold enough for you?" to one's neighbor, when it is cold. If he resents it, he, not the phrase, is "off"; if I misspeak it, I am in the wrong—I have put forward a different proposition than the valid one.

One often talks as though it is one's grasp of the usage in one's language, or the guidance of the language-system or of an impersonal standard like a dictionary, that renders a proposition valid, but actually validity rests on the assurance that one receives from the *others, through* one's sense of usage or the dictionary. For the others, however remotely they may have authorized a proposition in advance, remain quite presently its acid test. A few rebuffs from my neighbor will be sufficient to invalidate "Cold enough for you?" with respect to *him*. Failure with only a few of the people I say it to will destroy the presumption of *general* validity. We can easily imagine misfires with this sort of a proposition because it is so clearly a matter of one person's approaching another with a certain intention, at a level where intention is normally quite changeable. It is harder to imagine encountering any difficulty with a proposition like "It is 28 degrees Fahrenheit" uttered while looking at a thermometer in response to the question, "Just how cold is it?"—because the intentions in that scenario are standardized to a very great extent. Harder, but not impossible. The person asking the question might be one's estranged lover, who only wants to talk about the temperature metaphorically; to read degrees off the thermometer would then be nonsensical, or an insult. It seems that one can never be absolutely confident that a proposition will come off. Even as I say "It is 28 degrees" the words might sound as nonsense in my own ears, as I realize I should be saying something else to my lover, or as I am confounded by my inability to give a physicist's explanation of what "28 degrees" means. Saying "It is 28 degrees" is impeccable English but might still amount to perfectly executing a dive and then missing the pool. There is no use insisting it is a valid English sentence if it lets down the parties between whom it passes. (To be sure, it is not noise; as a well-formed English sentence it necessarily has a certain limited validity, sanctioned up to a point by the English-speaking community.)

The horizon of validity includes felicities and infelicities that vary infinitely with real interaction. Philosophically, however, one can do no more than point this out as a preamble to saying what can be said about general types and laws of validity. The importance of pointing it out is that we then lose any illusion that the "objective" generalities we arrive at could hold absolutely. The only principle from which no deviation is permissible is the pluralist one, that validity is constituted in reckoning with others as other. Then the principles of "grammar" (in the Wittgensteinian sense) valid for the time being and for the most part may and need to be drawn out of our actual practice.

But now we have other, more unsettled fields to survey. The validity of certain gestures considered merely as means of communication is, broadly, a matter for grammatical investigation. Yet we frequently do more than merely to try to bring off a communication (which is about all that "Cold enough for you?" does). Suppose that my neighbor and I are citizens of a state in the American South, the year is 1850, and as we walk out of our houses, I say to him, "Our moral duty is to abolish slavery." Though I had hoped in saying this to evoke his assent, or at least his thoughtful attention to the issue, my neighbor angrily tells me that I am either crazy or irresponsible. The problem is not that he did not understand my words or took them differently than I meant them; he appreciates my meaning perfectly, but he repudiates the position I have proposed. The moral content of my communication is, by his lights, invalid. How should we interpret such a case?

My proposition was a move leading my interlocutor to make a complementary move such that we would come down together in a tenable position, which here would amount to moral and eventually practical agreement. This did not happen. It seems that the assertion of slavery's moral intolerableness is not a gesture that my neighbor can make—although I made it in the first place because I judged slavery to be unjust, that is, interintentionally untenable in a certain way. But I do not actually know that he *cannot* make it; I only know that he *will not* make it. When I accuse him of arbitrariness, he claims he will not make the preliminary gesture of accepting a duty to abolish slavery because the whole gesture of rejecting slavery (which reaches far beyond the uttering of a few words or the entertaining of a sentiment) *cannot* be made; I am "crazy" or "irresponsible," intentionally or interintentionally disorganized, to think that it can. But neither he nor I *knows* for certain that it can or cannot be made. We may be "morally certain" of our positions, which means that we feel ourselves claimed by the judgments we have made and bound to honor them, fallible though they be, because the weight of probability or the luminosity of the good is so much on one side, as far as we can see. Undoubtedly, we are also strongly influenced by what we would like to do, how our intentions incline, distinct from what we can do or feel bound to do. However, insofar as our argument turns on the *validity* of a moral claim or the *tenability* of a moral position—and serious moral arguments frequently arrive at this formulation of the issue—we oppose to each other different judgments of what is possible for intention, that is, what, for you and me and others, individually and together, will come off. The same is true of all arguments over propositions as distinct from failures to understand propositions.

An ambiguity hovers over every such argument inasmuch as *will not* is never completely resolvable into *cannot*. Sympathetic readers of literature continually discover the possibility of intentions they once thought impossible. Thus, we are on much surer ground when we base validity claims on intentional moves that have succeeded than when we project that a proposed one will fail. Even in appealing to success, however, we speak with much less assurance and right of what has succeeded *with others* than with ourselves alone, and subject to doubt and criticism concerning whether success is being judged in the correct framework. The antebellum slaveowner will claim that his relationship with his slaves is just, beneficent, and tenable, confirming this with observations of his slaves' happiness and gratefulness. Not only that: some few slaves *are* happy and grateful. The slaveowner has to be gotten to ascertain more adequately the shape of his slaves' lives, which may require efforts going far beyond the bounds of that everyday interaction from which we normally gain our perceptions of each other's well- and ill-being. As for the happy slaves, if we want to say that they should not be happy, we may not ignore the fact that they are, as far as they know. But to have a validity-related argument against their position, it will not be enough to tell them that their intentions toward themselves are inadequate, for they may be content to occupy a social position of diminished freedom and responsibility as long as they live with others who want or accept the greater power. They must be shown that an intention they do have founders on some implication of the situation they are in. For instance, the propositions "We Africans (as a class) can be happy in slavery"—which an argumentative Uncle Tom would advance, since to except himself and others like him from his class as a whole would contradict the elementary spiritual intention of fairness—can be invalidated by confronting it with the evident unhappiness of numerous slaves who are inevitably ambitious of more freedom than they have simply because they are human. And a once-contented slave who has been persuaded to discontent now has reason to believe that one can never judge with certainty the true extent of the success even of one's own intentions. That lesson we should all take to heart.

In the broadest sense, "symbols" are simply the elements from which propositions are formed, bits of perceptible pipe from which conduits for intention can be constructed.[3] Many of them are not sufficient in themselves to make a move, as for instance my writing 'g' here, without the accompanying words that make of it an example, would mean nothing either to you or to me. But symbols can often function alone as propositions. They then become subject to the propositional conditions of validity discussed above in addition to the basic condition that they be instrumentally effective.

Certain symbols are pregnant with more meaning than one can explicitly assign them according to grammatical and lexical rules. They seem to be the indispensable mediators for our awareness of "higher" things, leading us beyond the secure and well-connected realm of what we "know" to marvelous rewards unencompassable by objectifying or rationalizing intentions. In them we make a move (it remains to inquire in the next chapter how a move can be made in or through a perceptible object) into the dark where something comes off, although we cannot see what it is or approach it from any other angle; and we credit the revelation of the move with "truth" when we detect a correspondence of the symbol with some permanent possibility of intention, whether we were obscurely involved with it before or came upon it this moment for the first time.[4] Now in the first place it is exhilarating just to have this happen. One has done something that one did not know one was capable of. In this expansion of one's performative repertoire there is a sense of strength, both one's own irresistible ability and the firmness of the carrying symbols—Chesterton somewhere speaks of poetic words as strong enough to build bridges with—and of "height," because the ceiling on one's operations has been raised, albeit into a dark zone. But this sort of height must be distinguished from the superordination of others in intentional encounter, which may also be accomplished through symbols. Meeting others as other is, to pursue the metaphor of a room, a backing away of the walls around one which creates an environing darkness charged with the possibilities open to the others, and to oneself as with the others.

Consider one short line of poetry:

Wild air, world-mothering air.[5]

The letters make words, the words make a thought, and the thought is an element of the larger proposition formed by the whole poem—we say the air is symbolized as a wild world-mother for the purposes of this poem. The thought can also stand on its own as a prescribed approach to the world, and latently does so (for which reason we speak of the "power" and "suggestiveness" of symbols) even when it is not asked to. Conversely, the whole poem will become part of our general vocabulary and an element for further propositions, thus a symbol.

We can discuss the similarities between the air and mothers by virtue of which comparison between them is thinkable, but it can never be shown, except in the poem, darkly, how it is *right* to aim at them together. In the poem one experiences the rightness, in the first place, as the sheer possibility of making the move after one has pulled it off. That success is a necessary condition of the line's validity, but not aesthetically sufficient. One must now dare to let the language refer to real air, world, and mothers (and indirectly to oneself as really being in and with air, world, and mothers), as one had not yet done in simply comprehending the words and mentally knitting them together. The line must become a vessel for intention as it meets those others. Such a line may actually introduce me to those others in the first place by jolting me out of my purely ideal grasp of the symbols that conventionally refer to them. Not from an extraneous moral point of view, but from the aesthetic point of view itself, which is concerned with the amplitude of life, we insist that a poem be thus lived, and not idly entertained. Beyond all this, the poem is matter for conversation and must be tested between *us,* who meet in the poem as critics both of poetry and of life. As a performance-possibility for intention, as a vessel by which intention approaches others, the symbol-proposition is at the same time a vessel by which one performing, other-approaching, speaking intention approaches others in a unique constellation of ways. "Wild air, world-mothering air" is thus charged with a multitude of motions and meetings that could not be specified or brought about otherwise.

Because of limiting assumptions concerning how symbols can and cannot relate us to the real, some rationalistic or morally sensitive philosophers have mistrusted the symbolism of art, seeing in it a seductive but cheap alternative to the reality in which moral demands are embedded. According to the best-known of such criticisms, that of Plato in the *Republic*, works of art are but copies of copies, that is, imitations of physical things that themselves only inadequately represent eternal Forms; this means that art is *retrograde* to the reality-seeking movement of philosophy—ultimately, to put this as baldly as possible, a way of hiding from the Good.[6] (I do not take up the problem of reconciling this view with the *Phaedrus* and *Symposium*, where it is suggested that the enthusiasm for beauty can spur one's attention on toward yet more excellent things; but note that even if art is blessed by this positive view, it remains something to be superseded.) Kierkegaard's critique of the aestheticist manner of living has inspired others. Ebner, for example, sees in the experience of art (for which his paradigm is music) a flight into I-aloneness, and in the longing inspired by beauty a substitute for the genuine transcendence of meeting other persons in the Word.[7] Grisebach's view of reality as ethical, that is, as interpersonally pluralistic and incorrigibly problematic, is similar to Ebner's. He, too, rejects works of art insofar as they smooth over our conflictual experience of reality with harmonies and solutions that are valid strictly in the sphere of the I, in *Erinnerung*. But he distinguishes, unlike Ebner, between the post-Renaissance cult of self-expressing, self-expanding art and art as such. He believes that art can stay related to ethical reality by holding back from the imposition of false harmonies. Its genuine positive aim is to provide a restoring pause, a clarifying disengagement from practice. The best example of this kind of art in literature he finds in Strindberg, who, following Kierkegaard, rejects aestheticist valuation of art.[8]

Buber, on the other hand, maintains a much more unqualifiedly positive view of art, even though he is not insensitive to the tension between aestheticism and the life of dialogue. In the language of *I and Thou*, art works are "spiritual beings" that inhabit one of the three "spheres of relation." Although we hear no "You" from them, we feel "addressed." [9] Buber's broad acceptance of art is correlated with his ability to affirm the *soul* (even while he must here and there deflate its pretensions in order to make his case for the "between") and the otherness of nonhuman beings. Two sentences are enough to reveal his crucial premises: "This is the eternal origin of art[,] that a human being confronts a form that wants to become a work through him. Not a figment of his soul but something that appears to the soul and demands the soul's creative power." [10] He does not portray the soul as essentially engaged in building an empire for its own security and enjoyment; though he feels the same polemical compunction that Grisebach and Ebner do (as witness his warning, "not a figment"), he does not feel it to the same extent.

The differences between these writers reflect the problems created by the inter- section of distinct validity conditions. I am intentionally related to myself as the intender, to the repertoire of forms of intention available to me with respect to myself, to other beings both speaking and nonspeaking, and to all the forms of possible intention with respect to them and with them. Other beings in their other- ness confront me with a power of exclusiveness, forbidding me to look through or past them to other beings in relation to which they would be mere means. If, therefore, my intention is subject to the demand of meeting and responding to other persons, it seems that it is necessarily invalidated if it gives itself to a performance of a piece of music *for its own sake;* while if it makes of that music a means for attending to others, as for example the background for dancing or, by stipulation, a message to a lover, the specifically musical intention is necessarily invalidated—for the "spiritual reality" of the musical form is not met as such. But obviously the principle of exclusivity requires some kind of qualification. It is not true that in the instant one gives one's attention to a certain being, every other being to which one could give one's attention is thereby dishonored. If it were, every intention would be invalid from all points of view but one. (Com- pare the argument in section 3.4 [1] above.) Exactly how, though, can a move be simultaneously valid from two or more points of view? This is a pressing question already at the elementary level of validity, the symbol, which is a servant at once of that which is symbolized and of the one with whom there is communication through the symbol.

Suppose that a woman says "Wild air, world-mothering air" to a man. She could say this looking out past him at the atmosphere and/or earth; looking at the atmosphere and/or earth while holding his hand; looking at him, gesturing toward the atmosphere and/or earth; embracing him with her eyes closed; or in some other way. Any of these utterances could in principle be valid objectively (for the sake of the world), personally (for the sake of the relationship), and poetically, all at the same time. In fact, to be valid poetically *means* (as we asserted just above) in part to be valid objectively, since a saying about the world unconnected with the real world could not be good poetry, and also personally, since a poem whose intention could not leap from one speaker to another and be shared could likewise not be good. The poetic form gives itself as a bridge to the world and the other person, meaning for all to exist together for intention in nonreductive fashion— in the way that the excellence of an actual dance step is essentially bound to the experience that two or more dancers will have with it.

The nonreductive togetherness of more than two beings through the symbol is possible for two reasons: (*a*) because my awareness of others is not in every case an active going forth to them, and therefore I can be aware of them simultaneously in *space,* seeing the open doors in the walls of my being without projecting myself through them; and (*b*) because there is *time* in which to participate in forming and maintaining a complex togetherness. I do not slight you in the moment I savor the poem because I can be in that very moment aware of you and ready for you, while in the next moment I can attend directly to you through the poem; and so with the world. Neither you nor things in the world require my totally concentrated attention at every instant; if you did or they did, I should never have room to maneuver in search of new symbolic approaches to you. What counts is that I am on my way to you and that the way is not blocked. The symbol can be viewed on the one hand as a multiple portal, on the other as a road system.

I conclude that the experience of art cannot be denounced as irresponsible until it is seen with what other intentions the art-savoring one is woven together, on the loom of the symbol. That depends on the intenders, whether they forget who and where they are in the dizziness of the climb upward into moves opened by art —which always also opens moves outward, toward the others. The critics of art speak against certain uses of art that they perceive to be blighting their age. It is impossible to speak against art as such.

6.3 Style

When we read the line "Wild air, world-mothering air," we are potentially acquainted with someone—not only personally, knowing something of the character of the one who uttered the line, but spiritually, taking the line as a way of being. But only potentially. One line is too little to go on. Who can predict with any confidence the other observations this poet will make? Who could go on to live in the manner of this poet, knowing only that he could declare the air both wild and motherly? It is not impossible that one could go on to live a wide-eyed yet cozy sort of life that one felt to be continuous with the initial impact made on one by the line. But obviously a nearly unlimited range of lives "inspired" in this way could be lived, all contradicting each other insofar as each claimed to be the one authentic extension of it.

Suppose, however, that we have the entire poem, or several poems—then we should have enough evidence to be able to recognize a sort of general principle of propositions which—taking over an aesthetic term to make a pre-aesthetic point —we may call "style." [11] Only with the emergence of a definite way of proposing, a showable general proposition rather than a sayable particular proposition, does there obtain the type of validity that goes to constitute intentional characters, which we conceive in our own case as personhood. I "know a person" in being able to follow and anticipate the propositions he or she makes. So also with intentional creations like texts, schools, cultures.

Not any series of propositions amounts to a style. Bad poets fail to create a style because making the moves called for in their poems does not put one in a position to make further moves. A style is a living rule, not merely a successful traversal of a given set of propositions but an ability to generate new ones that hang together with whatever has been given. New propositions that do not form a style from themselves lie around loose to be taken over by existing styles or forgotten.

Fortunately we do not have to be good poets to be persons. We are naturally endowed with knowability; whether we know it or not, our actions establish styles, admittedly of unequal richness and force but, in a minimal yet crucial sense, fundamentally valid. Even if I found myself unable to know you as a principle of propositions, it would be incumbent on me to try, on account of the respect and appreciation that are commanded for all others. For I know just by looking at you that you are not a being to be known merely as a spatiotemporally continuous locus of unrelated or infertile propositions. No relationship would be possible with you under these circumstances, and we both demand to flourish in relationship. However, except in very unusual cases the problem never arises. I do not have to try to know your style; I am aware of it, imperfectly but indubitably, from the first moments of our interaction. That is a psychological fact. A priori, it is conceivable that any given individual should pose an enigma, should, that is, fail to satisfy the conditions of validity that partly constitute the experienceable being called "person." But the general requirements of interpersonal life do not give me liberty to come to this conclusion about the putative Total Enigma without trying harder to know him or her.

As regards the style manifestations that establish relationships, it is similarly a fact that we are naturally able to get along in principle. Although we are often preoccupied by failures to get along with each other, even the most unsatisfactory relationships are still perceived as such against the background of a fundamental intended holding-together of our actions. At least we rely on the basal style supplied by the culture of which we are members. In meeting someone from an alien culture, however, one can have an overwhelming sense of the failure of a style of relationship to form. This cannot last very long, but it can last for all of a brief encounter. Spirit-style, therefore, having more complicated conditions, is less to be taken for granted than personal style. Yet it is certain a priori that valid relationship somewhere exists, since this is the condition of the possibility of uttering primary affirmations.

The enormous importance of style is partly reflected in the extent to which it claims our everyday attention. Misleadingly, we think of styles as things to be consciously compared and selected, picked up or dropped. That can only be done with relatively superficial manners of being, which are at most accessory to the styles that we *are.* Yet this mild insanity with respect to personal style that is characteristic of modern Westerners and all who have come under their influence is indirectly encouraged by the underlying imperative to live better with each other, which demands of us a perennial dissatisfaction with given principles of relationship and a certain straining toward reform.

6.4 Standpoints. Standpoint Conflict in the Problem of Determinism

On any road map of a country one will find that it is difficult to route oneself from one point to another at any distance without going through a city. The paths available are determined by where most people go most often, according to what is possible and desirable for them (on account of the terrain and weather and what they are carrying and when they want to meet). Since most business is done at the great meeting places, the cities, many persons and agencies have settled there, and everyone in the country knows the names of the cities and where they are.

On the analogous map of discourse one finds, within the multiplicity of things that can be done with language, certain settled language games or realms of discourse that are generally known and whose positions with respect to each other are, up to a point, generally understood. Some of these uses of language involve such an extensive commitment to speaking and mastering rules (becoming a physical scientist) that to enter upon them seriously is very like taking up residence in a large city (becoming a New Yorker).

If, however, we ask about the order among *intentions*—and we can do this in no other way than by examining gestures such as uses of language, but with an eye on the principles guiding them—then we meet with great concatenations of intention in the same places that language games showed themselves, but which we ordinarily refer to as "points of view" or "standpoints," by which we mean certain orientations in looking and thinking as well as certain ways of discoursing. One *occupies* a standpoint as one cannot occupy a language game; the standpoint is where one is, not what one is doing. But tenants of a standpoint are oriented toward particular classes of intentions, ready to identify, evaluate, feel, and act in conformity to the connections that are available within the class. Not that intention apart from standpoints is impossible; but in that case many fewer objects and directions are available to intention, just as travelers have fewer options on a country road than in a large city.

Standpoints are validity structures, loci of possible intentional coherence having import for the single intender, whose inner life they help to order, and, to an even greater extent, for the society, which they provide with meeting places for norming. We would often not know how to talk to each other if we could not plant ourselves together in, for example, the moral point of view, or the scientific. To a far greater extent than is true with propositions, symbols, and styles, we are *conscious* of the validity of standpoints. We deliberately resort to them for their security and order.

If there were only one intentional standpoint, intellectual life would be much more orderly than it is. But inasmuch as there are different classes of others to be mindful of and very distinct ways to be mindful of them, there are necessarily many standpoints, so that the problem is imposed on reason—the standpoint from which all standpoints are surveyed—of sorting them out when they prompt us toward the same objects differently. The intellectual problems that resist solution according to known rules are generally rooted in clashes between standpoints, each of which has been cultivated around rules that are absolutely valid within each. Should the government withdraw its support of art museums in order to give more money to international famine relief? May medical scientists experiment painfully and fatally with sentient, nonhuman animals? Is there too much gold in the churches? Questions of this sort would be clearer, if not necessarily more soluble by rule, if they merely forced one to compare the claims of different others present before one. But instead they involve *patterns of readiness to respond* to others who are typically *not* present.

It has been claimed that this or that set of standpoints must exist, wherever there is mind or society. For example, the scientific, moral, aesthetic, and religious points of view (corresponding to aspects of consciousness) enjoy a priori standing in neo-Kantian systems.[12] Husserl in the *Ideas* speaks of the fundamental "doxic modalities" corresponding to knowledge, feeling, and will.[13] Paul Taylor asserts that eight basic points of view, each corresponding to a universe of normative discourse, must pervade and govern life in all societies: the moral, aesthetic, intellectual, religious, economic, political, legal, and customary.[14] Arguments for the standpoints of respect and love have been offered here, based on the primary demands made by others (Chapter 3). The fundamental or derivative status of each standpoint could be debated, and perhaps some standpoints could be resolved into more specific ones—for instance, in Taylor's scheme "aesthetic" appears to take in the rather heterogenous interests in "beauty" and in "fun," as "moral" comprehends both respect and love. Whether we regard these more specific points of view as the true standpoints or substandpoints, they will certainly have their own rules and pose their own problems of priority. Therefore,

⌈our interest should turn from deducing a definitive list of standpoints, which is impossible, to ascertaining those characteristics that make for a higher or lower ranking of one standpoint, whatever it be, with respect to others.⌉

In connection with this issue, the most important characteristic a standpoint could have would be that of conferring priority on itself; and we would expect such a standpoint to exist, since the ordering of standpoints is a universal problem for rational beings. An initial difficulty is posed by the fact that not one but at least two such standpoints exist. They are (*a*) the moral point of view, which exists just so that we can decide what to do, and (*b*) the religious point of view, by which we relate ourselves to what appears to us to be unconditionally important. I do not place the intellectual-scientific and aesthetic points of view in this rank, because the former operates as a morality when it claims unconditional precedence, and the latter, when it is exalted, turns into a religion. What are we then to make of the confrontation between religion and morality? In the end, whatever tension there might be between actual religions and moralities on account of the different others they happen to be responsive to—when religion, in its most typical form, requires obedience to an invisible being who has communicated certain commands, whereas morality typically demands regard for the immediate interests of the visible beings surrounding us—there is not a tension between the standpoints as such. The action required by religion cannot be other than right, and the beings or aims honored by morality cannot be other than holy.

The "spiritual," considered as a standpoint, is therefore *functionally* equivalent to the religious standpoint, and just in this limited sense "spiritual" and "religious" are synonyms. (We do not of course make the claim that one Other steps before all others.) We discovered early the essential connection between the concept of the spiritual and the event of superordination of a claim.

This supreme principle of standpoint priority is also the only one. It is impossible to say that political demands always take precedence over economic ones, or that legal ones always come before aesthetic ones. We can easily imagine cases in which the alleged priority would be reversed. Such cases can be decided only in principle according to the relation of the acts and arrangements in question to the sacred other(s) and to religious response. Considered in the abstract, the religious *attitude*, "piety," is nothing other than readiness to do what is required, which presupposes holding to the standpoint according to which one weighs the ingredience of absoluteness in the demands confronting one. Thus, any serious attempt to mediate a standpoint dispute must proceed religiously. We see this relatively rarely because conflicts between standpoints are usually resolved by the sheer prevalence of one of them, not by any real mediation.

A glance at the problem of determinism will illustrate standpoint clash and confusion. Later, when we come to analyze concepts of causation (Chapter 8), we will try to resolve it; here we will only try to elucidate its relation to different forms of validity.

As a scientific knower of the world I am committed to the thesis (*Urdoxa*) that all events are necessarily and sufficiently determined by knowable conditions. I cannot exempt some events from approach on this assumption, for it seems that all events are ultimately related; to make any such reservation would impair my understanding of everything. At the same time I am a maker of decisions—a moral agent, a legal subject, and so forth. My decision making presupposes the genuine availability to me of the options I consider together with my spontaneous capacity to act righteously, lawfully, or prudently. Therefore, my actions may not be necessarily and sufficiently determined by knowable conditions. Now, given this prima facie conflict between the exigencies of two standpoints, I have, as I occupy each, four choices: (*a*) to abandon it in favor of the other, (*b*) to reinterpret it compatibly with the other, (*c*) to reinterpret the other compatibly with it, or (*d*) to abandon the other in favor of it. Let us assume that neither standpoint is so easily dispensed with that (*a*) or (*d*) is worth entertaining. That leaves us with two options of reinterpretation. In the present case, the position known as compatibilism offers a reinterpretation of moral freedom that leaves undisturbed the principal assumptions of scientific determinism. On the other side, teleological determinism is probably the best deal that the moral point of view can offer to science, although it is inconsistent with practical spontaneity to the precise extent that it meets the demand of science for determination.

If we picture the moral agent and the scientist negotiating a deal with each other, we will want to know what they have to deal with, what they can give away, and what they have to keep in order not to subvert the validity conditions that are constitutive of their standpoints and bound up with their respective Ur-theses.

The specific enterprises of morality and science cannot be put above criticism, even if we do project a resolution of the problem that does not involve a complete abandonment of either. Only the spiritual enterprise as such is impossible to criticize. It may be that an intention that is essential to morality in the particular form of it that the moralist is committed to, and that is a condition of moral validity, given that form, is yet invalidated by an exterior challenge; and so too for the scientist. For instance, a moral point of view amounting to a system of passive evaluation of human conduct, rather than a practical system of imperatives and sanctions, is conceivable. The moralist, deprived of freedom and responsibility as originally posited, could fall back to this position, which a certain brand of compatibilism would make available, without forfeiting all claim to a recognizably "moral" standpoint. (But there might be spiritual reasons against such a fallback.) Alternatively, we can conceive a recognizably scientific standpoint that posits universal sufficient but non-necessary causation or conditioning of events.

The validity network in which the deterministic thesis is embedded has, first, ideal constituents, comprising both the conceptual conditions of the possibility of "science" and the formulation of this particular version of "science"; and second, real constituents, among which are the actual concurrences of phenomena and colleagues with the scientist's intentions as well as the scientist's own intraintentional reward.[15] "Science" aims at and possesses the original validities of *seeing* or perception in general, that is, the definiteness and the forestalling of wheel-spinning that is granted to intention by virtue of the unhiddenness or "givenness" of that to which it is directed. But perception, especially when its spatial, temporal, and conceptual horizons are expanded by thought, always finds more hidden from it than is revealed. It sees a bird but does not see where the bird came from or where it is going or to what larger patterns its present behavior belongs, knowing which would enable one to say what it must have been doing before or what it must be going to do. The eye-mind is avid to be given these things too, avid with all its love for others (which cannot bear being separated from them), with all its fear of the impingement of the unknown, and finally with all its distaste for its own squinting, blinking, and dithering. (There is, besides, the dishonorable lust for mastery of the others, which is perhaps only a perplexed swelling out of these other motives.) We have, then, a strong reach for the phenomena, an unquenchable proposal that they should give themselves to us without reserve, which is ideally felicitated by the nature of "phenomenon" itself (as we learn from idealism). Our yen to know is happily met by to-be-knowns— or at least by beings that suffer themselves to be constituted to-be-knowns by the knowing intention. They allow us to know them to some extent, and since they do not unequivocally insist on the exact extent, our intention to know them fully waxes unhindered. As long as they exist for us as represented by essences, the others cannot effectually oppose this intention. (Only the special concept of otherness can limit the knowing intention by representing as "giveable" nongivenness itself; but this is an anti- and supra-essence.)

Accompanying the solitary knower's sufficiently felicitated proposal for unhiddenness is the cognitive community's project of arriving at a completely univocal account of the world. In other words, science wants to write a textbook, *one* textbook unconditionally reliable in mediating the phenomenal givenness achieved by investigation. That textbook represents the perfection of one of the primary exercises of speech, objective description, the intention to perform that therefore carries over into this project. But it cannot be written until the givenness is unlimited. As long as givenness is limited, scientific theory is underdetermined; rival theories will continually arise. On this front, the more important validity conditions are real rather than ideal, having to do with the impressive success of the scientific community in arriving at (or we should rather say, keeping itself oriented toward) descriptive unanimity. Many texts are written that do provisionally carry the authority within a certain domain of the one intended Text, without obviously absurd results. But there is an ideal validation as well in the possibility of constructing, free of decisive contradiction, a scientific "intersubjectivity" correlated with the phenomenality of other beings. The "givenness-to-me" of the phenomenon might just as well be a "givenness-to-us." Why not? If there is any correlation between object and subject at all, why not this more extensive one, accumulated out of everyone's actual and possible experience rather than just my own?—particularly since the language game of pure description has the essential task of uniting us by allowing us to forget our differences while we jointly attend to objective reality.

The preoccupation with causation, despite its obvious relevance to the project of control or technique, can be interpreted strictly as an expression of the predicting and retrodicting intentions that mean to clear away all clouds from the face of the knowable just to know, to be beyond doubt and surprises.

The scientific standpoint cannot limit its own validity. It cannot single out something to declare unknowable; its Ur-thesis is that everything it notices is knowable. Nor can we declare human action to be "nonphenomenal" and thus *ideally* exempt from the field where the scientific intention has jurisdiction, for although there undoubtedly is a nonphenomenal dimension of human action, we cannot deny that it is also, on its face, one class of perceptible happenings related to others. We cannot know all about the events that follow in the train of human acts—why, for instance, the surface of this planet is so encrusted with artifacts— if we do not know all about these acts.

However, this standpoint can be limited from outside. The range of phenomenality is limited by the presence for encounter of other beings as *giving* but not "given." This is a mystical assertion from the scientific point of view but, spiritually, the sober and requisite thing to say; further, it is implicit in the basic realist attitude of interest in other beings as other on which science unconsciously thrives. The others do not felicitate the phenomenalizing intention when, as in idealism and positivism, it dares to treat givers as givens. They then absent themselves and render hollow (for those scientists who are also spiritual beings) the scientific project. But we may not assume without further ado that the spontaneity of the moral agent maintained by the moralist is precisely identical with that ownmost otherness of the other that the sober scientist is bound to respect. Even the most sober approach to a rock or a tree does not demand that their worldly careers be unpredictable; so why should we be? A case must therefore be made for the necessary impingement of spontaneity in our experience of certain others, the intentional ones—"necessary" according to the validity conditions of some other intentional project to which we are committed.

Freedom is posited by the moral standpoint because the object of morality is interintentional norming. One cannot negotiate with or give direction to an entirely predictable being, for in that case the proposing intention would be false, a mere going through motions with nothing actually ventured. The "ought" *I* issue to *you* implies *your* "can," and vice versa. The moral Ur-thesis that what is right ought to and may be done finds its systematic intentional confirmation in the nearly universal readiness of intenders to act and account for themselves in relation to this demand. In principle, a moralist would not be committed to contradicting the claim that everything *has always* turned out as necessarily and sufficiently determined by knowable conditions, as long as it remained possible to propose doing what is right, because it is right, from now on. Morality would then be driven to adopt a desperate eschatological view of its work in the world. But even this much would defeat the theoretical unification that the scientist wants.

The fundamental intention of acting and responding in a mutually acceptable way gets represented by certain socially determinate principles of acceptability that offer themselves as objects of scientific comprehension ("mores") at the same time that they demand to be understood from the purely moral standpoint. Which interpretation will have force? The fact that these principles, unlike the principles of physics, are, *morally* considered, so various, so frequently flouted in practice, and so changeable does not invalidate the resilient moral intention, as contrariwise the deterministic intention of physics would be thwarted if physical phenomena were so unreliable. Thus, the moralist can concede this or that constitution of a rule and this or that practical outcome to the scientist, who can often make better sense of it. But the basic posture of being ready to respond and calling on others to do so is non-negotiable. It is validated by the ever-present opportunity to live affirmatively in relationship, an opportunity that is difficult to capitalize on but that beckons with such overwhelming import that intention reckons it home, however uncomfortable and difficult to understand that home may be.

We arrive at this standoff: the moral standpoint most familiar to us requires that an agent's actions not be grounded entirely within the determinable phenomenal realm where the scientific standpoint holds sway—yet this noncoincidence must not deprive actions of phenomenal effect, for that would make them unreal. But the scientific standpoint requires the inclusion in the phenomenal realm of anything that has anything to do with its being the way it is. We therefore must simply allow the world of morality to intrude, as a scientific surd, upon nature, on the strength of such spiritual credentials as it can prove; or else we must redefine "action" and "phenomena" in ways that do not violate the basic validity conditions in morality and science.

No solution may gloss over the fundamental tension between the intentions to have, to be secure, and to serve. The first intention of a spiritual being is to serve; the "religious" mediation of the conflict will therefore resolve it in that direction. But that will not necessarily lead to the hamstringing of science for the glory of morality. Science is not the hobby of the power-mad, to be given up when they become responsible. Nor is anyone's conception of morality and its prerequisites identical with responsibility as such. Theoretical determination and practical freedom are both instrumental in the service of the others, which spirit must allot to each principle its place.

6.5 Institutions and Culture. The Cultural Ideal

The validity structures called "institutions" are quite important for social-scientific purposes. They may be defined as loci of practical interintentional validity corresponding to the practical exigencies of social life. But we shall pass directly to the overarching network of institutions, standpoints, styles, and systems of propositions and symbols for which the most common name is "culture." What we find to be true of the workings of culture, that comprehensively valid way of living, will be true, when appropriately circumscribed, of institutions as well.

The simplest, most modest definition of "culture" is "how a people lives" (how they notice others of all kinds and classes and how they solve the awesome problem of what to attend to and what to do)—where we let the application of "a people" be fixed by our perception, at a given moment, of certain individuals living "together" or in a significantly similar way. With this purely descriptive use of the term we assume intentional performances without raising questions about their possibility or their implications. But we can hold to bare description only by keeping the meaning of "how" at its most superficial. Fuller senses of "how" crowd in on us immediately. We want to know "how" people live in the sense of how (that is, by what "mechanisms") some social events lead to others, and how social forms reflect human needs and interests; we want to know "how" people live in order to be able to identify each cultural alternative from a stylistic point of view and appreciate its import; and ultimately we want to shed light on the primary or fundamental conditions of the possibility of a culture, including the conditions of its meaningfulness and justification.

To these three areas of interest correspond three different conceptions of culture: technical, humane, and philosophical. Holding these categories lightly, we will use them to present pure *types* of thinking about culture, and not to limit investigators in any discipline. (In the so-called social sciences, for example, there has always been and must be a creative ferment involving all three. But we must be able to draw distinctions if the ferment is not to be a muddle.)

Culture in the *technical* sense is "institution" writ large. For the sake of explanatory force, technical thinking confers necessity on cultural forms by construing them as accomplishments of necessary generic tasks. For example, it is axiomatic for anthropology that a group must somehow arrange for its persistence through time, and therefore we expect to find customs governing reproduction, with other natural and historical conditions determining which particular customs arise. Similarly, a group must be able to settle conflicts and decide collective action to a certain extent in order to survive, and therefore we know that some form of authority system will always be present. Even awareness of the world and communication are tasks for a cultural symbol system to accomplish. Of course, we could dispense entirely with this talk of jobs getting done and use more abstract conceptions instead. But that would miss one main point of technical thinking, which is to orient us with respect to forms of collective existence by showing us *as members of them* how they work with us and for us (and against us). Technical concepts are the very ones by which we gain the cognitive high ground of being able to explain our culture without becoming at the same time completely alienated from it—because we in fact want to reproduce, to settle what is to be done, to know our way about in the world, and to communicate. We already identify with the ends in relation to which cultural forms are interpreted as means.

On the *humane* conception, culture becomes a theater of lived-out validity rather than an ensemble of instruments—costumes rather than props. Cultural forms are viewed as expressive of meaning, and differences of form are correlated with differences of expression. But since forms are unequally expressive, criticism and ranking enter into this sort of understanding. (Criticism in this sense is foreign to the purely technical approach.) In the humane mode, we consciously take a stand in relation to ends that are merely stipulated and accepted for the purpose of technical explanation, and at the individual level. We are interested not merely in "communication" but in the different specific things people can say to each other; not merely in "reproduction" but in specific forms of love, fatherhood, sisterhood, etc. And we seek those forms that accommodate the strongest and richest intentional moves, as appear in our own experiments with them. Yet, although we note the differences, we behold everything and reject nothing. Anything that can catch humane notice is valid in its own way. If our attention steers toward certain cultural forms, like "great works of art," that is not because they alone are worthy of attention but because a limited attention will find more reward in them than in alternative sets of objects. All costumes cannot be tried on at once. (There is an explanatory equivalent of this criticism in the preference for more causally "important" phenomena to study, those having larger effects of a sort that seem important to us.)

Philosophy complements the technical and humane approaches by elucidating the concepts and principles they presuppose—accounting for cultural forms as vehicles for the accomplishing of rational or spiritual programs, working toward insight into meaningfulness as such, and exhibiting relations between the two sorts of validity.[16] Beyond pure analysis, philosophy also undertakes an absolute criticism that is capable of ruling cultural forms in and out. A plain example of this is the extreme philosophy of Grisebach, for whom "true culture" (*echte Kultur*) is only that which faithfully reflects the conflict and suffering of ethical reality.[17] But any philosopher who prescribes principles of beauty or justice or "greatness" is, by implication if not expressly, legislating normative culture, which is to say, offering a spirit. This is more than noticing the pathways and configurations in which individual and collective intention *can* move; it is *leading* intention to some promised land, with the bait of the best grounds available. Notice that at the farthest pitch of criticism—as in Grisebach or Levinas or here, where the terminal focus for intention is the other as other—validity dissolves. The commanded intention is one that *cannot* be completed according to any knowable way. Since all other validities come under judgment against this horizon, they are undermined; of course, intentional *facts* remain, but as intentions *to be performed* (which is how the intender asking the validity question regards them) they remain with a question mark beside them, threatened by the unfulfillability of the ultimately requisite intention.

We peered into this abyss earlier and accepted the fact that we have to carry on with a certain unshakeable feeling of vertigo. Now we make the positive assumption that, thanks to the existence of cultural forms, spiritual life may go on, somehow; our intentional leaps may come down together, somewhere. This assumption makes of culture and all its constituents a *spiritual fact,* which is a very suspicious notion, but one that we already had to put on stage in anticipation of our inquiry into the real life of spirit in the world (section 5.4), and that is indispensable if culture is to interest us from the spiritual point of view, as it must. The reason we cannot avoid a spiritual interpretation of actual culture is that we meet the others in it, not outside it. They are other *than* cultural forms only in the sense of being distinct from any graspable object of consciousness; they are, in another sense, the otherness *of* those forms (commanding from a "deeper" position the otherness that belongs to the forms all by themselves), that is, others meeting me in them. For if I dissolve your facial expressions, your clothes, your language, and your principles in search of the real You, I am left with nothing. You are a *way* of making a face, wearing clothes, speaking, and following principles. Since we have met, and our meeting has amounted to something rather than perishing in the instant, something spiritual has been accomplished, not unconnected with the concrete cultural forms of our meeting. This spiritual fact, unlike other states of affairs that count as "facts," is not one that can be finalized and taken completely for granted as an instrument for further operations. It forms a location and starting point for reckonings that remain always, as regards their present and future, incalculable, and that perhaps change the meaning of their starting point as they are performed. But we could not even have these incalculable reckonings without the starting point, one that moreover is a spiritual "place," where from the start we know, indeed feel the knowledge incumbent on us, that we are facing each other.

A "spiritual fact" is a given interintentional validity. It is a place where I know I can move together with (some) others and that is therefore righteous, to the extent that righteousness is a condition of togetherness. What is true in a very limited way of symbols, that one can count on them to hold good for others as well as oneself, is true, in a larger and less definite but no less real way, of culture, which may now be defined as the sum of spiritual facts. Such "facts" must always be facts for certain individuals, the ones who "inherit" them by inhabiting them as starting points for moves of their own. Culture in this sense exists only for those who are committed to it. In saying this, we repeat our earlier formula for "a spirit" and thus tie the themes of culture and spirit together. Culture is the "factual" side of spirit: relationship as already created rather than purely as yet to achieve.

Philosophers sometimes project normative spirits-to-be-achieved that deprive actual culture of any validity, annihilating it as culture, by failing to establish any relation with it. This is called utopianism. It signifies an assertion of the spiritual in distinction from actual forms of relationship that are never adequate, never absolutely right enough; but, as an entirely negative assertion, it handicaps the spiritual standpoint by making it unable to recognize any real state of affairs as an actualization of the spiritual. A real state of affairs will inevitably appear as an obstruction of the spiritual, something to be overcome, never something to dwell in. The critical attitude is here a terrible fanaticism or paranoia that will never permit one actually to live with others. As Hegel maintained, it is necessary for spirit to reconcile its being at home in objective forms with the eternal discomfort it feels with anything determinate, being essentially free and able to surpass fixed forms by taking different attitudes toward them. But even though no one can outdo Hegel in professions of respect for the actual, the reconciliation with it is not, after all, attainable on his terms. Hegel loses hold of the ballast that would bring him back down to earth by refusing to acknowledge the *limit* of others. To the question "By virtue of what is the otherness of the others unsurpassable?" we answer, "By being precisely the way they are." Hegel gives the same answer to the opposite question: "others" *are surpassable;* that is precisely the way they are. But believing this subverts the point of saying such a thing as "That is precisely how they are," which is to hold us to something rather than to free us with respect to something. The others demand to be met through the actual, and in that way they check the pretentions of a critic who would ideally do them one better. This is especially true in the actual need and suffering of others. For this reason we must go very carefully in constructing "ideals" with which to confront and judge the factual.

We can think about this problem with reference to Apel, who, as we have seen, appeals to the norm of an "ideal communication community" at the same time that he recognizes the real communication community as a transcendental presupposition of sociality. The two are difficult to reconcile because the one is unlimited while the other is all-too-limited. Therefore he posits a dialectical contradiction between them. Must there not be such a contradiction between any normative, "ideal" vision of society and the imperfect status quo? There must certainly be some tension. But we ought to distinguish between two ways in which an ideal community can get conceived.

One way, Apel's, is reflectively to subtract in principle all hindrances to communication, including all dishonesty, delusion, ignorance, and oppression. Positively, the community thus conceived is quite indeterminate; one is aware of the conditions it satisfies rather than anything substantive about it. Further, there should be no difference between the unlimited communication community conceived by a German philosopher and that conceived by an American, or a Japanese; any differences that do exist are imperfections caused by the perspectival limitations of the individuals and cultures. If one has to say something positive about it, regarding, for instance, its members, one has to say that it is open to everyone who *could* exist.

The other way to conceive an ideal community is to proceed strictly from the real one: to try to conceive for the real one the ideal that it is groaning and travailing toward, that would comprise just those excellences, felicities, and fruitfulnesses that pertain specifically to the determinate others who surround me. This will always be a limited communication community, but the limit will have the sweetness of the limitedness of the others themselves. Philosophers who confront the present, relatively deficient form of the real community with an ideal arrived at in this way will of course still risk the misunderstanding and rejection of their consociates, not to mention being mistaken. But their critique will have the dignity or provisional validity of having been responsibly derived. They will not be offering abstract demands that could have been formulated by anyone, anywhere —even alone. Apel means to anchor himself in a responsible position by tying his ideal to the real dialectically, taking it for granted that, using a reflective method, his ideal has to be the abstract one. It counts as support for his ideal that anyone else reflecting would arrive at the same result—but this is true only because the result is vacuous. Apel's ideal will, in application, make a social difference only to the extent that it is, coincidentally, derivable in this second way (but therefore necessarily with particular determinations corresponding to the particularities of the real community). But in that case the reflecting philosopher would have been accomplishing the idealizing of the real community from the premise of itself, rather than bringing before it some genuinely contradictory prescription arrived at by independent means. Thus there is not really a contradiction between ideal and reality, only the embarrassment that the real community does not find itself where its appreciative critics acknowledge it ought to be.

The ideal community cannot be better *than* us; it must be a better *us*. But if we humbly accept the limitations that constitute us ourselves, others to each other, we cannot speak of an "unlimited" community. We cannot remove one limit without presupposing another. The principle of "justice for all," for example, removes limits on entry to a justice system, but for a particular class of beings, under particular circumstances. Otherwise, the concept of justice would be unintelligible. The same restriction applies even more obviously to communication. What could "unlimited communication" mean?

Another theory of normative culture escapes some of these difficulties by, in a sense, turning the ideal communication community inside out. That is the "ideal observer" theory, which we will discuss presently (section 6.8).

It may be objected that we cannot speak of "normative culture" unless we can exhibit a set of true a priori principles of culture, which in turn can never be derived from contingent experience. But these rules of the philosophical game have been upset by the others, who are, in the order of meaning, prior to all abstract rational principles even though we meet them contingently. Their demands function as a priori principles by determining in advance of anything that happens *between* us what that happening can mean. The cultural a priori is the validity foundation that has been constituted by social history, considered as an ongoing cumulative revelation of the claims of others and how they may and may not be responded to. Valid "ideals" are projections from this base, the base, so to say, judging itself. In that judgment, the principle of doing justice to the others here and now must always take precedence over the spiritual "facts" deposited in cultural tradition. For that reason, a relatively abstract rationalism will not only always be in the right against an empiricist historicism that respects nonspiritual facts too much, it will also often be in the right against normative traditionalism, which can imprison the spiritual in *Erinnerung*. But we must remember that rationalism derives its authority from encounter with the others, for which it offers itself as agent. If we lose this footing, we have nowhere else to stand.

6.6 "Values"

The concept of "value," crucial for recent Western thought about intention and forms of validity, needs special handling because its sense and reference are suspect.

The two great reasons for suspicion are complementary. The historical reason is that talk of "values" only arose in the later nineteenth century. Could a fundamental ethical or aesthetic or metaphysical fact have lacked an appropriate name until then? Is it not much more likely that "values" represent a peculiarly modern *preference* in conceptualization? The logical reason is that in today's ordinary discourse the concept of "value" is used *all too much*. It is so serviceable that one wonders whether it makes thinking or arguing too smooth by obscuring important issues.

I shall briefly expand on each of these points in turn.

The philosophical heyday of the concept of "value," extending a couple of decades on either side of the turn of the last century, coincided with a certain stage in the self-understanding of philosophy and at the same time with a climax in historical and cultural studies. In a philosophical school like the Southwest neo-Kantian, which had forsworn metaphysical speculation but still saw a greater role for itself than to be a handmaiden to science, "values" promised a new properly philosophical domain of inquiry with the right kind of universal normative application. In the broader intellectual scene, a heightened awareness of the differences obtaining among human attitudes across time and place also furnished a powerful motivation for the concept of "value." Students of cultures want, in the first place, to constitute everything in the realm of their investigation as "objects" or things to talk about; in the second place, they do not want to patronize or unduly psychologize a culture by speaking of the mere "attitudes" of its members toward goodness when these people evidently live in a certain kind of real-for-them world toward which these attitudes happen to be appropriate. The concept of "values" solves these methodological problems by positing something objective—not at any rate *individually* subjective—that is yet not an additional entity in the natural order, where, being invisible, it would be highly objectionable. Most importantly, whereas one cannot normally speak of "goodnesses"—for goodness is conceptually unitary—one can speak plurally of "values." (Then the ethicist can define "goodness" as a movement toward "higher" "values.") [18]

Now that there are "values," *I* can "have" some and *you* can "have" others. The very features that recommend the concept of "value" in an age of historical and cultural relativism also make it attractive in an age of individual relativism like our own. In order to validate the differing attitudes of individuals on questions of what is good and right, one may talk about their "values," by which one grants that their attitudes are correlated with something and are not simply arbitrary. This also makes moral tolerance distinguishable from moral indifference. But even if one is intolerantly disposed, one must now grant "values" even for the purpose of arguing with someone whom one thinks is wrong, for argumentative civility and order is easier kept when instead of attacking one's opponents' attitudes or imposing one's own attitudes on them one compares their "values" with one's own. Then the rules of objectivity apply, and in relative peace we can turn from direct confrontation to the joint examination of these other things before us. No doubt such advantages have much to do with the commonness of talk today about people's "values," about the need to clarify one's "values," about one person having "values" (or "good values") while another does not, about which values, if any, to try to teach, and so forth.

If we bear all this in mind, we can more alertly criticize the most interesting and instructive of all theories of "values," that offered by Scheler in his *Formalism in Ethics and Non-Formal Ethics of Values*. Max Scheler not only philosophized in an age of relativism, he was himself a historian and sociologist; further, he dedicated himself to responding, in defense of the ideal and reality of loving personhood, to the explicitly anti-Christian revolution in values advocated by Nietzsche. Scheler carried as far as possible the *objectification* of a concept which, after all, owed its origin to a perception of the subject-relativity of judgments concerning goodness. The irony in that did not give Scheler pause, for he believed in the historical progress of moral consciousness. His theory was a further turn of the screw; he respected this subject-relativity at the same time that he asserted the objectivity of "values." "Values," for him, are irreal essences given in phenomenological intuition that (*a*) are a priori, meaning that they are not abstracted from experience but are immediately given just as they are (such that they cannot possibly be contradicted by experience); (*b*) are qualitatively concrete or, in German, *material* or nonformal, like (say) colors; (*c*) occupy among themselves a determinate rank order, which is also immediately given to intuition; (*d*) are spontaneously acknowledged in intuition as worthy-to-be-realized, according to their own ranks; and (*e*) are differently intuitable according to the different capacities of individuals, as determined in part by culture.

One asks: Why must "values" be *objects* distinguished from the acts of valuation (preferring, prizing, etc.) by which we direct ourselves toward the ideas and beings that we value? The first answer is provided just by the phenomenological pose in which Scheler does philosophy. The philosopher's job is to bring to evidence the noemata or object-poles toward which intentional acts of any sort are invariably directed, and then faithfully to describe what is given. The methodological peace of mind that this descriptivism gives has already been rejected in our argument on the concrete. But we can accept the phenomenological pose for the moment in order to press our question in this way: Why are the phenomenological "objects" not our acts of valuation themselves, in the various ways in which *they* are intentionally correlated with ideas and beings? Why is this a philosophy of "values" rather than of valuations? In examining Scheler's answers to this challenge, we will see that in the end he falls back, without ultimate justification, on nothing other than the phenomenological pose for its own sake.

"Values" are conceived as *that which* we value. There must be a "that"; one does not value nothing. But what can the "that" be? Not, Scheler argues, any empirical property of things, for, on the one hand, we cannot abstract from empirical things any properties that consistently correspond to values—even if our sensory traffic with the world were entirely predictable in its results, there is not a predictable relationship between our perceptions as such and our feelings of value—and, on the other hand, we can contemplate a value without representing to ourselves any empirical property at all.[19] Values are sometimes given to us far more clearly than are their empirical bearers; "we can for the longest time consider a poem or another work of art 'beautiful' or 'ugly,' 'distinguished' or 'common,' without knowing in the least which properties of the contents of the work prompt this."[20] Values cannot be figures of our own striving and willing, for we can acknowledge them independently of conation; for example, I can feel the agreeableness of a drink without being thirsty, or the nobility of an act without positing it as a purpose of my own.[21] We are sometimes deceived in thinking that values are given when we are really only positing our purposes or the objects of our inclinations; but we can become undeceived. So we are faced with the conclusion that "values" are objects *sui generis* with which we have a special cognitive relation, which Scheler proposes to call "feeling."

These arguments all have force. Any naturalistic value theory must founder on the impossibility of identifying, beyond dispute, a value with any empirical property. Moore's "open question" test proves this elegantly.[22] Though it might be claimed that values sometimes appear more clearly than empirical properties because they are emergent qualities that still could not be given apart from unconscious perception of their empirical base, that would not naturalize "value" phenomenologically—any more than understanding mind as emergent from body would make mind a bodily thing. The last argument establishes the independence of value from my immediate willing, although whether it can be disconnected from willing in general is another question. Even Scheler's claim that a "value" is "there," apart from any particular experience, in the same way that "red" is "there," cannot be made sense of apart from counterfactual conditions in which it is given to someone—as he agrees.[23] But we can say that the intention that is directed to a "value" need not itself be desiring, striving, or enjoying.

Nevertheless, Scheler must be confronted with the basic implausibilities of "value"-objectivism. He cannot explain better than any other objectivist why this sort of object is binding or authoritative, or necessarily correlated with pro-feelings in a subject, except by making the dogmatic phenomenological claim that these are invariably the "acts" that belong together with the givenness of "values." Nor can he satisfactorily dismiss the prima facie difficulty for objectivism of the great variation in "value"-feelings among individuals and cultures; for the claim that individuals and cultures are differently able to feel "values," which are nevertheless in all cases "there" for the feeling, accommodates an infinite number of such differences, so that nothing is gained by asserting that the "values" are "there" anywhere but in the valuations (and why not, therefore, *as* the valuations?).

The strength of "value"-subjectivism lies in its ability to account readily for pro-feeling, inasmuch as it holds pro-feeling to be the fact constituting "value." (The internalist account of rational motivation has the parallel strength that it constitutes "reasons to act" those considerations which in fact move people to act; these considerations with regard to "values" apply, *mutatis mutandis*, to "reasons.") This point of view leads one to expect "values" to differ among preferrers and preference-communities, as they indeed do. What subjectivism cannot account for is the sense, essential to "values," that they are to be affirmed whether or not any given person affirms them at any given time; but this defect can be remedied by broadening subjectivism's base.[24] When I recognize someone else's action as "noble," yea, *really* noble, even though I may not be disposed to imitate it or be particularly pleased that it has been done, we may say that I am recognizing a type or possibility of intention, the valuing one, which is valid, first, intraintentionally in the sense that it *can* be done (and as a permanent possibility of intention it has Schelerian apriority), but also interintentionally, since it presents itself to me as blessed by the affirmative presence of others in it. A "really noble" action is an action that "one" looks up to, marks as exemplary, feels confirmed and grateful about, and so forth, *because* it involves someone's exemplary self-denying or self-restraining conduct. This "one" is the normative "one," a self-transcending position I take that confronts me "objectively," that is, as existing apart from my wishes and not to be changed by them. And "one" makes the distinctions between levels of "value" for which Scheler claims phenomenological evidence, for example, that spiritual "values" are "higher" than vital, generally using *reasons* which express the implicit logic of Scheler's more or less unargued presentation of the "value"-rankings.

Scheler held that "rightness" and "normative oughtness" are less original than "value"-phenomena and derived from the latter. A "value" is a *fact;* a "value"-claim is in the first place *true* or *false*. He argues:

> We can make value-statements in cases where it would make no *sense* to say that the bearers "ought" to be this or that. This is the case with all aesthetic predicates of objects of nature. Even in the moral sphere the ought is restricted to single acts of *doing* a deed. . . . In the case of deeds one can of course ask whether a proposition like "This deed is good" simply means that "this deed ought to be done," or that "there is a demand that it be done." This, however, is not the case when "good" is attributed to a man, i.e., a *person* in his *being*. Any ethics based on an "ought" must, as an ethics of the ought, err with respect to the true *value of the person* and indeed must *exclude* it; such an ethics can validly retain the person only as an X of possible *doings* that ought to be done.[25]

Scheler understands himself here and throughout his essay to be fighting a duty-fanaticism stemming from Kant and Fichte that empties everything actual of goodness. He holds that there is properly only an obligation to avoid disvalue, never to promote value (except when viewed as the alternative to disvalue). But our own argument meets his concern by holding to a primary obligation to promote the being of actual beings, who concretely face us always against the background of their possible nonexistence and thus energize intention "oughtly," rather than to an abstractly totalitarian or utopian obligation. (Scheler himself admits what he calls an "ideal ought" in the axiom that anything of "value" ought to be.)[26] We are also able to grant provisionally valid "facts" (what *is* affirmed according to spirits) to which judgments of "value" might or might not correspond, and thus we escape the necessity of positing a pro-feeling in every awareness of "value." But we deny that the beauty of a sunset considered as a "value" is, though admittedly distinct from the empirical characteristics of the sunset and the sensations, projects, etc. produced in us by it, also distinct from the attitude toward it that "one" has, which I therefore am called to have. We must insist on locating "value" in an attitude *toward the sunset* in order not to commit another sin against actuality by distracting attention from the really beautiful thing, the sunset, to some irreal "value."

No further grounds remain for holding "values" distinct from "normative valuations," which are sufficiently distinct both from valuable things and from individual valuations to pass Scheler's tests. Given Scheler's complete correlation between valuations and "values," the only reason to persist in talking about "values" would be commitment to the objectivist *façon de parler* of phenomenology, which in turn can be a way of declining responsibility for valuations by turning them into correlates of simply given "phenomena." The pitfall in talking of "values" is that no matter how one qualifies the conception, one is talking as though of some *things* that are *out there,* none of our doing. Careful readers of Scheler will be frequently reminded that "values" are *not* out there and *are* quite intimately bound up with our personal acts. But the concept of "values" drifts out of reach of this restraint.

Scheler believes we must move ethical thinking to a "value" standpoint in order to overcome the barrenness of Kantian formalism, which has long held the field by virtue of its conceptual strength. It is true that Kantianism, because of its lack of insight into the grounds of the spiritual gesture of universalization, is unable to give moral credit to nonrational features of persons such as nobility, lovingness, etc., where credit is surely due. But if Kantianism is endowed with a more adequate normative psychology, it can get around to crediting Schelerian "values," albeit too indirectly for Scheler's liking, by approving them for their universal affirmability. On my showing, Schelerian "values" can supplement Kantian formalism, but precisely because they derive their validity from the same source, the interintentional situation. It is this that orders the chaos Kant found in the human heart, which led him to dismiss all feelings and strivings not rationally determined as lacking in moral worth. Kant did not appreciate how the heart, *as ordered* by the principle of the interintentional situation, could attain objective validity, if not the superhard necessity that he believed to be the essence of apriority.

No individual could make a "value," simply because no individual is more than one individual. I cannot include an other. Since "values" are meeting-grounds approved by others, I must say that they are "there" for me. I do in fact hit upon some of them as already hallowed by tradition, for example, as I come to follow my parents in most of their judgments of importance. I also hit upon some experimentally and hypothetically. If I rebel against my upbringing and adopt iconoclasm as a "value," my positing of it is overcome by a sense of it meeting me as a preference that is tenable and best for everyone—if, that is, it really is a "value" for me and not just a policy of my own. I risk deception in this, naturally, but when do I not? Finally, if I meet and submit to the claim of a normative valuation, I cannot claim it as "my" "value" in the sense that my possessions or my personal style is mine. That would be a contradiction, a reduction of the more-than-me to my own scale. Could I call it "mine" in the sense in which the American flag is "my" flag, the one to which I proclaim myself loyal? But one takes satisfaction in expanding oneself into the flag-community, it is a way of being proud that takes advantage of the ambiguous overlapping of the transcendence of self-expansion by the transcendence of being claimed. I could not boast of my flag or my "values" if I really owned them.

Let us return to speaking of what is noble and fair, and call nobility and beauty kinds of goodness instead of "values," as though they could be added up, weighed, collected, and traded. Questions about the validity of claims concerning goodness should be turned to the claimants themselves rather than to separately existing "values" that the claimants either do or do not "feel." This brings us to an investigation of the ways in which validity inheres in persons.[27]

6.7 Being Valid, or Having Standing

An intender must exist for there to be intention; that is the priority of the being I call "I." On the other hand, only through specific intending moves does the intending sort of being have its peculiar existence—knowing, willing, feeling, and, cutting across these categories, being in relationship. It is thus a condition of the intender's being qualified as "wise," to be cognitively directed toward the things that matter; of the intender's being "resolute," to execute practical intentions tenaciously; of the intender's being "good," to keep faith with certain others; and so forth. I learn how to be and how not to be by studying intentions as such and trying them on. The "I" who tries on intentions is in turn a fundamental trying-on intention and not something different from intention. But in another sense the "I" (by which is meant here the person, not merely the epistemological or psychological subject) cannot be *an* intention, because it must be something that binds intentions together. It is, then, a *principle* of intention, which felt from the inside is the intentionality of selfhood and regarded from the outside is style. It is what Hume, being it, could not see in himself when he attended to his inner experience, but which everyone else could see in him.

The common philosophical view that rational beings are bound to respect rationality itself, in principle and as they find it in each other, has distracted attention from the broader foundation on which this norm exists, a normative foundation of concurrence among all intentional principles and performances. It is easy to overlook the broader norm because on the one hand it seems quite "natural" in its observance, while on the other hand so many exceptions to it are allowed that they often do not seem violations of principle. But we can readily see how departures from the norm can jeopardize the very integrity of persons.

Suppose a man on an airplane suddenly hears loud banging and rending noises. "Do you hear that banging?" he asks a woman next to him. "No, what noise?" she says. He describes it. His neighbor listens intently but still cannot hear anything untoward; nor can the second and third persons he asks. Now, one interesting problem concerns how this man's neighbors or he himself might come to decide that the evidence of his ears must be disallowed. But the more important point has to do with the original allowing of his evidence, the standing with which he begins. Whether they already know him or not, everyone begins by treating this man as a trustworthy reporter of reality. Of course, there are all sorts of known rules not infrequently invoked by which his standing could be impaired or lost— as, for instance, if he claims the sounds are caused by an attack of flying saucers, or if he simply looks crazy. But as long as his evidence is not disallowed on these specifiable grounds, he enjoys the presumption that what he experiences, "one" would experience; and the "one" in question here is not only the "one" of social inertia but also the normative "one."

Obviously, there is a lot to say about personal authority from a sociological point of view. Social existence would be unthinkable without a great deal of mutual crediting, as mediated by persisting rules of interpersonal and institutional crediting that are applied, infringed, and changed as a function of knowable conditions. But social problems and solutions are also spiritual problems and solutions. We have to see the spiritual issue in this, which involves a feat of aspection—like looking at an optically ambivalent picture and seeing the staircase that goes up instead of the one that goes down.

The fact is that intentional beings cannot be acknowledged and appreciated at all if their intentions are not respected. Respect for them therefore entails respect for the claims they make. One can have *dealings* only with a being who has *standing*. Some claims, like normal experience-claims, cannot be respected without being accepted, since their meaning is tied directly to the one factual world that we hold in common to be the theater of all our meetings. Other claims, like political opinions, need not be accepted as long as they are "taken seriously" (indeed, it is disrespectful for the one advancing political opinions to assume that everyone else will automatically endorse them). The man in the airplane becomes a nonperson to the extent that he loses his credit, whether because other subjects do not ratify his experience or because they laugh off or ignore the claims he makes on the basis of it. He has much more credit, to be sure, than what he stakes on this report of a noise, but it is alarming how quickly he could lose much of it. If he continued to be plagued by frightful noises, he might find himself in a psychiatric hospital, where his *prospects* would be honored, insofar as he would be expected to return to "normalcy," but his immediate behavior would constitute data for observation and no longer an argument for his fellows.

To put the point in different terms: If you say "The airplane is coming apart," that is a *reason* for me to think that the airplane is coming apart. Such a reason is hardly conclusive, in the real world, but if we imagine a void of reasons into which this one comes alone, impossible to supplement, then it would be. If I have no reason not to take your word, I have to take it so as to take you. If you and I and the airplane were alone in the void, and I saw the airplane integral and calm while you claimed that it was coming apart, I would still have to credit you and in so doing deem my own experience an illusion. Losing my relationship with you is a worse risk than losing my grip on myself. I can regain that grip, I can rehabilitate my own standing by pronouncing what I see to be an illusion; I cannot do that for you.

My good will toward you has to have some material to work on, the moves of your presentation which could be ratified by or excluded from the "one." But any intention of yours is prima facie valid interintentionally, an intention for "one" (and *thus* for me), because it came off in your case. If you hear a noise, then it is possible to hear a noise. If you think there is a noise, then it is possible to think there is a noise. Deception can enter in everywhere: you may say what you did not think, think what you did not hear, or hear what was not there. That is not to say that an intentional move was not performed by you, only that it was not what it seemed. One would find this out in taking it up, for example by deciding that the plane might be coming apart, forcing it to land, and finding nothing wrong with it. Such tests build up an experience from which individual experience can be criticized, and there is a corresponding "normative experience" from which individual moves can be criticized as wrong morally, aesthetically, and so forth. Nevertheless, the Hegelian view, according to which individuals gain validity just to the extent that they conform to an antecedently valid universal standard, has it backward. Universals in this realm are constructed from experience with individuals, which is constantly renewed and altered as new individuals come along making perhaps unheard-of claims that may yet very well survive all criticism. Once they do survive criticism, one can of course *say* that it was the universal "one" already in them by virtue of which their positions were valid. But to retroject the "one" before the individual's contribution to "one"-hood is only a hollow means of saving face for that universalism.[28]

Let us now go straight to the maximal case. If I *live* this way, then "one" *can* live this way; and if I live *well* this way, then "one" *ought* to live this way, in the absence of reasons to the contrary. We spoke earlier of the primordial command issued to our attention by all beings, and how that is qualified in the case of intentional beings. We must now add to that claim the normative interest an intender's style holds for any spiritual being, that is, anyone whose own style is qualified by the style(s) of the "one." The spiritual fact is that we find other intenders inexhaustibly fascinating—the people we know, the people we see on the bus, the characters we read of in literature, the monkeys at the zoo, our dogs and cats—for the possibilities of existence that they hold out to us. They all answer the question, How does one live? Some answers are splendid, some excite loathing or pity, but all of them count. The most alien are the most arresting. A rich woman's attention is captured by a pauper on the street: What would it be like to live like that? Can it really be done? Just to think about it is in a way to be sucked into it, taken over by it. Her own life seems momentarily unreal, like a tune playing faintly that no one is listening to. Or a college student reads a book about Gandhi and experiences the cogency of the Gandhian mixture of courage, compassion, and humor, bound up with an appealing individuality. He cannot be Gandhi, but he can form and judge his own moves in harmony and counterpoint with Gandhi. There can be no more powerful concrete reason for living in a certain way (insofar as immediate demands leave one room to ask the general question how to live) than the example of another person, who combines the demonstration of the validity of a style with an individual existent's solicitation of attention. These are the best possible credentials for a norm—but only as a proposal. One still has to see whether being like Gandhi is the right way to be with one's fated neighbors.

The reason one rarely thinks of "courage" or "unselfishness" entirely in the abstract, but more normally in relation to model persons, is not that the weak value-sense needs the help of the imagination, in the way that geometry students need to see pictures of triangles on a blackboard. It is that the "value" is in the persons first and only secondarily in their qualities. The unavoidable practice of citing qualities as reasons for judging persons as we do can be misleading in this regard. For example, one admires Gandhi because of his "courage." But actually Gandhian courage is quite a different thing from the courage of Attila. An admirer of Gandhi probably will not look up to the leader of the Huns. It is not after all the principle of courage entering into Gandhi and constituting him admirable, but the fact of Gandhi constituting that particular version of an abstract quality admirable. The fact of Gandhi speaks directly to our intention. When we are in another, reflective mode, attempting to evaluate or justify the model of Gandhi, we will make use of principles of the sort that have been developed in this essay, such as "other-respecting" and "other-promoting." However, we must remember that just as we do not know an Other-in-general, but only the real ones surrounding us, so we do not know what respecting and promoting or any other intentions are apart from the examples of people who have actually pulled them off. If we judge Gandhi by abstract standards, that is only our economical way of comparing him with other good persons in a regular and interintentionally acceptable way.

6.8 The Ideal Observer

We have established that intentional facts are the original reference points for intentional validation—valuations rather than "values," persons rather than qualities, and we might also say utterances rather than "language." What does this imply with respect to a philosophical theory of normative judgments of worth? It leads us toward a position that has already been taken by certain writers in ethics and aesthetics which now asks for elucidation with the help of the general outlook on validity we have attained.

The position in question may be called the "ideal observer theory." It is the theory that to call something good, bad, right, or wrong in the moral or aesthetic sense is to claim that a person having certain ideal qualifications would approve or disapprove of it. We find it, for example, in Adam Smith's appeal to the standpoint of an "impartial spectator" throughout his *Theory of Moral Sentiments*. Hume uses a similar approach not only in moral theory but also in normative aesthetics, tracing critical authority to the ideal of a maximally perceptive, practiced, and unprejudiced critic.[29] Recent refinements of the moral theory by Roderick Firth and Richard Brandt add to its plausibility in showing its ability to accommodate variations across cultures.[30] A Balinese "ideal observer" will not judge exactly as a Swedish one will, or even necessarily in a similar way, but it seems that what makes the moral standards of each culture recognizably "moral" is the formal property that they are keyed to such an ideal. In aesthetics, too, it seems theoretically advantageous to admit cultural and historical (and, thinking of how taste changes with age, we might add "generational") relativity in this way, without abolishing the possibility of tension between real judgments and an ideal.

The decisive virtue of the ideal observer theory is that it cuts through the dilemma of subjectivism and objectivism by positing an objective or interintentionally valid subjectivity, and it does this not in the suspicious manner of idealism —which argues toward an abstract subject-in-general or a purportedly concrete universal subject comprehending all possible experience—but by locating the culturally determinate ideal that belongs more or less immediately to the sense of normative judgments as they are actually made. This descriptive strength of the theory can also be taken for a normative weakness. For surely it is possible to criticize any conceivable ideal observer, on the "open question" principle; and surely criticism is often necessary. Slaveowners do not generally conceive of an ideal observer opposed to slavery. But what makes the ideal observer presupposed by abolitionists right over against the ideal observer presupposed by slaveowners? Are we to say that the mere fact that the slaveowners eventually give in and adopt the abolitionists' ideal observer as their own *means that the other was right?* It does mean that the other was right for *them;* but we want to know what is right in principle, and it seems a tell-tale absurdity of this account that it either makes a position right one minute and wrong the next, or makes its rightness at time T contingent upon how things turn out at time T'.

It is easy to embarrass an essentially descriptive theory by making normative demands of it, and rather unjust to do so. It is not at all absurd but rather highly plausible to say that slaveowners acting by their best lights are acting in a way they think model observers would approve, even if their best lights seem dark to us. Yet it is absurd to say that any given version of the ideal observer is necessarily interintentionally valid, hence valid for us. So it appears that a normative ethical or aesthetic theory must search for a *principle* by which to judge ideal observers and everything else, a principle that must be "abstract" enough to match the freedom vis-à-vis determinate ideas and beings that we have in meaningfully asking the question, "But is it good or right?" But before we flee into the arms of Kantian formalism or Moorean or Schelerian intuitionism, we should remember how our earlier investigations into valuation pointed in the direction of something like an ideal observer theory; and we should therefore give the theory more of a chance to function normatively. Evidently this can be achieved only by finding some link between the principle by which we ask such questions as "But is it good?" and the concept of an ideal observer.

Suppose that we accost a morally sensitive slaveowner and ask him, after he gives an ideal-observer justification of his defense of slavery, whether he realizes that the abolitionists base themselves on an ideal observer of their own. He says that he does. We ask him then how he justifies his ideal observer against theirs. He argues that his ideal observer is actually more "ideal" with respect to ideal qualities commonly acknowledged, such as being informed, fair-minded, consistent, and so forth. But we answer that the abolitionists make similar arguments and for all we can tell take into account the same facts and principles of judgment (although the principles might be ranked differently). Suppose he admits this. Finally he says: "Nevertheless, my ideal observer still seems to me to be the true ideal. Granted, it is only *my* ideal, but it is my *ideal;* I am not free to throw it over. I have to act by my best lights. I have known some very fine people who were abolitionists, but they and their ideal observer still seem to me to be misguided." Can it be denied that this slaveowner, if we assume his sincerity, has given an authentically moral justification of his views? And if we admit this, can we assert that the position that is morally, not just psychologically, valid for him is not at the same time valid, somehow, *in principle,* with a force we *too* would have to acknowledge? No, we cannot; it seems that moral validity is distinguished from psychological validity precisely by the blessing of a principle.

The point is crucial. We respect someone's moral position even if we do not always agree with it; respect it as moral, and not merely in the general, formal sense in which we respect all opinions. Yet to respect it as a moral position is to grant it authority. It is in fact a terrible thing to disagree with a recognizably moral view; it is to constitute oneself "wrong" with respect to an accepted authority, really "wrong" in a way because the authority is really accepted up to a point. Precisely herein lies the ambiguity of the relation between the descriptive content and the normative import of the ideal observer theory, or indeed of any metaethical theory. It presents an intentional fact, such as a conception of an ideal observer, an intuition, or a reflective procedure, as mediating a principle valid for all intention. We revolt from the fact, realizing that it must never be confounded with the principle; but we continue to find the principle in the fact (as with our slaveowner), and hit our heads against the impossibility of finding the principle apart from such facts. For how may we criticize the slaveowner's position, if not with reference to an ideal observer of our own, which could only be justified in the very way in which he justified his?

We may think to escape dependence on intentional facts by obeying a formal principle such as universalizability of maxims or, better, universal responsiveness to other beings. This gives us the principle we want disentangled from any fact. But it only gets us ready to make moral judgments by forbidding us to exclude any being's claim. If it told us any more, it could not apply a priori to all agents and situations. But actual moral judgments and substantive ethics always involve a synthesis of principle with concrete circumstances. For example, Kant can derive the duty of beneficence only from the application of the a priori law of universalization to a world of finite, vulnerable beings.[31] More concretely still, in determining on a particular act of beneficence, one must judge what constitutes the other's welfare, and one can exercise moral control of such a judgment only by making it, not simply as one wishes one would be judged oneself—for the other is not the same as oneself—but with as much sensitivity to the other's real needs as one could hope to benefit from oneself. So insofar as material discernment is necessarily involved in moral judgment, it is mandatorily the discernment of the wisest, fairest, and kindest possible subject, namely, the ideal observer, which admittedly is now a product of the law of universalization or the law of universal responsiveness, but a necessary one. Of course, the ideal observer is not timelessly valid, because our sense of our own and others' flourishing will change. That is its role, to change, so that the abstract moral law that generates it need not change yet may always apply to actual situations. It also has the role in the *ordo cognoscendi* of revealing the principle to us.

This is the solution, not to escape from intentional facts but to put them in their place—a place that still has authority. We respect in the slaveowner's position not his version of the ideal observer but the universal principle that constituted it. In arguing with the slaveowner we might wish to leap over our perspectival limitations to the principle itself; if only we could get hold of the naked principle, we would stand on the highest moral ground, free of the hindrances posed by the moral law's finite schematizations! But we *do* have hold of it through our ideal observer. The problem is that it will not cut against another of its own creations. It is impotent even to confute a fanatical Nazi, as Hare has shown.[32] Concrete ideal observers have been given authority in this world. One can only hope for critique of them directly from the others. And I believe we would want to say in any case that it is finally actual non-"Nordic" persons who make universalized Nazism untenable and not some principle in and for itself. A principle will come into the attempt to show Nazism's untenability, but the principle will function as a disclosure of the actuality of Nazism's victims.

If I seriously set out to judge how to benefit you, I will judge as "one" ought to judge, that is, as the best possible judge. The best possible judge is not Gandhi, or Goethe, or any other individual from whom I will have taken readings in finite theaters of intention; it will, rather, be a synthesis of all personal validities known to me. It will gain absolute standing by being placed above the contingencies that limit the standing that actual individuals have. Evidently this line of thought leads us to the equivalent of God. But the upshot of our argument is that the ideal observer or best judge is always a tribal god judging according to the tribe's horizon of discernment, just in order to be God for that tribe.

Knowing this, we know that any ideal observer is *not* God.

The ideal observer symbolizes the comprehensive spirit of a culture. It gains authority in the spiritual way, by being a place where we can meet, stay together, and flourish. This particular meeting place is an imagined subject whose acts are exemplary for us all. One would take this subject for an Olympian being were it not so close to us every time we open our mouths; for each of us becomes this subject every time we make judgments that are meant to be more than personal opinions. If I say, "Stealing is wrong," I am climbing onto the ideal observer's throne and speaking for all. What a presumption! No wonder that today, when we are more than ever aware of the presumption in normative discourse, we are afraid to engage in it. "Who am I to tell you what to do?" I *am* not really the ideal observer. But if I do not speak, neither will the ideal observer; and if the ideal observer is silent, the spiritual critique of life, the very nervous system of the spiritual life, will never awaken.

Chapter 7

The Spiritual as Material

7.1 The Concept of the Material

Under the heading of "validity" we considered spiritual forms only in their functional aspect. They were like money; it did not matter what intrinsic qualities they had, only that they counted to a predictable extent. This functional aspect is also the "formal" aspect, in the Kantian sense, for whether a spiritual object is (inter-)intentionally valid is determined by whether it satisfies the procedural requirements of intention(s), thus by how it stands with respect to intention(s) rather than by anything about itself. Of course, the properties of such an object are not irrelevant to its serviceability to spirit. But we can entirely ignore them just by positing that spirit works through them, as indeed spirit could conceivably work through anything at all concrete. It was not important to us, in thinking about the validity of symbols, whether they were written on paper or scooped out of cloud. For that matter, it was not important whether clouds or trees or anything in particular existed. However, such particular things as clouds and trees and human bodies and sharp marks on paper are evidently very important in some other connection, for it seems that life, yea spiritual life, would be different without them, and impossible without something like them. We now turn to examine the "material" aspect of spiritual forms, our starting point this inkling that the logic of the spiritual not only admits of such an aspect but requires it.

We are liable to be perplexed at first by the tradition that makes "spirit" and "matter" opposites. This is done both for good and bad reasons. The bad reasons all derive from an ontologization of the spiritual that makes spirit a higher and better *nature* than physical nature, with which "matter" is identified. "Spirit" has to be absolutely distinct from "matter" in the first place just because it is higher and better stuff, and any kind of mixing with matter would compromise that superiority. Then there are said to be specific essential attributes of spiritual beings that are incompatible with observable traits of material beings, notably, that the former are eternal whereas the latter are corruptible.

It has also been said that spirit is properly determining whereas matter is properly determinable. With this, however, the bad reasons begin to overlap with the good ones. The non-ontological doctrine that spirit is a network of claims between intentions also requires, as we have already seen, a freedom of intenders for and from each other, which is a freedom from determination qua objectification or supersession. But this freedom is not dissociation. To call a being "other" does mean that it is impermissible to take that being for no more than what is given and hence familiar and possessible of it. That is the good reason for saying that we still have to go on after we have said everything that can be said about material forms as such; we still face the twin issues of who or what a material being really is, and what our own attitude toward it ought to be. "Spirit" is beyond, distinct from, matter. However, it is just as impermissible to ignore what it is that is other as to ignore the otherness of what is. The agenda of concrete otherness is always set by a material form. That "material form" is the "matter" for spiritual "form." It enters conceptual opposition with "form" strictly in token of the basic division between our dealing and that through which we deal.

One other creditable reason for wrenching spirit away from matter is the principle that no determinate thing or order of things can ever be accepted as being absolutely as it should be. But the imperative of infinite rectification does not, in requiring us to hold material forms loosely, point us beyond all matter. Does a philosopher wishing to perfect an argument give up words, or an artist in search of a more beautiful picture give up paint and canvas? If some do, then they have gotten hold of the rule of infinity at the wrong end and impaled themselves on it. Even Plato, whom they might mistake for their patron, encourages them to live in finer and more lasting material, the "ideal," rather than to flee from material altogether. Even Hegel, who may make them restless, bids them settle down.

The immateriality that is proper to the spiritual is the perfect void yawning between me and the others, which I cannot collapse in order to be them or get hold of them. That is the open place across which the wind of spirit blows. For purely theoretical philosophy this void is at the outermost margin of the knowable, but it permeates my everyday experience, entangled at every point with what I am and know, like the warp vis-à-vis the woof. It is eminently the free over-againstness of materialized intentional beings who weave out of matter and freedom the shimmering, aerated form of relationship instead of the solid form of relation. Intentional qualities and qualifications are aerated or inspired in specific ways so that they turn into their spiritual counterparts—tenacity into fidelity, productivity into generosity, attractiveness into beauty, threat into evil, and so forth.[1] The discursive characterization of spiritual quality, to the meager extent that it can say anything, must resort to negation, referring intentional quality to what is *not* me or mine; but this theoretical shortfall is the inverse of an expansion of experience, which overflows in all those different spiritual ways, each present with, if not precisely *in,* a definite material form.

The "material" takes in all that is perceptible by the senses, and thus physical nature, but also anything that can be intuited. It includes all determinate forms given to our intentional grasp, whether natural or ideal. Mathematical concepts and characters in novels color our lives just as surely as trees and clouds do. That is how we will approach these forms here, as making up that which makes it what it is like to live as we do: everything we can feel of the consistency of the media we move through and the shapes of the walls we move between, our particular experience of the universal cohesion that Merleau-Ponty wanted to call the "flesh" of things.[2] This side of our undertaking is a first aesthetic. But the material as the feelable is only half the story. The other half is the material as the artifact of intention, its "expression" or design for feeling. It is crucial for the interpretation of language and action to understand how intention fits itself with material forms. The two riddles, aesthetic and hermeneutic, stand side by side. Somehow, intention and spirit inhabit matter. They know themselves in it and give themselves to be known in it. They change in it, and change it.

The Schelerian turn to the "material" makes an instructive comparison. Scheler wanted to rescue the emotional life of morality from the Kantian sword held over all "inclinations," the claimed impossibility of locating a priori moral validity in anything changeable and consequent restriction of apriority to the purely formal law of reason. According to Kant, true moral obedience can only be reason obeying itself, by the principle of autonomy. But reason cannot recognize itself in anything changeable, only in lawlikeness as such. (That is presently our problem, how we identify with what we are aware of, and how.) Now even though Scheler substitutes a rich realm of material value-essences for the hollow, abstract moral law of Kant, he still acknowledges the formal ethical primacy of apriority. His value-essences are immediately and eternally convincing to the spiritual beings who feel them. Like Kant's moral law, they cannot be criticized because they are that by which all else is criticized; and no more than Kant's moral law can they be treated as alien to the beings who feel them, since Scheler holds with Augustine that "where my love is, there I am." However, Scheler can only guarantee apriority by postulating a non-natural realm of value essences, and in doing this he has held back from a full overcoming of the Kantian abstractness. What he might have done—what we propose to do—is to spiritualize nature rather than erect yet another edifice behind it. He did what he did for the sake of apriority. But Kantian apriority, by virtue of the very formality that ties it (unlike Schelerian "value") inseparably to the matter of which it is the form, actually is friendlier to our purposes. It is necessary only to substitute intention for Kant's "reason" and the priority of spiritual demands for his necessitarian and legalistic apriority.

It must be said before passing from this point that Scheler's aesthetics and hermeneutics of the spiritual are without a doubt richer and more adequate by far, if not truer by far, than Kant's; and that his phenomenological method, though we do not accept all claims for its philosophical authority, has brought much into view that we can appropriate in our own way. His turn toward the "material" pioneers our own. And yet his argument would have reached further if he had stayed closer to Kant.

7.2 The Materialization of Intention

The "materialization" of intention is its taking on of a graspable form, so that someone can be aware of it, that it is and what it is. We view the event in our intentional quandary and with our intentional appetite: materialization figures for us primarily as something standing ahead of us to be accomplished, even though we obviously only have the questions and appetites we have on the basis of massive past accomplishment. From the biological standpoint one would more readily speak of the intentionalization of matter, meaning the phenomenon of (conscious) telic behavior. But to do that here would be to abstract from what we know first and are bound to respond to first, intention—to treat intention as something that comes along and is added to matter. To be sure, the *phenomenon* of intention does "come along" in the biological field of view, but the phenomenon is not what originally concerns us. What concerns us is that we *are* it, inseparably from *meeting* it. In due course we shall have to speak of the "intentionalization of matter" from the normative point of view, to reckon with the way intention meets us in material forms.

A "materialization" is an "object" in the broadest sense, a noticeable being of some sort, although of course not all objects are materializations of intention. (Certain definitions of "object" for scientific purposes can make it a materialization of cognitive intention.) The term "materialization" is preferable to "objectification" because it reminds us that that which has become graspable is the material of something forming it. According to the sense these terms have taken on in theoretical polemics of the twentieth century, an "objectification" or "reification" of intention could not be an authentic manifestation of it. The truth, however, is that intention can be manifested only materially. That is not to say that problems do not arise in the relation between intention and its material. Alienation between the two occurs, and is even endemic, but it is not automatic.

Materialization must also be distinguished from objectification or reification in the sense of mere fixing or standardizing. Most words, for example, normally function as standardized moves, purely instrumental and intermediate devices for conveying us to other things that we do grasp. They are more like readinesses than either acts or things. Although we could attend directly to them and treat them protopoetically as the material of intention, we do not. We inhabit them without indwelling them. The fixity of a language system is one kind of formal constraint for intention and spirit, not a "material" factor in our sense.

To see how the event of materialization occurs, I can think about what happens when my eye falls on a certain cream-colored Italian sports car. The appreciation I might feel for it as an independent being is swept aside by a kind of invasion of the car with my own being. Its fresh-mintedness, its formal and tactile perfection, and its speed become mine. My own body standing on a certain spot on the pavement barely exists for me any more, for I live over there in the car. I am not it; I am its rider, its driver. It takes me where and (more importantly) *as* I wish to go. My going becomes the going of this car, just as strong, fast, and fair. It is not a matter of my qualifying the car, thinking of the difference it would make to the car's life to have me as its driver (the way one sometimes thinks about a prospective spouse); it is all the car's qualifying me. And this qualification is, now that I think of it, so incongruously thorough and intoxicating that I recoil from it, dismayed. Surely my whole existence cannot be concentrated into a sports car? Sagely I remind myself that buying it (even if that were possible) would not finally gratify my inclination toward the car, that the true grounds of the mysterious fit with myself lie elsewhere than in having it or actually driving it. Still, it would be great fun to drive it, to "lose myself" in racing along mountain roads, which would really be a kind of finding myself in that experience.

But I am also always facing other people, not only explicitly, when I fancy myself showing up at friends' houses in a beautiful car, but implicitly, when I barrel down the highway feeling sheer speed and traction more and more purely. For the experience is a parable of personal efficacy and freedom from constraint that derives its full thrill from my consciousness of the real theater of action in which I might act so powerfully and freely. This is something different from the animal joy of going fast, or rather it is the spiritual complication of that joy; we are free from it only at that vanishing point of literally "losing ourselves" in the sense of losing consciousness, regressing to a temporary simulation of mere vitality. Therefore, the materialization of my intention in the car qualifies not only me for myself but me-with-others. It is for the moment my spiritual gambit.

The car can also figure as the gambit of another. Suppose it approaches me with a woman already driving it, and she owns the going of the car in such a way as to preempt all fancies of my own that might cling to it. Now, the sleekness and speed belong to her and are a presentation of her, whom I know only as she drives in that car. She is elegant, perfect, powerful yet precisely controlled . . . . But stop! Such a thorough identification of the car with her is no less absurd than my earlier identification of it with myself. Why am I so susceptible to such impressions? I appear to be avid to the point of foolishness for manifestations of intention, to have it to hold. And yet: what is more worth looking for? What else are we strictly bound to look for? The intentional others must be met. One searches for their hands to shake. Nor is it utterly wrong to see the woman in the car. She may not have made it herself, but she chose it, presumably, and now she drives it. The very way she now fits into it is a commitment to it on her part, a giving-herself-to-be-known through it. One hopes there is more to her than that car, but in any event there is not less. And so with me as well. In grasping my own motion as the car's, I know myself to be, formally or potentially, at least not less than that.

A concrete being supports the materialization not only of intention vis-à-vis itself and others but also of certain meetings between intentions. If I marry that woman and we then share the car, our very togetherness may indwell it. There are other materials that have been specifically designed to accommodate the intentions of indefinitely many intenders in a much more articulated and therefore adequate way; one thinks first of works of architecture and music. The solitarization of musical experience that Ebner lamented is by no means essential or original to music. One not only pours oneself into the rewardingly powerful and precise forms of a work of music, one holds one's motion together with the motions of others, which meet one, even if one is off by oneself listening to a recording through headphones, in the fact of the performance and in the cultural qualifications of the music. This holding together was not invented with ensemble playing or with polyphonic writing, but these institutions elaborate it and open it more to consciousness. Architecture and music are the arts of togetherness par excellence, but all works of art serve as meeting places, as we have already seen in the case of the poetic symbol. The Western spirit is decisively qualified by the "great" materializations to which we all attend—the cathedrals, the Rembrandt self-portraits, *War and Peace, Don Giovanni,* Michelangelo's *David*, and so on. It is a mistake to base the claim of such works entirely on the rewards they would offer the first person ever to behold them, or solely on what went into the artist's initial feat of materialization. The life of a whole culture has gradually materialized in these things and now filters through them. They have that much authority. They are no less public places than capitol buildings.

It might seem strange to attend first to cars and art works instead of to the intender's own body, but we should not be too quick to give the body the central place in the drama of materialization, for the striking fact is that our lives are not confined to our bodies. We do live in things outside of us.[3] The ability to do this is a requisite of spiritual existence, for my body and your body have grave drawbacks if they are considered as the materials of togetherness; mine is too much mine, yours too much yours. We begin to transcend our bodies by ornamenting and marking them or behaving with them in commonly intelligible ways. Once we have done that, it is merely convenient to transfer these independent marks or motions to physically independent bearers. Nevertheless, my body is an entirely decisive materialization of my intention in certain ways. It is what I cannot choose not to live in. It is the necessary bearer of all my real actions, that is, all actions that are toward others as opposed to mock actions of the imagination. It produces currents so strong that I can scarcely even think of trying to swim against them, currents (like sexuality) that account for a large part of my motion and its quality.

Its form is indispensable for anyone who would know me, the "best picture of my soul." [4] Precisely because I did not make it myself, it is a revelation of what I am—for I did not make myself, however much I may have influenced my own career. But it *is* not me, all the same. It is mine, something I ride, as yours is ridden by you.

Nothing is more certain than that a person's corpse is not that person, insofar as the body is regarded as a revelation of the other, for there is no dealing with a dead body. On the other hand, it is equally certain that a person's corpse *is* that person, if it is taken for the material of one's own intention aiming at that person (as the grieving parent cradles the body or the vengeful enemy abuses it). This contradiction mirrors the ambiguous position of intention in the body. The human (or canine, etc.) body makes it a tangible fact that a human (or canine, etc.) being exists. If you see mine, you know noninferentially that I exist, or did exist; it is not like a suit of clothes that might or might not have been worn by anyone. And yet if you did not know me when I was alive, you cannot get to know who I am by studying my body when I am dead. In that sense my body might have been ridden by anyone. (For all you know, I had multiple personalities, or felt myself to be of the other sex.) We can tie these perceptions together by saying that a certain body is *for* a certain being's motions toward others, not instrumentally, like a tool, but teleologically, which is to say that it awaits a fulfillment that is not simply immanent in it.

Intention inhabits material forms in different ways. It would be natural to say that intention is "expressed" in a work of art, but relatively odd to say the same of the body, which in fact prescribes for itself the more suitable term "embodied." "Expression" is a special case of the indwelling of matter that comes in for a large share of attention because it is communicative and often deliberate. It is impossible to understand except against the background of indwelling in general, which in the first place involves the material configurations we live in, our "bodies" in an appropriately extended sense—of which the forms that we ordinarily call our "bodies" make up a kind of hard nucleus. This indwelling, with the reverberations it sets up in things of all sorts, is certainly mysterious enough, but there is no additional mystery specific to expression. The importance that we attach to expression derives from the importance of the issue of how we live. Precisely from their felt responsibility to live better, some feel it imperative to act on the principle that where bare matter is, there shall expression be. But this gives rise to an expression-fanaticism that is insanely discontented with every form that has not been taken over for the manifestation of a consciously chosen form of intention; "insanely," because it ignores everything necessarily and properly unchosen in the world, the others in their otherness, the forms of togetherness with them that are already given as valid to some extent, and (perhaps to be counted among these latter) one's own identity. The principle finally shatters on the paradox of "self-expression": that the ones who express cannot become something expressed, at least, not by themselves.

———————————

The deepest mystery of experience is the solidarity between intentional, spiritual, and material quality. I listen to a piano piece by Mozart and the rising and falling, tripping and gliding, swelling and fading, thickening and thinning, hurrying and tarrying just are the very shape of an exhilarating piece of living, the order of lived time turned inside out for my ear and proved real. I listen to the third movement of his 40th symphony and am immediately convinced by the demonstration of a specific, eminently tenable social order that sounds in the fugal polyphony, where a number of different voices cause the whole to flourish in their very own flourishing. We already know that possibilities of "explaining" these qualities by bringing them into discourse are very limited. We can only strive experimentally to compose a likely account of how the qualities of distinct manners of being, the intentional and the material, come to be so intimately linked.

First, we must make a distinction between the qualities that a material being has in itself, as best we can tell, and the qualities that inhere in it strictly by our living in it. We may call these, respectively, "proper" and "received" qualities. A square, for example, has various qualities of regularity, such as straight-sidedness, in itself, and other qualities, such as stability, only by virtue of our trying it on and feeling what it is like to be in it. It is true that straight-sidedness as a feelable *quality* requires us to feel it. The quality is inactual apart from us, but it is still proper to the square in that it does not depend on any quality of our own to be what it is, in the way that "stability" depends on our own wild search for balance. Another way of putting this is to say that insofar as things are to have any qualities at all, it is inconceivable that a square could lack that of straight-sidedness, whereas we can indeed imaginatively place the square in a world where stability is not an issue or feelable quality in the same way.

That the distinction between proper and received qualities does not perfectly correspond to the classic distinction between primary and secondary qualities becomes immediately apparent in considering an example like red light, which for us *is* a material being in just that way and therefore is properly red. The older distinction, oriented to physics, would mark off the features (however you could see them!) of the independently existent waved photons as primary and the features of the color-reaction of the viewer as secondary. But a little pressing of allegedly primary qualities always shrinks them to a vanishing point. What are these photons apart from our perceiving them and conceiving them in some qualitative form, be it the more manipulable form of wave patterns that can be drawn and measured? The achievement of a quantitative grasp of light makes a large difference in our ability to do things with it, obviously, but it is also true that at any moment we know only that such a thing as light is before us, to measure or not, by virtue of a presentation of quality. Now the redness of *this* red light is not the same thing as "redness as such," not even the exact same hue, if it is only ideally conceived; for a purely ideal quality cannot be "proper" to any other being, idealization meaning precisely that the idealizer, not anything else, owns it. The redness of this red light is proper to it because apart from it we could not tell that we were seeing *this* light. The same cannot be said of a received quality like warmth, which, even though it is (in our culture) a more or less standard quality in redness, can be bracketed off without chasing the light itself away. We can pull ourselves out of the red and thereby remove its temperature. The red is "objectively" warm in the sense of secondary objectivity, that is, it is quite hospitable to the experience of warmth in it, supporting that experience for most people who are ready for it; but we say more when we say that it is "properly" red, namely, that its redness is a condition of the possibility of knowing what we are talking about if we try to talk about this light. As a proper quality the redness is primarily objective even if its secondary objectivity cannot be established, as it is not only not provable but extremely improbable that subjects have exactly equivalent qualitative experiences of the hues of things. In contrast, the older concept of "primary quality" is keyed to the conditions of secondary objectivity.

The same condition holds for us: apart from the qualities proper to our own existence we would not know what it is for us to exist. But intentional qualities are originally felt immediately and kinesthetically, whereas material qualities stand over against us, presenting themselves to be perceived and known. I feel what it is like to want or do something even though I may be at a complete loss to picture it to myself. I can be at one with myself or ill at ease, excited or depressed, interested or dull, without any perceptual or intuitive presentation of material at all—aware *in* the qualities without being cognizant *of* them. It is these qualities proper to my own existence that either fit into material housing and become elaborated therein, or do not. But how does that happen?

I see a red light. My attention leads me into it and out of it again, bouncing back toward myself; I move toward it, toward myself from it, and toward others through it. (The different kinds of attention are just these different extensions and displacements of my feeling-center, which might be loosely conceived as the saddle of my riding.) There is now warmth, cheer, boldness, or anger, as I become sure of myself in these ways with the confirmation of the material, which shines and thickens as I do and in harmony with other materials that I indwell— primarily my body. The red that is proper to the red light is *apt* to the entry of the qualities that are proper to me. It corresponds. And I am the sort of being that seeks such correspondence. Without me, there could not be that manifold of relationships, inadequately encapsulated by the idea of "harmony," between qualities, for they only come together in my riding.

The temptation looms to give up conceiving the self in the first place as a qualitative being of some distinctive sort that then comes into rapport with material qualities, and instead to conceive it as the being *of* the rapport between material qualities, such as those of redness and my body in anger. For after all I *know* of myself at any given moment only in such a rapport. But on reflection I know that I am not any one of these or even their totality, since my possibilities exceed the actual; rather, I am the power of instituting these rapports and the invisible center in which this power is seated. This reminds me that normally these rapports figure to me as a riding, meaning that I am a rider. I also frequently have the experience of "trying on" a material quality such as redness without any awareness at all of other material—my body is obviously active in some way, of course, but not for my consciousness. My own invisible qualitative existence purely as intention is the presupposition of "trying on," which otherwise would be nothing more than the occurrence of quality-feeling with no sense of fitness or unfitness.

I am not the rapport, but instituting it is my life. We cannot make a problem out of the relationship of my sort of being to material quality, because this is just what I do. The problem is not the relationship, but how one can conceive the invisible relatum on its own. We should remember at this point the freedoms of self and other that have already been enjoined on us from the spiritual standpoint. On these grounds we expect to be frustrated in principle in any attempt to fix the nature of intentional being, except for a highly general characterization of its manner of moving and positioning itself relative to other beings such as was given above (section 3.6). It is therefore entirely fitting that on phenomenological and speculative grounds the nature of intentional being as such remains a secret. We must be secret in order to sally forth freely. The intelligibility proper to this freedom lies in its being freedom-with-respect-to manifest beings.

To sum up, intentional qualities come into our field of vision in being received by materials. It seems most reasonable to say that the reception will be efficient or adequate in the measure that the proper qualities of the materials involved correspond to the qualities received from us. The nature of the correspondence cannot be specified more closely than can intentional qualities on their own.

What becomes of the other material being—or, as we should be especially careful to say in the case of intentional beings, the other being qua material —in the reception of my intentional qualities? Does the spiritual exigency of affirming others as other forbid the intentional invasion of other beings that has been described above as characteristic of all intentional being? Must I refrain from living in others to do them justice? We come across a sign that this is not necessarily the case when we notice that received qualities do not drive out proper qualities but rather fit with them; that fit seems to be their ticket of admission.

Thus, a rudimentary respect for others is presupposed by the successful act of living in them. Nor do received qualities necessarily occlude an other's proper qualities. The warmth I feel in a red light is present for me along with its redness. I attend to its redness "warmly," but I am not bound to attend solely to warmth and no more to redness. A familiar object on my desk does not lose its mass or outlines for being bathed in my fondness for it. On the contrary, my fondness gives me a sharper eye for its details, not only in making me pay more attention to it but by setting off those details in their presentation against a quasi-objective background of sturdiness, quaintness, and the like.

Our question may thus be turned around to this: *May* I refrain from living in others without thereby *failing* to do them justice? Respect cannot be defined so as to exclude love. My service of that red light or this object on my desk is precisely to live in it appreciatively.

A crucial complication is introduced when the other is intentional. In this case the material qualities that are apparent to me figure normatively as the material-izations of the intentional qualities of the other. According to idealist premises, it is no more possible for your materialization to be at the same time mine than it is possible for us simultaneously to eat the same food. Subjectivity's owner-ship of an experience is absolute. Dialogical philosophy traps itself in the same dilemma insofar as it defines itself in reaction against idealist or transcendental philosophy; it must hold the true, immediate "You" apart from the "It-You" that belongs to the I's experience, but in doing this it prohibits itself from any positive characterization of the true "You," and the encounter with the "You" that it so prizes becomes phantasmal. It becomes impossible to conceive how the qualities of the other, which make him or her who he or she is, can still be his or hers in the moment that they are present to me.

The root of the problem lies in taking a certain materialization of intention, "knowledge," as the only or paradigmatic kind. Knowledge as a determining of things and rendering them disposable for theoretical constructions—that is, as opposed to pure notice of things "present," which involves a standing back from proper qualities rather than an invading of them in that greedy and credulous way in which "presence" is sometimes equated with "givenness"—such knowledge is, indeed, incompatible with the presentation of the others as other, whether they be intentional or not. But I do not have to be materialized in a being as one who exhaustively surveys it and disposes of it. It is not a condition of my really living in a house that I must live in it as its sole owner and master; why then should I have to "have" the qualities of any of the beings that are present to me all to myself? The answer will be that I am the absolute owner of the intention that is materialized, since I am it, and that I have no basis on which to speak of a material quality as the materialization of some other intention, which would be absolutely owned by another. But this answer is just another dogmatic appeal to the principle that a *materialization* (as opposed to an intention) must be exclusively owned, which is decisively contradicted by my primordial realization that *I am not alone*—not alone in the world, since others are *present*, and feelably not alone in the very matter of my life, the places where I live. The other is in the house with me, making it our house, qualifying all of my feelings about the house interintentionally.

(If I were wrong about the claim of the others extending into feeling, the consequence would be that the life of feeling is nonresponsible. The unhappy Kantian exclusion of virtually all of the affections from the spiritual realm would be repeated. But I know that I am not wrong, because—as I confess and propose— my very feelings are better and worse, righter and wronger, things to be ashamed of or relatively at peace with. This is part of the knowledge that I cannot escape from, imposed on me by actual meeting of the others, where it actually happens.)

The principle that saves dialogical philosophy from the embarrassment that it inherits from idealism is that while the other is never mine, what belongs to the other can belong to me, too. For example, the face of my friend indubitably belongs to him. Its qualities are, for me, among the primary revelations of the qualities that are him. At the same time, I live in that face—feeling amusement in the smile, curiosity in the raised eyebrows—and, beyond that, I live in my conception of who he is. That he also lives in them is evident from the tension between how I fit myself to these materials and how they are moved and acted on by him. The tension is not just in his body; the whole world is our house. Obviously, neither he nor "his feelings" can ever be identical with anything in which I recognize my feelings, but our feelings can be in contact by virtue of a common indwelling, the ongoing infinitely ramified handshake between us.

7.3 Material Culture

When we live in things, they gain the force of the meaning that we ourselves are. Their qualities take on importance insofar as they are our own, and unsurpassable importance insofar as they belong to spirits. But how, if at all, do things keep an intentional or spiritual importance when we do not happen to be living in them? How can this importance be put into a thing, to be revisited later? Can matter be permanently "intentionalized" or "spiritualized"?

The issue concerns the nature and possibility of *significance*, if we apply this term to the specifically intentional or spiritual claim and interest held by material being for intention. By "meaning" we mean, in the last analysis, the actual moving or self-presentation of ourselves and other beings. What is meaningful is what is full of the existence of the beings that are. "Significance" is the herald, the potential of meaning; it is to meaning as a (good) check is to cash.

The realm of material beings that are significant is "material culture." This is the usual term for a spiritual community's material deposit by which it is recognized and in which it recognizes itself. (We still mean "material" in a broader sense than usual, however.) These beings point to or house the "spiritual beings" of which Buber says, "We hear no You and yet feel addressed." 5 We shall begin our discussion of them by considering two of the most interesting earlier approaches to the problem, first, Buber's description of an encounter mediated by a significant material, and next, Hartmann's ontological description of these materials as a class.

In the afterword to *I and Thou* Buber gives a supplementary account of the reciprocity specific to our relations with nonpersonal beings. His example of encounter with a spiritual being is his own beholding of an architectural form.

> Take the Doric column, wherever it appears to a man who is able and ready to turn toward it. It confronted me for the first time out of a church wall in Syracuse into which it had been incorporated: secret primal measure presenting itself in such a simple form that nothing individual could be seen or enjoyed in it. What had to be achieved was what I was able to achieve: to confront and endure this spiritual form [*Geistgebild*] there that had passed through the mind and hand of man and become incarnate.6

In this sophisticated report of the viewing of a Doric column, the material column is taken to be quite distinct from something else, the spiritual form, of which it is the "incarnation." The spiritual form so dominates the experience that the particular column is virtually eclipsed. Further, the incarnation is seen to have a twofold relation to human intention: it "had passed through the mind and hand of man," and it demanded of the beholder that he achieve something, the meeting and enduring of it. The word "enduring" suggests that Buber found himself lived in by something else, rather than going forth to live in it; the form was apparently formed in him.

As for Hartmann, it would raise false hopes to say that he offers a theory of objectivated spirit, because he endeavors only to describe the phenomena and never speculatively to explain them; and description of spiritual objectivation only deepens the mystery as to how it is possible. But in his own milder way he "confronts and endures" spiritual forms and gives a more general account of them than is offered by Buber.7 He, too, perceives the distinction between the "irreal" spiritual form and its material bearer, calling the latter a "material form" (*sinnliche Realgebilde*) and the former a "spiritual content" or "good" (*geistige Gehalt or Inhalt, Gut*). Material forms have the purely instrumental significance that they permit the detachment of spiritual forms from their creators and the survival of these forms over a longer or shorter period of historical time (depending on the material stability of the bearers), during which they remain available for recapture by living spirit. The irreal travels and enjoys duration courtesy of the real. But material forms are also, in varying degree, linked with spiritual contents qualitatively. In the supreme example of the work of art, the material "foreground" is necessary, just as it is, to the spiritual "background" of the work. The power of a beautiful work of art to evoke the right seeing of it is rooted in the determinacy of this material-spiritual connection. At the other extreme lie material forms like words, among which there is for the most part only a conventional relation between sound and sense.

Hartmann's theoretical objectivation of "spiritual content" is congenial with other important philosophical moves of this century, such as the theory of aesthetic semblance set forth in Susanne Langer's *Feeling and Form* (which Hartmann's own aesthetics anticipates), Husserl's noematization of logical objects in the *Logical Investigations*, and, of course, Scheler's theory of values. Again I suggest that we investigate the move suspiciously, as we did with Scheler. Is there a *being* that I behold when I see more in a painting than the paint or hear more in a word than the sound? Or is the truth just that I am *doing* something with paint and sound? Of course, Hartmann is composing an ontology of spiritual being in *Das problem des geistigen Seins*, and anything that comes into his view will be construed by him as some manner or other of being. But he gives a number of clues that the peculiar "being" of "spiritual contents" is different from anything subsistent, even from anything as objectively distinct from intention as "phenomena."

In the first place, these "irreal" "spiritual contents" owe both their creation and their maintenance to living spirit. The picture is not there when it is not looked at; it only exists in a *Gegenleistung* or encore performance of spirit.[8] If its paint were destroyed, it could not be looked at any more, and would be gone.[9] It is not like an "ideal" being, which exists for itself suprahistorically, grasped or not. Thus, in order to avoid positing a separate existence of spiritual contents that would not be warranted by the phenomena, Hartmann imputes to them a being-for-living-spirit that is difficult to keep conceptually separate from the being *of* living spirit (conceding for the moment the description of spirit as "being"). Second, Hartmann notes that a picture is not just a *sight* but a prescription or allowing of a *way of seeing*. "We can still see what Rembrandt saw; what is more, we can see 'as' Rembrandt saw."[10] This is eminently a feature of works of art, whose material foregrounds are strongly determinative of our sensibility and thus lead us in to see what is to be seen in them, but it is true in other content-realms as well. Hartmann gives the example that when we immerse ourselves in the Platonic dialogues, we are given not just the meanings of the words but a world, that is, a way of living in the world. Third, Hartmann finds that no ensemble of material form and spiritual content is wholly determinative of meaning, for the Rembrandt picture does not mean just the same to us as it did to Rembrandt and his contemporaries, nor does it even mean precisely the same to you as to me. There is some "free play" (*Spielraum*) in all spiritual contents such that their meaning must be completed by their beholders.[11] So we run into yet another way in which "spiritual contents" are a function of intention.

What prevents Hartmann from drawing the conclusion that "spiritual contents" are nothing but acts and meetings is their apparent over-againstness, or objectivity. When I look at the Rembrandt picture, something is there for me that I did not already have, something that was also there—if not in the same exact way, yet in an identifiable common way—for others who have looked at it. It seems that I am led to grasp it because it first grasps me. Now, we need to understand how we are "grasped"—Hartmann says this word can only be a metaphor since no one is actually present to make a claim—in order to understand how there *is* anything over against us.[12] The grasping must be the proof of the being. But Hartmann refuses to try to explain "grasping." Adhering to his phenomenological scruples, he leaves us in the lurch. And he can do no other than disappoint us in this telltale fashion, because he does not actually see an object that *could* grasp us. He only has a feeling of "objectivity."

Let us try to account for the true things Hartmann says about "spiritual contents" without ascribing being to them. I go up to a Rembrandt picture. Do I see anything more than daubs of paint? Of course—I see a woman bathing. There is not really a woman there on the wall, so one could say that I am seeing something "irreal." The daubs of paint get me to see a woman. But do they get me to see her by causing her to be there before me irreally, or by causing or allowing me to see as though I were seeing her? What does "irreality" mean, if not that she is *not* there? Is it not a contradiction to say that she is "irreally there"? She *seems* to be there because *I seem* to be seeing a woman. Precisely because she is a semblance, I would be mistaken if I concluded from my experience that she was there. But *something* is there; I am not hallucinating; you know the picture I mean, for we can talk about it. Beyond dispute, the painting qua "material form" is there. Now, why does anything else have to be there? Is not the material painting a sufficiently determinative point of reference for our illusory seeings to give us that possibility of comparing our impressions of it? Rembrandt has artfully painted a canvas so that when we look at it, we seem to see a certain woman in a certain setting, and in a certain way. (As regards the "certain way," the seeming becomes a reality, the painting's qualification of our real seeing.) If there were any point in bringing in an additional "spiritual content" to determine our seeing sufficiently, that point would surely be lost in allowing for a different "completion" of the content by each subject. It seems more reasonable to think that subjects complete their experiences of material forms differently precisely because there is nothing lurking behind a material form to determine how it is seen.

There is, to be sure, much besides the material form that determines how it will be seen; in our example, there is the whole body of knowledge and expectations associated with going to a museum and seeing a painting by Rembrandt. There is the title on the bottom of the frame, and everything the guidebook says. These accompanying indicators become more important as material form does less to determine the beholding, as is notably the case with words.

To return to our original question: Wherein lies the Rembrandt picture's "grasping," if there is not an irreal woman there to accost me? We must recall that I have learned to make something of pictures and that I have sympathy for them; that they are significant has been settled in advance, firmly if not irrevocably, by a conspiracy of the culture to which I belong. An uninstructed or indifferent viewer will not be accosted by the picture that accosts me. For me, Rembrandt's woman bathing is so vividly present because I have turned to the painting prepared and expecting to see such a sight. But I still strain to "see" anything in a certain canvas by Gorky; that is a seeing I cannot bring off, because I do not have a happy enough partnership with the material that faces me. A friend of mine loves the Gorky, so somehow it grasps her, which means that she "sees" something in it. What, then, is a painting's "grasping" one other than the actualization of one's ability to see something, something important, in it? Remember that by "seeing something in it," we mean seeming to see something by means of it.

There is a kind of stationary bicycle used for exercise that is called an exercycle. Imagine five of these standing in a row. Imagine getting on the first, the second, the third, and the fourth, finding that each has its pedals locked so that you can do nothing with it. Finally you climb on the fifth, push on the pedals, and —they go! This stimulating surprise makes you feel as though the pedals are pulling your feet. Your own motion is harnessed by them. Something analogous occurs in looking at a picture by Rembrandt: one feels accosted in the matching of one's own intentional energy with an opportunity for it to move in a certain way, materializing in the woman bathing.

The woman is now there for us to regard and think about, on the canvas, on reproductions of the canvas, and in our memories, as are her general qualities, for example, a Rembrandtian tenderness that we also know from other paintings and can think about as a theme in its own right. The woman and the qualities are there as materializations of our own intention, our act. But we feel ourselves acting under constraints of various kinds, and therein consists the objectivity of the materialization. We are constrained by what the daubs of paint will bear, by the knowledge we bring to the painting (including our knowledge of Rembrandt's style), and to some extent by what others make of it, such as the museum guide who explains its virtues and the friend standing next to me who understands it as I do and lives in the material with me. Above all, I find my seeing of the painting controlled by *her,* she whom I seem to see. She is the "content" or "spiritual being" in the case. Even though in one sense I make her myself, in another sense she stands over against me to be confronted and endured because she is a *certain* thing to be made who is sent to me from the world of real others —the one who painted the painting, the others who may and do look at it and think about it—as an instruction and reward for all our intention. She therefore "speaks" to me for the real others. If she did not have this twist, she would not be a specifically "spiritual" form or content, in our sense of that term; at any rate, when I face her I find that she does have this twist. This must be the spiritual dimension of the "claim" of the work, that it calls me toward humanity in one feasible, strongly affirmative way. "Spiritual significance" is thus the promise of this claim. A significant object is one into which I can find my way and in which I can take up my abode in a rewarding and answering way.

With this approach we end by understanding all the arts—for that matter, all dimensions of material culture—as performing arts. It is well-known that works of theater, music, and dance only fully "exist" in being performed, but also that they can be performed in different ways: in the imaginations of their creators, in the concert hall, or in the imaginations of persons able to read scripts and scores. For a trained musician, a reading of a score can be no less a performance of it than the physical playing of it is a performance for an ordinary audience. Our conclusion generalizes the score-performance relationship to all presentations of significant material. The sensory or intuitive material serves as the score, and the entry of intention into it on the part of the beholder is the final performance. Besides this, there is what we ordinarily call the "performance," the presentation of the material to the beholder, which indeed seems most like a performance because most of the beholder's sense of a performing comes from his or her own indwelling of the actions of players. Their activity is a materialization of the beholder's.

Any materialization of our intention is a way for us to be. A way of being has a structure. This structure does not have a being different from our being; it is simply a determinate way in which we may be. Hartmann says the same, in effect, by denying that objectivated spirit can exist apart from living spirit. His ontological scheme is surpassed, however, by the qualification of materialized intention by genuine spirit. Once we speak of ways in which we can be *together,* we may no longer ascribe to these ways even our own being—or, alternatively, we can continue to ascribe to them our own being, by way of participating in them, but avowing at the same time the inadequacy of this ascription. I perform my intention as an Ideal Performer and therefore as more than myself.

As we have seen, Buber holds that the spiritual forms are not figments of ourselves. "Tested for its objectivity, the form is not 'there' at all; but what can equal its presence? And it is an actual relation: it acts on me as I act on it. . . . Forming is discovery." [13] In this passage he has in mind the creation of the work of art rather than its later appreciation. Certainly the working artist furnishes a striking example of apparent interaction between intention and this structural opportunity that beckons to it from elsewhere, but this does not require us to find an ontological home for the spiritual form outside of intention and its real meetings. There is an intelligible sense in which intention neither is nor has *actually* what nevertheless is its own, namely, its own future possibilities. The artist does not confront a figment of his or her own soul *as it is* but rather attempts to wrestle that soul into a new and spiritually exemplary shape, this shape invading the artist from the future to the extent that he or she catches a glimmer of it. The work of art has this kind of "objectivity" in being something-to-be-reckoned-with for the artist; it is objective in another way as a materialization of intention, based on the material used (paint, stone, words, etc.); and in yet another way as a gathering place for intenders, based (with an entirely different kind of stability) on their actual meetings.

Supposing that we are now better positioned to understand the general nature of "significance" and materialized meaning—can we understand a material being as significant of the intention of *an other*? Can I ever directly read some material as the reach of an other toward me rather than my reach toward an other? This is a central issue for a general theory of interpretation. What artists mean may not be of primary importance for aesthetics, inasmuch as the significance of the work is not the same as the artist's intention. But outside of aesthetics we can hardly ignore the problem of how it is possible to establish what people mean, a problem that promises to have an intractable element in it somewhere since our first principles prevent us from knowing what any person is.

It might seem that the front door to this problem can be unlocked by a key we have already used, namely, the conception of intentional existence as a riding of all intellectually and sensorily available materials, based on a body but not confined to one. Speaking others are no more locked inside their bodies than I am; that they are not is of course the prime condition of the possibility of "speaking." However, I do not know this in the same way. My warrant for claiming this is that I *hear speaking, not* that I have the experience I earlier appealed to, wherein I found myself invading a sports car. I cannot merely reason by analogy from my own experience to the other's, as I did in the case of a sports car belonging to a woman, for by those means I only establish that it is reasonable to look for the other's self-presentation in such places, not that I find it. The possibility that she is presenting herself in the car is not the actuality. What makes for an actual meeting via a materialization of the other's intention, and what makes the meeting determinate, so that one is in *some* position (not necessarily omniscient or infallible) to say nonarbitrarily what the other means?

I receive a letter from a friend. As I am opening the envelope, the sense of my friend and our relationship, remembered, grows upon me to establish the context for the letter. I read it. It is written in the English language, which I understand; let us say, using the analogy we have just adopted, that the symbols make up a score that I am capable of performing. I take these in and play them in order to attend to the propositions that are formed by means of them, already with a sense of my friend's style to fit these expected propositions into. The moves, although I am making them at what we might call the technical level, are not mine; they are not the ones I would make, except in the unusual case where I am imitating my friend. Nevertheless, they are makeable, they hang together comprehensibly, they add up to something *one* would say if one were a certain person.

We are driven to speak of "one" in this connection insofar as my friend, though permanently other, enters into the realm of the intelligible, the logos. "One" is the spiritual speaker in general, the owner of language; even the things I say are things "one" can say. (To be sure, I do not normally think of myself, nor does my friend figure to me, as a specification of "one." I am inclined to say that we *are* not one, we *are* ourselves. But then I remember that as a spiritual being I am not simply myself but also "one," and this "one" is not something I own, but rather something I am a member of.) As the speaker of intelligible language my friend comes before me as a *certain* "*one*." We have to say this, but we must take great care not to fall into the error, which this formulation encourages, of interpreting the other as a species of an intelligible genus. The horizon of language is there for my friend to step into. The unlimited range of moves that can be made with language by such beings as my friend is actually the transcendental horizon of language as a system of intelligibility, and not the other way around. My friend's otherness is the spin that makes the "one" who speaks other than the "one" of my own speaking. In other words, when we communicate by language, we are other to each other as other "ones," his otherness of course superordinate to his onehood.

My friend's other-oneness is like a twisting of the rope that I am holding when I understand language. Actually, it is one degree more complicated than that, because I myself am twisting the rope in making out the propositions, and I discover that the way I am twisting shows that my twisting is being twisted. I expected to discover this from the moment I saw my friend's return address on the envelope; without that context I could read the letter as though it were a cereal box or newspaper, more as loose matter for propositions than as an actual set of propositions. I expected to discover this and now, in this case, am confirmed. A twisting occurs that does not come from myself but has a recognizable style, his.

We may generalize the rope and the twisting in this account to all communications, even those that involve "language" and "speaking" only in a very loose sense. When archeologists find an ancient Mesopotamian pot in the sands and it "speaks" to them of a lost culture, there is a medium, the common practice of forming and using such objects, and the qualification of that medium by a strangeness with a style. In this sort of case there will be a lot of argument about what that style actually amounts to. But doubt about who is communicating does not mean that no one is communicating. My wife and I will likewise give different interpretations of some of the finer points of my friend's letter; our disagreeing about what he means does not dissolve him. The crucial difference between the cases is that we can write back to my friend and solicit another self-presentation, while the Mesopotamians rely entirely on our conscientious approaches and re-approaches to their message. We can dig for more pots but we cannot get them to act again with our own moves among their reasons.

The field of intentional materialization and interintentional meeting is much broader than the field of deliberately composed and "read" messages. But philo-sophical theories of interpretation are dominated, not unnaturally, by the paradigm of reading texts, which fails to bring to our minds the other ways we indwell material beings together, acting and undergoing happily and unhappily in our bodies, using tools and delighting in objects and environments, working and play-ing under the guidance of materially symbolized purposes. Through all of these modes of common life the issue of interpretation confronts us: each is called upon to know what the others mean in order rightly to respond to them.

7.4 Conditions for Solidarity of the Spiritual with the Material. The Example of Zionism, and Chesterton's Mistake

Once we entertain the concept of materialization (or incarnation), we are bound to try to measure the adequacy of materialization with respect to that, distinct from it, which is materialized. The question of the adequacy of *my* material existence to *me* gives rise to the philosophy of subjective authenticity or ownness, wherein a doctrine of what would count as an actualization of my true self is matched with a doctrine of what it is possible for me to actualize in the materials of the world. The parallel question of the adequacy of material forms to culture or spirit produces the philosophy of objective authenticity or genuineness. Both questions drew much attention in the first half of this century. That the latter is now comparatively neglected is a sign of the conceptual eclipse of spirit. The movement of our argument takes us back toward it; but we may not do this in ignorance of the perils threatening anyone who presumes to declare which materials spirit is at home in. These dangers can be summed up by the word "fascism." What is wrong with fascism in this extended sense is that the others cannot, in principle, justly be *defined* through being tied together in a material bundle, the *fasces*. Let us keep and even cultivate our fear of fascism. But we ought to see if we can be duly averse to fascism and still get on with undertaking and understanding a mutually affirmative life together in the world. Fascism has the last laugh on us if it forces us to define ourselves merely in opposition to it; then it has crippled us.

What clues can we take from the much-studied difficulties that intention as such has in living in matter?

In order to tell what sort of being "I" am, I, the one who intends, must grasp myself as the one who is *not* what is intended. Whenever I assert my own existence, it is by negation, as the reaction "But I!" to any X, Y, and Z. I fail to coincide with X, Y, and Z in two ways: by remaining on their near side, as the other to whom they appear or for whom they exist, and by surpassing them in projecting toward other possibilities that I see beyond them (X', Y', and Z'; not-X, not-Y, not-Z; etc.). Now, since any given circumstances of life, including one's body, amount to some X, Y, and Z for the "I" in the moment when it asks itself what it is, it would appear that a perfectly adequate materialization of the "I," one in which it would contentedly recognize itself, can never be achieved.

But it would be going overboard to conclude on these grounds that the "I" just is a factor of nihilation set over against materializations that invariably figure to it as un-ownable reifications. An intender is not in the first place a negator or recoiler, but a mover-in-and-toward-things. Moving does imply negation, but negation for the sake of a movement. The negativity is subordinate to a positivity. It appears as the healthy restlessness of a living "I" embarked on the project of living better, never settling down to be comfortable in a given form of life, though sometimes tempted to. The "I" who appears in the self-querying of the movement has to be the sheer negativity in the movement's disentangling itself to confirm itself, perhaps to stir up intention out of one of its congealings. Cartesian doubt has its moment when it is sovereign. But then what? One moves on *to* something, just as one resumes breathing after holding one's breath for a moment to listen. The breathing, not only the holding of breath, must be conceived as the I's own.

These considerations suggest that a given material will be accepted by the I as its own if it figures for the I as something moved-in-and-through rather than as a stationary obstruction. The actual material that most obviously meets this condition is the very one with which we most closely identify, with which, in fact, we have some trouble not identifying, our bodies. Of course, the bedridden body of a very ill person is quite a different matter from a body that is sound and active. Normally, however, the body is home; everything I do radiates from it and conforms to the shape of actions of which it is capable, and to separate myself from it would be unnecessary and absurd. How else other than this way would I be? What other face besides this one would be mine? And even if my body is sick, enfeebled, and a drag on my life, what would I want other than for *it* to be healthy, strong, and apt for enterprise? That there are not seriously felt alternatives to being in our fated bodies, provided they are healthy, shows the normal solidarity of intention with this material. The solidarity is not absolute. Some of us who are men wish we were women, and vice versa; some of us wish we were fish or birds; some of us cannot be reconciled with our own looks. But we do not have to claim that the body as such is absolutely adequate to intention as such in order to establish that under normal conditions the body is not a problem for intention, but, indeed, a solution for it.

Now what of spirit? Can its blowing, like the movement of intention, be on friendly terms with matter? There is precedent for distinguishing spirit more sharply from the material forms with which it is associated than we did with intention, to picture it, for instance, as generating forms rather than as itself formed.[14] Whereas intention is a movement that must have a determinate worldly form and place, spirit is a calling upon that movement, of its essence a provocation or solicitation, a kind of implacable restlessness that is superordinate to any impatience intention might feel on its own account. When Hartmann describes the association of living spirit with its objectivations over historical time, he is obliged to refer to a dialectic of two negations, the "fettering" of spirit in forms that are inadequate to it and its "liberation" from them.[15] Living spirit and objectivated spirit are basically at odds because the latter is lifeless—a husk always to be outgrown. But living spirit can change only by setting what is in it outside of itself where it can be contested. For that reason, objectivation is an essential part of the very life of spirit. The living lives in negating the lifeless. That, at least, is what Hartmann maintains, marching rather close to Hegel. But it seems that in this view we encounter a repetition of the false opposition in which doctrines of selfhood go astray, that between freedom as nihilation of the determinate and determinacy as reification. Let us see if we can make a parallel correction in the case of spirit.

If determinacy *were* reification, freedom *would* have to negate it. But freedom is not bound to negate a living determinacy in and through which it moves; that is to say, so long as it is, if not the sole determiner, at least the happy codeterminer of that determinacy. Similarly, on the plane of the issue of spirit, a spirit would have to be regarded as negating any intentional determinacy, if such determinacy were a thought, deed, or experience possessible by a single intender. However, a spirit is not bound to negate an interintentional determinacy that it itself is determining so as to gather intenders. When one person's hand conveys food to another person who is hungry, that is a solution, not a problem, for a spirit. The other person's face, qua presentation to me of that other's existence as other, is likewise a spiritual event, of which the face's very determinacy is a necessary condition.

Consider a particular facial expression, like a look of compassion, with eyes open as if to embrace what they see and lips formed as if starting to say "Oh"; or a certain action with a recognizable meaning, like putting coins into a beggar's plate. The question can be raised whether and how these materializations are ade-quate to the norms of compassion and charity that give them their spiritual identity —whether the quality of a spirit is accommodated by their material qualities. Is the look of compassion an event of response and leaguing with another to affirm him or her against threatening circumstances? It might only be a social cipher, unconnected with the uncommanded inner life of the one with the look. Is the giving of alms an adventurous act of service? It might rather be a convenient act of conventional virtue. Just when we have made our civilization wholly expressive, as we fancy, of a lofty spirit, a prophet may arrive and expose us all as Pharisees and hypocrites. The prophet will know that our designedly "spiritual" moves are selfishly controlled or merely automatic, and not manners of being commanded by others or by norms of togetherness with them. But how does the prophet know that our spirit is not in our materializations, that our tears are crocodile tears? (Let us rule out for the moment grosser clues like the fact that those who give pennies to beggars keep fortunes for themselves.) Is this a matter of aesthetic criticism? Does our conduct contain false notes, like a flawed theatrical performance?

Looked at in one way, "aesthetic" evaluation must always be completely destructive of the relationship between spirit and matter and so cannot be given authority over it. For even more damning than the judgment "His look of compassion seemed put-on" is the praise "He has the look of compassion to a T!" Such a description makes the compassion evaporate for us, no matter whether its subject was expertly simulating it or sincerely expressing it. (A novelist can wreak havoc with our perception of sincere characters simply by meticulously describing them as "sincere characters.") A spiritual quality is annulled when posited as an intentionally graspable quality; the values of aesthetic surface all fall into the latter category.

If I can look at you and tell that you are genuinely compassionate, the mark of the genuineness is not on the surface. You do not avoid seeming false by seeming true, in the sense of accurately modeling some conceivable quality. Something different happens. We might say that you "ring" true. The notion of ringing true suggests a vibration of the surface coming from behind it, from a hollowness wherein there is room to be struck by something other. The surface takes an effect into itself without owning it. Rather than acting, you reveal that you are first acted upon (in the peculiarly spiritual way) and that this being-acted-upon qualifies your own acting. You are not entirely self-possessed. But this being-acted-upon and not-being-self-possessed are not discernible *elsewhere* than on your "surface," in a material. Where else is there? Therefore we should draw the conclusion, not that spiritual genuineness transcends aesthetic evaluation, but that aesthetic evaluation properly deals with more than the intentional production and grasping of "surfaces." Of course, good stage actors *seem* to register the effects of what others say and do rather than to produce all the details of their comportment out of themselves, and they garner aesthetic praise for the accuracy of this seeming. But the technical praise of the seeming is subordinate to an appreciation of the ungraspable reality that is modeled by the performances and the play. A play is finally good because it is an orientation to life with the real others. It is important here that we designate the question of the adequacy of materials to spirits an "aesthetic" question, in order to rescue aesthetics proper from superficiality.

If we accept the principle that spirit can be at home in matter, then we will next ask whether there is a certain material in which, under normal circumstances, spirit is fully at home, to the same extent that my intention is at home in my body. Much twentieth-century thinking proceeds consciously or unconsciously on the assumption that language is to spirit what the body is to intention; let us explore the same path.[16]

We looked at language earlier with the problem of validity in mind. Then it appeared as a system of moves available to speakers that (they could be more or less confident) would be received and appropriately answered by others. In short, language *works* as an interintentional apparatus. But *how* does it work? Largely by pure stipulation, it seems. We know that words do not generally resemble things, though fancy can always find the horns of a cow in its *w*; do we also know that propositions need not resemble gestures? Is it similarly fanciful to find fundamental spiritual qualities mirrored in acoustical and grammatical materials? For example, Ebner argues (taking a cue from Jacob Grimm's lecture on the origin of language) that German pronouns appropriate the "natural possessiveness" of the *m*-sound and the pointingness of the *t*-sound in taking on their different pneumatological meanings. *Du* and *Du bist* ("Thou," "Thou art") are vocative pointings to the other in which, so far as this goes, the I relates itself to the other as other and does not close itself off. "In the nominative, the I (*Ich*) is inwardly open to the Thou . . . [but the] I secludes itself from the Thou in *Mein-Mir-Mich* ("my, "me"), wherein it becomes itself the object and goal." He relates the *m*-forms of the self to "the 'hateful' *moi* of Pascal, fallen from God, the I of the 'will to power' and also the 'object of psychology'."[17] Language thus has inscribed in it both an original, spiritually acceptable relationship and a "fall" into pathological manners of being spiritual. That is to say that one can read off of language indications that spirit is partly at home and partly ill at ease in it.

There is nothing to object to such a view as Ebner's, provided we understand that the "possessiveness" of the *m*-sound or the "pointingness" of the *t*-sound are *already* gestures and not merely natural phenomena that parallel spiritual events. It is not surprising that the tissue of language should be composed in part of such spiritual molecules and atoms. It is true, moreover, just as this theory predicts, that we sometimes feel at odds with language not because it fails us as a means of expression but because it puts us in a position we feel to be false—as when, because of the conjunction of certain circumstances with grammatical rules, one finds oneself forced to use the words "me" and "my" too much, in what seems an unholy way.

Others have written far more interestingly and instructively on the spiritual physiognomy of language than I am prepared to. I refrain from embarking on the same project here because any "pneumatological grammar" would be an appreciation of *a* spirit rather than an essential qualification of spirit as such. Many of Ebner's observations have quite wide application, throughout the Indo-European language family and perhaps further, but evidently not to dolphins or Martians. Our business is to think through the fundamental conditions of a fit between spirits and matter, in the course of which we certainly should note the general spiritual fact that language, that endless train of vanishing but qualitatively distinctive emissions in which we launch ourselves invisibly through the air toward each other, is very much like a body to spirits. Even the withdrawal from speaking to a communing silence between dialogue partners—which has been held up as an ideal by, for example, Buber and Binswanger, in their different ways—parallels the Cartesian withdrawal of intention from bodiliness.[18] It, too, is like a holding of the breath, after which breathing must resume.

With any repertoire of gestures like language, we are given an instrument that is very much a spirit's own, not alien to it. It is sufficient to constitute "home" for a spirit, in the sense that a spirit would genuinely live wherever and under whatever conditions its proper gestures were made; but it may not be adequate, all by itself, to its spirit. It may be the home of a spirit that is in the larger sense homeless, like the shell on the back of a hermit crab. By analogy, a person's body shows itself inadequate to his or her intention if we remove it from a theater of action in which intention can regularly be materialized and confirmed. Inmates of prisons are subject to this deprivation. They cannot be alienated from their bodies, but they are nevertheless denied adequate scope of existence. What is called the "quality" of their life, actually their life itself, is impaired.

Zionism is an excellent historical example of spiritual discontent with material deprivation because of its explicit connections with "spiritual" issues. Turn-of-the-century European Jews concerned for the future of Jewish spirit were divided between those who favored rapprochement with the dominant society, those who favored the creation of a wholly Jewish society (somehow, somewhere), and those who preferred to pursue distinctiveness where their historical scattering had landed them—in their ghettoes, to put it in a way that is now entirely pejorative. Supporters of rapprochement believed that the spirit of Judaism could survive and flourish as an enrichment of the general European spirit, which it had in any case done much to create.[19] Zionists, with the example before their eyes of a recent large-scale social "assimilation" of Jews, saw Jewish spirit losing all shape in the melting pot of secularized Christian civilization, and saw this happening, moreover, without the supposed accompanying advantage of the Jews ceasing to be offensive to the Christians, hence more secure. They argued that the long-term well-being of the Jewish spirit would be inseparable from the existence of Jewish land. The third point of view, finally, rested not so much on a distinct conception of the spiritual as on a different way of respecting divine providence.

We may pass over here the debates within Zionism over goals and means, even though they offer very important study material for political, social, and cultural theory. Of greatest interest to us is the notion that a spirit requires a land. According to two of the chief reasons why this should be so in the case of the Jews, the land is involved only extrinsically. First (for those for whom the land must be Palestine), it happens to be the same land that figured in a divine mission given to the Jewish people long ago, still waiting to be fulfilled. It is a history that requires the land rather than anything about land as such. Second, the possession of a land is practically necessary for the existence of a durable community. There must be a place where what Buber calls "ingathering" can occur, so that the separation that does exist among members of a spirit does not count as a dismemberment.[20]

But in addition to these reasons, there is another for which the land's material qualities are essential. The Jewish spirit is taken to regulate the being-together of Jews concretely as a *working*-together that aims at the significant result of the land's bearing fruit. Buber writes: "I believe in the great marriage between man (*adam*) and earth (*adamah*). This land (Palestine) recognizes us, for it is fruitful through us: and precisely because it bears fruit for us, it recognizes us." [21] The spirit wants to bring forth these works, would be frustrated if it did not, because they are the signs and confirmations of the happiness of spirit as such, just as vigor and good color confirm the well-being of an individual intender. Looked at in this way, the cultivated landscape of a country is the true body of a spirit, forming (as does the body for the person) the real base of the conversations and literature in which the spirit more purely but more vulnerably blows. It is the great steed that a spirit rides.

Let us only venture to speak of spirit's riding with due regard to the difference between spirit and intention in themselves. A spirit is not itself a being that rides. Nor, for that matter, does it flourish; rather, there is flourishing of intention through it. We really mean that the riding and flourishing of intenders is expanded over a language or landscape as qualified by a spirit. To meet the Jewish spirit in Israel is not the same kind of event as to meet the intention of a Jew. The Jew is someone to deal with. The Jewish spirit plucks at me as a way to be.[22] There is no question of being the Jew, but there is a live question of being Jewish—Israel is something *I* might ride with the others.[23]

For Zionists, the Jewish spirit demands a country to dwell in because it feels constricted by the lack of a homeland. It expands to fill the land. However, when Jews who live in (say) England are told by an English Christian that they ought to live in their own place, the effect on them is not an expanding one. This point was not sufficiently appreciated by Chesterton, an English Christian who said such things; he understood himself to be a Zionist yet was not unjustly taken to be anti-Semitic. Because of the lucidity with which Chesterton entangled himself in this irony, and also out of my affection for him, I propose to call his position Chesterton's Mistake and generalize from it.

Chesterton's view is most fully presented in his travel book *The New Jerusalem*. He writes:

There is an attitude for which my friends and I were for a long period rebuked and even reviled. . . . It was always called Anti-Semitism; but it was always much more true to call it Zionism. At any rate it was much nearer to the nature of the thing to call it Zionism, whether or no it can find its geographical concentration in Zion. The substance of the heresy was exceedingly simple. It consisted entirely in saying that Jews are Jews; and as a logical consequence that they are not Russians or Roumanians or Italians or Frenchmen or Englishmen.[24]

By this last remark he means that Jews can never be at home in Russia, Roumania, Italy, France, or England. They are foreigners there. They will always have the vices of a "cosmopolitan financial" point of view—historically associated with the evils of usury—because they in fact have no land of their own in these places. They will never exercise political responsibilities in a way that would satisfy a patriot because they in fact have closer ties with each other, scattered among the nations, than with any nation (of the early twentieth century). Popular prejudice against Jews in European countries accurately reflects these facts and ought not to be disregarded as a manifestation of the truth even if not adopted as the right sentiment toward it. "Only a few years ago it was regarded as a mark of a bloodthirsty disposition to admit that the Jewish problem was a problem, or even that the Jew was a Jew. Through much misunderstanding certain friends of mine and myself have persisted in disregarding the silence thus imposed; but facts have fought for us more effectively than words. By this time nobody is more conscious of the Jewish problem than the most intelligent and idealistic of the Jews." [25] Chesterton hastens to draw attention to the positive side of the "Jewish problem," the Jewish identity that is foreign only through being misplaced. He asserts that the Jews are an oriental nation with glorious traditions and values proper to them. He flippantly proposes that England grant full social and political equality to Jews but adopt a law requiring all of them to dress like Arabs. "The point is that we should know where we are." [26]

The irony is that Chesterton's version of Zionism really is a form of anti-Semitism, however much he complains of being misunderstood: not because it alleges false facts about the Jews (whatever the real facts and their real explanations might be), but because he who does not belong to the spirit of Zion has presumed to say what it is. It does not matter that Chesterton takes fully seriously the responsibility to attend to his neighbors as they are and to promote them and rejoice in them. One would have a hard time committing Chesterton's Mistake more lovingly and nobly than Chesterton did, but his lovingness does not cancel his mistakenness. It is as though I presented you with a beautiful coat and then told you that you had to wear it. Even if the coat fit, you would not find it comfortable. It would be a loathsome imposition on you by someone else instead of a dwelling of your own. So, too, even Jews who might want to dress in brightly colored flowing robes cannot let themselves be dressed in that fashion by Chesterton.

Chesterton's Mistake is in principle a seductive one because of its close relation to the affirmation of others. It is a condition of real love and respect to reckon with others as they actually are and not as fond fictions would have them be. Should not, therefore, all "facts" about an other or class of others enter into our dealings with them? Let us take the individual case first. Clearly, what you are for me is inseparable from how you actually appear, what you actually do, and your actual history. But your otherness also means that you are free from that; your intention as such is a secret with respect to all that. To know you is to know that I do not know this, but have always to wait for new showings of it. Consequently, it would be a mortal insult to you to show someone else a photograph of you or a letter you had written and say *"That* is Y; now you know Y precisely, and may act accordingly." Facts cannot be fitted on you in that way, relieving us of the obligation to wait for your own showing.

Now, in the case of the interintentional showing of a spirit we also have to wait to meet it, for it is just a way in which we meet the others who are members of it, and requires the same courtesy. But a spirit, unlike a person, holds itself out as something that can be joined. To join a spirit would be to include oneself in its constituency and thus to become a fellow prescriber of it, even a possible leader and changer of it. A Chesterton committed to Judaism could be a Zionist. But Chesterton has not precisely joined this spirit. He has done something rather similar that can be confused with joining it, and can wrongly be taken to confer the same entitlements, namely, he has *appreciated* it. Appreciating a spirit resembles joining it insofar as it involves making the prescribed moves imaginatively. But these moves are not him, nor are its materializations his. He knows, for instance, what it means that Palestine is a holy land, but it is not a holy land for him in the Jewish way. Therefore, although he could not but participate in the showing of Jewish spirit were he Jewish, and although he is obliged even as a non-Jew to call attention to the showing of the Jewish spirit by the Jews with whom English Christians are confronted, he is still not entitled to define that showing. A nonmember cannot lead a spirit.

This reasoning does not prove that a proposition like "Send the Jews to Palestine"—or the blacks to Africa, or the women back to their kitchens—is necessarily invalid *politically*. It only knocks out of our hands the most holy-seeming reason we could give for advocating such politics, namely, that the spirits of the groups concerned are such that they are thereby best served. "*Allow* the Jews to go to Palestine" is, of course, another matter. The only trouble is that many a Send masks itself as an Allow.

(I believe it is important to remark in passing that in a political realm like that of the United States which is *constituted* by the enterprise of gathering ethnic spirits and dis-spirited individuals into a kind of super-spirit and which therefore makes a new kind of spiritual home, a call to send or "allow" anyone to go elsewhere becomes impertinent in a new way.)

We found earlier that the ideal of an unlimited communication community, as posited by Apel, is incoherent if we take in all the implications of "unlimited." There is another ideal qualification of communication, however, also put forward by Apel and Habermas, that is not incoherent because it is relative to the real characteristics of a particular communication community, and that pertains to the materialization of spirit. That is the notion of *undistorted* communication. Chesterton's Mistake, though based on a respect for facts, is one of the primary roots of distortion in the presentation of spirits. It is possible to avoid making it, and to that extent a community of undistorted (if not unlimited) communication can be envisioned. To each spirit its own materialization, and let others only wait and witness.

Chapter 8

The Causation of the Spiritual

8.1 The Problem of Spiritual Causation

We saw that speculation on *pneuma, psyche,* and *nous* revolved from the first around the question of spirit's role in constituting the world as we find it or in influencing it to change. Now that we have worked our way toward a more determinate conception of what spirits "are" and how they are identified in and through material forms, it falls to us to confront this last great problem. We must try to understand how spirits *act* on the world, their contribution to the determination of what happens. In other words, we must think how spirits can be causes.

Our position now differs from that of the Greeks. Classical Greek metaphysics resorts to "spirit" as an explanatory principle precisely in order to make sense of everything that happens, whereas we have registered it as a class of demands that *condition* the meaning of world-experience by laying claims on what we make of it but do not constitute or explain the world, except in what might be called a weakened Leibnizian sense. This world full of beings, each sacred in its distinctiveness, each to be affirmed and none to be denied, is the best of all possible worlds—more precisely, the best possible base for possible worlds, since we are permitted to add to it. No world-population not compossible with the actual one may be preferred, whatever objections one might have to what *happens* in this world (and whatever difficulties may arise in distinguishing the affirmable being of a Hitler from what a Hitler has actually done). It makes sense in that way that this world rather than any other is actual. There is sufficient reason for it. But the fact that the actual world is, in this restricted sense, approvable does not entail that the grounds of our approval are what in fact brought it about. Indeed, the possibility must be taken seriously that the grounds of our approval of things, or the meaningful imposition on us of things, had in no case anything to do with bringing them about, and that causally speaking the spiritual is only froth on a natural wave.

But the "spiritual" order is no other than the concrete intentional order. Thus, the possibility of divorcing spirit from cause is broadly and deeply threatening. It would undermine the sense of all intentional ascriptions, not only special providential claims like "It was meant to happen" but also everyday statements like "I did it because it was the right thing to do," which avow the influence of a spiritually qualified end.

Although we define the spiritual nontheoretically, we cannot waive the question of spiritual causation on the grounds that normative gestures are free of entanglement with theoretical schemes. The concept of causation certainly belongs in the realm of theoretical representation of the world rather than in normative discourse, but then we ourselves live in the representable world as well as in normative discourse, and we are correspondingly mental as well as spiritual beings. Spiritual causation is just as much a condition of our genuine worldliness as is materiality. We cannot help but suspect at the start that spiritual causation will turn out to be *in some respect* non- or supratheoretical, for that is the trademark of the *spiritual;* but if *causation* is also involved, we will expect to pick up the trail of spiritual causation in the effort of mental beings to understand the world.

If spiritual causation is thinkable, we would expect it to belong in the realm of causation "for the sake of," which we term "final causation." Meanings act on the world in being acted *for,* that is, in being ends. But the Platonic-Aristotelian category of final causation is today nearly out of use. It would appear that Spinoza's argument has carried the day—to wit, that humanity assigns final causes to events only from its habit of estimating everything in relation to its own desires, and from ignorance of true (necessitating, formal or efficient) causes.[1] As our knowledge of formal and efficient causes grows, it would indeed appear that our reliance on final causes and even the possibility of appealing to them for explanation shrinks. The modern revolutions in biology and psychology seem amply to have borne Spinoza out. Therefore, in order to equip ourselves to conceive of spiritual causation, we first have to inquire into the place of final causation in a total understanding.

8.2   Final Causation

We do not ordinarily mean by "cause" nearly as much as Aristotle meant long ago by *aitia.* Our word "cause" means something close to what Aristotle called "that by which movement is started," the *arché* of *kinesis,*[2] which later came to be called "efficient cause"—namely, a prior event that makes it necessary that an event occur or "produces" it, and thereby accounts for it.[3] The complexities addressed by the Aristotelian scheme of causes are still with us, but in our language they attach themselves to the word "because" instead of "cause." Statements beginning with "Because" are offered in response to questions beginning with "Why," and why-questions can point in several different directions, asking for different sorts of "becauses," or reasons.

Two sorts of "because" are more or less standardized and thoroughly studied. One, the theoretical "because," resolves the question "Why does (or did) X occur?" by identifying the preceding events and conditions that in all cases of X make it necessary for X to occur. "The airplane flies because of the thrust of its jets and the lift of its body in air." A second type of "because" is practical. It normally concerns events that have not yet occurred or at least, for purposes of evaluation, are viewed without regard to whether they in fact occurred. "Why should X occur?" or "Why should I do X?" demand answers that exhibit a possible future determination of an event rather than an actual past or predicted future one, and a determination by our own decisions, at least in part, rather than by natural factors outside our control. "You should pay your debts because that's only fair if you wish others to pay their debts to you."

There is, in addition, a third important type of "because." When we ask "Why does (or did) X occur?" we are often asking neither about what leads up to X and "produces" it, nor about whether we should bring X about, but rather what it *means* that X happens, to what *end* X happens, what X is "all about." This "because" largely coincides with Aristotle's "wherefore," *to ou eneka*,[4] later called "final cause." Aristotle is generally more inclined than we are to consider questions of this sort settled by the apprehension of a thing's form, its *eidos*, since he holds a thing's end to be the actualization of its own proper nature. Yet it can be said that final cause distinctively involves a means-end relationship: it orders the explanandum with respect to something else rather than constituting the explanandum as does formal cause.

Finality could be defined more precisely and narrowly if we took the final cause of X to be not "what X means" but "what purpose X serves." Purposiveness, the ordering of means to an end, is a much more definite idea than "meaning." However, to restrict finality to purposiveness either hides or begs the most interesting questions about finality, as we shall see presently. For any instance of purposiveness itself needs a "because" and can be understood only according to its finality.

We begin with a relatively better grasp of the logic of the theoretical "because" and the practical "because," and for this reason a good opening move would be to see whether we can interpret the final "because" as a variant of one or the other of these. The first reduction would go like this: when we ask what an event "means" or what it is "for," we are really asking to be shown how that event hangs together with other events in a larger nexus of efficient and formal causation. Events occur only grouped with other events with which they are structurally compossible, so that they cannot be fully understood unless the patterns of coexistence and interaction that constitute their event-systems are seen. You can learn all about the biophysics of the kidney without yet finding out why, in an important sense of "why," the kidney does what it does; you have to see how the kidney contributes to the operation of the whole organism before you understand it. A complete list of the conditions that make it necessary for the kidney to exist and do what it does would have to include the larger structure to which it belongs, which both enables and requires it to be. Therefore, a "teleological" explanation of the kidney, such as, "Your kidneys remove certain elements from your blood because you need a certain balance of those elements to live," is not radically different from a "mechanistic" explanation. It simply serves up efficient and formal causes in a special format.

This reduction of final cause to efficient-formal cause will not solve our problem, however, because it fails us when we grasp perfectly a structure of events and still wish to ask, "But what is its meaning?" or "What is it for?" That is, in order to find a final cause, we must find not only some kind of causal link between events but a genuine end. This is so even though our habit of asking "What is it *for?*" suggests that we will be adequately answered once we are shown the structure of the pertinent system of events to which the questioned event belongs, whatever the nature of that system may be. The event's having certain consequences is the necessary condition of its coexistence with certain other events, allowing them to exist as well; that is what it means to say that the event is "for" the system or the other events in the system, related as a part to a whole. But in fact we often mean something different when we say "What is it for?"—something like "So what?" And this is not just a demand to be shown the yet-larger system of events that the system that is already perceived constitutes together with other systems. The question of finality is, from this standpoint, curiously open. One could be shown a Spinozan vision of the structure of the entire cosmos and still ask, "So what?" We can ask "What does it mean?" or "What is it all for?" even when there is no more comprehensive structure to relate things to. Hence, structure as such cannot be the principle of the final "because."

Let us then try the other tack. On the practical interpretation, the superficially theoretical question "What does it mean?" should be translated into a practical question such as "What is it *good* for?" We would be asking what we ourselves are to do about it or feel about it. In one sense an issue of structure is raised here, too, for to answer such a question we must relate the structures of our own lives (always kept out of the picture in purely theoretical questioning) to the questioned event so as to arrive at a more comprehensive structure in which event and attitude are compossible. This greater structure is not entirely known, since we do not and cannot know ourselves in the way we know the world, but *lived* and thus guided by practical reasoning. Confronting future possible thoughts and actions that are ours to determine, we follow the lead of feelings or rules of conduct in building a world pattern that has "meaning" or finality because of this investment of ourselves in it. We meet finality in whatever thing we have set ourselves in motion toward, as an echo of ourselves; and we often feel that a thing is unaccounted for until we have heard the echo.

If the practical approach is correct, then to cite a final cause of X is really to give a reason of a practical sort for having a certain attitude toward X's occurrence.

But here we seem to hit a snag. On this account it makes much more sense to ask of a future event X, "What *would* X mean?"—since a future X might be in someone's power to determine—than to ask of a past event, "What *did* X mean?" There is indeed a certain absurdity in taking a practical attitude toward any past event, which is now beyond our influence. What difference does it make to a past X what our attitude to it is? Yet talk of final causes is often directed to events not under our control; rather than avoiding them, it seems almost to have been designed to apply to them. It is a way of making sense of what *happens,* even of what happens *to* us.

The solution of this apparent anomaly could be that when we ask the question of a past event's final cause, we are regarding that event, like the future events that are envisioned by the practically reasoning agent, as something that could be replaced by other possible events or that could have different consequences. It is in some way, in some measure, yet to be determined. For illustration, imagine the way in which a group of atheistic but morally zealous Israelites might think about their escape from Pharaoh. (We make them atheists so that the problem of the meaning of their escape cannot be solved by a claim about what an omnipotent Being meant by bringing it about.) They remember that on the day of their flight the Red Sea was in an unusual condition such that they could cross but the pursuing Egyptian army could not. The "meaning" (in the sense of consequence) of this event was that the Israelites were delivered from slavery. Their attitude toward it now is not simply "Lucky us!" but: "This event means that we can live freely [the consequence] and therefore justly [the practical determination]." The event occurred *so that* they could found a just community. It gains meaning from being the precondition of their now proceeding to do something meaningful. "Why *did* the Red Sea part?" is thus asked in the same spirit as Israelites would ask before the event, "Why *should* the Red Sea part (what good would come from it)?" To look back on the event in this way is, we might say, to "appreciate" it, that is, to comport ourselves affirmatively under its complex claim.

But why would "appreciating" a past event in this sense be indispensable for understanding it? The accounting required for comprehension of an event would, it seems, be satisfied by discovery of the necessitating antecedent events and formal conditions, the efficient-formal causation. Appreciation is just icing on the cake. Yet it is frequently complained that an accounting in terms of "blind determinism"—no better than "blind chance"!—is no accounting at all, in some decisive sense. This "blindness" that is felt to impair understanding must amount to the absence of any end in view, a "happening for no reason," that is, an absence of finality. (This was the "blindness" for which Leibniz, champion of final causes, reproached Spinoza's *Deus sive natura*.)[5] It follows that "appreciation" is essential to understanding, because it brings ends into view. Practical reasoning cannot take place without ends in view, obviously, for without them there is nothing on which to deliberate. And finalistic understanding also requires ends to be "in view" so as to be active in the determination of what occurs, for otherwise ends would be attained only coincidentally, by the inadvertent help of other (efficient-formal) causes. Ends must be in view to be active as ends, having their proper causality.

At this point it appears that the implications of finality relate the final "because" closely to the practical "because." It is not at all clear yet, however, why causality is attributed to finality. Are the atheist Israelites transplanting an end that is only in view for them to the earlier event to lend it meaningfulness, as though what actuates them could be at the same time what stirred the Red Sea? If so, it seems they have only two choices, both unacceptable to them: they can attribute their intention to an Agent who could have made the event occur, which would be to embrace theism; or else they can retract their demand for a finalistic accounting. They will want a third way. To find it, we must first explore the range of the concept of "cause" and of the intellectual demand to which it responds. Then, armed with a preliminary notion of finalistic determination, we will be prepared to learn more about final causation from a closer encounter with finality itself.

A rock, dislodged by rainfall, rolls down a hillside. As far as we know, the rock just goes, never considering that it might go down the hill at one time rather than another, or not at all. But the rock is observed by conscious beings who are able to conceive of something other than what happened happening. Since for consciousness the actual is the possible, and appears embedded in a range of possibilities,[6] conscious beings want to know why the rock did just what it did, why one possibility and not others became actual. These knowers are in a position similar to that of agents who are wondering which of the future events that are possible through their action should be actualized, but they participate in the determination of events in a different way. The knowers do not (as such) cause the rock to fall, of course; that happens apart from them. Just the same, however, they require a way of making the mental transition from envisioned possibilities to perceived actualities, from the world that could be to the world that is. If they do not have a way of making this transition, they will be unable consciously to orient themselves with reference to possibilities in the real world. Estimation, explanation, and prediction will all be out of the question.

Knowing beings have an analogous need with regard to the *essences* of things that collectively make up the semantic world-map presupposed by all of their mental operations. The principle that "makes" a thing a case of X, gives it a nature or essence, is, like the causal principle that "makes" a thing happen, a fixed way of determining which one of a range of possibilities is to be actualized —in this case, which groups of characteristics, constituting the definitions of names and concepts, will in fact order experience.

We seek to anticipate the actualization of possibilities on some basis other than a random one, for if selection from possibilities were random, it could be a positive hindrance to us to conceive of possibilities at all. One basis besides random choice, long prized most highly, is necessity, from *ne-cedere,* "no withdrawal." In the cause-and-effect scheme, the effect cannot withdraw from the cause; it cannot exist apart from the cause and it cannot fail to exist with the cause. As regards essence, the characteristics that make a thing the sort of thing it is cannot withdraw from each other, cannot exist separately, without undoing the thing. Now, it is possible to view the cause-and-effect and essence cases as commonly based on the essence principle, namely, that conjoint existence of certain constituents uniquely enables a "thing" or "event" (where the latter comprises a prior constituent called the cause and a consequent constituent called the effect) to be. The necessity by which the effect is preceded by its cause would be like the necessity by which one right angle in a rhombus requires three others; we notice that a composite form can exist only in a certain way. Let this essence principle be called "necessity." But it is also possible to view cause-and-effect and essence as commonly based on the causal principle, namely, that the existence of certain things *brings it about, makes,* or *produces* the existence of certain other things. It can even be said that the geometer "produces" the theorem that the other three angles of the rhombus are right from the premise that the first one is. Here let us speak of "necessitation" rather than "necessity," since something is imagined to act.

"Necessity" and "necessitation" are both mind-presupposing concepts, of course, since possibilities must be envisioned before they can be excluded. "Necessitation" is, in addition, a practical concept. To claim that one thing's occurrence as cause necessitates another thing's occurrence as effect is to envision the first thing *compelling* the other to occur, shutting off all possibilities of its non-occurrence in favor of the actualized possibility of its occurrence. Obviously, the rainfall does not literally "make" the rock roll down the hill. The rain leads necessarily to the rock's falling—we cannot have the rain without the rock's falling, too—but the one thing does not compel the other. Only agents compel, because only agents can perform the act of shutting off possibilities, which involves choosing. And choosing is done only with an end in view. Theorists transform necessity into necessitation, "make" the rock fall with the rainfall their imaginative instrument, for the sake of the sheer determination of the event, which is the compulsion's end, and which (presumably in a different way) brings it about that the compulsion occurs. Thus, the very concept of efficient cause, which rests on necessitation, requires completion by the principle of final cause—in our example, the end of theoretical determination and understanding.[7]

If there is any mode different from necessity by which the transition from possibility to actuality may be mentally negotiated, it cannot differ from necessity in the number of possibilities it selects as actual. The number must remain one; this much is required by the most general notion that can be used in analyzing causality, which is determination (of which the subjective counterpart is decision).

Now, there is reason to think that finality indeed works as a principle other than necessity by which one actuality can be chosen from many possibilities. Practical reasoning, more obviously than theoretical reasoning, employs this principle, deciding for the "desirable," "right," and so forth, though even here the distinction between final and necessary determination is sometimes obscured by the entry of necessity into the technical dimension of practical reasoning, where means are chosen to reach willed ends. For ends and conditions of action together dictate means. But the non-necessity of ends (except abstracted, analytic ones such as "getting what one wants") is notorious.

The choice of ends of action is not, at any rate, *experienced* as a necessary event. Such choice is normally experienced as free response to the appeal of the end that presents itself as "best," not "only possible." So if the theoretical understanding of human choice is achieved by ascribing necessity to its occurrence, the human being so understood is bound to be alienated from such an understanding. (This implies that there are contradictory requirements for "understanding"; we will have to sort out presently where necessity does and does not belong in understanding.) The deep perplexity in the issue of the freedom of the will lies in the irreducible heterogeneity of these two modes of deciding the actuality of human behavior. Necessitarians pose the unsavory alternative of randomness in human behavior over against their own view that human acts occur as they do necessarily. On the other side, libertarians appeal to our experience of nonarbitrary freedom, our sense that we are intelligent causes rather than necessitated effects, to prove that necessity is not the only mode of determination. Necessitarians seek in turn to show that this "nonarbitrary" mode of actualization, properly understood, is really a type of necessitation. The two standpoints cannot be reconciled. Believing in free will, I insist that my wife is the only woman for me *because* she is the best; the determinist replies that she is the "best" *because* she is the only, that is to say, the woman I would necessarily prize, she being what she is, I being what I am, conditions being what they are and have been. The different priorities of these "becauses" conflict.

If libertarians interpret the experience of free will as evidence that the agent is active as a cause, this leaves the free-will thesis readily reducible by the necessitarians. For the agent could then very well be defined as a certain point in the causal chain (or invariable pattern of occurrence) after which effects take a different form than that taken by the preceding effects, physiological and psychological, that serve as their causes. The phenomenon of "action" would be this transition from one type of effect to another. And this would be why being an agent does not feel like being a billiard ball in the middle of a billiard-ball chain reaction. Therefore, if there is something non-necessitarian about being an agent, it cannot lie in the mere feeling of being an uncaused cause. It must rather lie in the feeling of being a cause that is available and responsive to an end in view, which in its peculiar way "beckons" or "appeals." This "feeling" will be a mandated self-interpretation, not just an experience but a way of being responsible to ends.

Suppose that human agents cannot but act as they do, owing to their physical structure and environmental conditions. And suppose also that when agents see things as ends, as "bests," they are feeling from the inside what it is like to be a being with that sort of biological programming. But, even if this is factually the case, three points must be insisted on. The first is the logical and experiential distinction between finality and necessity. Finality is not felt and does not signify as a kind of necessitation, nor does it function in the offering and examination of warrants and justifications as a kind of necessitation. The second is the sufficiency of finality to determine actuality, whether or not actuality is also determined by necessity. That is to say, if indeterminism were true with respect to efficient causality, choice would not perforce be random. Efficient-cause determination could, to some extent, be lacking, and each agent could still understand how to act and why other agents act as they do. Third, and crucially, we must be aware that finality itself only exists non-necessarily, so that a finalistic determination cannot be fatalistic.

The right understanding of finality is often vitiated by a tacit presumption in favor of what might be called a crypto-efficient finality. Final causes become efficient causes that happen to be lurking in the future instead of the past. They pull rather than push, but just as forcibly. Very well; if finality does not necessitate occurrences, how does it actually determine them? An end's finality picks it out as a possibility that is *meaningful* to actualize. This determines occurrence in at least two ways. First, although the meaningful end does not necessarily bring about any particular event, what does come about gains *its* meaning from its relationship to the end. For instance, the end of virtue determines the meaning of an action of mine not congruous with this end as wicked. Second, experience, which apart from finality is a continuum of indefinitely many configurations that could be called "actualizations" or "events," is mapped, gains articulation, according to the interest that meaningfulness arouses. Final causes cause, then, by "giving orders," that is, by choosing benchmarks of meaning by which experience is ordered. For this additional reason efficient causation is comprehensible only in partnership with final causation, because apart from final causation we would be at a loss concerning what it *means* that what happens happens, and thus it is difficult to see how we could have any knowledge of *what* it is that happens.

Just as finality or meaning does not operate in the same way as efficiency or power to compel, so too we meet it differently. The otherness that is decisive in the original claim of other beings on our attention (and in the claim of spirits or ways of being with other beings, like "virtue") figures in this context as their gratuitousness or absence of ground; one cannot say why an end-in-itself is such, and thus it escapes theoretical comprehension even as it incites the desire to know.

Taking an evening walk on my street, I notice for the first time an oak tree in a neighbor's yard. It has a distinctive Y-shaped separation of its trunk not far from its top. It rustles in the breeze. In the dusk, its greenery has a quality both delicate and deep. It is not especially beautiful, though it has its beauties; but *it* is *there*. Once it has my attention, I wonder why this tree is and why it is the way it is. There is something enormously improbable about this tree, I first, and inaccurately, reflect; it is a miracle that this particular tree is in the world at all. Refining this reflection, I find that it is not so much improbable that this tree is here now—for what else would more probably have taken its place?—but *unaccounted for except by the tree itself*. Viewing the actuality of this tree against the background of possible worlds lacking such a tree, it seems to me that the tree has its own secret reason for being. I cannot provide one for it. Precisely the impossibility of compelling this tree to be, its non-necessity, makes of the tree an end-in-itself. The same can be said of the appreciative way of comporting myself toward the tree that stands before me along with the tree itself—tree-determined yet uncompelled.

Suppose the tree fascinates me so much that I become a botanist. I take a series of biology and botany classes to learn about the processes that make it necessary for such a tree to be in such a place. One might expect this scientific investigation to do away with the tree's finality, but that is not what happens. The finality is actually expanded, for the processes are themselves gratuitous; the larger pattern is itself an end. Science's excitement does not lie in abolishing the finality of things by imposing necessity on them (even though there does exist a properly technological excitement in becoming able to control nature as a means to yet-unspecified human ends). The excitement proper to science lies in taking the meaningful intimation of a single tree, a "word," and tracing it out to find its place in a more extensive meaningful intimation, the "sentences" of botany and ecology, which tend to refocus wonder on generalized nature instead of on particulars in their own right. Only thus can we begin to account for the apparent contradiction that science stimulates us by adding to experience's meaning while at the same time it seems to remove the finality of particular things. The real roots of this contradiction, however, lie in the relationship between necessity and non-necessity that is internal to the command of finality.

I return for another look at the oak tree that caught my eye earlier. It originally excited me because it was an excess over what might have been. It might not have been there, yet it was, and just as it was. Now this "just as it is," the tree's essence, means that the particular relationship obtaining among the ingredients of the tree is necessary. Of course, it is analytically true that any named set of particulars must include the designated particulars to earn its name, but the ensemble of ingredients called the "tree" is not arbitrarily selected but rather presented to me as a configuration of things that *belong* together. The necessity that binds them is rooted in the tree's own command, its self-definition, without which there would be no tree. Since the necessity of relationships among a thing's ingredients is constitutive of the thing's being, therefore, I must perceive those relationships as necessary in order really to know the thing (cf. sections 4.4 [a] and [b] above). Knowledge searches for necessity (formal cause) and necessitation (efficient cause) while interest is commanded by the gratuitous. Our intellectual life in general and our understanding of things in particular are produced by interplay between knowledge and interest. I see a tree as at once a necessary component of a whole natural process (a means to that end) and as an instantiation and revelation of the gratuitous end, the process, partaking of its gratuitousness.

A world experienced as a strictly necessary order, its actualities never appearing against a background of possibilities, would no longer be "necessary"; it would just be. The Spinozan view of the world, premised on the sole reality of necessity, produces a meaningless world. It is not a defect of our understanding, as he held it to be, that we understand and evaluate the actual in relation to nonactual possibilities; instead, it is in virtue of that capacity that we transcend unconscious nature and have such a thing as understanding.[8]

Both necessity and non-necessity are required for the occurrence of finality: necessity insofar as there are essences to perceive and understand, non-necessity insofar as an open question is present concerning the actualization of these essences. Necessity has traditionally been assigned to essence but withheld from existence (except from the existence of a god or cogito that grounds all other existence). Existence seems inferior to essence. Whereas the mind is compelled by necessity and respects it as a master, the mind seems in turn to master the existence of things. By no effort can I conceive a square circle, but I can readily conceive that New York or the Himalayas do not exist. Moreover, existence is disesteemed because you cannot count on it absolutely in an argument. Contingent premises yield only hypothetical conclusions.

But this attitude can be turned on its head. Our contempt for the non-necessary becomes wonder and gratitude as it rises above us, exceeding our grasp, instead of sinking below us, lying under our heel. It can sink below us only when it is regarded as a tool—for example, as a premise in an argument that would ideally coerce assent. For tools, non-necessity is a deficiency, because one must be able to count on them. Conversely, necessary things have to be tools, have to be instrumental to something non-necessary, since the merely necessary, as such, is not interesting. Necessity sinks below us in turn. The necessity in the make-up of a meaningful thing is instrumental to its finality, which is rooted in its non-necessity.

We may speak of contingency in relation to essence in two respects. First, we recognize that whether an essence is or is not instantiated in a really existing thing is contingent. At least as important, however, is the contingency of the very ideal existence of the essence. Who could have told that there would be *such a thing* as this oak tree, whether on the street or in my fancy alone? It may be necessary, given the prior occurrence of certain events, that this tree grow on my street; it may be necessary, given the opportunity offered by earth, water, air, and sunlight, that any growing thing would adopt a certain configuration; and so on. But all of these considerations expand rather than shrink the mystery. It now becomes a wonder that this entire order of things exists (ideally) of which the tree is part. It does not have a discernible cause; it is itself the (final) cause of the experience of meaning, which is felt to be at once discovered by the subject and bestowed by the end. That finality is found or bestowed, but in any event not made, means that its provenance is exterior to the realm of the known; it comes from who-knows-where.

To experience finality is to enter into relation with the unknowableness "behind" the end, the who-knows-where from which it comes, its secret principle of actualization—these negations articulating the "otherness" we earlier assigned to beings in our account of relationship and primary objectivity. (Thus final causation is justly called an *asylum ignorantiae*.)[9] Finality enters into our experience as a kind of excess. The excess can be seen darkly, as a nauseating *de trop*, if the subject cannot live with the end's command. Contrariwise, if the end has a form in which senses or intellect can delight, then the excess is an occasion of joy, thanks, and obedience. "Because" can be rendered "Thanks to." The subject in the presence of finality relishes the excess, wonders.

Wonder and joy, not satisfaction, are the ultimate subjective points of reference in the analysis of meaning, although satisfaction has a subordinate place of its own in the economy of understanding. Satisfaction signifies the making good of a lack or the completion of a requirement; the provisional transcendence in looking forward to it is superseded in the attaining of it. But the making good of a lack merely brings one to equilibrium or stasis; then what? And the completion of a requirement is meaningful only if the requirement itself is meaningful; is it? Neither its completion nor its lack of completion seem to decide. Satisfaction is the wrong norm by which to try to control the relationship with an end-in-itself. That relationship cannot be brought to closure, to a standing pat, as would be required for satisfaction, without losing its character as a relationship with transcending and commanding finality. If our botanical training removes the states of excitement with respect to the oak tree that are called "curiosity" and "wonder," then botany dies as science, though it may survive as a technical handmaiden to, say, the logging industry. Understanding both begins and ends in wonder.

Because finality's way of determining events is in the nature of a bestowal of meaning, it would be best to say that X, the final cause of Y, causes Y by *allowing* Y to occur, this "allowing" to be contrasted with the compulsion of necessitating causation. Y occurs "thanks to" X. Y must be the response of an intentional being, if we hold to the principle that ends act only as ends in "view." In that response, final causation modulates into efficient causation. What was allowed to happen is then made to happen. (The starting point for a definition of agency must therefore be the principle that things are made to happen because they are allowed to happen.) I perform virtuous act A because of M, the meaning of virtue; proximately, my own efficient action, B, is what brings A about, but originally M, the end in view, is what calls forth my action and allows my action or simply my attention to have a point. We cannot understand A's having occurred without M's permitting it, and we cannot be aware of M's permitting A without holding M in view ourselves and thus opening the spiritual question of how we should respond to it. Hence, spirits are not only possible ends in themselves, they are always present in the forming of responses to ends, which is to say that they are the eminent formal factor in the effect stage of final causation.

For the Israelites who wonder how to articulate their obscure sense of provi-dence, the correct question is not "What was the final cause of the Red Sea incident?"—a question that most naturally relates to the intentions of a divine agent. It is, instead, "How does the Red Sea incident, taken together with the chance it gave us to build a just society, constitute a meaning in relation to which our own action is allowed to have a point, and thus a correlated, finalistically caused meaning of its own?" The Red Sea incident was cause, not effect, and the effect will be the Israelite response, grateful and possibly creative. The analysis of final causation always takes this *ad hominem* turn from "Why did X happen?" to "What does X mean to you?" to "What do *you* mean?"

8.3 Finality and Freedom (Kant and Buber). The Sixth Primary Affirmation

"What do you mean?" is not a question with one answer. You are free to mean in different ways, and your freedom is directly correlated with the transcendence or exteriority of the ends that beckon to you. A determinism of efficient-formal causation threatens both the exteriority (gratuitousness) of ends and the freedom of the self. Both require the slack of non-necessity. One must be to a certain extent free to make of things what one will, bound to them (by their command) but on a tether of some length. I can look at the oak tree in my neighbor's yard a year hence, as my neighbor fells it and chops it into firewood that I will share, and find nothing wonderful in it at all. The tree asks to be understood, and it is clearly wrong to avoid attending to it, but our eventual understanding of the tree depends on our ability to respond to it. My freedom with respect to a spiritual end such as virtue consists in being able to regard it as a practical obstacle or opportunity rather than as an authoritative challenge. Finality and freedom are correlated, therefore, and not only because by imposing finality on an otherwise arbitrary freedom we can give it meaning through responsibility, but also because freedom and finality are two aspects of one event, the event of meaning, outside of which neither one is thinkable. To experience oneself as free is to experience oneself as commanded-but-not-compelled to "make something" of the world and one's life. Moreover, this command gives one the opportunity to be a certain someone. Therein lies its allure. One jumps toward it to actualize oneself, to be one who means as well as one who is receptive to what other things mean.

Kant makes the modern era's greatest attempt to conceive of intentional freedom as neither arbitrary nor subject to necessary natural determination. We must consider now how he goes wrong through failure to link freedom with final causality.

Kant's understanding of finality is based on the correct assumption that true ends must be unconditionally final, impossible to convert into means to further ends. By thematizing "meaning" strictly as a function of rationality, however, he unduly narrows finality. Once finality is limited to teleology, and teleology to human purposiveness, Kant can do no other than assert that morality alone is an unconditional end.[10] Even so, in the "Critique of Aesthetic Judgment" he glimpses an interruption of his system when he admits that the beautiful is a manifest purposiveness for which the purpose cannot be conceived.[11] In other words, there are things in the world besides our own reason that are capable of commanding our attention—although our attention remains commanded, according to Kant, thanks to our rational satisfaction in the play of our cognitive faculties as they are engaged by the beautiful object.[12]

The true home of finality for Kant is the moral law. And the moral law is not only the aim but the basis of personal freedom. Moral reason (rational freedom) is both that which is obeyed and that which does the obeying. Yet Kant does not go down the path, taken later by Hermann Cohen, of interpreting the causality peculiar to freedom as a final causality.[13] He conceives the causality of freedom as immanent push rather than transcendent pull. He does this fundamentally because he cannot see how to relate freedom to anything without determining it by that thing and thus destroying it as freedom. Consequently, the "causality of freedom" can only mean freedom's own efficiency, not its responsibility.

Kant deals with the dilemma of free will and determinism by, first, upholding the rule of efficient causality in the realm of phenomena while securing the transcendental possibility of freedom in the realm of things-in-themselves.[14] As a free being, I spontaneously express my own rational nature. But this activity of mine takes place in the "intelligible world" of things-in-themselves rather than in the natural world where everything, including my perceptible behavior, is brought about by efficient causation. Kant is thus faced with the problem of understanding how we can be determined at the same time in two different ways. It would seem that either the two sorts of determination must always determine me to the same result, in which case the point of distinguishing the sorts of determination is lost (except for Leibnizian metaphysical consolation), or else the two sorts of determination must determine me with different results that are yet compossible. If the intelligible world existed alongside the natural world as its constant companion, never acting on it to change it but perennially offering a kind of higher-order commentary on it, then this second condition would be satisfied. This would give Kant a theory of the moral *meaning* of all that occurs in natural human existence, but it would put us in the position of appreciating the moral significance of our acts without having any power to control and alter our acts according to that meaning. Not only would this require us to hold a strange notion of "appreciation"—can "appreciation" be entirely unresponsive?—but it would be far from what Kant declares himself to be after, namely, an understanding that free action produces results in the natural order. The point of morality is not to interpret the world, but to better it.

Kant's solution is to conceive the causality of freedom as an efficient (results-necessitating) causality parallel to that of nature which determines nature without interfering with nature's own causality. Freedom can do this because it is not in time. We are invited to imagine all rational beings timelessly determining their free actions, and the natural history of human affairs as the spatiotemporalized outcome of this determination. Natural experience is the product of timeless decisions made by moral agents.[15]

Now, suppose we could overcome the logistical problems posed by this scheme by stipulating that a deity shapes the occasions of choice in such a way that everyone's choices can be reflected in one world history. Even so, a more serious problem remains. These timeless free decisions are not recognizable as moral decisions (or, more broadly, as responsible actions) precisely because they are outside of experience.

In the first place, this freedom is spontaneous and therefore arbitrary; it takes no bearings outside of itself. Reason is Kant's horizon of justification. He does not think it possible to account for the initial decision of free beings to be rational. Free beings are meaningfully free only if they act rationally, within the horizon of justification—and "freedom" then means "freedom from natural compulsion." But since reason has been pictured as a rival necessitation, the "freedom" of the agent is only another kind of compulsion. (There *is* such a thing as self-compulsion, willfulness, although Kant cannot admit it in this context.) The freedom that is appreciated and presupposed in the praising and blaming of agents, however, has to do with the original decision to follow reason, the susceptibility to, or amount of "respect" for, the call of reason; but Kant is committed to interpreting this call or susceptibility as the epiphenomenal product of the competition of reason's causality with our self-forgetful subjugation to natural inclinations. He cannot say that moral value attaches to one's *responsiveness* to reason; he must say that moral value attaches to the *strength* of reason in one. This view is belied by our sense that the moral reachability of people counts as more fundamental than their strength of character and is just what makes the difference between a saint and a prig.[16]

In the second place, timeless decisions are not recognizably moral because they cannot be made in evaluation of and response to natural events, which are the very stuff of the moral life. If moral character were truly determined timelessly, we would be forced to regard most of what is understood as the moral *drama* of life as a kind of charade: the building up of resolve, temptation, fall, remorse, repentance, all make sense only in a temporal frame of reference.[17]

Kant does provide a means of escape from his own unsatisfactory conception of freedom. By placing the causality of freedom in the noumenal realm, he appeals to an "asylum of ignorance"; he refuses to try to understand the possibility of freedom. We cannot doubt that we have it, but there is no way of finding out how, and no meaningful way of asking why, for it is grounded outside of experience.[18] Now Kant's positive view of freedom, like other doctrines in his theoretical philosophy, invites criticism for illicitly applying phenomenal principles to things-in-themselves. He conceives the causality of freedom to be the same kind of necessitation that understanding imposes on appearances, in the form of efficient causation. But we may question this, following Kant's own procedure of taking guidance from the way in which the moral demand announces itself.

According to Kant, our only valid reason for thinking we have freedom at all is the initial demand of the moral law, an "ought" that implies a "can." [19] The categorical "ought" requires a real capacity to respond to it, or else it is fundamentally incongruous with reality and thus not a command in any meaningful way. The demand of the moral law, the perception of moral meaning, thus *creates* the freedom that is correlated with it. There was no "can" before there was an "ought." Kant refers this priority of the "ought" to the "can" to the conditions of our knowledge, rather than to the real being of freedom. According to him, it is just that we become aware of the freedom we already have, which really grounds the moral law (by the doctrine of autonomy), in encountering the apparent conflict between rational and natural causation that is manifested in our feeling of obligation.[20] But how are we in a position to impose this interpretation on moral freedom, since the experience of the "ought," and not any other intuition into some mode of acting unconstrained by natural causality, is the only ground we have to stand on in talking of freedom?

If we do not stray from this ground, the conception of freedom we will arrive at is that of a responsiveness to perceived meaning rather than a supernatural quasi-efficient causality producing sensations of "obligation" and "respect" as its impact on the phenomenal order. The efficient causality of the moral life is simply the ordinary embodied human will. The moral demand is an end-in-itself that commands attention, superordinate to any other consideration that might be brought forward—and in this, moral meaning is not fundamentally different from other meanings, all of which make their claims; it is *first* among them, superordinate among the superordinate. However, it is not *necessary* to rise to it, either by the natural necessity that is comprehended by theoretical reason or by the alleged immanent necessity of reason in its practical employment.

Buber must have the Kantian treatment of freedom and finality in mind when he formulates his more adequate but less clear idea of the two in *I and Thou*. His parallel to the distinction between phenomena and noumena is to divide the It-world, where "causality holds unlimited sway," from the realm where I and You confront each other, where "man finds guaranteed the freedom of his being and of being."[21] Mortal life should be an oscillation between these two realms. What guarantees my freedom in the You-world is "the one that intends me,"[22] my fate (*Schicksal*) meeting and blessing my will. "He that forgets all being caused as he decides from the depths, he that puts aside possessions and cloak and steps bare before the countenance—this free human being encounters fate as the counter-image of his freedom. It is not his limit but his completion; freedom and fate embrace each other to form meaning; and given meaning, fate—with its eyes, hitherto severe, suddenly full of light—looks like grace itself."[23] This account cannot be said to smack of compatibilism, not at least of the Nozickian "tracking" sort.[24] "Freedom" is not a matter of hitting on the right ends thanks to the work of certain specified causes, the *right* causes, rather than others that are *merely* causes. It is a matter of being completely free from causes, "bare," so as to be *available* to "fate." Fate is a determinacy that freedom needs so as not to be caprice, but it is a different kind of determinacy than that of "natural" or "efficient" causation. And yet Buber does not declare for natural indeterminism, either. His version of "ought implies can" is the idea that one "forgets all being caused" in rising to the occasion of encounter. That means not that one is not caused but that one is not conscious of being caused and acts for another, better reason. He might be the sort of compatibilist who merely denies the relevance of natural causation to estimations of final causation. We will have to return to this point presently.

Buber calls the response to a You the essential act of the spirit. Therefore this freedom *of* relationship is the sort of freedom that is essential to spirit and which spirit essentially is; and clearly the philosophical agenda that is presented here, if not finished with, is to go beyond the Kantian problematic of freedom-as-reason and rational causation to take in freedom-as-spirit and spiritual causation.

Buber has started this thinking along two lines that seem correct. First, he points out how a spiritual being moves in response, in correlation with an other that appears necessary, imposed, in a sweet way—the fate that is grace. That is to say that I am with and able to act for the other *thanks to* the other, without whom I would lack aim. Second, he connects the focusing of the energies of a spiritual being's will, which occurs just in encounter with others—never in the "capricious" life unrelated to others—to the eventual creativity of that being. This is again a more general category of which Kantian dutiful action forms only a special case. "Only he that funnels all the force of the other [i.e., the unchosen possibilities] into the doing of the one, absorbing into the actualization of what was chosen the undiminished passion of what was not chosen, only he that 'serves God with the evil impulse,' decides—and decides what happens."[25]

Buber represents the spiritual being's own causality as its aimed energy: will and passion harnessed by the aim granted in encounter. We met this earlier under the name *thumos*.

It is tautologically true that a spiritual being is actualized and active *qua spiritual* only in the service of "fate" so conceived. But the spiritual actuality and activity of persons is, besides, the commanding aspect of persons and offers them their only true fulfillment. Whoever lives only in the It-world is not human, as Buber asserts, for whoever lives sometimes in the You-world recognizes the supremacy of You-saying, hence cannot but let the meaning of "human" be controlled by You-saying.[26] This implies that spiritual causation is the eminent determinant of what happens.

In sum, Buber's conception of freedom is an advance on Kant's in that it renders personal spontaneity nonarbitrary and admits all the powers of the person into spiritual life, under the umbrella of the responsive aim. He has substituted the duality of I-You responsiveness and I-It unresponsiveness for the Kantian war between reason and inclination, which so narrows the Kantian person.[27] But the great conceptual problem of freedom's relation to natural determinism, which Kant wrestled with mightily if unsuccessfully, is not solved by Buber, either. It may be enough, in describing the self-understanding of free persons, to say that they "forget" natural causation; it may be appropriate not to let natural causation intrude on an account of the original claims of beings or eclipse the eminence of spiritual causation; but we can hardly continue to forget it now that we are thinking out implications.

Assuming that compatibilism versus indeterminism is the interesting choice as regards the position of natural causation in our thought, do any of our primary affirmations constrain our decision between them? None of the affirmations were directly practical. We could deduce from the premises that the other is most-high and that happiness consists of living affirmatively with the others this primary practical affirmation: I ought to do that which will maximally affirm the others. But this is not an original, unconditional "ought" like Kant's. It does not guarantee me freedom; it only disposes of whatever freedom I happen to have. The sense of it is not destroyed if we qualify it as follows: I ought to do that which will maximally affirm the others, so far as I am free to control what I do. The "ought" would dissolve if no freedom obtained, but that would create no conceptual scandal, since we derived it from the bestness of maximally affirming the others rather than vice versa.

On the other hand, what would "bestness" mean if it were not always possible in principle to respond to it? Does the primary affirmation of a mandate require a complementary primary affirmation of the possibility of response? It would appear so; but to be sure that we are not introducing the sixth primary affirmation arbitrarily, we must feel our way toward it by setting out an appropriate supporting argument.

The strongest available argument to a strong "ought" appears to be one based on *irreducible guilt*. It can be stated as follows: Whenever I have failed to act for the best—that is, so as maximally to affirm the others—I cannot excuse myself, because I cannot believe that I could not have done better. No knowledge about the natural causes determining my action is sufficient to excuse me; I cannot escape the fundamental practical conviction that by *trying harder* I could have risen to whatever occasion I found myself in. (We might qualify this by saying "under normal conditions," meaning to rule out pathological compulsions, but I maintain the harder claim because I think that morally sensitive persons cannot entirely cease to reproach themselves no matter how apparently overpowering the causes of their moral insufficiency were.) If, however, determinism is true, then "could have tried harder" and "could have done better" are meaningless in the sense presupposed by my self-reproach, which is not merely a guise taken by my disappointment with my own character but primarily a form of responsibility, an *apology*, essentially inadequate, to the others; not merely a feeling but a *position* in relationship commanding me prior to my feelings. It is only vis-à-vis the others that there exists this infinite exigency for trying, whereby nothing I actually do can be enough. Therefore, an "ought" that necessarily implies a "can" (from which the theoretical thesis of indeterminism can be deduced, since the "can" is one of availability rather than Kantian spontaneity or counterfactual causability) is rooted in the original situation of encounter.[28] We are appropriately constrained to add a practical primary affirmation to our original set: "I can and should always act so as to affirm the others." Rendering the principle maximal, we can add this second clause: "I have never done as much as I could and should have to affirm the others." [29] To deny this principle is fundamentally impermissible. It is a letting oneself off the hook that one is never entitled to do.

One might object by putting forward another interpretation of the position of being in the wrong that does not imply "could have done better" in the strong sense. Can I not feel that I am in the wrong for having acted badly, and will be in the wrong for acting badly, without believing that under identical influences I might have tried harder to act well than I did, or might try harder than I will? That is, can I not feel the "stain" of badness without believing that the stain is avoidable? The adjudication of this objection will rest on the distinction between regret and remorse—the former a spectator's emotion that allows the unchangeability of what has occurred, the latter an emotion of agents unable to separate themselves from the live issue of their agency. The objector will interpret the irreducibly guilty feeling that one should have done better as regret for failure, and what we call "remorse" as a particularly acute regret in which we admonish ourselves in the present by the example of an unsatisfactory past. The defender of the sixth affirmation will reply that "remorse" so construed would only be an illusion, for which lucid regret and resolve should be substituted; but that, on the contrary, relationship with others does not permit the dissolution of remorse, which would in effect lift the practical weight of the past, or the future regarded as past, from the back of the guilty one.

The solution of this problem will properly be somewhat ambiguous and unstable. We may not diminish the responsibility of the agent confronted with others, and therefore wherever it is possible to attribute freedom to the agent, we must. But we cannot say certainly in advance to what extent it will be possible to regard the agent as free (and thus to what extent a sane agent would be liable to remorse). No one thinks that I am to blame for pushing you off a cliff if a falling boulder knocked my body into yours, or that I ought to have pulled you out of the way of the bus that ran you over while I was disabled by a seizure. A sane agent would feel regret, not remorse, for those . . . misfortunes. But our knowledge of neurological causes could progress to the point where many actions that now seem to us freely choosable are in fact compelled by causes as irresistible as boulders and seizures, though more subtle. Although it seems unlikely that any causation of that sort will ever become as flatly *knowable* and unquestionable as the causation of a falling boulder—considering the typical invisibility of such alleged causation—it is at least not inconceivable.

At any rate, we can say that within the *known* constraints of any situation of encounter, an ineliminable burden of responsibility to act for the best is on agents insofar as they are free, and that this burden makes us interpret ourselves as maximally free, and never as wholly unfree. "Knowledge" of necessitating causes is never beyond suspicion and never furnishes the last word in our interpretation of events involving persons. Even our knowledge that my body could not but be thrown as it was by a falling boulder does not prevent us wondering whether I somehow managed to use that boulder to get rid of you, or neglected to watch for it as I should have. However it may be limited by knowledge, the burden of responsibility can never be reduced to zero. That would annihilate the principle that under any circumstances whatsoever *we could have done more*. Here and only here is an a priori guarantee of freedom.

8.4 "Human Science" and the Explanation of Gesture

According to the distinction drawn by Kant, we judge a state of affairs differently depending on whether we approach it as spectators or as agents. In the most perplexing case, we regard ourselves as entirely subject to formal and efficient causation, if we are spectators; but as free causes, if we are agents. And this difference in outlook is correlated with a difference in basic interests: on the one hand, to know what is; on the other, to bring about what ought to be. The two standpoints are not entirely cut off from each other. Theoretical knowledge enters into the calculations we make regarding circumstances of action and means to ends; practical orientation affects the setting of scientific strategy and also the metaphysical background of science. But these are partnerships rather than mixtures. Even in our practical reckoning with what is, we strictly distinguish it from what ought to be; even in our normative theorizing we acknowledge the difference between what we intend and what is.

Evidently a paradox will arise if we rashly want to know what *is* the case as regards *practice,* or action. Then we will have to constitute action an object, thus as something caused and explicable through being caused. But action that is a necessitated effect is neither a free nor a responsible cause, and so is not action, but something else: "behavior." Agency eludes the spectator. (Spectation could elude agents as well if their refusal to settle for anything as it is made it impossible for them fully to affirm things as they are, in all their necessary connections.) It follows that "human science," conceived as in some way or other systematically distinct from natural or structural science, cannot exist.

Our own approach to the possibility of "human science" is different from the Kantian one just given, but equally subversive. For us the "spiritual" is that about the human which would distinguish "human science" from other sciences. But the spiritual is not a being, not a subject of true descriptions; it has actuality only in normative gesturing, which is in turn a function of relationship with other beings as other or as indescribable. Again, it seems plain that "human science" or "spiritual science" (*Geisteswissenschaft*) cannot exist.

Yet distinct human sciences do exist. It would fly in the face of the practice and concrete achievements of legions of historians, philologists, critics, humanistic psychologists, philosophers, and students of religion if we were to deny that it is possible to have *knowledge* of the exercises of human freedom in language, images, thought, and conduct beyond the bare historical record of the outward characteristics of what has been done or can be done; possible, that is, to have *insight* into what has been or can be done based on connections between actions and reasons, and more than mere insight, a framework of *reason,* a "discipline" within which to accept or reject claimed insights. All of these ingredients belong to the human sciences as their practitioners understand them. The difficulty is to vindicate the knowledge, insight, and reasonableness of the human sciences in face of the rival paradigms of natural science. I see no prospect of relieving the tension between the two standpoints, but at least at this point the conceptual means are available for better understanding their relation.

Knowledge, as bare notice of what is apparent, is the starting point of sciences of any sort. It cannot be disputed that the human sciences have data, for human freedom is not shut away from all view, it manifests itself, so that apparent beings and events can be assigned to it and it to them. What can be disputed is that the human sciences deal with that data scientifically, yielding us the requisite kind of insight on the requisitely reasonable basis. One can hold with Cassirer that human science is purely a science of the *what* with which we are confronted—more precisely, the *expressive* "what," comprising all materials that happen to be materializations of intention—and thus consists in an endless and disciplined refinement of perception.[30] The insight and reason of human science would be those proper to description, albeit description of a different sort than the naturalistic; the principles of "form," "style," and "structure" would rule instead of "cause."

We have already seen why it is mistaken to think that there can be mere description of "style," a spiritual principle.[31] To leave style out of the question and assign to human science only describable form or structure is to credit it with too little in the way of insight and reason, as will become apparent when we see what more can be said for it on these two heads.

Insight into beings, events, or conditions implies the grasping of connections between them and other beings, events, or conditions so that they no longer appear accidental but as they have to be or should be. Natural-scientific explanation reveals necessary sequences of events according to which each may be expected with certainty to come to be, just as it is; structural explanation reveals formal necessity. Humane explanation, if such there be, cannot provide insights based on necessitation and necessity, not if it wants to remain an explanation of how free beings comport and may comport themselves. One might believe against this that there is a "necessary" relationship between, for example, the aesthetic properties of an individual painting and the general principles of style pertinent to it that have been discovered by art historians; but we meet here only with a "law" of the structure of *accomplished* intentions, a posteriori, no doubt suggestive but not predictive.[32] Significant art cannot be produced by formula, no more than language or history or philosophical or religious thought.

Now that we have taken the trouble to clarify the nature and working of final causation, we cannot be rushed to the conclusion that human science therefore lacks insights and explanations of its own. Humane explanation invariably shows the data, not as they have to be, but as they should be, finalistically intelligible in relation to ends that appear simultaneously as ends for the sake of which the data exist and ends for those who understand the data. For example, a historian may state that President Truman decided to use atomic bombs against Japan in order to shorten the war and save lives. In fact, we do not know with certainty what Truman's (or any individual's) motives were; we will argue among ourselves, perhaps indefinitely, whether we would have done the same; we may not be able to settle once and for all the relative importance of the various factors that brought the bombing about. But it cannot be denied that the historian's claim, even though it is non-necessitarian, does give insight and explains. It does this, not exactly by allowing us to "empathize" with Truman—as one form of the *Verstehen* theory of human science would have it—but by presenting to us the end that contributed to the determination of that historical event, as a real end. We do not need to become Truman in any sense, we only need to stand beside him and see what he saw (or might have seen). We have insight into the decision when we know what it means to act in order to minimize evil and when we know enough of the particulars of Truman's situation to read it as a challenge so to act. (We may learn what it means to try to minimize evil precisely in becoming acquainted with Truman's situation.) The significant "forms" studied in the human sciences appear *primarily* as things to be interested in, for which reason they invariably (if usually implicitly) put the question to us as to what *we* mean, how *we* propose to be responsive partners with them.[33]

Reason does not amount to something fundamentally different in the two types of science. Both possess authoritative procedures that order inquiry and argument. The most important difference is that theoretical scientists have subjugated their own freedom, as much as they can, in order faithfully to study what is not free or not regarded as other, nature or structure. The norms of their disciplines, those that do not directly pertain to intradisciplinary conversation as such, are just those of description. As mere describers they can treat their data as merely given. Humanists, on the other hand, have gratuitous data with which to enter an unnecessitated relationship. Their givens are more and less than "given," they are personal challenges and teases. To deal with this data reasonably is always a matter, therefore, not just of obeying norms, as any scientist must, but of actively engaging in norming. Astronomers cannot believe that what the solar system actually is depends at any moment on what they make of it, no matter if they hold a sophisticated view of the dependence of scientific cognition on changeable theoretical paradigms. But what the *Iliad* actually means—what literary science can know about it—hangs right now and forever, in small but irreducible part, on my own interpretation of it.

It is necessary and salutary to draw these distinctions in principle between the human sciences, for which final causation is dominant, and the theoretical sciences, for which nonfinal formal and efficient causation are dominant. Otherwise we will always be subject to confusion about their warrants and constraints. But we cannot keep them entirely separated, either. The human sciences are avid to incorporate theoretical knowledge in their jumping-off platforms; for instance, critics of the *Iliad* want to learn everything that can be known about the natural and formal conditions governing ancient Greek life and poetic art, on the one hand, and their own reading, on the other. For their part, the theoretical sciences are unhappy so long as they are cut off from the dimension of finality in their objects of study. Astronomers who do not wonder at the heavens have no sense of significance in their work. The necessary but problematic partnership between the two modes of insight comes to a head very pointedly within psychology, in which province there should be the greatest amount of intellectual suffering. Psychologists have to study motivated conduct as caused behavior and caused behavior as motivated conduct.

The large problem of the relation between spiritual and theoretical insight, "understanding" and "explanation," requires to be given here its setting under the aspect of the spiritual. The two foremost principles of that setting, as in every other matter we have dealt with, are the separateness of the order of the spiritual from the order of describable being (which is *not* a separation of intention from matter), and the superordinate or commanding position of the spiritual with respect to other standpoints. These principles should guide us in deciding how we stand with respect to one of the greatest philosophical programs of modern times, coeval with our independent and powerful natural science. The program, undertaken by Leibniz, Kant, and Hegel, and more recently by Dewey, Cassirer, and Ricoeur, consists of working out a comprehensive world-understanding in which the spiritual order fully accepts natural science and takes it into itself without being essentially compromised. The basic faith of this program has been well expressed by René Le Senne:

> Every precious advance of the human spirit consists of a conversion by which something that first seemed to it extrinsic, which was presented to it as other than itself, is now by its art assimilated to the degree that it becomes capable, on the basis of its own inwardness and by its operation, not only of generating but of transforming the other at will, transcending it. At the beginning of this conversion, spirit felt itself to be an outsider; it was inferior to what it apprehended, which excluded it; but once the appropriation is accomplished, spirit is on familiar terms with the other, which has become its own.[34]

The question for us is whether spirit as we propose to conceive it can assimilate or possess nature in this manner, or whether such assimilation is patented by spirit-as-mind.

The mind can deal with the knowledge that its own thoughts are factually determined in two ways. One is to assert that knowing a fact always means being free with respect to it. Science would in that case never be a threat to us but always a savior, because real unfreedom consists in being unaware of the factors determining one. Psychoanalytic patients, for example, become (in theory) capable of freeing themselves from compulsion when the grounds of their compulsions are laid bare. Interpreters of texts become capable of rising above their prejudices once criticism has brought those prejudices out in the open. And so forth. It does seem true that anything established as a "fact" becomes at the same time something toward which various attitudes and policies may or may not be adopted. Even massive, unchangeable, life-permeating facts, such as the fact of thought's dependence on sense-perception and language, are objects toward which we can choose different attitudes. But how can thought-as-free really outflank thought-as-determined if we know in principle that even apparently free thinking is, insofar as it confronts facts, another determined fact in turn, though not (yet) a fact for itself to confront? The freedom of thought, which seems essential to genuine thought, would in any case be only apparent and provisional if thought is actually a natural product. This difficulty might turn us to the second attitude toward the factual determination of thought, which is to regard all knowledge as additive rather than reductive. We comport ourselves as free thinkers and doers according to one standpoint, as products of nature or our own artificial structure according to another. Full knowledge of ourselves must admit both of these aspects. There is a contradiction between them only if we insist on reducing one to the other; why not have both?

Spirit-as-mind may not be entirely comfortable with this arrangement, which calls for something like permanent schizophrenia. Nevertheless, spirit-as-mind fundamentally wants to keep every possible thought in its head and could never bear to get rid either of freedom (for its own creative exercise) or determination (for the possession of the world in knowledge). Thus the best solution for it is the "additive" one. With spirit-as-relationship, however, the situation is different. Here, too, there must be a place for knowledge, minimally the knowledge that identifies the others, notifying the knower of the features without which the others would not be what they are. But the rule of wonder and (when the others are speaking others) fellowship supervenes upon and limits knowledge and necessitarian explanation.[35]

We can illustrate this by letting two researchers M. (for spirit-as-mind) and R. (for spirit-as-relationship)—representing anthropology's endemic push and pull —study a remote island tribe, the Waki. M. carefully describes the insect worship of the Waki and relates it to structural and historical invariances according to established principles. (We prescind from any difficulties that might be encountered in completing this kind of account, even though they may be insuperable; the fundamental purpose is in question, not strategy and tactics.) In order to perfect his knowledge of their religious rites, he secures their permission to participate in them one night, and on that night, so long as he wears nothing but a pair of antennae and crawls before the totem in the torchlit darkness, he feels many of the same fears and exhilarations that the Waki do. Nor does he cheat himself of this excitement by reflecting then and there on the causes of the practice. He lets it mean to him something like what it means to them. His sympathetic retelling of the experiences will enrich his account of the Waki and furnish clues for further investigation.

R. like M. aims to give a theoretically objective presentation of Waki culture, but she approaches and qualifies this presentation in a different way. To R., the religion of the Waki figures as a spirit, its structure as a style, and its history as a story. The necessities R. discerns in Waki life will be allowed to condition their existence in the same way that the human body and a mother-tongue are ordinarily allowed to be conditions of the existence of any individual; they will be understood as indwelt and ridden rather than as themselves determining, themselves riding, like unruly or ungrateful steeds. R. does not cross a boundary line between objectivity and subjectivity when she takes part in their rites. She does not primarily gain an "experience"; she gains sensitivity to or mastery of the Waki way. Her view has a unity that M.'s view lacks, but it excludes something of great significance that M.'s view includes, namely, determinism and the powerful type of explanation that is founded thereon. The dominant strand of her explanations will be the elucidation of why people in the situation of the Waki *might well* act, responsively, as they do; she will be exhibiting ends and referring to final causation. Necessitarian knowledge and explanation can be admitted to a very great extent without eclipsing this interest, but will be excluded when they would eclipse it; and this is a limitation that is totally foreign to M.'s approach.

M. has made Waki experience his "own" according to Le Senne's program, transcending it, overcoming its otherness. R. has not done away with Waki otherness, but she has become "familiar" with it by *joining* it, so far as an anthropologist could. That is a spiritual "appropriation" too, if not an "assimilation"; she appropriates the Waki way in being appropriated by it. She gains responsive freedom by losing theoretical control.

The object of R.'s science is not unequivocally present. Other anthropologists using R.'s approach might be, indeed will be, appropriated by the Waki way differently, perhaps very differently, in which case they will accuse R. of leading cheers for her own Waki-sentiments, and she will charge them likewise, and only with difficulty, if at all, will they resolve their disagreements by seeing how well the unequivocal data bear their varying interpretations. Some of them, disillusioned by the problem of equivocalness in the data and scientific agreement, may turn to M.'s approach. Note, for example, how Ivan Pavlov decided against ambiguity and for theoretical control in psychology:

> While making a detailed investigation of the digestive glands I had to busy myself also with the so-called psychical stimulation of the glands. When, together with one of my collaborators, I attempted a deeper analysis of this fact, at first in the generally accepted way, i.e. psychologically visualizing the probable thoughts and feelings of the animal, I stumbled on a fact unusual in laboratory practice. I found myself unable to agree with my colleague; each of us stuck to his point of view, and we were unable to convince each other by certain experiments. This made me definitely reject any further psychological discussion of the subject, and I decided to investigate it in a purely objective way, externally.[36]

R. does retain some advantages over M. notwithstanding the messiness of her approach. Her "object" is intrinsically a challenge to her and can never be finished with. Scientific discussion of her "object" is intrinsically *interesting* for the same reason that it is intrinsically interminable, namely, that it is an issue to which one is called on to bring more or less good provisional theses for dialectical argument, rather than a being to fix descriptively.

Teachers of the human sciences meet constantly with Pavlov's reaction in their students. The "results" of research in philosophy, religion, language, and the arts are not textbook-objects, which students (preoccupied with theoretical control not only for psychological reasons but because of the grade race into which they are thrown) often would like them to be so that the question of how to deal with them could be settled once and for all. Only with difficulty, if at all, can teachers convince their students that what they think is a privation is actually a bonus: that these disciplines are interesting precisely because they are permanently equivocal and unsettled, and reasonable precisely because they demand responsive thought and endless conversation. It is both more stimulating and truer to the spiritual condition to stand on air, as the humanities so obviously do, than to stand on firm ground. (The natural sciences are stimulating, too, because their ground is not actually firm, either; they are constantly in revolution as regards their possibilities of description, and they begin and end in wonder.) This is so even though philosophers have perversely been trying to supply firm ground to stand on, in the form of ontology, from the beginning of philosophy. If they had had their way, there would be no further possibility of gesture either to make or to explain.

8.5 The History of Spirit in the World

Spirits are affirmative relationships between intentional beings for whom the task is set of trying to live with each other as rightly as possible. The task is *set*, without a doubt, but can anything be said about a tendency toward successful *accomplishment*?

Anaxagoras' claim that "spirit" (*nous*) is the primordial motion from which all motion begins, more and more governing all motion with its own regularity, is hard to improve on for simplicity and grandeur. The same grand idea is enormously developed by Hegel, for whom Anaxagoras' "motion" becomes the meaning-constituting action of one final cause, the Idea or absolute spirit. It is certainly not open to us to say what Hegel also said, that "spirit" *makes* things what they are. Spirit is the matrix of the realizing of the meaning of beings, not the manufacturer of their meaning. However, spirits are also repertoires of response comprising whole constellations of standing possibilities of *our* meaning, the approaching to others that is inseparable from their coming to us. Bearing this in mind, we can say that the program of absolute idealism errs not in the breadth

[handwritten annotation:] Spirit = "matrix for realization of the meanings of beings, NOT the manufacturer of their meanings"

of its claim but in its attachment to comprehension. That program cannot be too grandiose, for it is true that everything we manage to mean is spiritually determined, and that the mission of philosophy (to position ourselves most rightly) extends to every pocket of our experience and every branch of our discourse; only it is not right to project knowledge as the consummation of our approach to other beings.

Although each of us is directed by all others to understand the world spiritually and thus as finally caused by beings and spirits as ends, it does not follow that the events in the world are more and more spiritually governed. *I* can straightforwardly affirm that a spirit makes a difference when I act in one, notwithstanding the possibility of self-deception and the myriad rereadings of my action that may be made later. This affirmation is always the nerve of my practical response to the others. It is a separate question, however, whether the spiritual acts of individuals add up to the kind of lasting and progressive world-difference that Anaxagoras envisioned. How, if at all, does "spirit" get hold of the world and change it?

Our question must be distinguished at the start from the question of culture's effect upon nature, meant such that "culture" is to us as dams are to beavers. No one doubts that the earth's biosphere has been significantly changed as humans have acted under the guidance of language, art, scientific problems and propositions, and so forth—suprapsychological forms assigned by Popper to "World Three" and rightly placed in causal relation with physical World One by the mediation of psychic World Two.[37] But these forms could have had their effect if they were simply possibilities of thought and action innocent of spiritual qualification. They could be valid or invalid simply to the extent that they are reliable or unreliable in working with the world, without any trace of the higher problematic of validity pertaining to intentional fellowship. They could all have evolved for technical rather than spiritual reasons. If a spirit amounts to more than a complicated beaver dam or the readiness to build one, then the proliferation of libraries, museums, and atomic reactors does not prove that the world is becoming spiritually altered.

Hegel's coup was to exhibit "world" as nothing other than spirit or the Idea playing itself out. But he could not convincingly subsume nature under the Idea, not without disrespecting the very factual nature that the natural sciences were interested in. His achievement was thus not as inclusive as he wished it to be. Still, he did disclose what appeared to many of his successors to be the true theater of operations of spirit, namely "history," that world-within-the-world constituted by the free and responsive acts of intenders in community. "History" would be the effect of the causation of spirit. But the actual science of history can and must involve itself with the "natural," unfree, unresponsive dimension of human affairs over time, so that "history" in the spiritual sense becomes something smaller (if not lesser), the interesting, elusive ghost in that machinery.

Buber, proceeding with the rival conception of spirit as relationship, thinks of spirit as "grasping" nature through humanity (whom he calls "spirit's cosmic risk") through a historical rhythm of separation and return. Persons are alienated from each other and from what is common, turn back, are alienated again more perilously, then re-engage themselves yet more profoundly.[38] How can we measure whether there is a rhythm such as Buber sees? What would count as proof of it? The political and technological horrors of the twentieth century might be adduced to support the claim of unprecedented spiritual peril; but do we know that the world is more unglued and alien for us, taking everything into consideration, than it was for all those would-be citizens who shuddered through the crumbling of ancient empires? Do we see in today's constructive responses a profounder spiritual movement than in earlier responses to earlier trials? A religious vision might have it so. Apart from such a vision there does not seem to be reason to think so. It does not seem possible to make the necessary comparative measurements of profundity.

But apart from any consideration of profundity it might be thought that the advances of human civilization constitute an irrefutable argument for the progressive spiritualization of the world. The "advances" are not unambiguous, naturally; but the fact is (it might be claimed) that whereas 10,000 years ago the vastly greater part of the natural world was unseen and unaffirmed by spiritual beings, who moreover where they did live were mainly hostile toward each other, group against group, now billions of spiritual beings live in relatively high and appreciative consciousness of nature and each other. Many of us make this optimistic assessment of history more or less unconsciously; it will not stand examination. First, it is probably untrue and certainly unprovable that people today are more appreciative of others than they were earlier. The existence of countless books and films celebrating the wonders of nature and countless sermons instructing us in our global responsibilities (to feed the hungry, etc.) is no proof, for we do not surely know just what these things mean to their audience; in fact, the very multiplying of such stimuli suggests a massive insensitivity. Second, the world is not more "spiritual" because a billion spiritual beings live in it instead of a million or a thousand, and we could not make it yet more spiritual by more thickly populating the earth or spreading ourselves through the galaxies. Fruitfulness and multiplication are good things in themselves, to be sure, on the more-the-merrier principle, but the spiritual program is the affirmation of such beings as are, not the creation of beings. The world will not be more spiritual for having more things in it; it will be more spiritual for having the things in it better attended.

If we take a longer view, and compare the state of affairs before the appearance of humanity with the state of affairs after, can we say, with Teilhard de Chardin, that the universe took a huge and specifically spiritual leap forward with us which it would not have taken had the lure of that possibility not existed?[39] And has not the evolution of the natural order shown a deep affinity with the spiritual not only by producing spiritual beings in the first place but by promoting them, selecting in their favor?

To rebut the first part of this version of the belief in spirit's causal impact on the world, we need only point out the possibility that the universe hit on spirit either by accident or by necessity (that is, just in the course of running through all its possibilities), but in any event answering no "lure," and that on the longest view spirit may be found to have had no more durable or influential a career than any of the other realizable organizations of energy. The "lure" is supplied by prophetic vision, not by evidence that demands that interpretation.

To answer the second part of the claim, we need to reckon with a striking coincidence between the logic of natural selection and the logic of the spiritual. By "natural selection" we refer to the elimination not only of competitively disadvantaged genotypes but also of incompossible ensembles of being. To put it positively, the universe produces and maintains beings who can live together. For example, only those parasitic organisms who do not kill off their host populations can survive. Further, those groups whose members flourish individually while at the same time aiding each other are the more competitively successful. This law of coexistence resembles the law of mutual affirmation, but it is not at all the same. The relation between coexisting parties is not destructive, to be sure, but neither need it be affirmative beyond a technically necessary minimum. It can be, and for all we know usually is, entirely utilitarian—that is to say, it is not governed by the intrinsic meaning or finality of the beings involved, which may figure as no more than "cattle" to each other in the most derogatory sense. It is incidentally true that good cattle ranchers must have a good eye for their cattle, and that in this sense even exploitative coexistence promotes appreciation. Indeed, opportunities for appreciation will be increased when cattle language and lore develop. But the most competitively successful ranchers will be the ones who rigorously subordinate any respect or appreciation for their cattle to their exploitative purposes. This holds for our relations with each other and the whole civilized fabric of such relations as well. Nothing, not the most elaborate courtesy of mores, not the nicest public network of parks and galleries, not the most widespread and consequential religious ministry, is proof that we are not cattle to each other and ranchers of each other. (But the evolution of technical culture provides more and more pipes through which the wild air *could* blow.)

In facing the question of spirit's place and power in the world, we are like the Israelites whom we pictured earlier trying to make sense of the parting of the Red Sea. Was it mere accident that events unrolled in just such a way as to give us such occasions to which to rise? What do *we* mean? Whether the causation of spirit is actual, whether the world really existed for the sake of spirit and will be shaped according to it, depends always on the future, where we will or will not live well. Whether a hidden, original world-wheel is spinning us into a better future, we cannot determine. There could not in any case be a proof of non-necessary causation, could there?

Notes and Index

Notes

Prologue

1. Martin Heidegger, *Being and Time*, trans. John Macquarrie and Edward Robinson (New York: Harper & Row, 1962), p. 19.

Chapter 1

1. *American Heritage Dictionary of the English Language* (Boston: Houghton Mifflin, 1973). On *Geist*, see "Geist" in the *Historisches Wörterbuch der Philosophie*, ed. Joachim Ritter (Darmstadt: Wissenschaftliche Buchgesellschaft, 1971–), 3:156.

2. Deuteronomy 30:19.

3. Aristotle, *On the Soul* 405a19 (on Thales); Plato, *Laws* 899b.

4. *Metaphysics* 983b20.

5. Selection no. 160 in G. S. Kirk, J. E. Raven, and M. Schofield, *The Presocratic Philosophers*, 2nd ed. (Cambridge, Eng.: Cambridge University Press, 1957).

6. Ibid., no. 602.

7. Ibid., pp. 294–96, 314–16, 320–21.

8. Ibid., no. 196.

9. *On the Soul*, 404a–405a.

10. Walter Wili, "The History of the Spirit in Antiquity," trans. Ralph Manheim, in *Spirit and Nature*, ed. Joseph Campbell (Princeton, N.J.: Princeton University Press, 1954), p. 84.

11. "Reason, however, is nothing else than a portion of the divine spirit [*spiritus*] set in the human body"—Seneca, Letter 66:12 (trans. Richard M. Gummere).

12. But A. Debrunner urges for *nous* a root *snu* related to Germanic words for the nose and sniffing—reported in the *Theological Dictionary of the New Testament*, ed. Gerhard Kittel and Gerhard Friedrich, trans. G. W. Bromiley (Grand Rapids: Eerdmans, 1964–76), 4:952. In that case *nous*-perception would originally require moving air to enter the nose!

13. *The Presocratic Philosophers*, no. 476.

14. Plato, *Phaedo* 97c, trans. Hugh Tredennick.

15. *Laws* 893–99.

16. *Phaedo* 79.

17. Cf. Plato, *Symposium* 211.

18. *On the Soul* 412b.

19. Cf. Plato, *Timaeus* 35a.

20. E.g., Plato, *Meno* 81.

21. *Timaeus* 41d–42e; *Republic*, Book IV; *Phaedrus* 244–56.

22. *Theological Dictionary of the New Testament*, 3:167.

23. *Symposium* 208c.

24. As in Paul Ricoeur's revival of *thumos* theory in *Fallible Man*, trans. Charles Kelbley (New York: Fordham University Press, 1987), pp. 106–132. The *Republic* swerves away from this possibility in attributing *thumos* to children and animals who are supposed to be utterly nonrational—441b.

25. *Timaeus* 48a.

26. Ibid. 29e.

27. Ibid. 69b.

28. Ibid. 28–29.

29. *On the Soul* 406a et seq.

30. Cf. *Laws* 898e–99a.

31. *On the Soul* 415b.

32. Ibid. 413b25, 429b4.

33. Ibid. 408b18.

34. Ibid. 430a15.

35. Aristotle, *Metaphysics* 1072b20.

36. *On the Soul* 432a.

37. *Metaphysics* 1072b22–25.

38. Ibid. 1072b18–29.

39. *Republic* 508.

40. Ibid. 509b (trans. Paul Shorey).

41. *Timaeus* 29e–30b; *Laws* 899d–905c.

42. *Euthyphro* 7d (trans. Lane Cooper).

43. *Theological Dictionary of the New Testament*, 6:372–75.

44. One reason he is able to do this is that the Septuagint uses a distinct word for breath, *pnoé*.

45. *Phaedrus* 244a–49e.

46. Philo of Alexandria, *On the Account of the World's Creation Given by Moses* 139; *Allegorical Interpretation of Genesis II, III*, 1:36–42.

47. See Marie E. Isaacs, *The Concept of Spirit: A Study of Pneuma in Hellenistic Judaism and Its Bearing on the New Testament* (London: Heythrop College, 1976).

48. *On the Soul* 430b25.

49. I Corinthians 12:8–11. Cf. I John 4:1.

50. I Corinthians 15:35–50. John 4:24, "God is a spirit," is not informative either.

51. Augustine, *Confessions* VII, 1 and 4.

52. But see *On the Trinity* XIV, 16, and XV, 5.

53. *Confessions* XII.

54. Ibid. VII, 1.

55. Ibid. XII, 17.

56. Ibid. VII, 1.

57. *On Free Will* II, paras. 14–39; *Confessions* XIII, 9.

58. *Confessions* VII, 1.

59. Ibid. VII, 12 (trans. Vernon Bourke).

60. Thomas Aquinas, *Summa Theologica* I, Q. 36, art. 1 (Dominican trans.).

61. Augustine, *Confessions* XIII, 9 (trans. Bourke).

62. René Descartes, *Meditations on First Philosophy* II.

63. Augustine, *The City of God* XI, 26; cf. *On Free Will* II, para. 7.

64. Immanuel Kant, *Critique of Judgment*, para. 49.

65. See "Geist" in Jacob and Wilhelm Grimm's *Deutsche Wörterbuch* vol. 4 (Leipzig: S. Himzel, 1897), senses II.18.h and II.24.d (4:2678, 2716–17), and the *Historisches Wörterbuch der Philosophie*, "Geist," VII.

66. For numerous word references see "Geist" in the *Historisches Wörterbuch der Philosophie*, 3:186, and in the *Deutsche Wörterbuch*, sense II.29.b (4:2733–34); for Herder's thought on national cultures see especially *Ideas for a Philosophy of the History of Humanity* VIII and IX.

67. Baron de Montesquieu, *The Spirit of Laws* XIX; see David W. Carrithers' introduction to his edition of this book (Berkeley: University of California Press, 1977), pp. 23–30.

68. See "Geist," VII, 3, in the *Historisches Wörterbuch der Philosophie*.

69. For Hegel's definitional remarks on spirit (or the Idea realized as spirit) see esp. G. W. F. Hegel, *Phenomenology of Spirit* VI, introductory, and *Encyclopedia of the Philosophical Sciences*, introduction to the "Philosophy of Spirit," paras. 377–86.

70. Hegel admits that "spirit" is a determinate notion only in opposition with the notion of "nature" (or "matter"), but the opposition here is between the alienation of the Idea from itself and its returning to itself. "Spirit" is thus an *aspect* of reality but the aspect of *consummation*. See his *Lectures on the Philosophy of World History*, Introduction: *Reason in History*, trans. H. B. Nisbet (Cambridge, Eng.: Cambridge University Press, 1975), pp. 44–53 (the beginning of part B).

71. *Encyclopedia*, paras. 385, 387.

72. Wilhelm Dilthey, *Der Aufbau der geschichtlichen Welt in den Geisteswissenschaften* III, 2, 3, 1–2—pp. 177–85 in the 1970 Suhrkamp ed. (Frankfurt-am-Main). Dilthey's and Nicolai Hartmann's treatments of the theme of objective spirit were anticipated by the mid-nineteenth century theorist of "Völkerpsychologie," Moritz Lazarus—see Hans-Ulrich Lessing, "Bemerkungen zum Begriff des 'Objektiven Geistes' bei Hegel, Lazarus und Dilthey," *Reports on Philosophy* 9 (1985): 49–62.

73. Hegel, *Encyclopedia*, paras. 385, 553–55.

74. Ibid., para. 204.

75. Ibid., para. 377.

76. Søren Kierkegaard, *Philosophical Fragments*, ch. 3.

77. Søren Kierkegaard, *The Sickness Unto Death*, in *Fear and Trembling* and *The Sickness Unto Death*, trans. Walter Lowrie (Garden City, N.Y.: Doubleday, 1954), p. 146.

78. *Søren Kierkegaard's Journals and Papers*, ed. and trans. Howard and Edna Hong (Bloomington: Indiana University Press, 1975), vol. 4, no. 4350.

79. *The Sickness Unto Death*, p. 146.

80. Augustine, *Confessions* I, 1.

81. Cf. Kierkegaard, *Either/Or*, trans. Walter Lowrie (Princeton, N.J.: Princeton University Press, 1972), 2:218, 266–67.

82. Wilhelm Dilthey, *Gesammelte Schriften*, 5th ed. (Stuttgart: Teubner, 1959), 5:144.

83. See e.g. Rudolf Eucken, *Life's Basis and Life's Ideal* [Die Grundlinien einer neuen Lebensanschauung], trans. Alban G. Widgery (London: A. & C. Black, 1918).

84. See Friedrich Nietzsche, *The Will to Power*, trans. Walter Kaufmann (New York: Vintage, 1968), fragments 477, 480, 524–26, 529, 644, 659, 676, 687, 709, 820, 899, 1045, 1052; and Walter Kaufmann's *Nietzsche* (Princeton, N.J.: Princeton University Press, 1974), ch. 8.

85. Max Scheler, *Formalism in Ethics and Non-Formal Ethics of Values*, trans. Manfred S. Frings and Robert L. Funk (Evanston, Ill.: Northwestern University Press, 1973), p. 389 (my translation).

86. Ibid., 6, B, 4, ad 4—pp. 519–61.

87. Ibid., p. 521.

88. Augustine, *Confessions* X, 7–8.

89. Max Scheler, *Man's Place in Nature*, trans. Hans Meyerhoff (New York: Noonday, 1961), pp. 54, 62.

90. Ibid., p. 66.

91. Ludwig Klages, *Der Geist als Widersacher der Seele* (Leipzig: J. A. Barth, 1929, 1932).

92. Plato, *Phaedo* 64a, and I Corinthians 15:50.

93. Bruno Bauch, "Natur und Geist," *Zeitschrift für deutsche Kulturphilosophie* 4 (1938): 272f. As much as Klages' argument owes to Nietzschean inspiration, Nietzsche's positive use of the term "spirit" accords with Bauch's claim.

94. Julius Kraft, *Die Unmöglichkeit der Geisteswissenschaft* (Frankfurt-am-Main: Offentliches Leben, 1957; first published in 1934), p. 28.

95. Nicolai Hartmann, *Das Problem des geistigen Seins* (Berlin: Walter de Gruyter, 1933).

96. Ibid., pp. 90–92. For example, the ideal of educating everyone is untenable, for it destroys a nation's "reserves"—p. 92. Presumably he means we will fail to eat or reproduce sufficiently if we have too many scholars, artists, etc. and not enough farmers.

97. Cf. Erich Rothacker's identification of *Geist* with a *Verantwortungsbewusstsein* which, instead of oppressing the soul (as Klages thinks), opens its doors—"Das Wesen des Schöpferischen," *Blätter für deutsche Philosophie* 10 (1937): 418.

98. Hartmann, *Das Problem des geistigen Seins*, pp. 77–78.

99. Ibid., p. 95. Cf. Helmuth Plessner, *Die Stufen des Organischen und der Mensch* (Berlin: Walter de Gruyter, 1975), ch. 7.

100. Hartmann, *Das Problem des geistigen Seins*, p. 148.

101. Ibid., p. 174. Hartmann's conception of objective spirit is an overlooked predecessor of the "World 3" sketched in Karl Popper's later work. See Popper's "Epistemology Without a Knowing Subject" and "On the Theory of Objective Mind" in *Objective Knowledge* (London: Oxford University Press, 1972), and (with John Eccles) *The Self and Its Brain* (New York: Springer, 1977), pp. 36–50. Heinrich Rickert incidentally employs the phrase *drittes Reich* for a comparable purpose in his *Die Grenzen der naturwissenschaftlichen Begriffsbildung*, 2nd ed. (Tübingen: J. C. B. Mohr, 1913), p. 181.

102. Ibid., pp. 260–66.

103. Ibid., p. 267.

104. Ibid., pp. 157–59.

105. Ibid., p. 283. Cf. Hartmann's countertheses against Hegel, ibid., pp. 122, 172–76.

106. Ibid., pp. 348ff.

107. Bertrand Russell's comparable specification of "spirit" in distinction from "mind" is discussed in section 2.4, below.

108. Ludwig Feuerbach, *Principles of the Philosophy of the Future*, paras. 32, 62, 63. Cf. the history of dialogical thought in Harold Green's introduction to *The Word and the Spiritual Realities* by Ferdinand Ebner (Ph.D. diss., Northwestern University, 1980), which discusses the place of Jacobi, Geijer, and Humboldt in the development of this idea.

109. An exception, not connected to the *Fragments* argument, is Kierkegaard's distinction between *Thou* and *other-I* in *Works of Love*, trans. Howard and Edna Hong (New York: Harper & Row, 1962), p. 69.

110. Gabriel Marcel, *Metaphysical Journal*, April 23, 1914.

111. Cf. ibid., Jan. 5, 1914.

112. Ibid., Aug. 23, 1918.

113. Ibid., Feb. 25, 1919.

114. Ibid., March 5, 1923.

115. Ibid., Oct. 17, 1922.

116. Ebner, *The Word and the Spiritual Realities*, pp. 128ff., 217.

117. Ibid., p. 6.

118. See Eberhard Grisebach, *Gegenwart: Eine kritische Ethik* (Halle: Max Niemeyer, 1928).

119. Martin Buber, *I and Thou*, trans. Walter Kaufmann (New York: Scribner's, 1970), p. 89.

120. Ibid., p. 89.

121. Eugen Rosenstock-Huessy, *Die Sprache des Menschengeschlechts*, 2 vols. (Heidelberg: Lambert Schneider, 1963).

122. Buber, *I and Thou*, p. 68.

123. Ibid., p. 143.

124. Ibid., p. 85.

125. See "Replies to My Critics," in *The Philosophy of Martin Buber*, ed. Paul A. Schilpp and Maurice Friedman (LaSalle, Ill.: Open Court, 1967), p. 693.

126. Ibid., p. 102.

127. Ibid., p. 149.

128. Martin Buber, "Afterword" to *Between Man and Man*, trans. Ronald Gregor Smith and Maurice Friedman (New York: Macmillan, 1965), p. 218.

129. Emmanuel Levinas, *Totality and Infinity*, trans. Alphonso Lingis (Pittsburgh: Duquesne University Press, 1969), p. 23; Emmanuel Levinas, *Otherwise than Being or Beyond Essence*, trans. Alphonso Lingis (The Hague: Martinus Nijhoff, 1981; first published in 1974).

130. Levinas, *Totality and Infinity*, p. 40.

131. Martin Heidegger, *Being and Time*, trans. John Macquarrie and Edward Robinson (New York: Harper & Row, 1962), para. 26.

132. Emmanuel Levinas, "On the Trail of the Other," trans. Daniel J. Hoy, in *Philosophy Today* 10 (1966): 44. Cf. Exodus 33:12–23.

133. This point was made in conversation with the author.

134. *Totality and Infinity*, pp. 290, 25.
135. Emmanuel Levinas, "Transcendance et hauteur," *Bulletin de la Société Française de Philosophie* 56 (1962): 96 (my translation).
136. *Otherwise than Being*, p. 116.
137. Ibid., pp. 180–82.
138. Ibid., p. 143.
139. Emmanuel Levinas, "Questions et réponses," *Le Nouveau Commerce* 36–37 (1977): 74 (my translation).
140. Buber, *I and Thou*, p. 180.
141. Michael Theunissen develops an objection like this in *Der Andere*, 2nd ed. (Berlin: Walter de Gruyter, 1977)—partial English translation by Christopher Macann (Cambridge, Mass.: MIT Press, 1984); see esp. the "Postscript."
142. Buber, *I and Thou*, p. 69.
143. But cf. Levinas' analyses of paternity and sexual relations in *Totality and Infinity*, pp. 154ff., and *Time and the Other*, trans. Richard Cohen (Pittsburgh: Duquesne University Press, 1987).
144. *Otherwise than Being*, p. 198, n. 28.
145. René Descartes, letter to Princess Elizabeth, May 21, 1643.
146. Buber, *I and Thou*, pp. 100–110.

Chapter 2

1. François de la Rochefoucauld, *Reflections*, no. 102.
2. "Reflective" or "interpretative" social scientists *can* be as much oriented to pure description as behaviorists, even if the objects of their observation are more difficult to establish reliably. They can be, in effect, mental behaviorists. One can be aware of possible or possibly preferable intentions without responding to the challenge to intend thus, even if a kind of virtual responsive performance is requisite to understanding meaningful acts. Cf. Jürgen Habermas' discussion of this point, and particularly of Hans Skjervheim's view of it, in Habermas, *The Theory of Communicative Action*, vol. 1, trans. Thomas McCarthy (Boston: Beacon, 1984), pp. 102–41, esp. 111–13. The account of humanistic social science developed below, section 8.3, is an activation of the role of performative involvement to which Skjervheim has drawn attention at the conclusion of his "Objectivism and the Study of Man," pt. II, in *Inquiry* 17 (1974): 298f.
3. John Locke, *An Essay Concerning Human Understanding* II, 23, 5; George Berkeley, *Of the Principles of Human Knowledge*, paras. 2, 7.
4. Samuel Taylor Coleridge, *Biographia Literaria*, ch. 12, thesis VI. Cf. F. H. Bradley, *Appearance and Reality*, 2nd ed. (London: Oxford University Press, 1930), pp. 441–42.
5. *A History of Western Philosophy* (New York: Simon & Schuster, 1945), pp. 288–89.
6. Bertrand Russell, *Principles of Social Reconstruction* (London: Allen & Unwin, 1916), p. 207.

7. Ibid., p. 210.

8. Ibid., pp. 223–24.

9. J. N. Findlay gives a plain statement of the inside-out view, speaking for both Hegel and himself: "Our conscious life does regularly tend to sharpen itself into just that perceptive, intelligent state, analytic yet synoptic, in which characters are disengaged, relations and likenesses made to flash out, and the results of quite elaborate surveys resumed in the deeply felt grasp of a whole. . . . [T]he rise to a consideration of the points of view and interests of other persons, and to co-operative work with them, is no more than a natural extension of the same organizing self-collection of thought and behavior which occurs in the simplest exercises of intelligence. We have therefore reason to say that conscious life, to the extent that it sharpens itself into intelligence, will show some tendency to move towards the rigorous intersubjective canons of science, the impartial directives of morality, the detached appreciations of art and the 'self-naughting' surrenders of mystical religion. It seems plain, in fact, that the source of our various impersonal norms and values is to be found in the universalizing tendencies native to the human mind"—*Hegel: A Re-examination* (New York: Oxford University Press, 1958), pp. 54–55. Even if it were psychologically true that formal structures of intelligence emerge independent of social experience, we would still have to ask what constitutes the *meaning* of the attainments of intelligence. If unreduced otherness is an ingredient of the meaning of spiritual universality (as we find it in theoretical and ethical universalizations), then Findlay's assertion, if it means to be more than a psychological observation, is backward.

10. Although Grisebach does not use spirit-words to characterize his "Outside," the logic of his argument places him in accord with Levinas on the ontological issue.

11. *Republic* 611d–e (trans. Francis M. Cornford).

12. Cf. the metaphysical "self" spoken of by Ludwig Wittgenstein, *Tractatus Logico-Philosophicus* 5.641.

13. The Latin *intueri*, "to contemplate," stems from *tueri*, "to look at, watch, protect," which stems in turn from the reconstructed Indo-European root *teu-*, "to pay attention to, turn to"—"Intuition," *American Heritage Dictionary of the English Language* (Boston: Houghton Mifflin, 1973).

Chapter 3

1. G. W. F. Hegel, *Phenomenology of Spirit*, trans. Allen V. Miller (Oxford: Oxford University Press, 1977), pp. 321–55 (VI, B, I.b–II.b).

2. Ibid., pp. 111–19 (IV, A).

3. Stendhal, *On Love*, ch. 2.

4. C. S. Lewis explores the problem of compelling but apparently private encounter with an other in his novel *Till We Have Faces*, where the Eros and Psyche legend is adapted to serve as a parable for religious faith.

5. "The highest and first law of the universe—and the other name of life, is . . . 'help'—John Ruskin, *Modern Painters* (New York: J. W. Lovell, n.d.), pt. VII (vol. 5), ch. 1 ("The Law of Help"), p. 175.

6. Martin Buber, *I and Thou*, trans. Walter Kaufmann (New York: Scribner's, 1970), p. 175.

7. Hans-Eduard Hengstenberg claims that the fundamental determination of human existence is our capability of *Sachlichkeit* (similarly defined), which we must decide for or against, in a decision before all decisions. The decision for concreteness spoken of in this chapter corresponds to the Hengstenbergian *Vorentscheidung*. See his *Philosophische Anthropologie*, 2nd ed. (Stuttgart: W. Kohlhammer, 1960), pp. 45, 126. After addressing the phenomenological question about how *Sachlichkeit* is realized in the reception and communication of meanings, Hengstenberg asks what he calls the metaphysical question about the principle that grounds human *Sachlichkeit*, and answers, *Geist* (p. 131). He then attaches attributes to spirit in a manner not basically different from Scheler's or Hartmann's, despite various specific disagreements with them, especially the latter.

8. Robert Nozick argues that organic unity is the principle of value in his *Philosophical Explanations* (Cambridge, Mass.: Harvard University Press, 1981), ch. 5. The plausibility of this aestheticist approach to a universal theory of value lies in the coincidence of organic unity as satisfyingness for contemplation (its more usual significance) and organic unity as bindingness on response. Nozick is sensitive to both sides of the coincidence but continually collapses the second side into the first.

9. It seems that the cat will never step over the threshold, but there are other beings not yet over it who will. Different ambiguities, therefore, obtain in our dealings with other human beings who are not present in the standard way yet make their claims on us, such as fetuses and future generations. Fetuses are actually present beings who are prospectively certain to become persons, barring mishap; the ambiguity in their status has two aspects, (*a*) the merely psychological ambiguity in our awareness of them caused by their hiddenness, and (*b*) the spiritually important ambiguity concerning *who,* which persons, they will be. Future generations are prospectively certain to exist, but here we know neither who they will be nor (as we do know with the fetuses) to which actuality the who-question attaches.

10. Albert Schweitzer, *The Philosophy of Civilization*, trans. Charles T. Campion (New York: Macmillan, 1960), p. 309 (ch. 23).

11. Schweitzer, *Out of My Life and Thought*, trans. Charles T. Campion (New York: H. Holt, 1933), p. 188 (ch. 13).

12. Buber notes that the "exclusiveness" of the tree-encounter does not involve a narrowing of awareness: "This does not require me to forego any of the modes of contemplation. There is nothing that I must not see in order to see, and there is no knowledge that I must forget. . . . Whatever belongs to the tree is included: its form and its mechanics, its colors and its chemistry, its conversation with the elements and its conversation with the stars—all this in its entirety"—*I and Thou*, p. 58.

13. Cf. G. W. Leibniz, *Monadology*, paras. 64–67.

14. The focus on generalities as crypto-individuals is characteristic of Platonism, as classically in the *Symposium*'s call for the devotion of attention to Beauty. I repeat the Ockhamist point that this move destroys the very generality of generalities—see the texts on the problem of universals in William of Ockham's *Philosophical Writings*, trans. Philotheus Boehner (Indianapolis: Bobbs-Merrill, 1964), pp. 35–48.

15. I would not have been able to describe intention as I do here and in Chapter 7 if it had not been for Maurice Merleau-Ponty's *Phenomenology of Perception* and the essays

translated in *The Primacy of Perception*, ed. James Edie (Evanston, Ill.: Northwestern University Press, 1964), and *Signs*, trans. Richard McCleary (Evanston, Ill.: Northwestern University Press, 1964). My brief descriptions are no substitute for his, of course; they amount to a proposal to put an extra spin on his from my different vantage point. (For a good example of this, compare my section 6.3 with his remarks on style in "Indirect Language and the Voices of Silence," in *Signs*, pp. 39–70.) Because Merleau-Ponty has already wrestled with the demons of intellectualism and reductionistic naturalism in order to rescue our understanding of subjective existence from false problematics, I am free to reproblematize existence under the aspect of the spiritual.

16. G. E. M. Anscombe, *Intention* (Ithaca, N.Y.: Cornell University Press, 1957), p. 84 (para. 47).

17. Jean-Paul Sartre, *Being and Nothingness*, pt. 3.

Chapter 4

1. This objection is articulated by John Macmurray in *The Self as Agent* (London: Faber and Faber, 1969), pp. 72f.

2. See R. M. Hare, *The Language of Morals* (Oxford: Oxford University Press, 1952) and *Freedom and Reason* (Oxford: Oxford University Press, 1963).

3. On subjectivity, see esp. Emmanuel Levinas, *Otherwise than Being or Beyond Essence*, trans. Alphonso Lingis (The Hague: Martinus Nijhoff, 1981; first published in 1974); on time, see esp. Emmanuel Levinas, *Time and the Other*, trans. Richard Cohen (Pittsburgh: Duquesne University Press, 1987), and *Totality and Infinity*, trans. Alphonso Lingis (Pittsburgh: Duquesne University Press, 1969), pp. 220–47, 281–85.

4. Emmanuel Levinas, *De l'existence à l'existant*, 2nd ed. (Paris: Vrin, 1978), p. 11 (my translation); cf. Alphonso Lingis' translation *Existence and Existents* (The Hague: Martinus Nijhoff, 1978), p. 15.

5. The work of Karl-Otto Apel and Jürgen Habermas (partly of Peircean inspiration) is a major exception.

6. Ludwig Wittgenstein, *Philosophical Investigations*, para. 199.

7. Cf. Apel's argument for this point in "The Problem of Philosophic Fundamental-Grounding in Light of a Transcendental Pragmatic of Language," trans. K. R. Pavlovic, *Man and World* 8 (1975): 239–75.

8. Sufficient grounds are typically non-necessitating when the "ground" is a reason for doing something, because a plurality of acceptable reasons exists in most situations. With respect to natural causes, however, only an imperfect science admits a plurality of acceptable explanations of a particular natural event.

9. Leibniz' most important reason for positing this world as the best of all possible ones is not, however, to cater to a necessitarian principle of sufficient ground, but to avoid subjecting the intelligent creator of the world to "blind necessity." He frequently refers to the difference between logical necessity and the "necessity" by which an intelligent being chooses the good; unfortunately, he does not explain the latter.

10. Hobbesian arguments that try to constrain intenders to remain interintentionally

oriented with the force of their own self-interest (considering that everyone will be happier if all cooperate) not only fail on their own terms but miss a more important point, namely, that interintentional existence as such is, though non-necessary, beckoning and commanding, and that herein (rather than in any calculations of utility maximization) lie our first-order reasons for living it. They fail because the "cooperation" of self-interested parties that they envision, not amounting to genuine interintentional comportment, is inevitably fractured by temptations to selfish prudence. Unless intenders know that other intenders *will* cooperate—which they can never know—it remains in their interest not to cooperate in many situations. See Stephen Darwall's critique of the Hobbesian approach in *Impartial Reason* (Ithaca, N.Y.: Cornell University Press, 1983), ch. 13.

In the fullest contemporary Hobbesian argument, David Gauthier's *Morals by Agreement* (Oxford: Oxford University Press, 1986), moral constraint is grounded on selfish utility-maximizing via a quasi-Rawlsian bargaining scenario. Agents without interest in each others' interests nevertheless want to enjoy the greater benefits of cooperative life and thus place themselves in the context of interaction; as interaction must be governed by fair, impartial rules if cooperation is to come off, however, agents must adopt a *virtually* other-interested bargaining standpoint, choosing dispositions (including actual unselfish interests) that may not promote their greatest benefit in particular situations. Yet Gauthier admits that this argument does not shut off the ring-of-Gyges escape hatch for the individual who is willing to cheat for selfish advantage. In order to get over this difficulty, he appeals sweetly to a socialized human nature geared to uniquely social benefits.

11. David Hume, *A Treatise of Human Nature* (Oxford: Oxford University Press, 1888), p. 415.

12. This formula was introduced in Levinas' "Philosophy and the Idea of Infinity" (1957), in *Collected Philosophical Papers*, trans. Alphonso Lingis (Dordrecht: Martinus Nijhoff, 1987), p. 56.

13. René Descartes, *Meditations on First Philosophy*, in *The Philosophical Works of Descartes*, trans. G. B. S. Haldane and Elizabeth Ross (Cambridge, Eng.: Cambridge University Press, 1911), 1:166, Meditation III.

14. Levinas, *Totality and Infinity*, p. 305.

15. Levinas relates this mode of existence to the paradigmatic figure of Abraham, who goes forth to an unknown destination, in contrast to Ulysses who is always homeward bound—"On the Trail of the Other," trans. Daniel J. Hoy, in *Philosophy Today*, 10 (1966): 37.

16. Husserlian transcendentalism, which exposes *knowable* conditions on the constitution of ordinary knowledge, is in our terms a foundationalism.

17. The arguments of Thomas Nagel and Stephen Darwall on the objectivity of reasons have the effect of norming intention by making it choose between crediting the impersonal standpoint and falling into a manifestly life-distorting solipsism. See Nagel, *The Possibility of Altruism* (Oxford: Oxford University Press, 1970), and Darwall, *Impartial Reason*. These arguments are, quite properly, less coercive than Gewirth's and Apel's, but for that very reason they are caught in a kind of no-man's-land where anyone can say that he or she "fails," that is, comes up short. The present essay attempts to come to their aid by making clearer the nonnecessitarian fashion in which a good intention-norming argument proceeds.

18. Alan Gewirth, *Reason and Morality* (Chicago: University of Chicago Press, 1978).

19. Ibid., p. 135.

20. Ibid., pp. 43–45.

21. Ibid., p. 80.

22. R. M. Hare makes essentially the same criticism in "Do Agents Have to be Moralists?" in *Gewirth's Ethical Rationalism*, ed. Edward Regis, Jr. (Chicago: University of Chicago Press, 1984), pp. 52–58.

23. See Apel, "The Problem of Philosophic Fundamental-Grounding."

24. Ibid., p. 266.

25. Apel, "The *A Priori* of the Communication Community and the Foundations of Ethics: The Problem of a Rational Foundation of Ethics in the Scientific Age," in *Towards a Transformation of Philosophy*, trans. Glyn Adey and David Frisby (London: Routledge and Kegan Paul, 1980), pp. 277–78.

26. Ibid., pp. 280–81.

27. Ibid., p. 285.

28. Ibid., p. 268.

29. See Hans Albert, *Treatise on Critical Reason*, trans. Mary Varney Rorty (Princeton, N.J.: Princeton University Press, 1985), p. 18, and Apel, "The Problem of Philosophic Fundamental-Grounding," p. 240.

30. As also for Aristotle—see *Metaphysics* 1006a6–18.

31. The most significant critique of Husserl along these lines known to me is Jacques Derrida's "Speech and Phenomena," in *Speech and Phenomena and Other Essays on Husserl's Theory of Signs*, trans. David B. Allison (Evanston, Ill.: Northwestern University Press, 1973).

32. Cf. Levinas' practice in *Otherwise than Being* and esp. his appreciation of skepticism, pp. 165–71.

33. Plato, *Republic* 509b; Hume, *A Treatise of Human Nature*, p. 469.

34. Robert Nozick, *Philosophical Explanations* (Cambridge, Mass.: Harvard University Press, 1981), p. 4.

Chapter 5

1. Such as, for example, Michael Theunissen is concerned with in *Der Andere*, 2nd ed. (Berlin: Walter de Gruyter, 1977). His determination to construe dialogical philosophy as a contribution to theoretical inquiry (since philosophy for him *is* theoretical inquiry) distracts him from dialogism's main point and leads inevitably to the disappointment expressed in his "Postscript."

2. I owe this example to Daisy Thorp.

3. Joseph Conrad's Marlow says: "No, I don't like work. I had rather laze about and think of all the fine things that can be done. I don't like work—no man does—but I like what is in the work—the chance to find yourself. Your own reality—for yourself, not for others—what no other man can ever know. They can only see the mere show, and never can tell what it really means"—*Heart of Darkness* (New York: Norton, 1963), p. 29.

4. Jean-Paul Sartre holds in *Being and Nothingness* (pt. 3, ch. 3, sec. 1) that the

fulfillment of the love-relationship is not merely improbable but impossible; it requires subjectivities to confirm each other as subjectivities, whereas (for Sartre) a subjectivity can remain subjective only in reducing an Other to an objectivity. Our argument against Sartre's presupposition as to the nature of subjectivity has already been given in section 3.6. It should be noticed, however, that his account suits the conception of love as a *project* of the self undertaken to redeem its own facticity—whereas the real possibility of love lies in the transcendence of "project." Similarly, Marcel Proust's portrayal of love as torture suits the predatory aestheticism of romance, which love's fulfillment transcends. But the torture witnesses ironically against itself; the remark, "We love only what we do not wholly possess," both turns the screw of the contradiction of romance and points beyond romance —*Remembrance of Things Past*, trans. C. K. Scott Moncrieff and Terence Kilmartin (New York: Vintage, 1982), 3:102.

5. Cited from John Noss, *Man's Religions*, 5th ed. (New York: Macmillan, 1974), p. 133.

6. Max Scheler thinks that love will always evoke love in return, in the absence of any interfering circumstances—*The Nature of Sympathy*, trans. Peter Heath (Hamden, Conn.: Shoe String, 1973), p. 102. Given the prevalence of interfering circumstances, this principle does not inspire optimism.

7. Heidegger, *Being and Time*, trans. John Macquerrie and Edward Robinson (New York: Harper & Row, 1962), para. 27; Scheler, *The Nature of Sympathy*, p. 248; Martin Buber, *I and Thou*, trans. Walter Kaufman (New York: Scribner's, 1970), pp. 69–73.

8. Adapted from Else Holmelund Minarik, "Mother Bear's Robin," in *Little Bear's Visit* (New York: Harper and Row, 1961), pp. 24–37.

Chapter 6

1. This is Herbert Spencer's approach; see the criticism of it made by John Stuart Mill, whose basic position was not dissimilar to Spencer's, in his *System of Logic*, Book 2, ch. 7.

2. Empirically oriented understandings of reason come into the vicinity of the pneumatological approach in the measure that they locate the grounds of rationality or objective validity in a group of reasoners' negotiat-*ing* and in group standards *as* fruits of that process. This perspective is variously represented in Stephen Toulmin, *Human Understanding. The Collective Use and Evolution of Concepts* (Princeton, N.J.: Princeton University Press, 1972); Stephen Darwall's *Impartial Reason* (Ithaca, N.Y.: Cornell University Press, 1983); and Kurt Baier's paper "The Social Source of Reason," *Proceedings of the American Philosophical Association* 51 (1978): 707–733. It is at least latent in the work of Wittgenstein and Austin. But these writers all risk falling into sociologism, in which the normative authority of group standards would evaporate, so long as they fail to pin their empiricism explicitly to the exteriority principle, which superordinates the issue of how to agree to actual agreements. This superordinated issue, however, is met and lived in factual existence. The claim of others as other is the intersection of the a priori with the empirical, the transfiguration of natural facts into spiritual facts. The affinity one can see between the

apriorization of the empirical and empiricalizations of the a priori is thus partly deceptive, partly significant.

According to the promising proposal of Paul Lorenzen, the significance of historical-cultural actuality for norming lies in our need to carry out a "normative genesis" of the concrete situation in which we make our choices—as, for example, a philosophical essay proceeds in part by rehearsing the philosophical history of the problem of interest so as to create a publicly acceptable venue for argumentation, or a legal argument reviews precedents. This "material" supernorm or "cultural principle" is to operate in conjunction with the "formal" supernorm or "moral principle," which requires publicity or "transsubjectivity" in the first place. See Lorenzen, *Normative Logic and Ethics* (Mannheim: Bibliographisches Institut, 1969), pp. 73–89.

3. As will become apparent, I do not distinguish "symbol" from "metaphor" as does Paul Ricoeur in *Interpretation Theory: Discourse and the Surplus of Meaning* (Fort Worth: Texas Christian University Press, 1976), ch. 3. My purpose is to get clear on conditions of meaningful thought and communication that are prior to the points typically dealt with by hermeneuticians (the meaning of a text vis-à-vis the intentions of author and audience, how metaphorical differs from non-metaphorical discourse, etc.).

4. The "permanent possibility of intention" contains the "sense" of the symbol, that is, an intentional configuration available to all subjects, and with this sense a particular *way* of being aware of the symbol's referent(s)—as, e.g., the distinctive sense of a metaphor puts a revealing new twist on the ordinary referents of the metaphor's terms just in the subject's new positioning with respect to those terms, without introducing a new referent. Thus it is possible to deny that every distinct symbol has a distinct referent yet affirm that every symbol has a unique semantic force. This answer seems to me to end the conflict between positions like Donald Davidson's in "What Metaphors Mean" and Max Black's in "How Metaphors Work"—both papers in *On Metaphor*, ed. Sheldon Sacks (Chicago: University of Chicago Press, 1979).

5. Gerard Manley Hopkins, "The Blessed Virgin compared to the Air we Breathe," in *The Poems of Gerard Manley Hopkins*, ed. W. H. Gardner and N. H. MacKenzie, 4th ed. (Oxford: Oxford University Press, 1970), p. 93.

6. *Republic* 595–608.

7. "No doubt the 'sense' for beauty, the aesthetic need, is nothing other than an expression and a form of the need for a 'renewal' of life, which is deeply inherent in man and is justly to be termed 'metaphysical.' Barely comprehensible psychologically (but difficult so to interpret) is the feeling underlying this need, that the life one is living is not the real one, a feeling which is certainly not entirely strange to any man, but which most misunderstand. . . . The aesthetic fulfillment of life is only an apparent fulfillment; it is dream and not reality. And therefore it just fades away, born of longing, into longing again" —Ferdinand Ebner, *The Word and the Spiritual Realities*, trans. Harold Green (Ph.D. diss., Northwestern University, 1980), p. 84. Emmanuel Levinas calls the aesthetic fulfillment an "evasion"—see "Reality and Its Shadow" in *Collected Philosophical Papers*, trans. Alphonso Lingis (The Hague: Martinus Nijhoff, 1987).

8. Grisebach claims that his view of art is not moralistic; "moralism" is yet another reality-falsifying system, not the encounter with reality itself. See Eberhard Grisebach, *Gegenwart: Eine kritische Ethik* (Halle: Max Niemeyer, 1928), pp. 396–402.

9. Martin Buber, *I and Thou*, trans. Walter Kaufmann (New York: Scribner's, 1970), p. 57.

10. Ibid., p. 60.

11. It could be said that this is a *hermeneutical* appropriation of the concept of style, along Hans-Georg Gadamer's lines—cf. his discussion of the history of the concept of style in *Truth and Method*, trans. Garrett Barden and John Cumming (New York: Seabury, 1975), pp. 449–52—for I, too, take it that the hermeneutical question, How is it possible to recognize a certain way of being? is inseparable from the question, How is it possible to be? In our context the latter question, as it applies to spiritual being, is actually the primary one.

12. These are, for instance, the *Kulturgebiete* treated in Heinrich Rickert's *System der Philosophie*, First Part: *Allgemeine Grundlegung der Philosophie* (Tübingen: J. C. B. Mohr, 1921), ch. 6.

13. *Ideas*, para. 147.

14. Paul Taylor, *Normative Discourse* (Englewood Cliffs, N.J.: Prentice-Hall, 1961), p. 300.

15. A Husserlian phenomenological analysis will disclose to us the constituents of the ideal sort, but not the real ones. We cannot even find an essential form for the scientist's intentional reward, since it depends contingently on the individual's actual performance, which, eidetically speaking, is in the dark. The principle that the meanings of the contingencies are controlled by ideally discoverable essential intentional relationships has been controverted by our earlier arguments for the primordial transcendence of others as meaning-controlling.

16. These culture concepts recall the "explanation"/"understanding" dichotomy but represent only one of the many facets of a complex underlying issue; the terms of this analysis should not be equated with the terms of discussions of other aspects of it, e.g., of the relationship between "objective" or "distanciating" and "subjective" or "appropriating" approaches to the interpretation of texts. For an analysis of the relation between instrumental and intrinsic validities in the sciences, see sections 8.2–8.4. In 8.4 the category of the "humane" is more fully investigated and a statement of the general "explanation"-"understanding" issue is given.

17. Grisebach, *Gegenwart*, pp. 385–402.

18. Max Scheler, *Formalism in Ethics and Non-Formal Ethics of Values*, trans. Manfred S. Frings and Robert L. Funk (Evanston, Ill.: Northwestern University Press, 1973), p. 25.

19. Ibid., pp. 12–14.

20. Ibid., p. 17.

21. Ibid., pp. 36f.

22. G. E. Moore, *Principia Ethica* (Cambridge, Eng.: Cambridge University Press, 1903), p. 15.

23. Scheler, *Formalism in Ethics*, p. 265.

24. The same move is made by Darwall in *Impartial Reason* to strengthen internalism.

25. *Formalism in Ethics*, p. 184.

26. Ibid., pp. 206ff.

27. Scheler himself points in this direction in his claim for the supremacy of person-

values—see, e.g., *Formalism in Ethics*, pp. 100, 109, 396f.—and in attaching such importance to model persons—pp. 572 et seq.

28. The Hegelian universal need not be understood simply as antecedently valid, however. One can posit a dialectically, i.e. temporally constituted universal that is always to be newly grasped according to the contributions of individuals and groups to it; this is how Sartre thinks of the *intelligible* universal or the "totalization" in his *Critique of Dialectical Reason* (see the Introduction).

29. David Hume, "Of the Standard of Taste," in e.g. *Essential Works of David Hume*, ed. Ralph Cohen (New York: Bantam, 1965), pp. 448–66.

30. Roderick Firth, "Ethical Absolutism and the Ideal Observer," *Philosophy and Phenomenological Research* 12 (1952): 317–45; cf. his discussion of this paper with Richard Brandt in *Philosophy and Phenomenological Research* 15 (1955): 407–23.

31. Immanuel Kant, *The Doctrine of Virtue*, para. 30.

32. R. M. Hare, *Freedom and Reason* (Oxford: Oxford University Press, 1963), ch. 9.

Chapter 7

1. *Without* aeration, however, intentional virtues become interintentional vices— tenacity becomes stubbornness, thoroughness evasiveness, etc.—as Eberhard Grisebach points out in *Gegenwart: Eine kritische Ethik* (Halle: Max Niemeyer, 1928), p. 550.

2. Maurice Merleau-Ponty, *The Visible and the Invisible*, trans. Alphonso Lingis (Evanston, Ill.: Northwestern University Press, 1968), fourth part.

3. Max Scheler shows in *The Nature of Sympathy* how we live in the experience of other persons, although the cognitivist conceptual framework in which his insight appears is different from our own. "It is not the case . . . that we have to build up a picture of other people's experiences from the immediately given data furnished by our own. . . . What occurs, rather, is an immediate flow of experiences, *undifferentiated as between mine and thine,* which actually contains both our own and others' experiences intermingled and without distinction from one another. . . . [I]f there is a general human *tendency* to err in one of these two directions rather than the other, it is certainly not the error of empathy, so-called, whereby we impute our own experience to others, but the *opposite* tendency, in which we entertain the experiences of other people as if they were our own. In other words, a man tends to live more in *others* than in himself; more in the community than in his own individual self. This is confirmed by the facts of child-psychology, and also in the thought of all primitive peoples. The ideas, feelings, and tendencies which govern the life of a child, apart from general ones such as hunger and thirst, are initially confined entirely to those of his immediate environment, his parents and relatives, his elder brothers and sisters . . . and so on. Imbued as he is with 'family feeling,' his own life is at first almost completely hidden from him. . . . Only very slowly does he raise his mental head, as it were, above this stream flooding over it, and find himself as a being who also, at times, has feelings, ideas, and tendencies of his own"—trans. Peter Heath (Hamden, Conn.: Shoe String, 1973), pp. 246–47.

4. Ludwig Wittgenstein, *Philosophical Investigations*, para. 178.

5. Martin Buber, *I and Thou*, trans. Walter Kaufmann (New York: Scribner's, 1970), p. 57.

6. Ibid., p. 176.

7. Nicolai Hartmann, *Das Problem des geistigen Seins* (Berlin: Walter de Gruyter, 1933), ch. 46, pp. 360ff.

8. Ibid., p. 362.

9. That is so even though it *appears as* "timeless." See the interesting discussion in ibid., pp. 400–406.

10. Ibid., p. 361.

11. Ibid., p. 425.

12. Ibid., p. 395.

13. Buber, *I and Thou*, p. 61.

14. As does Buber—ibid., p. 176.

15. Hartmann, *Problem*, pp. 446–66.

16. In philosophy the outstanding developments of this idea are to be found in the grammatically oriented thought of Ebner, Rosenzweig, and Rosenstock-Huessy, because of their lucidity with respect to the spiritual horizon, rather than in the language philosophies of Heidegger and Wittgenstein. Nevertheless, one can and should read Heidegger and Wittgenstein from this perspective. In Heidegger's case one has to put Being in spiritual brackets, regarding it as a normative construction, which unfortunately is totally opposite to his intentions.

17. Ferdinand Ebner, *The Word and the Spiritual Realities*, p. 142. Cf. Jacob Grimm, "Ueber den Ursprung der Sprache," in *Kleinere Schriften*, vol. 1 (Berlin: F. Dümmler, 1879), pp. 285–87.

18. See Michael Theunissen, *Der Andere*, 2nd ed. (Berlin: Walter de Gruyter, 1977), pp. 287–91, 457.

19. Hermann Cohen was the prime philosophical representative of this view.

20. Buber, "The Land and Its Possessors" (from the 1939 open letter to Gandhi), in *Israel and the World*, 2nd ed.(New York: Schocken, 1963), p. 227.

21. Ibid., p. 233.

22. For Hartmann, on the contrary, a *Gemeingeist* like the Jewish spirit (or one of the competing and overlapping spirits that is taken in by a global notion like "the Jewish spirit") is a real being. His chief positive reason for thinking this is that we can so unmistakably *encounter* it when, say, we visit a Jewish community. Negatively, he argues that if such spirits were only abstract types, ways for individuals to be rather than realities in their own right, their validity would have to be timeless—which we know not to be the case, since we acknowledge the difference between, e.g., living and dead languages (*Problem*, pp. 163–68). However, both the encounterability and the historicality of a spirit may entirely derive from the encounterability and historicality of its constituents. If it is not thus derivative, what is to distinguish it from the *natural* fact of a social phenomenon? (Our question across the board: Can one keep "spiritual being" distinct from other forms of being, as one should, without adopting our radical distinction between normative issue and describable matter which knocks the concept of being from our hands as we approach the spiritual?) Besides, any spirit's validity *is* timeless in one sense, inasmuch as a *dead* language is still a dead *language* that can in principle be spoken.

23. The possibility is virtual, not real. If Israel is constituted strictly by God's election of Abraham's seed, then a Gentile lacks genetic qualifications to join that spirit. It is, however, the virtual possibility that determines the real collectivity as a spirit.

24. G. K. Chesterton, *The New Jerusalem* (London: Nelson, n.d.; first published 1920), p. 221.

25. Ibid., pp. 227–28.

26. Ibid., p. 227.

Chapter 8

1. Benedict de Spinoza, *Ethics*, appendix to pt. I.

2. Aristotle, *Metaphysics* 983a30.

3. This wording is Richard Taylor's, from his article "Causation" in the *Encyclopedia of Philosophy*, ed. P. Edwards (New York: Macmillan, 1967), 2:56.

4. *Metaphysics* 983a31.

5. G. W. Leibniz, (the long) *Theodicy*, paras. 173–75.

6. Whatever is actual may be, *for us,* possible as well, as an axiomatic implication; but it is not quite right to say that the actual is by its very nature possible. For "possibility" is a permissive rather than a compulsive notion. It is odd to say that a thing "can" be if it cannot not be. Therefore, there is always more than one possibility, and to see a thing as possible means to envision at least the two possibilities that it be or not be.

7. R. G. Collingwood does not make this claim in precisely this way, but it can be inferred from his argument in *An Essay on Metaphysics* (Oxford: Oxford University Press, 1939), pt. IIIc.

8. Spinoza, *Principles of Cartesian Philosophy*, appendix, pt. I, ch. 3.

9. Spinoza, *Ethics*, appendix to pt. I.

10. Immanuel Kant, *Critique of Judgment*, paras. 82–84.

11. "*Beauty* is an object's form of *purposiveness* insofar as it is perceived in the object *without the presentation of a purpose"*—Kant, *Critique of Judgment*, trans. Werner S. Pluhar (Indianapolis: Hackett, 1987), para. 17, p. 84.

12. Ibid., para. 12.

13. See Hermann Cohen, *Kants Begründung der Ethik* (Berlin: F. Dümmler, 1877), esp. pt. II, ch. 3; and Heinrich Barth, *Philosophie der praktischen Vernunft* (Tübingen: J. C. B. Mohr, 1927), ch. 8.

14. Kant, *Critique of Pure Reason* A 532–541 = B 560–569.

15. Ibid. A 542–558 = B 570–586.

16. John R. Silber argues that Kant advanced beyond Plato in incorporating the freedom to choose rationality itself within rational freedom, thereby making irrationality culpable; Kant "defined freedom and reason as spontaneity and pointed to rationality and autonomy as fulfilled and to irrationality and heteronomy as deficient modes of its expression"—"The Ethical Significance of Kant's *Religion*," published with Kant's *Religion within the Limits of Reason Alone*, trans. Theodore M. Greene and Hoyt H. Hudson (New York: Harper and Row, 1960), p. xciii. If this interpretation, which places heavy emphasis

on the *Religion*'s contribution to Kant's ethical theory, is right, then my objection is certainly blunted. Against this, however, must be placed Kant's declaration in the *Metaphysics of Morals* that freedom of will cannot be defined as the capacity to choose to act for or against the law (Akademie ed., p. 226).

17. Silber ("Ethical Significance," pp. xcviii–xcix) articulates this objection.

18. Kant, *Groundwork of the Metaphysic of Morals*, Akademie ed., pp. 458–59.

19. Kant, *Critique of Practical Reason*, sec. 6. Karl Ameriks provides an interesting discussion of how Kant earlier thought that transcendental freedom is provable from the "I think," even before the "I am obliged" appears on the scene, but later believed that freedom is only warranted by moral considerations—"Kant's Deduction of Freedom and Morality," *Journal of the History of Philosophy* 19 (1981): 53–79.

20. *Critique of Practical Reason*, Akademie ed., p. 4.

21. Martin Buber, *I and Thou*, trans. Walter Kaufmann (New York: Scribner's, 1970), p. 100.

22. Ibid., p. 101.

23. Ibid., p. 102.

24. As expounded in Robert Nozick, *Philosophical Explanations* (Cambridge, Mass.: Harvard University Press, 1981).

25. Buber, *I and Thou*, p. 101.

26. Ibid., p. 85.

27. Cf. Buber, "The Power of the Spirit," trans. O. Marx, in *Israel and the World* (New York: Schocken, 1963), p. 175: "Spirit, then, is not just one human faculty among others. It is man's totality that has become consciousness, the totality which comprises and integrates all his capacities, powers, and urges. When a man thinks, he thinks with his entire body; spiritual man thinks even with his fingertips. Spiritual life is nothing but the existence of man, insofar as he possesses that true human conscious totality, which is not the result of development; it goes back to the origin of mankind, though it may unfold differently in different individuals. Nowadays the word spirit is used in a very different sense by persons who forget or scorn its great past in both the East and the West, and designate by it that part of human thinking which essentially regards all totality as something alien and hateful; the severed intellect. Severed from totality, yet greedy to govern all of man, for a number of centuries the intellect has been growing greedier and more independent and is attempting to reign from on high, but without the ability to flow freely into all organic vitality as the spirit it has dethroned can and does."

28. We can specify the difference between our "can" and the others by comparing their conditions.

I can do action A in a Kantian sense if I am the kind of being to whose nature the doing of things like A belongs intrinsically. Thus, (A) will obtain if (I) and (I do things like A) both obtain.

I can do A in the counterfactually causal sense if I am the kind of being who will do A when appropriately acted on by something else. Let C/R be a sufficient Cause, which might also be taken for a Reason. Then (A) will obtain if (I), (C/R), and (If I and C/R, then A) do.

I am "available" to do A, however, not because anything makes me do it, but because nothing prevents me from doing it. I *may* do A for a reason R, in the absence of interfering conditions (IC). My contingent decision D must be added to bring about A. Thus, (A) will obtain if (I), (R), (If I and R and D and not-IC, then A), (D), and (not-IC) do. R is a sufficient *reason, and* a necessary condition, but not a sufficient or necessitating condition, of my deciding to do A. R is indispensable for D if D is not arbitrary.

29. "I could have done X" means that no ascertainable factor whatsoever excluded my doing X.

30. See Ernst Cassirer, *The Logic of the Humanities*, trans. Clarence Smith Howe (New Haven, Conn.: Yale University Press, 1961).

31. It is interesting to see how Cassirer takes a descriptivist stand against Rickert's keying of the *Kulturwissenschaften* to "values" rather than to being: "What style-concepts present is not an ought but simply an 'is'—even though this 'is' is not concerned with physical things but with the persistence of 'forms.' When I speak of the 'form' of a language, or of a definite art 'form,' this, *in itself,* has nothing to do with value reference" —*Logic*, pp. 26f. What Cassirer says is just, on its face, yet he misses the background normative framework which makes these "forms" figure as the sort that the humanities are interested in.

32. Still, Cassirer is surely right not to accept Windelband's contention that the human sciences are merely "idiographic," for they do give insight by relating particulars to universals—*Logic*, pp. 120ff.

33. In recent theories of interpretation (Collingwood, Gadamer, Popper) which correctly maintain that an interpretandum must be approached as the answer to a question or solution of a problem, there is a tendency to dwell on the transpersonal form of the question/problem more than on its personal challenge to the interpreter. It is true that the interpreter poses the question/problem transpersonally, for everyone, and that the question/problem supports this, having a discoverable "objective" form (as an element of objective spirit or denizen of Popper's "World Three") on which the commonality and reliability of interpretative science is based; but it is also true that *he* or *she* so poses it, qualifying his or her own individuality by presuming to decide objective meaning and at the same time individually qualifying that meaning. Gadamer appears to understand this best. See Hans-Georg Gadamer, *Truth and Method*, trans. Garrett Barden and John Cumming (New York: Seabury, 1975), pp. 325–41, and Karl Popper, "On the Theory of the Objective Mind," in *Objective Knowledge* (Oxford: Oxford University Press, 1972), pp. 153–90, both of which include discussions of Collingwood.

34. René Le Senne, *Traité de Morale Générale*, 5th ed. (Paris: Presses Universitaires de France, 1967), p. 5.

35. Both Gadamer and Richard Rorty build this limitation of knowledge into the philosophical posture called "hermeneutical." Gadamer rightly derives the limitation partly from the claim of the to-be-understood You as other; interpretation occurs in relationship (*Truth and Method*, pp. 321–25). Rorty, on the other hand, makes the limitation a function of whatever obstacles to comprehension happen to obtain at a given moment, denying that any beings, even we famous human beings, are essentially obstacles: "If one draws the hermeneutics-epistemology distinction as I want to draw it, there is no requirement that people should be more difficult to understand than things; it is merely that hermeneutics is only needed in the case of incommensurable discourses, and that people discourse whereas things do not. What makes the difference is not discourse versus silence, but incommensurable discourses versus commensurable discourses. . . . There is no metaphysical reason why human beings should be capable of saying incommensurable

things, nor any guarantee that they will continue to do so" (*Philosophy and the Mirror of Nature* [Princeton, N.J.: Princeton University Press, 1979], p. 347). For Rorty, the hermeneutical-conversational approach is a technique for "coping" with things that elude science, not (as I have argued) the prescribed way to approach beings originally absolved from comprehension; it is merely the embarrassment of science and not an originally other warrant. "Spirit is whatever is so unfamiliar and unmanageable that we begin to wonder whether our 'language' is 'adequate' to it" (ibid., p. 352).

36. Ivan P. Pavlov, "Lectures on the Work of the Cerebral Hemispheres" (1924), in *Experimental Psychology and Other Essays*, trans. unk. (New York: Philosophical Library, 1957), p. 177.

37. Popper, "On the Theory of the Objective Mind," pp. 155–61.

38. Buber, *I and Thou*, pp. 144f., 149, 163, 168.

39. In *The Phenomenon of Man*, trans. Bernard Wall (New York: Harper & Row, 1959), Pierre Teilhard de Chardin (like most writers) runs the "spiritual" together with the "mental," the soul, consciousness, etc.; on the other hand, he does recognize the importance of distinguishing between the intentional and interintentional realms, as for instance when he criticizes a confusion between mere individuality and personality and looks ahead to an ultimate "intercentric" union brought about by love (pp. 263ff.). I daresay he would have been able to make this point more clearly if he had started from a sharpened concept of the spiritual. But then it would also have been clearer that the extrapolation of spiritual from psychic evolution can be only a prophetic gesture, not a theoretical one.

Index